The
Vanishing
American
Dream

The
Vanishing
American
Dream

Immigration, Population, Debt, Scarcity

Virginia Deane Abernethy

Transaction Publishers
New Brunswick (U.S.A.) and London (U.K.)

Library of Congress Catalog Number: 2016018033
ISBN: 978-1-4128-6280-6 (hardcover); 978-1-4128-6337-7 (paperback)
eBook: 978-1-4128-6230-1
Printed in the United States of America

Library of Congress Cataloging-in-Publication Data

Names: Abernethy, Virginia, author.
Title: The vanishing American dream : immigration, population, debt, scarcity / Virginia Deane Abernethy.
Description: New Brunswick : Transaction Publishers, [2016] | Includes bibliographical references and index.
Identifiers: LCCN 2016018033 (print) | LCCN 2016025690 (ebook) | ISBN 9781412862806 (hardcover) | ISBN 9781412863377 (pbk.) | ISBN 9781412862301
Subjects: LCSH: United States--Economic conditions--2009- | United States--Economic policy--2009- | United States--Social conditions--1980- | United States--Social policy--1993- | United States--Population policy. | United States--Emigration and immigration.
Classification: LCC HC106.84 .A24 2016 (print) | LCC HC106.84 (ebook) | DDC 330.973--dc23
LC record available at https://lccn.loc.gov/2016018033

This book is dedicated to young Americans who reach for
Responsibility and Liberty

Contents

Preface

This artificial suppression of interest rates is also necessary to prevent the insolvency of the US government itself. It could not afford to pay a higher rate to borrow, and must continue to borrow just to continue functioning. And as government continually expands, just the cost of its functioning will drain the rest of the economy dry.
—Mark J. Lundeen, May 15, 2015

Quoting one's parents is a sign of age and, revealingly, I lead with one of my father's favorites: "Figures don't lie but liars figure." An early ideal was trying to not lie to myself. The articles in this volume are dedicated to all Americans who want to face reality and do not appreciate concerted lying from government, central banking, and the media.

The volume includes a number of academic writings, many on fertility rates and population, well documented and published in professional journals. These are my credentials and placing them at the beginning of this retrospective was a temptation; but they landed mostly in the middle. The beginning and end of this collection incline toward articles written for popular journals or as editorials over the ten years that I edited the journal *Population and Environment [1989–1999]*. While I edited it, *Population and Environment* was cutting edge. The editorial board was honored to publish all papers contributed to ecologist Garret Hardin's festschrift, and we were fortunate to introduce several younger authors who have gone on to become influential.

The cultural, economic, and environmental condition of the United States has been a major interest over my career. Citizens have a responsibility for themselves, their families, kin, communities, and nation—an ever-widening circle. Kinship is central, the key, and must hold—one conclusion among several that are controversial in mainstream academia. Cracked crystal balls chart tangents that lead far from the mainstream and cause commotion.

Sociologist Talcott Parsons held that the function of politics is the management of conflicting values. In that definition, politics infuses almost all social activities, certainly education and science. Has any science not passed through political flames fueled by values? Can one forget that the pursuit of astronomy, so mathematical today, once carried the risk of being burned at the stake? In relative calm, German-Polish renaissance scholar Nicolaus Copernicus published his thesis that the Earth circles the Sun—rather than the Earth being the center around which other heavenly bodies revolve—despite opposition by both Protestant and Roman Catholic Churches. Galileo, however, was twice tried as a heretic for supporting Copernican theory and spent his later years under house arrest. The Vatican maintained official opposition to heliocentric theory until the early nineteenth century.

Biology today is in a similar transition. Genetics is fraught with conflict over the heritability of intelligence. Evolution and creationism still contend, and their arena is often a State Legislature. Founder of sociobiology E. O. Wilson was once drenched by a bucket of water emptied on him during a formal public address. And geology? In gradualism and Charles Lyell's uniformitarianism, which laid groundwork for the Darwinian theory of evolution, did geology not tread perilous ground?

New paradigms rarely have a smooth ride. I, personally, came late to the discovery that science of any kind entails a fight more vicious than its antiseptic self-image projects. My publisher may have known that when she named my 1993 book *Population Politics*. The indictment of being politicized—value laden—applies in full force to the "social sciences." Its research findings are seldom testable, that is, cannot be falsified through observation or experimentation, so they are not scientific. In agreement, certain practitioners of demography say that their craft is not some "bloodless" count of populations.

Economics is still more political, often a set of theories built to advance values and special interests. So it is with the current (2015) hue and cry about deflation. Deflation can mean either that the quantity of money is shrinking (the monetarist view), or (the usual view) it can mean that prices are falling. The two are closely linked, and the Federal Reserve cabal uses its power of creating money to manipulate prices.

Governments, central banks including the Fed, and the compliant media want inflation. Debtors want inflation because more plentiful dollars make it easier to repay debt. Governments are among the largest debtors in the world. And central banks, thanks to quaintly named quantitative easing (QE) own huge amounts of low-quality debt, assets carried on their books at face value rather than true market value, and they want those debts repaid. Carrying water for the US federal government and its biggest owner/client banks worldwide, the Federal Reserve's "annual inflation target" is 2 percent. The media do their best to program "we the people" to fear deflation and want 2 percent annual inflation, too.

The reality, however, is that savers and those on fixed incomes benefit hugely from *deflation* because, when prices fall, their dollars buy more. Many older people are on fixed incomes. Populations in most industrialized countries are "aging," say demographers. So deflation immediately favors a large, and increasing, share of the population. Many citizens should applaud deflation! They should resist inflation.

The rarely explained relationship is that, under the condition of 2 percent annual inflation, a dollar loses half its buying power every thirty-five years. So who can count on a pension, Social Security, or savings to maintain a future standard of living? With the buying power of a dollar halving every thirty-five years, how is that going to work? The Fed and US government are pulling all the ropes to fire up inflation: flooding financial markets with money through quantitative easing, zero interest rates in perpetuity (ZIRP), borrowing for everyone, and—coming full circle back to demography—an ever-growing consumer base to fuel demand.

The Census Bureau plays its part by tamping down citizen concern over exploding population size. The media trumpet low-ball Census Bureau projections but hide upward revisions. On-board-with-the-program environmentalists cope with resource scarcity and growing pollution through every expedient other than advocacy for stabilizing demand by stabilizing US population size. The power elite—but not most Americans—want inflation and see massive population growth as one way to get it.

So what, besides theoretically driving price inflation and, incidentally, pressure on the natural and man-made environment, does explosive population do for the United States? Effects are both economic and cultural.

Unfortunately for about 80 percent of Americans and the vast majority of newcomers, the United States is no longer the job-producing machine it once was. Even were capital investment robust, it might not drive job creation because robotics is making less-skilled labor increasingly obsolete and surplus. A GM upgrade to its Rochester, New

York, plant entailed a $100 million investment and hiring an additional 30 people. That is, each new job was backed by a capital investment of more than $3.3 million ("GM Announces Rochester Plant Investment," April 12, 2011. Autoevolution.com). For comparison, the standard 20 years ago was that an investment of approximately $250,000 would create one good new job.

Immigration and children born to recent immigrants are the principal source of US population growth. For thirty years, it appeared that business lobbied for mass immigration to procure cheaper labor, create a labor surplus, and force American labor into compliance with lower wages and fewer benefits. However, except in service industries that compete on price, low wages for unskilled labor are rapidly becoming less important to business success. Labor may no longer be the scarce (more expensive) factor in the US economy. One now suspects a second motive in the push for mass immigration, and the impetus comes only secondarily from industry: bankers and government, especially, want more bodies to swell consumer demand and drive price inflation.

The banking elite and federal government—chief cheerleaders for inflation—ignore at their peril the effect on the middle class when more people seeking work and services are admitted into the country. At all skill levels, surplus labor displaces Americans and competes downward the wage scale and job benefits. Moreover, the immigrant sector does not pay sufficient taxes to cover the additional costs incurred by them for education, health care, and criminal justice services, so added infrastructure and the operational expense of accommodating more people are invariably borne by local communities and States.

Also ignored is that more people need more basic resources including water, and that residential expansion eats up agricultural and forest acreage and habitat essential to the survival of many animal species. Further, is urban crowding and loss of spacious recreational opportunity conducive to good relations among people? How is that going to work, when already the nation's highway system is crumbling, bridges are unsafe, water quantity and quality are at risk, national parks sometimes close for lack of funds, and housing costs are rising?

Current immigration policy amounts to importing, and spreading, poverty. How will that work for bankers and government that are putting their chips on creating consumer demand? Will demand be "effective" when the middle class can no longer afford to buy?

Where was the United States when I began writing? Where is it headed? Are the actual changes those foreseen decades ago, and do Americans want recent trends to continue? Will the center hold? Readers can judge for themselves the extent to which the essays in this volume, written over a lifetime of work, anticipated some of these questions or present possible answers.

Virginia Deane Abernethy
Nashville, Tennessee,
July 4, 2015

1

Trust

Introduction

I grew up in the American generation that trusted government implicitly. My patriotism probably got its edge from being abroad during wartime, with American parents, until age nine. Ex-pats, both American and British, attended the Fourth of July picnic at Buenos Aires' American School. I said "American" when an Argentine teenager asked about my nationality, but he corrected: "Norteamericana." Point taken!

I believed in my country right or wrong, and it was never wrong. Elected and appointed officials merited their offices and deserved respect. Politics ends at the water's edge.

Time and exposure to the morass of mass immigration, explosive population growth, massaged unemployment statistics, and counterproductive policies have shaken me. The Bureau of Labor Statistics changes methodology in ways that hide price inflation and unemployment. Bankers and mega-tycoons call the Census Bureau's tune. Politicians bemoan low fertility rates and urge accepting immigrants as a replacement population. But in twenty years, by resisting mass immigration, Japan, Singapore, Korea, and Eastern Europe will be envied for their declining numbers.

For decades, Census Bureau projections have underestimated annual US population growth and its principal drivers: legal immigration, the uncounted flows of illegal aliens and visa overstayers, and their offspring who, absent past immigration, would not have been born in the U.S.. A 1995 legislative effort to reduce legal immigration was derailed when the Immigration and Naturalization Service (INS) commissioner testified before Congress that immigration was spontaneously declining by 10 percent annually. Shortly thereafter, it was leaked that numbers would increase significantly, soon, and that the INS had known it all along. Fruitlessly and furiously, Senator Alan Simpson protested, "If the INS had projections about the dramatic hike in legal immigration and did not release it to Congress before debate on the effort to lower immigration numbers, its actions were unconscionable."

Also questioning intent, physicist Albert Bartlett critiqued INS Statistical Division Director Robert Warren's flawed arithmetic: "Is it Warren's or a desire of the INS to make immigration figures look as small as possible?" Toeing the line, bureaucrats ignore immigration and immigrants' US-born children as the drivers of surging school enrollments, the 1990s fifteen million increase in the medically uninsured population, and the dramatically increased prevalence of diseases long thought eradicated in the United States.

I no longer trust. Perhaps that is my problem. I hope to make it yours, too.

Jobs, Politics, and Immigration*

Unemployment and underemployment are trends becoming more noticeable as the twentieth century draws to a close. Eighteen million new jobs were created in the United States during the expansionary 1980s but, ominously, structural unemployment—the seeming base level in our society—was redefined upward from 4.5 to 5.5 percent of the workforce. Worse, new job creation fell far from this pace in the early 1990s and remained sluggish even as the production of goods and services grew. All the while, the category of "discouraged worker," describing those who have ceased looking for work, rises uncounted. The root cause of these developments is, arguably, a rapidly growing population. More people mean more workers. Some few contend that this bodes well for Americans in the long run. But there is room for doubt.

First, review some characteristics of labor. It is a factor of production; labor productivity puts an upper limit on the wage that can be paid without igniting inflation. In other respects, labor is a commodity; wages, or the price paid for labor, respond to the law of supply and demand. Wages usually rise in a strong economy. The trigger is unemployment falling to near its structural level, which allows labor to command, as well as demand, higher wages.

Consider the decade and a half after World War II. The economy boomed, the labor supply did not expand, wages went up very, very fast,

* In *Chronicles*, The Rockford Institute, Rockford Illinois, pp. 47–48 (October, 1993).

and the consumer market was strong. This was not too inflationary, however, because productivity also rose quickly; industry responded to expensive labor by substituting new technology and automation, which increased productivity. Almost everyone prospered. Most people thought easy times had come to stay and each generation would do better than the one before.

Too soon, the worm turned. A 1987 *Wall Street Journal* article identified a large increase in the supply of labor as the cause of stagnant real wages during the 1970s and 1980s. Baby boomers and women entering the labor force for the first time were depressing wages. When this temporary bulge was absorbed, the story went, real wages would rise again.

Historical demography supports the point that a tightening labor supply stimulates general prosperity, whereas a growing labor supply damps wages. Ronald Lee at Berkeley, studying nineteenth-century England, found that a 10 percent rise in the labor supply led to a 22 percent increase in rents (return on land or, broadly, on capital) and to a 19 percent decline in wages. The picture that emerges is of the polarization of society into rich and poor, based largely on a change in the supply of labor.

Now turn to the labor supply in the United States. Is the general impression that it is growing quickly or slowly? Slowly? To be sure, the baby boomers are just about absorbed into the labor force, as are the middle-aged women who entered it during the 1970s. In 1987, indeed, a labor shortage, particularly among skilled workers, was predicted by the "executive summary" of Workforce 2000, released by the Hudson Institute of Indianapolis. The "executive summary" stated that, from 1987 to 2000, white males would account for only 15 percent of new entrants into the labor force. Every CEO in the country heard this number and knew its implication: the traditional source of skilled labor was drying up. The gap would have to be filled by women, minorities, and immigrants.

Almost immediately, however, some people noticed a mistake in the "executive summary." But word about a correction never really got out, that the *true* fraction of labor force entrants who are (will be) white and male is nearly 32 percent.

The "executive summary" had omitted the word "net," distorting the intended message that 15 percent more white males are to enter the labor force than leave it (through attrition and retirement). This means that from 1987 to 2000 the economy must grow at least 15 percent to absorb just the extra white males.

Add to this the extra black males and other minorities and the extra females—a very large change because of low female labor force participation in earlier generations—and the number of new jobs has to expand very fast indeed just to keep up with the supply of young American workers. In fact, nearly one million more young Americans enter than older Americans leave the labor force each year.

How well is the country doing with its growing supply of labor? A few sectors hold surprises. One-half of young black men are unemployed, and virtually all of them are in the unskilled sector. The cost of this unemployment (and related alienation) is significant, not only in the taxes and direct private sector money that it takes, say, to rebuild Los Angeles after mob violence, but also in what it means to the American Dream. What happened to integrating most people into mainstream America? And will this staggering unemployment creep upward into the next levels of education and skill? Maybe. Disappointed college graduates report that a bachelor's degree is worth very little in today's job market.

Science magazine reports that several hundred (out of fewer than 1,000) new PhDs in mathematics in 1991 could not find jobs; they were competing with Chinese students who had sought asylum and professionally established Russian mathematicians. Among the latter, *Science* reports, as many as 300 had sought employment in the United States within the previous two years. As recently as March 1993, 13 percent of mathematicians with PhDs were unemployed.

Engineers are experiencing the same. The 1990 Immigration Act tripled the number of visas for engineers and scientists. The rationale—the expected skilled labor shortage—is derided as "lies and fraud" by the president of the American Engineering Association (AEA); companies prefer to hire foreign engineers, he states, because they work for lower wages. The AEA is currently petitioning Congress to reconsider the 10 percent of visas set aside for skill-based immigration.

Congress should no doubt reconsider its entire legislative package concerning immigration. It should certainly reconsider the effect of immigration on unskilled Americans. Fully one-quarter of workers with less than a high school education are immigrants; so the impact on America's own poor and minorities (including recent immigrants who now make the United States their home) can hardly be overestimated. New econometric studies are at last documenting the job displacement and decline in wages resulting from current immigration. In round numbers, over one million immigrants, refugees, and asylees enter legally each year; 90 percent of them have "family reunification"—not skills-based—visas. And an estimated half-million more enter without coming to the attention of the Immigration and Naturalization Service (INS) but intending to stay.

The population of the United States is growing by 58,000 a week. Nearly half of that growth is immigration; some additional portion is due to children born to immigrants, who have significantly more children per woman than native-born Americans. The immediate impact of this on the labor force is significant, and down the road the numbers are immense. In the next sixty years the American population is set to grow 50 percent by Census Bureau projections, and by nearly 100 percent if one extrapolates our present growth rate.

Now, how does immigration relate to unemployment? The INS issues work authorization papers, either as "temporary work permits"—many of these to people who arrive in the United States without documentation of any kind—or as "green cards," which are issued to refugees and legal immigrants. In the first six months of 1992, 439,000 temporary work permits and 390,000 green cards were issued. Even if only 75 percent of all those newly authorized to work entered the labor market immediately, we still get 659,000 new foreign workers competing for the total number of new jobs. This very nearly matches the number of new jobs (864,000) that were created nationwide within the same period.

In all of 1992, the economy created well short of 2 million new jobs while the potential labor force grew by nearly 1 million net new American workers, by 1.3 million legal immigrants, refugees, and asylees who received work authorization papers from the INS, and by approximately one-half million illegal foreign workers. Clearly, workers exceed jobs. Without immigration of any kind, the job market could come into balance by reabsorbing the unemployed, reengaging the "discouraged" worker, and inducing certain of the more productive older workers to postpone retirement.

Under present conditions, I need hardly say, native-born Americans, especially those just coming into the job market and particularly the least skilled, are having a tough time. An economic slowdown is hard enough to overcome, but our continuously and rapidly growing labor force, driven by the highest level of immigration this country has ever seen, is putting paid to any prospect that the majority of the young or their children will enjoy the American Dream.

No administration or government program, and no foreseeable private investment of the quantity needed, can expect to overcome unemployment in the face of 1.5 million immigrants every year. If the administration and Congress want to improve employment prospects for Americans, let them establish a policy that limits immigration, from all sources combined, to under 200,000 a year. This level would about equal the annual voluntary flow out of America. Only then can unemployment cease to burden job-seekers and taxpayers alike, the consumer market regain strength, and joy return to the land.

Effects of Mass Immigration*

George J. Borjas's (1996) method for estimating the economic effects of immigration is insightful and important. It reveals that immigration creates both an "immigration surplus" which benefits primarily employers and a "redistribution of wealth" to the detriment of those who depend for their living on wages. Depressed wages, which underlie both effects, are caused by growth in the labor force: more workers must compete in a relatively slow-growing job market.

Borjas makes a crucial decision in accepting the estimate that "a 10 percent increase in the number of workers lowers wages by about three percent." The source probably is Claudia Goldin's (2001) findings; she uses data from immigration and labor markets in the rapidly industrializing US economy of 1880–1920.

The effect of a growing labor force may be magnified in economies that are developing less dramatically (creating fewer jobs) than the United States was at that period in its history. For example, studies of preindustrial England by the historical demographer Ronald D. Lee, of the University of California at Berkeley, show that a 10 percent increase in population depressed wages by 22 percent. That is, Borjas cites a 3 percent wage decline; Lee estimates 22 percent. The present effect is probably somewhere between.

Lee's data span several generations. In contrast, the United States is experiencing a 10 percent increase in population every nine or ten years. Direct immigration plus the children born to post-1970 immigrants account for 60 percent of that very rapid increase. (Immigrants accounted for 18.5 percent of 1994 births although the foreign-born are no more than 10 percent of the U.S. population.) And, population growth soon translates into labor force growth.

---

* Letter to the Editor in *The Atlantic Monthly*, p. 11 [March, 1997].

Thus it is easy to conclude that the immigration surplus for employers is larger, and the redistribution of wealth away from Americans who work for wages is greater, than Borjas estimates. Moreover, Borjas appears to underestimate the public sector costs of immigration. Taken together, these effects suggest that the immigration of low-skill people (who make up more than 90 percent of the stream under "family reunification" policy) is a serious net drain on the economy and also counterproductive in terms of the long-standing social policies for giving opportunity to least-advantaged Americans and strengthening the working middle class.

Immigration Misinformation: Teeming Masses and Funny Numbers*

The debate over immigration policy has been marked by inaccurate reporting in an astonishing number of instances. Errors and material omissions by the US Immigration and Naturalization Service (INS), the Census Bureau, and the Department of Education are only the beginning of the misinformation. News releases and publications by experts, including some associated with the federal government, add to the confusion about the population explosion most Americans observe in their communities.

The mistakes are systematic. All direct the reader (listener, viewer) to believe that the US population is not growing unusually fast compared to that of other industrialized countries, that immigration is a negligible source of this growth, and that immigration is not contributing to many of the nation's social problems.

In 1998, months of congressional debate over increasing the number of H1-B visas to allow additional skilled immigrants to enter the United States culminated in raising the number of visas from 65,000 to 115,000 for two years and then 107,500 in the third year. Additional provisions of the so-called American Competitiveness Act of 1998 gave amnesty to 50,000 Haitians who were illegally in the United States and delayed for 30 months the implementation of provisions of a 1996 law to expedite deportation of illegal aliens.

The H1-B and refugee debates were revisited in March 2000. Congressional subcommittees on immigration voted on proposals ranging from an additional 45,000 H1-B visas this year to as many as 195,000 additional visas over the next three years.

---

* In *Chronicles*, The Rockford Institute, Rockford, Illinois, pp. 21–24 (August, 2000).

The debate was marked by acrimony and conflicting statistics. Invited to testify before Congress, the presidents and chief executive officers of numerous information technology (IT) companies explained that they needed to import computer software specialists in order to remain competitive. American universities, they claimed, were graduating insufficient numbers of IT specialists. T. J. Rodgers, president and CEO of Cypress Semiconductor Corporation, struck the prevalent note: "[W]e have strong feelings about the value provided by immigrant engineers—and also about the factually hollow, emotion-driven claims of those who insist the US semiconductor industry could retain its current global leadership without an adequate supply of high quality engineers, including immigrants." Rodgers added that "The need for skilled workers in the high-tech sector is growing exponentially. . . . Foreign skilled workers do not take jobs from Americans . . . but, in fact, create additional jobs."

Industry representatives and congressional allies, Sen. Spencer Abraham (R-MI) foremost among them, relied on several sets of data to bolster personal testimony. For example, they argued that, between 1994 and 1997, the Labor Department and the Commerce Department nearly tripled the number of job openings it "certified," a declaration that no American was trained and available to do these jobs. A 1995 Information Technology Association survey found that "half of all respondents cited [a lack of high-skilled workers] as the biggest barrier" to growth. Finally the Hudson Institute concluded in *Workforce 2000* that the skilled labor shortage could "shave 5% of the growth rate of GDP."

Others argued that the labor shortage is a mirage. Edwin Rubenstein suggests, "The alleged shortage of highly educated worker in the U.S. is a myth. In fact, we're suffering from a chronic surplus of PhDs." In June 1998, Rep. Lamar Smith (R-RX), chairman of the House of Representatives Immigration Subcommittee of the Judiciary, released a survey showing that 21 American high-tech companies had dismissed 121,800 workers since December 1997. As Norman Matloff, a professor of computer science, said in an interview with Investors' Business Daily: "The problem is that most employers prefer less-expensive talent. Most software firms surveyed hire less than 5% of the software professionals that apply for jobs. Microsoft Corporation hires 2%. Brodebur Software Inc. hires just 1%." Also see Matloff, 1998, letter to the editor, Wall Street Journal.

The General Accounting Office (GAO) is likewise skeptical of the purported labor shortage. Its assessment of the US Department of

Commerce study is that it "has serious analytical and methodological weaknesses that undermine the credibility of its conclusion that a shortage of IT workers exists." The GAO further criticizes the Information Technology Association of America findings, saying that the association had relied "on two employer surveys with 'unacceptably low' response rates of 14 percent and 36 percent."

Hardly mentioned in this debate is the long-term effect of responding to labor market shortages by importing immigrant labor: namely, to dampen wage increases that would otherwise occur, which is, of course, the subtext in industry's lobbying for additional immigrant workers. However, higher wages for skilled labor are not necessarily bad for the economy.

Demand-induced market adjustments in the price of labor are the traditional capitalist mechanism for overcoming labor shortages. Higher wages signal those seeking employment, or considering an area of specialization, to select the sector where wages are rising. In addition, higher-cost labor is an inducement for industry to invest in capital projects or training that increase productivity. Such investment raises the quality of American jobs while ensuring that the shortage will be temporary. These facts have lately been submerged by the concerted lobbying of groups that have an interest in high levels of immigration.

In tandem with the Competitiveness Act, Congress passed a weak version of the Religious Persecution Act sponsored by Rep. Frank Wolf (R-VA) and Sen. Arlen Specter (R-PA). In its original form, this bill would have authorized a new State Department office to certify religions whose adherents are persecuted, granting automatic refugee or asylum status to any practitioner of a certified religion in the specified countries. This bill would have put the burden of proof that an individual was not a bona fide adherent of the certified religion on US agencies, essentially opening American's borders to unlimited immigration at the discretion of the State Department. Its enactment in a weaker version raises the possibility that its provisions will be strengthened over time until its sponsors' original goals are achieved.

In March 1996, Rep. Lamar Smith and Sen. Alan Simpson (R-WY) sponsored legislation to reduce immigration. The bill had substantial bipartisan support despite being opposed by the leadership of both parties, notably President Clinton, Senators Edward Kennedy and Spencer Abraham, and Representatives Newt Gingrich and Dick Armey.

Doris Meissner, commissioner of the INS, testified before House and Senate Sub-Committees on Immigration that immigration had declined 10 percent in 1994 and again in 1995. One month later, when the bill's momentum had dissipated, it was leaked that legal immigration in 1996 was expected to increase by 41 percent over 1995 and that a similar increase was expected in 1997. The INS had apparently been in possession of these facts at the time of Meissner's testimony.

"If the INS had projections about the dramatic hike in legal immigration and did not release it to Congress before debate on the effort to lower immigration numbers, its actions were "unconscionable," charged Senator Simpson (Puente 1996).

The effort to reduce legal immigration ended with the 1996 bill. Provisions to control illegal immigration—many of which have subsequently been gutted by the INS—were substituted for the original bill. It is likely that no immigration restriction legislation will be enacted unless the United States enters a recession.

Robert Warren, director of the statistics division of the INS, has also found occasion to use immigration data creatively. In *Population Today*, the house organ of the Population Reference Bureau (PRB), Warren concludes that "immigrants currently account for 20% of the gross annual additions to the population." The statement is technically correct as the answer to the question, "What fraction is immigration of the sum of births plus immigration?" The catches, however, are the word "gross" and the misleading title of Warren's piece, "Immigration's Share of U.S. Population Growth," which suggests a calculation of the net demographic impact of immigration. Using Warren's own figures, the correct answer to the query posed in the title of his paper is 39 percent, not 20 percent.

Physicist Albert A. Bartlett's comment on Warren's procedure is trenchant: "The substitution of the answer to one problem as the answer to another superficially similar problem is an old and honorable art that shows no sign of decline. But it is surprising nevertheless to see this strategy used in an article by an author who is identified as 'Director of the Statistical Division of the U.S. Immigration and Naturalization Service.'"

Bartlett continues: "A separate but related issue is the significant difference between the data used by Warren and those from another source that uses INS data to record and report the number of immigrants entering the United States." Warren's percentage figure is applied to a population increase of just 2.8 million. But the Center for Immigration Studies (CIS) tabulated immigrant categories for the same year, 1993–1994, and concluded that the annual immigrant flow accounted for 43 percent of a 3.1 million increase in the population. Asks Bartlett, "Is it Warren's [desire], or a desire of the INS, to make immigration figures look as small as possible?"

The sleight of hand continues. As demographers Dennis Ahlburg and James Vaupel observe, "Population projection is not a bloodless technical task, but a politically charged craft of great interest to policymakers and the public." Not surprisingly, scenarios for future population size and composition vary enormously.

For example, the National Research Council (NRC) takes 1995 as the baseline year in its projections. With "zero" immigration hypothetically beginning in 1995, the population would grow to 310 million and begin to decline before 2050. Under the "medium" immigration scenario, however, the population grows without stopping, reaching 387 million by mid-century. By making this the middle projection, the NRC appears to imply that this is the most likely scenario.

It is not. At present, the US population is growing by about 1 percent annually. A growth rate of 1 percent causes a quantity to double in seventy years. Given the estimate of approximately 274 million in late 1999, the United States will have a population of 546 million by 2069. Indeed, one of the more recent (but less publicized) Census Bureau estimates puts the US population at almost 500 million by 2050.

The pattern of Census Bureau projections—repeated upward revisions—does not inspire confidence. Past assumptions about immigration, fertility, and mortality rates resulted in several years of unrealistically low projections of future population size. In 1989, the Census Bureau's middle projection was just 300 million by 2050. Its high projection, 414 million, received little media attention. Within the year, however, Ahlburg and Vaupel wrote that, under assumptions which seemed plausible, the US population in 2050 would likely be at least 400 million and possibly as high as 553 million.

The composition of the population is another important consideration. Polls suggest that most Americans, especially blacks, want large reductions in immigration and would prefer that the future population of the United States be composed of their own descendants, rather than immigrants. The keys to evaluating the makeup of the future population are immigrant flows, ethnic group fertility rates, and the year used for the baseline population.

If one projects to the year 2050 from 2040, immigration accounts for relatively little population increase. But in 1996, the US Census Bureau released a report stating that, by the middle of the twenty-first century, immigrants and their descendants will account for 60 percent of all population growth since 1994 if current trends persist. If the baseline year is 1970, when the impact of the 1965 immigration law that elevated the criteria of diversity and "family reunification" first became manifest, the scenario is far different. According to demographer Meredith Burke, "immigrants after 1970 and their descendants account for three quarters of current American population growth" and will account for "90 percent of the growth between 2000 and 2030—and all of the growth after 2030." Move the starting line and the numbers change.

The same misdirection occurs in examining the impact of immigration on education. US Secretary of Education Richard Riley announced an enrollment crisis in American education in a special report titled "The Baby Boom Echo," released on August 21, 1996: "Twenty-five years after the baby boom generation set a national record for school enrollment . . . it is fitting that the children of the baby boomers are doing the record breaking."

The problem with the report's title and conclusion is that the recent large and rapid increases in the school population are not primarily the result of children born to baby boomers; Riley's attribution is disingenuous. The baby boomers have below-replacement-level fertility; they are not reproducing themselves.

Linda H. Thom, a retired statistician from the Santa Barbara (CA) County Administrator's office, attacks the US Education Department's report with the department's own data—which can be found in the report itself or in the *Digest of Educational Statistics*. Analyzing enrollment trends between 1975 and 1990, Thom finds that "nationally, average daily attendance (ADA), excluding California, declined by 3,542,207 students. In California, however, ADA increased by 699,030. Large enrollment gains were also experienced in Florida and Texas."

These three border States lead the list of immigrant destinations in the United States. In California, the major immigrant destination, county-by-county comparisons of the school-age population show that the children of immigrants and children who have themselves immigrated account for the higher enrollment numbers.

The increase in child poverty is a related issue. Secretary Riley states that many more of America's young people live in poverty now than three decades ago: "In 1970, near the peak of the last [school] enrollment high, the number of young people living in poverty barely exceeded 10 million. In 1995, the number of young people who were struggling reached 15.7 million." Riley offers no useful explanation of what caused this increase.

However, Thom suggests, "If immigration caused the enrollment increase, then immigration caused the poverty increase." During the 1980s, California, Texas, and Florida accounted for 98 percent of the increased caseload in the Aid to Families with Dependent Children (AFDC) program. The US General Accounting Office reports that, for the same decade, "the total number of school children declined by 2.3 million," and the number of white and black school-age children also declined. But the number of poor students increased. Thom concludes: "Hispanic and Asian/Pacific children accounted for all of the added poor, school-age children."

Educational achievement often reflects parental education and values. Unfortunately, Mexican and Central American immigrants average less than an eighth-grade education. Mexico and Central America are not only the source of the largest annual immigrant flows into California and the United States in general; Hispanic women now account for approximately 18 percent of all births, up from 14 percent in 1989. Mexican, Central, and South American women (not Cuban) account for most of this increase.

These facts are never mentioned in connection with the problems of population growth—overcrowding, budget deficits in local governments, environmental stress—that trouble Americans. Child poverty, bloated school budgets, and a poorly educated, unskilled labor force have multiple components, but a common denominator appears to be the very high level of immigration into the United States.

Many statistical reports require a second look. The National Center for Health Statistics, in reporting on illegitimacy rates, plays with the categories, "white, black, and Hispanic," in a way that seems to inflate the rates for whites and blacks in comparison with Hispanics.

The illegitimacy statistics are not an isolated instance of creative reporting. FBI crime statistics report the ethnic group of victims and perpetrators, but they do so differently. Victims are classified "black, white, Hispanic or other"; but the perpetrator classification drops "Hispanic." Under the system in place at least as late as 1999, an assault on a Hispanic by a Hispanic is reported as either black-on-Hispanic or white-on-Hispanic crime. Clearly, this is an irresponsible irritant to race relations.

Similar errors are found in a range of publications. *Workforce 2000* (Packer and Williams 1987), released in 1987 by the Hudson Institute, includes a particularly grievous error. The report's Executive Summary announced that only 15 percent of the entrants into the workforce during the thirteen years leading up to the year 2000 would be white males. The alarm was raised in every newsroom and every Fortune 500 boardroom in the United States.

The correct datum, however, is that white males were expected to be 31 percent of all entrants into the labor force, with 15 percent more entering than retiring by the year 2000. The error crept in through omission of the word "net" from the Executive Summary. In effect, net new skilled jobs had to grow by 15 percent just to keep pace with the job needs of young white American men, to say nothing of minorities and women.

Richard C. Atkinson, chancellor of the University of California (San Diego), exposed the error in a letter to the editor that appeared in *Science* shortly after the publication of *Workforce 2000*. But for approximately one year, no mass news media broke—or perhaps even knew—the complete story.

The erroneous report and the near-panic reaction in some quarters helped create momentum for the 1990 legislation that raised legal immigrant (green card) visas by 40 percent. H1-B visas for skilled workers were added without an offsetting reduction in other visa categories. Indeed, almost every visa category was enlarged.

Three weeks after Congress increased legal immigration visas, a sidebar in the November 19, 1990, issue of US News and World Report exposed *Workforce 2000*'s mistake. Were the error and the lack of timely corrections the work of gremlins?

Distortions also characterized the initial press release and certain editorial comments regarding the NRC study of immigration, *The New Americans* (1997). Sen. Spencer Abraham and the chair of the NRC study panel coauthored a piece for the *New York Times* that provoked NRC panelists George J. Borjas and Richard B. Freeman to respond with an article titled "Findings We Never Found." Outraged at various misrepresentations, Harvard economists Borjas and Freeman objected that certain public figures, specifically Senator Abraham and Rand Corporation economist James P. Smith, "make it seem as if immigration is a free lunch for Americans. . . . [They] simply failed to mention that the bulk of the increase in the GNP [due to immigration] goes to the immigrants themselves as wages and salaries, not to the native born."

The economic benefit to natives is on the order of one to ten billion dollars annually—trivial in an eight-trillion-dollar economy.

Moreover, the economic benefit of immigration (growth in Gross National Product [GNP]) may be more than offset by public and social costs. Referring to the widening gap between rich and poor, Borjas and Freeman explain, "The Academy report also concluded [that] the 44 percent of the decline in the real wages of high school dropouts from 1980 to 1995 resulted from immigration . . . There are 13 million such workers." Immigration creates winners and losers: employers who can substitute cheaper immigrant for native-born labor win, to the tune of approximately $140 billion annually. At the same time, workers whose wages are driven down by rapid growth in the size of the labor force lose by approximately $133 billion annually. Immigration has negated forty years of US social policy designed to end poverty.

Yet the beat goes on. The INS, between August 1995 and September 1996, gave citizenship to an estimated 39,000 ineligible aliens, including 11,500 criminals, according to independent auditing and consulting firm Peat Marwick. The Peat Marwick study found that over 90 percent of the INS naturalization and processing procedures that resulted in 1.05 million new US citizens eligible to vote in the 1996 election were flawed.

On November 11–12, 1998, the annual conference of the State Department's Office of Refugee Resettlement attracted 1,200 participants to the Mayflower Hotel in Washington, DC. Approximately half of those present were government officials, including Secretary of Health and Human Services Donna Shalala. Speakers and workshops addressed the means by which private and government organizations could secure public health care and welfare programs for refugees (and asylum seekers), and how antidiscrimination legislation could be invoked to circumvent welfare limits and prevent the denial of benefits.

Secretary Shalala stated that over 39 percent of active tuberculosis cases and approximately 60 percent of hepatitis B cases in the United States are found in the immigrant population. She suggested that the prevalence of disease among immigrants could be used as a wedge to move the United States toward the national health care model proposed by Hillary Clinton's health care task force in 1993–1994.

Of lesser importance but indicative of the mood, the moment of silence at the conference in observance of Veterans Day was not for American vets, but rather for Red Army veterans (Russian refugees) who are drawing Supplemental Security Income (SSI) benefits in New

York City. In fact, the increase in SSI benefits to immigrants, especially refugees, is several hundred percent greater than to the native-born population.

The refugee authorization for 1999 was 78,000 persons, not including about 20,000 Cubans who entered under a separate program. Refugees enter under the 1989 Lautenberg Amendment, which grants them immediate entitlement to any benefit available to citizens, including Social Security. Those who apply for asylum after entering the United States were not included in the 78,000; they numbered about 50,000 in 1999.

The category system for allocating immigrant and refugee visas—whether the criteria be country or continent of origin, religious affiliation, skills, or family reunification—leads to jockeying for position and logrolling among ethnic, business, and other interest groups, and results in larger numbers of newcomers and unstoppable population growth. The only strategy that will stabilize US population size is to enact an all-inclusive immigration cap or moratorium. The number need not be zero, because some people emigrate each year; and the number probably ought not be zero because American citizens who marry foreigners should expect to be able to bring in their spouse after some reasonable period of time. However, the expectation that all "family reunification" should occur in the United States rather than in some other country is unreasonable. Immigration of 100,000–200,000 persons annually is compatible with a stable US population.

By large majorities, white, black, and Hispanic voters have endorsed immigration reduction. Nevertheless, the issue has not become politically salient, unlike, for example, improving education, saving Social Security, and reducing taxes. Each of these goals, however, becomes more difficult to achieve as the immigrant population grows.

A vocal minority of wealthy contributors to both major political parties, representing left and right, have forged an alliance in support of high levels of immigration. Pro-immigration activists including the National Lawyers Association and "many Jewish groups," according to *Washington Jewish Week* (March 28, 1996), engaged in a "concerted lobbying campaign" to preserve the current refugee and other immigrant flows. Barring a recession, the latent disgruntlement with high levels of immigration is unlikely to coalesce into a strong grassroots movement except in border States. The mis- and disinformation campaign have been a resounding success.

Census Bureau Distortions Hide Immigration Crisis: Real Numbers Much Higher, Part I*

Publications on the size and growth rate of the US population seem designed to confuse rather than enlighten. The Census Bureau made up for large annual underestimates of population growth during the 1990s with a twelve-million-person bump in the census year. Unfazed, it perpetuates error through massively undercounting illegal aliens.

The Census Bureau is not unique in massaging statistics, possibly in the service of policy rather than accuracy. As an example, economist John Williams' website (www.shadowstats.com) addresses other seriously misleading statistics. Williams computes current unemployment and inflation numbers using criteria standardized by the government during the 1940s–1970s, criteria since altered to the extent that past and present cannot be meaningfully compared.

A Twelve-Million-Person Bump in One Year

A smoking gun that reflects on the Census Bureau's underreporting is that a 12 million increase in the US population, from 272.7 million in 1999 to 284.5 million in 2000, had to be accommodated in one year. The startling twelve-million-person one-year increase in the Census Bureau's 2000 report reflects findings of the ten-year census.

For comparison, the Census Bureau's population growth estimates in other years of the 1990s decade center approximately on 2.5 million annually. Allowing for the standard 2.5 million increase in the tenth year and spreading the remaining 9.5 million increase over each year of the decade would add 0.9 million in annual growth. A better estimate of US population growth during the 1990s would have been 3.4 million annually.

Someone should possibly have asked if the twelve million leap in 2000 was enough. Much was made of failure to count the homeless in censuses before 2000. However, the 1990s underestimates seem mostly the result of not taking into account illegal aliens settling in the United States, particularly in view of reports that illegal alien border crossings were increasing dramatically. Systematic undercounts of the illegal alien population result in the Census Bureau estimating five–seven million present in 2000, whereas other sources [including retired Border Patrol officers and an independent analysis by accounting firm Bear Stearns

---

* Online in *Population-Environment Balance,* www.balance.org [October, 2006].

17

Asset Management] were quick to estimate eighteen–twenty-eight million illegal aliens at the least.

If 11–23 million more illegal aliens than the Census Bureau expected—and failed to count—actually were in the United States in 2000, then the real population of that year was already close to exceeding 300 million. In fact, the evidence overwhelmingly indicates that the 300 million mark was passed in the year 2000. This October's much-heralded announcement that the United States just reached 300 million in 2006 will be another scene in a great charade.

Long-Term Estimates Also Revised But Still Short

The Census Bureau also revises upward its long-term projections but perhaps not enough. An example pointed out in demographer Lindsey Grant's newest book, *The Collapsing Bubble*, is that the Census Bureau projects the likeliest size of the US population in 2100 to be 600 million. This is 100 million greater than the Census Bureau's middle projection made as recently as 1994—a 20 percent revision upward!

Reviewing Grant's book, Andrew Ferguson hazards that the Census Bureau's new middle projection should have been still higher. If the "U.S. population continues to grow at the rate of the three closing decades of the last century, 1.06% per year, then by 2100 [the] U.S. population would be 810 million" (Ferguson 2006).

The Census Bureau Perpetuates Error

Going forward from year 2000, a chastened Census Bureau might have been expected to correct the assumptions that had led to massive underestimation. But no, the 2001 through 2005 estimates return to the fiction that the US population grows each year at the relatively stately pace of slightly less than three million, at a rate of 0.9 percent annually in the latest year, 2005 (PRB 2006). The illegal alien addition to the population is assumed to be 500,000 annually.

Massive Undercounting of Illegal Aliens

Reports of much higher-than-reported illegal aliens entering, and in, the United States are solid.

In February 2002, a Border Patrol (BP) Supervisor of twenty-seven years' service testified before Congress that the number of illegal aliens was several times the Census Bureau estimate. He stated, "According to various Mexican media and official Mexican government sources, the country of Mexico has 18 million of its citizens residing illegally in the United States at this very minute" (Stoddard 2002). Besides Mexicans, what of Filipinos, Indians, Chinese, Koreans, Vietnamese, Eastern Europeans, Irish, Brazilians, Guatemalans, Hondurans, and Haitians living illegally in the United States?

Using financial and employment data, analysts for Bear Stearns Asset Management also estimate a number much higher than anything considered by the Census Bureau. They concluded in early 2004 that, "The number of illegal immigrants in the United States may be as high as 20 million people, more than double the official 9 million people estimated by the Census Bureau" (Justich and Ng 2005).

Time Magazine asserted, also in 2004, that more than 4,000 illegal aliens simply walk across the Mexico/Arizona border each day! Nationwide, an estimated three million enter annually, and as many as "fifteen million" are thought to remain in the United States (Barlett and Steele 2004).

Department of Education reports are also suggestive. Comparing projected and actual enrollments for the latest years, the data yield this: the projected K-12 increase in public school enrollments from 2002 to 2003 was 11,000 pupils. But "actual 2003 enrollments came in 339,000 above 2002's level—more than 30 times the projected rise" (Rubenstein 2006). Where did these children come from, if not illegal immigration?

Patrick Buchanan's 2006 book *State of Emergency: Third World Invasion and Conquest of America* states that the BP apprehends 150,000 illegal aliens breaking into the United States each month, amounting to 1.8 million apprehensions annually (Buchanan 2006). The BP estimates that, for each illegal alien apprehended, 3–5 succeed in entering. Assuming 4, the middle figure, then 4 × 1.8 million annual apprehensions = 7.2 million aliens enter illegally each year.

Some illegal border crossers may be apprehended more than once, although most—70 percent— make it in a first or second attempt, and 92 percent make it eventually according to the Center for Comparative Immigration Studies at UC, San Diego (Gonzalez and Carroll 2005). In recent testimony before the House Judiciary Committee, Wayne Cornelius, director of the center, stated that 92–97 percent succeed on two tries or less (Cornelius 2006).

Moreover, many foreigners enter supposedly for a visit but never leave. In 1992, approximately 150,000 more foreign passengers arrived in US airports than left (Grant 1992). *USA Today* reports that "at least 3.8 million" illegal aliens arrived legally but remained after visas expired

(Editorial 2006). This could be, in part, H1-B workers who stayed—contrary to the terms of their visa—after termination of their job.

Conservatively, assume that just 5 million—rather than 7.2 million plus visa overstayers—actually enter the United States each year. Of these five million, assume that 40 percent remain indefinitely. This calculation suggests that two million illegal aliens melt permanently into the US population annually. If 60 percent stay, then approximately three million new illegal aliens remain in the United States annually. Compare that to the Census Bureau's puny estimate of 500,000 illegal aliens staying annually!

A high proportion of illegal aliens planning to stay on a permanent basis seems reasonable on various counts. Recent [*circa 2004–2005*] polls show that 46 percent of Mexicans would like to move to the United States (Schodolski 2006). Once here, illegal aliens seemingly wish to stay: a 2005 poll found that 4 to 1, or 80 percent, would stay if given a good opportunity (Pew Hispanic Center 2005). Rather than risk repeatedly recrossing, illegal alien men are increasingly likely to be joined by their families (Gonzalez and Carroll 2005).

Also suggesting long-term residence in the United States is the calculation that "Mexico will take in a record $24 billion in remittances this year" (*Investor's Business Daily* 2006). Transients do not earn that kind of spare change, particularly in the low-skill jobs available to most Mexican and Central American workers.

Unrealistic Estimates

Our estimated low figure, two million illegal aliens staying annually, more than explains why the 2000 census required the Census Bureau to show a leap of twelve million in the population in one year. The high figure of three million strongly suggests that the census missed a good many! That is likely: which illegal alien family member will hop up and say, "Count me"?

The question arises: does the Census Bureau have an agenda other than factual reporting of population statistics? Errors since 1990 have all gone in the same direction: underestimation of absolute growth and growth rates. Moreover, the revisions and catch-up numbers are underplayed. Who knew that the 2000 census forced a hike of twelve million in the estimated size of the population? Rarely is the public told that the US population is growing very fast—by far the fastest rate of any developed country in the world. Or that the growth *rate* itself appears to be growing?

The Census Bureau's misinformation appears consistent with the intent to soothe a public that is becoming alarmed at the scale of immigration and the rapidity of population growth. Underestimates also go far to discredit those who call for a moratorium on both legal and illegal immigration, and for ending automatic citizenship awarded to children born in the United States to illegal alien parents. Accurate reporting of numbers would make ending birthright citizenship politically compelling and would strengthen the argument for a catch-our-breath moratorium on legal immigration.

One may fairly conclude that the Census Bureau is a willing participant to misinforming the public on the state of the nation. Perhaps this is a strategy designed to redirect and lull voters into complacency so that they forgive their representatives and senators who legislate in favor of illegal aliens and massive legal immigration, rather than in the interest of citizens of the United States.

Massive Undercounting Begins with Legal Immigration

Throughout the 1990s, the Census Bureau has nailed legal immigration at approximately one million annually. This entails omitting the annual refugee number, which has varied from 45,000 to 142,000 and the asylee number, approximately 150,000 annually. Arrivals under student programs and the H1-B and other employer-sponsored programs and their families, and "extended voluntary departure" categories are also ignored, although these "temporary" visa categories often become de facto permanent residents.

Since the 1970s, the Census Bureau has been the target of legal actions by state and local government because census numbers are the basis for allocating billions of dollars in federal funds. Recently, the Census Bureau acknowledged undercounting the population of Washington DC by 6 percent (University of Mississippi 2006).

Also, compare Census Bureau numbers with those of another government agency, the CIS constituted under the Homeland Security Department. For 2005, the CIS Yearbook estimate of permanent legal additions to the US population is 1,224,078 (including legal permanent residents, refugees, asylees, and orphans). This is the same year for which the Census Bureau estimates less than one million immigrants altogether.

The Census Bureau appears to be missing one-quarter million persons who legally entered the United States in 2005, people who will be permanent additions to the US population.

Real Population Numbers

The US population passed 300 million in year 2000. The current US population is approximately 327 million.

The latest year for which vital statistics are reported, 2004, saw approximately 1.7 million more total births than deaths. Of the approximately 4.1 million total births, 945,000 or nearly one-quarter were Hispanic births (National Vital Statistics Reports 2005). Additionally, the data suggest that between two and three million illegal aliens stay in the United States and more than one million legal immigrants arrive in the United States annually. These numbers indicate a faster rate of population growth and a shorter doubling time than the Census Bureau estimated for the 1990s (1.2 percent annual growth, projecting fifty-eight years to double) (PRB website).

Summing annual growth figures (1.7 million natural increase, 1 million legal immigrants [Census Bureau count], and 2 or 3 million illegal aliens who stay), one sees that, each year, the population grows by 4.7–5.7 million. The growth rate is between 1.4 and 1.7 percent annually. If it is 1.4 percent, the population doubling time is fifty years.

The rate of growth has itself been increasing. If acceleration of the growth rate continues, we are on trend to pass the one billion mark in approximately seventy years.

Is today's 327 million "many"? Consider that the United States fought and won World War II with a population of 135 million—less than half!

Note: Going forward, the Census Bureau estimates sedate growth centering approximately on three million or less annually. The World Population Data Sheet published in 2001, 2002, 2003, 2004, 2005, and 2006 state that the population for preceding years, respectively, was 284.5 million, 287.4 million, 291.5 million, 293.6 million, 296.5 million, and 299.1 million. This quiet sequence brings one to gently anticipate the announcement that the United States will pass its 300 millionth person in October 2006.

The 300 million in October 2006 is nonsense. That number was passed some years ago. The Census Bureau undercounts legal immigration by omitting whole categories. Illegal immigration accounts for more misinformation. Whereas the Census Bureau estimated approximately eleven million illegal aliens in the United States in 2005, and now apparently concedes up to twelve million, various credible sources put the number much higher.

To Reform Welfare, Reform Immigration*

All welfare reform proposals have the same goal: to get people off of public assistance and into jobs. But the US Department of Health and Human Services estimates that 2.3 million net new jobs would be needed to absorb present welfare recipients into the active work force. A commitment to creating these jobs would cost billions of dollars. A more efficient strategy is to dry up a principal source of unskilled labor.

Welfare reform can be linked, cheaply and fairly, to immigration control. In 1992, the US INS issued 1.3 million work authorizations, and the US Census Bureau estimates that another 300,000 aliens entered the United States illegally. The economy created nearly two million net new jobs, a vast improvement over recent net job losses, but with an annual net increment of about 900,000 native-born Americans entering the labor force, the demand for jobs still exceeded supply.

Americans most directly harmed by immigration are the poor. This is nothing new. A century ago, Booker T. Washington exhorted the people to rise up against immigration on grounds that blacks were passed over for jobs in favor of immigrants. Today's depressed neighborhoods in high-immigration cities show how little has changed. Demographer William Frey of the University of Michigan documents an outflow of unskilled native-born blacks and whites from California, where they have been displaced from jobs, schooling, and other opportunities. Americans have been displaced in the janitorial, restaurant, motel/hotel, construction, meatpacking, and service station industries. A consensus is developing among economists that one unskilled American worker's job is lost for every six or seven immigrants who enter.

A labor force that grows too rapidly also debases jobs, seen in the Third World's disregard for worker safety and shown historically by the effect on wages. A study of nineteenth-century England by economist R.D. Lee (1980) shows that a 10 percent rise in the labor supply led to a 19 percent wage decline. Economist Claudia Goldin of Harvard finds that our last great surge of immigration, from 1890 to 1920, caused wages in the immigration-impacted cities to rise 1–4 percent

---

* In *Governing*, pp. 10–11 (August, 1994).

less than they would have done in the absence of immigration. And in economic recessions, she writes, "wages were distinctly depressed in cities having an increase in the percentage of their populations that was foreign-born. A 1 percentage point increase decreased wages by about 1.5 to 2 percent" [Goldin 2001]. Indeed, during the past fifteen years of heavy immigration, Americans' real disposable personal income has been declining.

Labor surplus, not shortage, is the abiding issue at every educational level. As of March 1993, 13 percent of PhD mathematicians remained unemployed. Until the better prospects of 1994, college graduates and engineers faced underemployment even as the economy recovered. High school graduates are bumped downward and, in turn, bump those below them. The United States' rapidly expanding labor force, driven by the most immigration this country has ever seen, continues to diminish prospects that all young Americans and their children will enjoy the American Dream.

Immigration accounts for nearly half of US population growth, and births to post-1970 immigrants—who have significantly more children per woman than the national average—add more. The population of the United States is growing by 58,000 people a week. The Census Bureau's most recent projection suggests a population of 400 million by 2050.

Facing demographic trends of this magnitude, no administration or government program and no foreseeable private investment can provide enough jobs to implement welfare reform humanely. The nonchoice will be rising unemployment/underemployment, and more people on the welfare rolls as both native-born Americans and those who have already immigrated to this country contend against incoming job-seekers.

A pause in immigration would let welfare reform proceed smoothly. The market could absorb the unemployed, reengage the discouraged worker, and relieve the welfare burden. A genuine labor shortage, if it materialized, would encourage a substitution of technology for labor, enhancing productivity and leaving room for noninflationary wage raises.

These benefits are realizable from a time-out on immigration, aiming in the long term for an annual flow of 200,000. This approximates a "replacement level" number where those entering the country are balanced by others leaving. Paralleled by two-child-per-couple fertility, this reform of immigration policy would gradually stabilize the US population, again making all of the people stakeholders in their communities and in the national enterprise, America.

Immigration and the Nation's Health*

Nothing is more vital to the safety and survival of Western nations than the enduring health of their population. During earlier periods of population migration, countries that encountered high immigration levels, such as the United States during the 1880s and early 1900s, took stern measures to restrict the flow of immigrants, in part out of public health concerns. Poor hygiene among immigrants and inadequate screening measures by public health officials during these high-influx periods triggered legislative reforms that severely restricted immigration levels to the United States. Lately, public health officials have considered another potential risk: importing infectious diseases.

A panel discussion at the annual meetings of the American Association of Public Health (Boston 2001) and featuring speakers from the Harvard University School of Public Health warned of diseases being newly introduced into the United States. Increasing risk, they said, was linked to twenty million Americans who travel annually (but usually briefly) to third world countries. Who would have considered that American tourists could become such a risk to their local communities, contaminating hearth and home with infectious diseases from abroad!

What, then, of infections brought into the United States through immigration, by the approximately 1.2 million legal and half-million illegal aliens who settle in the U.S. each year? American travelers are the threat, not immigrants, insisted the Harvard panelists. Their insistent message was that nothing could be blamed on immigration. Audience skepticism regarding this conclusion was dismissed and eventually suppressed.

The US Centers for Disease Control (CDC) deal, rather more forthrightly, in facts. An impartial concern for public health drives their frequent reports on the rising incidence of tuberculosis, hepatitis (A, B, C, and E), malaria, and various contagious or infectious diseases long thought to have been defeated—or never before seen—in the United States.

Tuberculosis (TB) is a prime example. The bacterium that causes tuberculosis "infects one third of the world's population."[1] Keeping pace with the increasing impact of post-1965 immigration from the third world, America's TB rate has been growing since 1984. The prevalence of TB in the countries of origin of most immigrants to the United States is ten to thirty times greater than in this country.[2] Risk is greatest where

* In *The Occidental Quarterly* 2(4) pp. 27–32 (Winter 2002/2003).

recent immigrants concentrate. For example, a 1996 investigation of an Alexandria, Virginia, high school found that one-quarter of the students carried tuberculosis bacteria.[3]

In December 2000, the *Journal of the American Medical Association* cited the CDC's conclusion that tuberculosis is continuously being reintroduced by new immigrants.[4] The TB rate among foreign-born US residents was 32.9 per 100,000 persons over a six-year observation period ending in 1999, more than five times as great as the native-born rate of 5.8 cases per 100,000. Through late 1999, immigrants accounted for 42 percent of the 18,000 identified cases of TB.[5] The CDC estimates that the rate among the foreign-born will continue to escalate, as it has already in California, New York City, and Northern Virginia.[6]

In Canada, immigrants account for two-thirds of active TB cases; 20 per 100,000 of foreign-born persons carry the TB bacterium, a rate 15 times as great as among native-born Canadians (excluding American Indians).[7]

Until recently, legal immigrants to the United States were screened only for active disease, and illegal immigrants have evaded screening measures altogether. The majority of foreign-born with active TB tend to have had a reactivation of a latent condition. Their impact on the US health care system is magnified through transmission to the native-born population. Approximately half of cases among US-born persons are new. That is, they result from contact with someone who is infected, rather than from a reactivation of a latent infection.[8]

On average, a person with active TB infects twenty others annually,[9] although, at the high end of the range, a boy adopted from the Marshall Islands into a small town in North Dakota infected fifty-six persons, including his unrelated legal guardian.[10] In Toronto and Hamilton, Canada, dozens of people infected by one Gaspare Benjamin, recently arrived from the Dominican Republic, are suing the Canadian government for shortcomings in its health-screening process.[11]

A complicating factor is multidrug-resistant cases of TB, which develop if the (six-month) treatment program stops before the bacillus is totally eliminated from a patient's system. The World Health Organization reports that countries formerly part of the Soviet Union, the Philippines, Peru, India, Bangladesh, China, various sub-Saharan African countries, and South Africa have a high proportion of drug-resistant strains among their TB caseloads. In 1999, multidrug-resistant strains accounted for 1.3 percent of TB cases in the United States,[12] and the proportion is rising.

Crowded housing, early childhood and old age, or compromised immune systems linked to other medical conditions are associated with contracting TB. The bacterium is airborne, so risk is also associated with being eight hours or more in confined spaces, such as trains or planes.[13]

Children Especially At Risk

American children are increasingly at risk not only from introduced diseases, but also from preventive measures against these diseases. For example, since 1991 the CDC has recommended that all babies born in the United States should receive vaccinations against hepatitis B virus. The three-shot vaccination confers lifelong immunity against a disease that is transmitted by blood or intimate contact, much like HIV, except that it is many times more contagious than HIV.

Areas where hepatitis B is endemic include Asia and the Pacific Islands. The foreign-born account for 40–60 percent of all US cases. As of 1991, an estimated 1.25 million carriers, capable of infecting others, lived in the United States, and an estimated 22,000 newborns, annually, acquire the virus from their mothers.[14] Only half of hepatitis B carriers show early symptoms, but up to a quarter eventually die of liver failure or liver cancer.

The hepatitis A virus also affects the liver and is highly contagious. On the US side of the Texas-Mexican border, and in California, residents have a disease rate that is two to three times the national average. The virus is transmitted through unclean food and water and spread by infected food handlers or processors. In 1997, frozen strawberries grown in Mexico and processed in San Diego sickened consumers as far away as Michigan.[15] Young children are at highest risk because of unreliable hygienic practices in school and play environments.[16]

Vaccinations against measles/mumps/rubella (MMR) are routinely administered to American-born babies, and immunization records must usually be provided before enrollment in kindergarten. Nevertheless, epidemics break out in school systems because immunization may not be checked when children, even those from countries that lack preventive public health programs, enter at later grades. American children are subjected to repeat MMR booster shots if epidemics break out in their school.

North Carolina leads the nation in incidence of rubella, and "Latinos" account for 80 percent of the cases. The measles-like viral infection causes severe birth defects if contracted by a woman in the early stages of pregnancy.[17]

Assorted Disease Agents

Americans who come into direct or indirect contact with immigrants are exposed to an array of infectious agents that they would otherwise not encounter in this country. Infection may result in discomfort, severe illness, or death.

Public health alarms near ports of entry or in single communities have been raised in connection with many conditions in addition to the more commonly introduced diseases, such as TB and hepatitis. Among these are cholera (endemic in South America), the West Nile virus (identical to a strain identified in Israel that killed four people in New York City), bubonic plague, ebola virus, and leprosy. Then there is the neurocysticercosis parasite, increasingly prevalent among children in the United States and endemic in Mexico, where it is a principal cause of seizures; the parasite uses pigs as a vector and is spread through accidentally ingesting infested feces or eating pork infected with the parasite's ova.[18]

Public Costs

Public health measures as well as treatment for disease are costly to taxpayers. Public expenditures directed toward the care of individual immigrants have been most studied, but are not the whole story. For example, New York City allowed a decline in tuberculosis surveillance and care because it seemed largely unneeded when the disease was receding. The city's 1989 budget for all expenditures on TB was $2 million. The shock of discovering the immigrant-driven resurgence in TB rates drove the 1991 budget to $50 million, with annual increases to come.[19] The wake-up call to treat multiple-drug-resistant TB eventually cost the city $1 billion.[20]

Economist Donald Huddle, at the behest of the Carrying Capacity Network (CCN), evaluated the fiscal impact of health-related payments and medical care for immigrants. The 1996 cost of Medicaid for legal and illegal immigrants was found to be $14.55 billion, net of contributions by immigrants. The net cost of SSI was $2.76 billion. Legal immigrants accounted for more than 80 percent of these costs.[21]

Social Security records obtained under the Freedom of Information Act show that elderly and disabled immigrants apply for SSI shortly after arriving in the United States, despite promising the U.S government that they would be supported by relatives. The Associated Press reports that "Immigrants made up 11% of SSI rolls in December 1992, up from 3.3% a decade ago."[22]

The Center for Immigration Studies (CIS) in Washington, DC, focuses on how immigration affects the number of US residents without health care insurance. Principal findings of a July, 2000, CIS study are that "[i]mmigrants who arrived between 1994 and 1998 and their [US-born] children accounted for an astonishing 59 percent or 2.7 million of the growth in the size of the uninsured population since 1993." Compared to the 13.9 percent without health care insurance in native-American households in 1998, "32.4% of persons living in immigrant households . . . lacked health insurance."[23]

Not surprisingly, immigrants are heavy users of the nation's hospital emergency rooms. In 1997, New York City hospitals provided $1.2 billion in care to immigrants "who could not pay."[24] The foreign-born also account disproportionately for use of maternity services. In 1999, 20.2 percent of US births were to the foreign-born, contributing to the fifty-six million foreign-born residents and children of immigrants who were in the United States at the time of the year 2000 census.[25] Approximately half of married, illegal Latino aliens have a child who is a US citizen by birth.[26]

Informing Public Policy

Immigration's costs are varied and high. Children, the poor, and those with compromised immune systems are at greatest risk from deteriorating public health, crowded clinics, and higher ambient levels of contagious disease. Local and state taxpayers bear the increased fiscal weight of disease—both for treatment and prevention.

The principal beneficiaries of immigration are the immigrants themselves and employers who benefit from cheap labor. Business profits from paying low wages while shifting certain of their labor force costs to the public at large. Employers enjoy the concentrated benefits of low-wage labor, whereas the cost of public services—including health care, education, and the infrastructure used by immigrants and their children—are widely distributed.[27] Public debate on the costs and benefits of immigration, and the national interest in receiving approximately 1.2 million legal and half a million illegal newcomers annually, is long overdue.

Notes

1. "A Weak Link in TB Bacterium Is Found," *Science* 289 (August 18, 2000), 1123.
2. Virginia Abernethy, "Third World Hospital De Luxe," *Population and Environment* 17, no. 3 (1996): 191–3.

3. "Carrying Capacity Checkup and Connections," *Network Bulletin* 1–2, no. 5 (1996). Carrying Capacity Network, Washington, DC.
4. August Gribbin, "CDC Report Links TB, Immigration," *Washington Times*, December 13, 2000.
5. Samuel Francis, "Uncontrolled Immigration Creates Serious Health Threat to U.S. Citizens," *Tribune*, January 2, 2001: sec. A, 7.
6. Leef Smith, "TB Still on Rise in No. Va.," *Washington Post*, March 18, 2002.
7. Andre Picard, "TB Threat," *Toronto Globe and Mail*, May 18, 2002.
8. E. Geng, B. Kreiswirth, et al., "Changes in the Transmission of Tuberculosis in New York City from 1990 to 1999," *New England Journal of Medicine* 346, no. 19 (May 9, 2002): 1453–8.
9. August Gribbin, "CDC Report Links TB, Immigration," *Washington Times*, December 13, 2000.
10. J. McConnaughey, "Immigrant Child Takes Tuberculosis to Country Town," *San Francisco Chronicle*, November 11, 1999: sec. A, 16.
11. Greg Weston, "Every Canadian's Health Nightmare," *Toronto Sun*, January 28, 2001.
12. M.C. Raviglione, D. Snider, and A. Kochi, "Global Epidemiology of Tuberculosis," *Journal of the American Medical Association* 273, no. 3 (1995): 220–26.
13. Andre Picard, "TB Threat," *Toronto Globe and Mail*, May 18, 2002.
14. Centers for Disease Control, "Hepatitis B virus: a comprehensive strategy for eliminating transmission in the United States through universal childhood vaccination," MMWR 1991; 40(RR-13); Gale Scott, "Hepatitis in Infants 'Ticking Time Bomb,' " *Nashville Banner*, September 8, 1992.
15. *Oakland Tribune*, April 3, 1997: sec. A, 9.
16. Philip Rosenthal, "Assessing the Hepatitis A Threat to California," *Liver Lifeline* (American Liver Foundation, San Francisco), Spring 2000: 6.
17. Charlie Frago, "N.C. Leads Nation in Rubella," *The News and Record* (Piedmont Triad, N.C.), January 9, 2001.
18. R. L. Glass, M. Libel, and A.D. Brandling-Bennett, "Epidemic Cholera in the Americas," *Science*, June 12, 1992: 1524; "New York's Lethal Virus Came from Middle East, DNA Suggests," *Science* (November 19, 1999): 1450; "Plague Fever," *Science*, July 31, 1998; Ken Kilpatrick, "Woman from Congo in Hamilton Hospital," *Toronto Globe and Mail*, February 6, 2001; T. D. Mastro, S. C. Redd, and R. F. Breiman, "Imported Leprosy in the United States, 1978 through 1988," *American Journal of Public Health* 82, no. 8 (August 1992); E.H. Kossoff, "Neurocysticercosis," *EMedicine Journal*, December 13, 2001.
19. "Disease Fights Back," *The Economist*, May 20, 1995, 15–16.
20. Eric Stokstad, "Drug-Resistant TB on the Rise," *Science*, March 31, 2000, 2391.
21. Donald Huddle, *The Net Costs of Immigration: The Facts, the Trends, and the Critics*, Washington, DC: Carrying Capacity Network, October 22, 1996.
22. "Immigrant Welfare," *USA Today*, May 7, 1993.
23. Stephen A. Camarota and James R. Edwards, *Without Coverage. Immigration's Impact on the Size and Growth of the Population Lacking Health Insurance* (Washington, DC: Center for Immigration Studies).
24. R. Kennedy, "Desperately Ill Foreigners at U.S. Emergency Rooms," *New York Times*, July 1, 1999, 1.

25. Janny Scott, "Foreign Born in U.S. at Record High," *New York Times*, February 7, 2002, 18.
26. M. L. Berk, C. L. Schur, and L. R. Chavez, "Health Care Use among Undocumented Latino Immigrants," *Health Affairs*, July–August, 2000.
27. Cosman, Madeleine. Spring, 2005. Illegal Aliens and American Medicine, *Journal of American Physicians and Surgeons* 17:1. http://www.japands.com/.

References

A (Sore) Loser That Won't Heal. 2006. *Investor's Business Daily*, September 5, 2006.

Ahlburg, Dennis A., and James W. Vaupel. 1990. "500 Million Americans by 2050?" *Demography* 27 (4): 639–47.

Barlett, Donald L. and James B. Steele. 2004. *Time Magazine*, September 20, 2004.

Borjas, G. 1996. "The New Economics of Immigration." *The Atlantic Monthly*, November, 72–80.

Buchanan, Patrick. 2006. *State of Emergency: Third World Invasion and Conquest of America*. New York: Thomas Dunne Books.

Cornelius, Wayne. September 2006. *Testimony to House Judiciary Committee on Immigration*. San Diego, CA: Marine Corps Recruit Depot.

Editorial. 2006. "Think All Illegal Aliens are Sneaking In? Think Again." *USA Today*, May 1, 2006.

Ferguson, Andrew R.B. 2006. "Review of *The Collapsing Bubble*, by Lindsey Grant." Optimum Population Trust, Great Britain, September, 2006.

Goldin C, Katz L. F. 2001. Decreasing (and then increasing) inequality in America: A tale of two half centuries. In *The Causes and Consequences of Increasing Inequality*, edited by F. Welch, 37–82. Chicago, IL: University of Chicago Press.

Goldin C, Katz LF. Decreasing (and then Increasing) Inequality in America: A Tale of Two Half Centuries. In *The Causes and Consequences of Increasing Inequality*, edited by F. Welch, 37–82. Chicago, IL: University of Chicago Press; 2001.

Gonzalez, Daniel, and Susan Carroll. 2005. "Siege on Border: Costly Fortifications Fail to Deter Immigrant Flow." *Arizona Republic*, June 19, 2005.

Grant, Lindsey. November 1992. *What We Can Learn From the Missing Airline Passengers. The NPG Forum*. Teaneck, NJ: Negative Population Growth.

Hansen, K. A. and Bachu, Amera. August 1995; revised September 1996. *The Foreign-Born Population, 1994, 1900–1994*. Washington, DC: US Census Bureau.

Haub, Carl, and M. M. Kent. August 2005. *Frequently Asked Questions About the PRB World Population Data Sheet*, 1. Washington, DC: PRB.

Justich, Robert, and Betty Ng. January 3, 2005. *The Underground Labor Force is Rising to the Surface*. New York: Bear Stearns Asset Management.

Lee. R. D. 1980." A Historical Perspective on Economic Aspects of the Population Explosion: The Case of Pre-Industrial England." In *Population and Economic Change in Developing Countries*, edited by R. E. Easterlin, 517–56. Chicago: University of Chicago Press.

Lee, R. D. 1980. "A Historical Perspective on Economic Aspects of the Population Explosion: The Case of a Pre-Industrial England." In *Population and Economic Change in Developing Countries*, edited by Richard A. Easterlin, 517–56. Chicago, IL: University of Chicago Press.

Matloff, Norman. 1998. "Visa Program for High Tech Workers." *Wall Street Journal*, June 5, Letters.

National Vital Statistics Reports: Preliminary Data for 2004. Births: Vol. 54(8), December 29, 2005. Mortality: Vol. 54 (19), June 28, 2006. National Center for Health Statistics, Hyattsville, MD.

Packer, A.E. and William B. Johnston. August 1, 1987. Workforce 2000: Work and Workers for the Twenty-First Century. Diane Publishing, released by Hudson Institute.

Pew Hispanic Center. 2005. Press Release: Extensive Survey Examines Mexican Migrants' Views Toward Immigration Reform Proposals. Washington, DC, March 2, 2005.

Population Reference Bureau. 2006 *World Population Data Sheet (WPDS)*. Washington, DC: Population Reference Bureau.

Population Reference Bureau web site, www.prb.org.

Puente, Maria. April 25, 1996. "Immigration Numbers to Surge." *USA Today*, 3A.

Rubenstein, Edwin S. 2006. Immigrants Blindsiding U.S. public Schools. www. VDARE.com September 6, 2006.

Schodolski, Vincent J. 2006. Mexicans Like the U.S. Merida Insider, August 19, 2006.

Stoddard, David J. 2002. Testimony Submitted to U.S. Subcommittee on Criminal Justice, Drug Policy and Human Resources, Representative Mark Souder, Chairman. February 22, 2002.

Tech Firms. 1996. USA Today, February 28, p. 1.

University of Mississippi. 2006. Press Release: Sociology Professor Testifies at Congressional Hearing on Census Bureau's Population Estimates. Oxford, Mississippi, September 15, 2006.

Ventura, Stephanie, Martin, Joyce A., Mathews, T. J., and Clarke, Sally C. (June, 1996). Advance Report of Final Natality Statistics, 1994. *Supplement* 44 (11), Tables 10 and 11 (pp. 41–42). National Center for Health Statistics, Division of Vital Statistics. (Foreign-born)

2

Carrying Capacity and Complexity

Introduction

Carrying capacity is a relatively simple concept, but estimating the carrying capacity of a region or Earth is complex. Estimates take into account changing technology, per capita impact on resources and the environment, and feedback loops. The feedback loops are often unanticipated. The intricacies of Earth systems defy policy fixes, a difficulty intuited by 1950s media personality Eric Sevareid: "The chief cause of problems is solutions."

Ecologists assume that every area, nation and community in the world experiences some natural constraint on further growth. The constraint is often referred to as "the limiting factor." Land area, land fertility, water, or power (human, animal, or mechanical) to till fields are common limiting factors in agricultural areas. Constraints on urban growth are more diverse: infrastructure to move clean water and food in and waste out is among the more obvious. Despite efforts to discern what may be potential limiting factors, ecologists no doubt miss some. For example, what of the Sun, the variability of its heat emissions and their effect on Earth systems? What of the natural system's capacity for neutralizing polluting emissions? What of keystone species? What of bee populations, which provide uncountable pollination services?

Carrying Capacity Network (CCN), a nonprofit organization dedicated to studying and preserving the carrying capacity of the United States, states on its website:

> A common fallacy is to equate existing and seemingly open or "unused" spaces with the kind of resources and ecologically productive land needed to support human life under modern conditions. In fact, the criteria for determining whether a region is overpopulated

are not land area, but carrying capacity. Carrying capacity refers to the number of individuals who can be supported in a given area within natural limits, and without degrading the natural, social, cultural and economic environment for present and future generations. (www. carryingcapacity.org)

Current literature on carrying capacity typically warns of eroded topsoil, salinized soils, rivers that no longer reach the sea because of upstream withdrawals for supplying urban populations and agriculture, land subsidence because of depleted ground water, air quality, crowding, disease transmission, and depletion of fossil fuels. "Peak oil" coming approximately in 2005 was widely expected to be a watershed moment in human history, but a modified view is that nonconventional oil delays the production peak until 2020. Oil including liquid natural gas (LNG) supply, which had been constant for years at approximately eighty million barrels per day, rose to ninety-nine million barrels per day in the decade after 2005.

Recovery of oil far below the ocean floor and the process of "fracking" shale oil rocks tap new sources, with environmental, monetary, and energy costs of oil becoming paramount. Concern that earthquakes can be triggered by fracking as well as that water quality is contaminated by nearby fracking sites sometimes retards projects. In a cynic's view, however, policies responsive to politics and profit—but framed as essential for meeting human needs—usually override environmental values. In the foreseeable future, economic and energy considerations are most likely to slow fracking. The depletion rate of oil production from the average fracked well is estimated at 60–80 percent annually. Companies maintain the flow of oil by regularly bringing new wells online, but well drilling is expensive and uses energy. Logically, the limiting factor in oil production is energy return on energy invested (EROEI). If the ratio falls to 1:1, should one bother?

The economic calculation is separate. In 2015, fracking was said to repay capital investment in new wells only if the price of oil remained at approximately $60/barrel or higher. Indeed, US frackers suspended drilling new wells within a month of a precipitous price decline. Deployment of fewer rigs, "shutting in" least productive wells, and improving technology reduced the cost of recovered barrels, so that the break-even point had fallen by mid-2015.

The oil price's precipitous decline early in 2015 to below $60/barrel had political and business causes: the United States attempted to squeeze Russian and Iranian oil revenues at the same time as Saudi "swing producers" continued normal production, allegedly to drive US frackers out of business. Able to produce conventional oil at $15/barrel, the Saudis can do it.

The tale lets one speculate. Oil will almost certainly remain the most valued form of fossil fuel and, so long as some oil can be accessed by some technology, it will be used. Peak oil has been delayed, not averted. Saudi Arabia, with possibly the world's largest remaining supply of conventional oil, is betting on higher prices. Reportedly, the government promotes solar energy for residential and commercial uses: Why use oil domestically, a sheik might reason, if its progressively higher price virtually guarantees a huge future income stream?

The potential for applying technology—such as fracking—to a resource or pollution problem is one reason that the carrying capacity of the world and any region remains unknown. Some analysts focus on the expense of technology, seeing money as the limiting factor. An over-emphasis on money, however, carries its own risks. The financial system is itself complex; and the Earth is, after all, finite and fragile. The limits of Earth's resources and capacity for healing are unknown. "Nature bats last" is more than a sound bite.

Nevertheless, technological optimists are inclined to deny absolute limits. Consider the late economist Julian Simon's assertion that knowledge "in our libraries" guaranteed resources sufficient to do us for seven million years. On a finite planet that position is ludicrous, revealing only that Simon lacked an appreciation for large numbers. (Simon's original contention, politely corrected by physicist Albert Bartlett, was for seven billion years).

Several decades ago ecologists David Pimentel and Robert Costanza estimated, independently, that the US carrying capacity is 150,000,000–200,000,000 people. By 2015, with the population possibly exceeding 330 million, no one knows by exactly how much the carrying capacity has been degraded through overuse. Pimentel calculates that "For every person added to the population, one acre of natural habitat or farmland is converted to developed uses." Water shortage in California's prime agricultural region—or population longage as Garrett Hardin would have said—has not been slow to come. California supplies the nation with the majority of its fresh plant foods. The United States' absolute environmental limits, and at what standard of living, remain unknown.

The true complexity of systems could not be ignored after the 1969 publication of MIT professor Jay W. Forrester's *Urban Dynamics*. Using the power of computers, Forrester showed how variables interact and cause unexpected pressures in unanticipated ways through "feedback loops." Complexity theory was on its way; technological optimists would have much to explain, or explain away.

Dennis and Donella Meadows with collaborators at MIT applied Forrester's method to the interactions of environmental systems and population, reported in *Dynamics of Growth in a Finite World* (1974). A range of values (quantities) for depletion or growth of key resources and population was the beginning point from which their computers projected multiple pathways into the future. Without exception, a limiting factor before the end of the twenty-first century emerged from every analysis, and was confirmed by an update indicating that many Americans now alive will see the tipping point. I value an afternoon spent with Donella Meadows at Dartmouth College, where she identified the passage in *Dynamics of Growth* which projects the interaction between resources and fertility rates, similar to relationships that I find in historical and cross-cultural records.

Also building on Forrester, financial analyst Jim Rickards uses complexity theory to project possible economic scenarios. Financial strength should be taken into account because environmental remediation has costs. Desalinizing water is expensive in money, energy, and even beach front property. Environmentalists might usefully take account of Rickards, and Rickards take account of population and the environment, in order to project landing places for the nation and world. Money, water, territory, and energy limit the possibilities for applying technology to expansion of the usable resource base; each domain depends upon the health of the other.

Conservation and saving do not occur naturally; they are handicapped because enjoyment or profit which might be had today is put off until tomorrow. Natural resources are overexploited when treated as a commons, or if those who conserve are not assured of being able to capture the future benefit of past frugality. Mechanisms such as private property rights contribute to assurance that the conservationist and his heirs will have rights to the future use of protected resources. Incentives for conservation, population stabilization, and efficiency are musts, or solutions are illusory. Neoclassical economists should desist from reassurances that redistribution is sustainable because growth can last forever. In the centuries-old Lockian tradition, government's contribution to society should be to guarantee security in property and use rights.

In light of the foregoing, one may say that carrying capacity is a range which it is important to estimate and reestimate. System complexity is virtually beyond the capacity of the human mind to assimilate although the interaction of variables, the feedback loops, can be projected with the aid of high-powered computers. Even then, human failure to enter one variable into the computer program, or anticipate one "black swan" a la Nassim Taleb, throws off projections. Highly esteemed ecological economist Herman E. Daly wrote, "The economy is a wholly owned subsidiary of the environment, not the reverse." He followed up, "There is something wrong with treating the Earth as if it were a business in liquidation."

The Politics of Conservation*

Since the first Earth Day in 1970, environmental protection strategists have concentrated on regulating individual and corporate behavior. The Clean Air and Clean Water Acts, the Endangered Species Act, and similar legislation—enforced by dint of judicial activism—have done much to restore and preserve the nation's national treasures. Even at the apogee of success, however, victories were sometimes partial—a series of such "victories" left only devastation. For illustration, repeated standoffs between loggers and environmentalists, when each compromise entails saving 70 percent of a forest, results after ten compromises in all but 3 percent of the forest being logged.

Never wholly satisfactory, environmental outcomes are about to get worse. Public antagonism toward regulation which deprives landowners of the full economic value of property, or which forces the private sector to bear the cost of environmental protections, has spawned a political backlash. Environmental legislation seems certain to be progressively rolled back.

Environmentalists will regroup defensively to examine what can be salvaged, what are the root causes of the devastation, and which new strategies hold promise. New thinking is essential. One promising direction turns on the concept of carrying capacity.

Carrying capacity refers to the number of individuals who can be supported without degrading the physical, ecological, social, and cultural environment, i.e., without reducing the ability of the environment to sustain the population at the desired quality of life over the long term. A degraded environment produces less. Thus, exceeding the carrying capacity today impairs the future viability of nature's life-support systems, so that smaller and then smaller numbers can be

---

*Editorial in *Population and Environment* 17(2), pp. 100–3 [November, 1995].

supported without further damage. Thinking about carrying capacity suggests that the sheer growth of population size combined with the high consumption levels to which all Americans and immigrants aspire is the ultimate threat to the topsoil, forests, energy, clean air and water, and other resources of our national home.

David Pimentel and others (1995) show, for example, that topsoil is being eroded twenty to thirty times faster than its natural formation rate and is being paved over or made useless for agriculture at the rate of three million acres annually. No known technology can create or substitute for topsoil. If present trends continue, arable land will shrink from the 1.8 acres per person available in the United States currently to only 0.6 acres per person by 2050 (1.2 acres per person is needed to provide a diverse diet).

Moreover, underground aquifers which accumulated over millennia are being depleted 25 percent faster than the water is replenished (Pimentel et al. 1995). Transport of water from ever-more distant sources and desalination are energy-intensive and expensive; foreseeably, water-short areas (much of the US West) will cease to be agricultural in order to release water to dense urban populations.

Reed F. Noss, J. Michael Scott, and Edward T. LaRoe III report for the National Biological Survey that whole US ecosystems are endangered. Thirty systems have declined over 98 percent of their natural area, imperiling habitat for countless species (Stevens 1995). Five hundred species are known to have vanished already as humans encroach on habitat (Ling-Ling 1995). George Robinson, Steven Handel, and Mary Yurlina attribute the 40 percent loss of Staten Island's original species to population growth. Man and Biosphere (MAB) reserves in New Jersey, the outer islands of Maryland's Chesapeake Bay, and Southern Florida are similarly at risk (Long 1995). The critical shift is from agricultural to more intensive uses of land as population density increases.

Even prehistorically, human population growth threatened biodiversity: "We have no evidence that the processes responsible for prehistoric extinctions differed fundamentally from those that continue to deplete surviving species today. The differences are mainly technological (snares versus guns, and stone adzes and fire versus chain saws and fire, for example)" (Steadman 1995, 1123).

Losses in biodiversity have economic as well as moral and esthetic implications. Biodiversity contributes in uncounted ways to productivity and income, e.g., honeybees pollinate billions of dollars worth of crops and we have no good substitute! Microorganisms restore eroded topsoil, a contribution because "about 10% of all the energy used in U.S. agriculture today is spent just to offset the losses of nutrients, water, and crop productivity caused by erosion" (Pimentel et al. 1995, 1120).

Seventeen percent of US petrochemical use is in the agricultural sector, and some experts consider it to be the most crucial of all petrochemical uses (Gever, Kaufman, Skole, and Vorosmarty 1986). But population growth explains why America's thirst for oil and energy seems insatiable. Nearly all (93 percent) of a 25 percent increase in energy use between 1970 and 1990 was driven by population growth. That is, consumption per capita levelled off, but this conservation effort was, and continues to be, overwhelmed by growing numbers (Holdren 1991).

Already, 60 percent of the oil used in the United States is imported and accounts for a major portion of the balance of payments deficit. Domestic oil is expected to be effectively gone in twenty-five years (meaning that the energy recovered will be less than the energy used to get the oil). This shortage will greatly impact food production, prices, and the $40 billion/yr in export income from agriculture. Our increasing reliance on foreign sources threatens both agricultural productivity and policy options vis-à-vis oil-producing nations including Mexico, Russia, Iran, Iraq, Egypt, Libya, and Saudi Arabia.

Other factors (deforestation, pollutants, traffic congestion) could be chosen to illustrate carrying capacity limits. Resources are being depleted and biodiversity decimated even at the present rate of use: more people demand more space and resources; in using them people create more pollution. After a system has been degraded, it supports fewer people than formerly; the carrying capacity shrinks. This means that a given population and quality of life that would have been in balance within the pristine environment no longer is so; thus the carrying capacity enters a downward spiral in which systems are increasingly vulnerable.

Some systems have no substitute and if they are used up or degraded, the loss is irretrievable. Other systems can be remediated but only at great cost: e.g., implementation of the Clean Air Act is estimated to cost $25 billion annually. Such uses of money further aggravate economic and fiscal problems that the country faces already.

Environmentalists inveigh against consumption, but often choose to deny the population factor and have zero understanding of the economic drivers. In fact, Americans are progressively losing control of the use of domestic resources because use is being decoupled from domestic consumption. This may sound odd, but consider the export of food, logs, and other products (with varying degrees of value-added manufacture). These exports account for part of the use of American resources although none are consumed in America. Exported goods help put the foreign trade account into balance to pay for past consumption. As the largest debtor nation in the world, the United States is already exporting natural resources that should be conserved. The United States might someday have to earn foreign exchange by exporting food needed by its own poorer citizens—on the model of any third world country.

Resource use traceable to domestic consumption is the evil to which the greenest of the green address their purest hatred. But does consumption not support jobs? Consumption, face it, is a system that has worked for the betterment of many in the United States and which, moreover, establishes a goal (having more things) that is antagonistic to large family size. The consumption ethic creates a perception of scarcity in America. Whatever one has, it could be more. Consumption goals function as an incentive to limit dependents. If classic consumption goals were not the general rule, many people (it seems logical to speculate) might commit resources to having more children.

High fertility rates, setting population on the road to prolonged growth, are the ultimate environmental threat. The United States can ill afford higher fertility, especially when growth receives an extra push from immigration. Counting refugees and asylees, the United States accepts over one million legal immigrants per year. This number together with illegal immigration and the high fertility of the immigrant sector (those arrived since 1970) accounts for 50 percent of annual US population growth. The proportion is growing and can be reversed only by congressional action to limit immigration.

Calls for an immigration "moratorium" resonate with the rank-and-file electorate and may result in a succession of legislative moves to scale back the numbers. A moratorium of 100,000 a year could leave room for the United States to meet long-standing humanitarian goals, provide for the rare skill category not available in the United States, and permit reunification of spouses and minor children. In memory of the "St Louis," 25,000 slots of the 100,000 could be reserved for refugees; the Holocaust Museum retells the tale.

America's environment remains at stake while we fashion population policy. The policy should reflect primarily the national interest. Yet, through choice, America often lets guilt dictate policy even when more guilt is accepted than, strictly speaking, is due. A population policy driven by guilt poses hard choices because reparation must be apportioned among competing interests: the nation's own citizens whose land was taken or whose forebears were enslaved; the wanderers and persecuted among all nations; and the suffering of all species where stewardship is in our hands.

Environmental protection is, at bottom, habitat protection; this responsibility can be honestly discharged just one way: population stabilization. Environmentalists, facing setbacks in one legislative agenda, have the opportunity to regroup around the real answer.

Doing Government to the People*

Gallup News Service poll results released in May, 1996, suggest that Americans favor certain changes in national policy but often find that their government is unresponsive. On some issues, the public consensus attains the level of 6 to 1. Nevertheless, initiatives to enact desired changes either fail in Congress, remain bogged down, or (in 1995–1996) were vetoed by President William Clinton (Benedetto 1996).

A healthy natural environment is among the quality-of-life indicators that most Americans appear to value. Yet key government policies are undermining this highly prized national endowment, a heritage which makes an essential contribution, indeed, to US prosperity and perhaps to life itself. Encouragement of population growth is one government policy which is supremely antagonistic to preservation of environmental quality. Words by Nathan Keyfitz put the population/environment relationship into perspective:

> If all else is equal, action damaging the environment is directly proportional to the number of people. That at least seems the most appropriate initial hypothesis. . . . The burden of proof is on anyone who argues against the proportionality hypothesis in either way. (1993, 547)

In this light, the three million annual US population growth assumes great seriousness. Increasing competition for space and resources

*Editorial in *Population and Environment* 18(3), pp. 227–31 [January, 1997].

41

creates the conditions for conflict, so that mitigation of environmental harm will become increasingly contentious, costly, technologically challenging (Kinsley and Lovins 1995), and even (in certain realms as, for example, protection of aquifers) unattainable.

Nevertheless, the federal government's progrowth policy persists. It is manifested in financial inducements to have the extra child (aimed at virtually every income level of society), a tenuous posture toward family planning services available to medically indigent women, continuing high levels of legal immigration, and ineffectual enforcement of laws barring illegal immigration.

Prolife policy and cash subsidies to families with dependent children (AFDC) have an arguable, if minor, effect on population size, but that issue rarely enters into the acrimonious disputes which surround them. These debates, while very important, are not our subject. In another realm entirely is immigration policy. Immigration has an undeniably major effect on US population growth, and the electorate is remarkably united in opposing the present large flow.

A February 18, 1996, Roper poll shows that 70 percent of all respondents support limiting immigration to 300,000 or less per year. This preference unites 73 percent of blacks, 72 percent of whites, 52 percent of Hispanics, 73 percent of political liberals, 72 percent of conservatives, and 71 percent of moderates (Mittelstadt 1996).

These results track increasing dislike of current immigration policy under which a minimum of 1.3 million immigrants net (including family reunification and skilled immigrants, refugees, asylees, asylum claimants who vanish into the population, visa overstayers, and illegal border crossers) enter annually to remain as settlers. A *Times*/Mirror Center Poll in November 1994 (published by *USA Today*) found 82 percent of Americans saying that the United States should restrict immigration, up from 76 percent in 1992. Similar trends are found in CBS/*New York Times*, CBS, Time/CCN, and other national polls, without exception (Carrying Capacity 1995).

The American people have reached this consensus despite being relatively uninformed on key supporting facts. What would opinion be if the popular media linked population growth to its real and pervasive environmental consequences, or repeated data which show that immigration, including children born to post-1970 immigrants, presently accounts for 60 percent of US population growth? Or if it reported mainstream demographic studies, where projecting present annual immigration and its inflation of the US fertility rate leads to a population size of half a billion to 800 million people by AD 2080, with immigration accounting for virtually all of the increase? (Ahlburg and Vaupel 1990; Heim and Austin 1996). (For baseline comparisons, the United States fought World War II with 135 million people, and today's population is in the vicinity of 270 million.)

Despite ample data and the clearly expressed will of the people, legislation to reduce legal immigration is exactly the type of initiative that Congress was unable to enact in 1996. Bills introduced by Lamar Smith (R-TX) in the House of Representatives and Alan Simpson (R-WY) in the Senate included provisions for modest reductions in legal immigration—about 10 percent distributed across every major category—but were amended to death and finally scrapped after being split off from provisions designed to address illegal immigration.

Perhaps Congress believed that the public would be appeased by bare-bone action on illegal immigration because the media has largely presented the illegal number as the major law enforcement, financial, and environmental problem. While very serious, because lawbreakers are precisely the element whose presence is troubling on its face, illegal aliens in fact account for less than half of the $51 billion annual net public cost associated with immigration (Huddle 1995), and they represent less than one-third of the total immigration flow. Thus, Congress also must reduce legal immigration or break faith with the electorate.

So what happened to the bills to reduce legal immigration, minimal as the reforms were to be? First, the Immigration and Naturalization Service (INS) under Commissioner Doris Meissner presented incomplete and seriously misleading information. Second, a powerful array of well-funded liberal and conservative lobbies (unlikely allies except on this issue) combined to protect special ethnic entitlements and foreign sources of cheap labor.

Meissner, formerly with the Carnegie Foundation, was appointed commissioner of the INS by President Clinton. Although somewhat streamlining the asylum process, Meissner's principal activities have gone toward expediting the process of naturalizing immigrants as US citizens. To this end, citizenship applicants have been actively recruited, and requirements of English language proficiency and demonstrated economic self-sufficiency have been largely waived.

Meissner's role in the 1996 congressional immigration debate commenced with her March 28 testimony that 1995 legal immigration had fallen 10.4 percent from 1994 levels, thereby implying that legal immigration would decline of its own accord, without legislative action. This apparent reprieve was followed by the Senate Judiciary Committee adopting, in that same afternoon, an amendment proposed by Senators Edward Kennedy (D-MA) and Spencer Abraham (R-MI) that "served to increase legal immigration. What Ms. Meissner had failed to mention, however, was that the INS already expected legal immigration to rise dramatically—from 720,461 in 1995 to almost one million in 1996 and 1997" (Bordering on Disaster, May 20, 1996).

The INS confirmed this expected 41 percent increase in legal immigration only after the information was leaked. Representative Lamar Smith reacted angrily to Meissner's apparently intentionally misleading testimony, stating that, "The administration has engaged in a pattern of deception by leaving a false impression that decreases would continue" (Puente, April 25, 1996); Senator Simpson's comments were no less pungent.

Ultimately, the legislation was defeated by the weight of the counterproductive amendments and lobbying-inside-the-Beltway. Pressures came from the media and public foundations interested in maintaining high levels of immigration, ethnic lobbies, and certain corporate interests pleading labor shortage.

The Ford Foundation, for example, is a longtime supporter of immigrant advocacy groups. According to the Annual Report of the Ford Foundation, their 1993 charitable giving included $567,000 to the National Immigration Forum headed by Frank Sharry, $850,000 to the Mexican American Legal Defense Fund (MALDEF), $2,850,000 to La Raza, and $1,115,282 to the Urban Institute.

A second major foundation, the PEW Charitable Trusts, also appeared less than even-handed in the immigration debate. An October 18, 1995, letter from Susan Sechler, executive director of the PEW Global Stewardship Initiative, announced a "roundtable discussion" cosponsored with the National Immigration Forum to "discuss contentious issues which have the potential to cause a schism between population and environment groups on the one hand, and pro-immigration organizations, on the other." Suffice it to say that interested representatives of the "population and environment groups" were overtly excluded. Your editor had additional, firsthand knowledge of PEW Stewardship Initiative bias: the convener of a fall, 1995, environmental conference received three telephone calls from PEW staffers urging that I be disinvited from the roster of speakers.

The reporting and editorial pages of the *New York Times, Washington Post, Los Angeles Times,* and other papers that fall into line seem equally reluctant to provide space for open discussion of the linkage between population growth and environmental problems. The *Wall Street Journal* is unique, with a news department largely independent of its proimmigration editorial stance.

Foundations and the media cannot, of course, single-handedly defeat popular legislation. It appears that a major lobbying effort combined the efforts of the National Association of Manufacturers and the American Trial Lawyers defending their interests in cheap labor and litigation opportunity, respectively, Jewish lobbies defending their Russian refugee status entitlement (Barnett 1996; Dorf 1995, 1996), and shell organizations including MALDEF and La Raza, allegedly representing a Hispanic membership but in fact virtually devoid of members.

Also count the leadership of the Christian Coalition in the column of open-door advocates. At the last minute they jumped on this wagon, possibly at the urging of the head of Americans for Tax Reform, Grover Norquist. It subsequently became public knowledge that, in February, Norquist had registered as a lobbyist for Microsoft, collecting $10,000/mo. for his services (Rough Road 1996). Bill Gates, founder of Microsoft, himself traveled to Washington to lobby for maintaining high levels of immigration. He makes no secret of his company's use of Indian programmers; but given the communications technology available, it seems inexplicable that Gates would court the eventual public relations fiasco of bringing programmers to the United States rather than content himself with using their services elsewhere.

The power blocks arrayed against the 80 percent of Americans who want less immigration, and the 72 percent who want 300,000 per annum or less, suggest that the electorate has some work to do. Their task will not be easy. Five senators are retiring of the mere twenty who voted to trim immigration by the modest 10 percent which Senator Simpson proposed, whereas just three senators are retiring from among the eighty who voted to keep immigration at present levels or higher. In the meantime, public costs resulting from the flow of predominantly unskilled immigrants go on rising, and the environment (all else equal) groans under the weightier press of human activity.

Carrying Capacity: The Traditions
and Policy Implications of Limits*

Abstract

Within just the last few centuries, science and technology have enlarged human capabilities and population size until humans now take, for their own use, nearly half of the Earth's net terrestrial primary production. An ethical perspective suggests that potentials to alter, or further increase, humanity's use of global resources should be scrutinized through the lenses of self-interested foresightedness as well as respect for non-human life. Without overtly invoking ethics, studies of the carrying capacity achieve just this objective. Carrying capacity is an ecological concept that expresses the relationship between a population and the natural environment on which it depends for ongoing sustenance. Carrying capacity assumes limits on the number of individuals that can be supported at a given level of consumption without degrading the environment and, therefore, reducing future carrying capacity; that is, long-term sustainability. Worldviews differ in the importance accorded to the carrying capacity concept. This paper addresses three world-views—ecological, romantic, and entrepreneurial—and explores the ethics and the policy implications of their contrasting perspectives.

Introduction

Environmental carrying capacity is a venerable, if hypothetical, ecological concept that has acquired fresh currency in light of the growing human population. It relates individuals to quantity of resources and quality of life, so it implies limits. Familiar to stock growers—year in and year out, for example, it takes thirty acres to support a cow-calf unit on typical Wyoming-range land—the concept of carrying capacity in the modern context refers to the number of humans who can be supported without degrading the natural, cultural, and social environment. Exceeding the human carrying capacity implies impairing the environment's ability to sustain the desired quality of life over the long term. The appropriate comparison is to a too-dense cattle herd that finds sufficient feed for several years, but at the cost of overgrazing so that the land's future yield is reduced to below the original level.

*In *Ethics in Science and Environment* [ESEP], pp. 9–18 [Jan. 23, 2001].

The concept of carrying capacity is widely discounted, in part because it is fluid and virtually unquantifiable. Past discoveries and technological breakthroughs have, many times, raised carrying capacity, and much Western science encourages the belief that technology's potential is unlimited. Technological optimists typically reject scientific warnings that no substitutes exist for topsoil, fresh water, clean air, and the "free services" of many species, or that technology and its deployment to replace existing uses of petrochemical energy will take twenty years to bring online, minimum. The standard answer to evidence that a nonrenewable resource is being depleted, or a renewable one degraded, is that if a resource becomes "scarce" or pollution too detrimental, prices will rise sufficiently to call forth either substitutes or innovative technology that overcomes the problem. Technology and market mechanisms, it is said, will always enable humans to overcome putative natural limits.

Economic cornucopians point to low (even falling) prices for essential commodities and staples, arguing that they give no sign of impending scarcity. Economic pricing theory is conveniently ignored, although this suggests that a purely competitive market—which describes many agricultural sectors -- as opposed to a monopolistic market, often induces producers to go on producing regardless of price signals. Pure competition may, indeed, promote increased production as a strategy for maintaining a constant income stream in the face of declining prices.

Oil production in the late 1990s, when a barrel of oil was priced at approximately $10.00, exemplifies the price and production effects of relatively pure competition even when the resource in question is actually limited. Producer countries in the Mid East are dependent on oil revenues to maintain the various consumer subsidies to which their populations have become accustomed. In the face of low prices, production surged in order to maintain the needed revenue. Only when the Organization of Petroleum Exporting Countries (OPEC) reexerted production caps did prices rise.

The leaders and the citizenry of industrialized countries seldom interpret the higher price of oil or natural gas as a sign of scarcity. Many remain convinced that prices are arbitrarily manipulated. The production quotas set by oil-producing countries are not seen as sensible responses to knowledge about the limited quantity of the underlying resource.

Mixed evidence often leads to rejecting the concept of carrying capacity, possibly because it is reassuring—inherently more pleasing—to believe that humanity has escaped from limits that constrain the growth of all other species. Moreover, much in Western history warrants such confidence. For example, in the last decades of the nineteenth century, just as the United States' eastern forests were about depleted, crude oil was discovered and put to multiple uses formerly met by wood fuel.

Ecologists, partisans in the ongoing debate, not only assert that limits to essential resources and the threat of both local and global pollution are apparent already, but also warn of a threshold effect. They point out that a boundary condition can be encountered suddenly. Simplistically, a person jumping off a forty-story building might enjoy the ride until brought up short by the landing.

A standard requiring total certainty—such as the landing—carries a risk. This risk is that proof of the carrying capacity's being exceeded may come only after much damage—and perhaps irretrievable damage—has been done. If optimistic forecasts are wrong and a natural threshold is crossed, the consequence could be calamitous. Nevertheless, proof sufficient to convince skeptics remains elusive. Many experts and opinion makers contend that most difficulties are temporary, requiring only the right fix. The inexactness of carrying capacity models encourages that perspective. An exact limit for a local population is rarely if ever established. Yet, population studies in human and other animal populations repeatedly show that exceeding this uncertain limit, the carrying capacity, results in catastrophic change.

When do problems start to be seen as intractable? When does the perceived cost of being wrong about unlimited technological potential outweigh the perceived cost of being wrong about limits where none, in fact, exist?

Realms of Disagreement

Disagreement about the theoretical validity of conceptualizing and estimating ecological limits, and its practical ramifications, is only the beginning. Attitudes toward limits can be expressed in different realms, including existential values. One major philosophical tradition denies limits to humanity's moral capacity. Others assume limits. The divergence in schools of thought reaches into policy.

In mid-eighteenth-century France, controversy over limits hinged on human moral capabilities. Francois-Marie Arouet de Voltaire dramatized the conflict of worldviews in *Candide*. Early in the plot, a trusting Pangloss confidently reassures Candide that they are living in the best of all possible worlds. Ultimately, a world-worn and soberer duo settles for improving their own backyard, "Cultiver son propre jardin."

Opposed to Voltaire's eighteenth-century rationalist view were the romanticists Jean Jacques Rousseau and Condorcet in France and William Godwin, father of Mary Shelley, in England. Central to their belief was the imagining—untroubled by anthropology—of the uncorrupted "noble savage" of the Americas. Proven to the romanticists' satisfaction was the (re)perfectibility of man and of society in the context of living harmoniously with nature.

Historical Notes

The eighteenth- and nineteenth-century controversy about physical limitations was concerned less with absolutes than with the balance between population and resources. A maelstrom swirled around Thomas Robert Malthus, whose famous first edition of his essay on population was published on June 7, 1798. Malthus argued that most humans would reproduce up to, or even surpass, the limit of resources available to them.

The Malthusian observation invites the conclusion that most people find sustained prosperity elusive because technological progress or other addition to wealth stimulates population growth. This growth eventually restores the original ratio of resources to people.

Malthus is remembered for the elegance and force of his argument; however, the essential element of his thought had been anticipated. Writes ecologist Garrett Hardin, "Two thousand years ago Koheleth, the Preacher, said in Ecclesiastes 5:11: 'When goods increase those who eat them increase.'" Similarly, "the English philosopher David Hume, in 1752, played a variation on the theme in Ecclesiastes: 'Where there is room for more people, they will always arise'" (Hardin 1998a). Malthus, a theologian and political scientist, surely knew both sources.

Three Worldviews

The conflicting worldviews on limits to both resources and human moral capacities descend to the present. The taxonomy proposed here identifies three patterns and is admittedly an oversimplification. But a division into entrepreneurial, romanticist, and ecological traditions— loose classification though it is—may partially illuminate present-day coalitions that might otherwise seem mystifying.

Entrepreneurs. The entrepreneurial tradition relies on individual initiative and contractual relationships for the betterment of mankind and society, and is mainly skeptical of the moral perfectibility of human kind. In the tradition of John Locke, it assumes that pursuit of private ends can serve the common good because the incentive to increase personal property often results increasing the total wealth that a society may ultimately enjoy. Proponents are pragmatists and, often, self-styled conservatives. The dominant motive acknowledged in oneself and generally attributed to others is not altruism but self-interest—as in the Declaration of Independence' guarantee of the right to "pursuit of happiness"—which is taken to be a virtually universal human characteristic that can be socially channeled to become usually positive in effect.

Competitive self-interest reinforced by good information and accountability is expected to yield a well-regulated society, rational markets, prosperity founded on market principles, and fair government. The entrepreneur advocates free trade and ample immigration so long as these policies appear to enhance net profits. They rely not on perfecting human moral instincts but, rather, on the social contract for mutually agreed governance.

The entrepreneur's view of limits varies depending upon whether the reference is to a moral or physical realm. The situation-specific use of criteria suggests a pragmatic rather than ideological orientation. Pragmatists are swayed by evidence.

Technological innovations that quadrupled carrying capacity since the Malthusian era are the basis for the entrepreneur's skepticism that material limits are real and close. A 1997 essay in *The (London) Economist* points out that "predictions of ecological doom, including recent ones, have such a terrible track record that people should take them with a grain of salt." The essay continues, "journalists and fame-seekers will no doubt continue to peddle ecological catastrophes at an undiminishing speed. These people, oddly, appear to think that having been invariably wrong in the past makes them more likely to be right in the future" (Environmental Scares 1997, 19).

Reasonably enough, this essay appeals to the historical record. Why would the future be different? As the twentieth century closes, many entrepreneurs accept the assumptions relating to technology and the physical world that have been provided, in large measure, by Julian Simon. This is the late University of Maryland economist, author, and editor of the rose-colored-wrapper compendium *The State of Humanity* (1996) and proimmigration tracts such as *Immigration: The Demographic and Economic Facts* (1995).

Simon's premise is that limits to natural resources as well as the environment's capacity to cope with pollution invariably yield to the transformations made on nature by technology. Thus, natural constraints are merely challenges, ultimately irrelevant to the economy. Technology will refresh or give us substitutes for clean air and water, rich topsoil, cheap fossil fuels, and Earth's services in detoxifying pollution. That is, man-made capital can substitute for natural resources indefinitely and without end; repeated doublings of the size of the economy and population present only opportunity. Whatever accelerates growth should be pursued. In 1995, a Washington, DC, think tank, the Cato Institute, published Simon's nigh-incredible cornucopian assertion that "Technology exists now to produce virtually inexhaustible quantities of just about all the products made by nature." Extending his foray into science, Simon writes, "We have in our hands now—actually in our libraries—the technology to feed, clothe and supply energy to an ever growing population for the next 7 billion years. . . . Even if no new knowledge were ever gained . . . we would be able to go on increasing our population forever" (Cato Institute 1995, 14).

Note that "seven billion years ago" is about two and a half billion years before the first one-celled life form appeared in Earth's newly formed primal ooze. Can one have confidence in the author of prognostications for seven billion years into the future?

Physicist Albert A. Bartlett of the University of Colorado is a gentleman inclined to give adversaries the benefit of the doubt. Therefore, he was pleased to report that Simon did not entirely mean what he wrote: "Simon said that the '7 billion years' was an error and it should have been '7 million years.'" But, Bartlett continues, "It is too early to breathe easily." Given the 1996 world population of approximately 5.7 billion and an annual population growth rate of 1 percent, world population after 7 million years would be equal to 2.3×10 to the 30410th power. "This is a fairly large number!" (Bartlett 1996).

Nonmathematicians might like to know that 2.3×10 to the 12th power is 2.3 trillion (American definition of "trillion"). So how large is a number with the exponent of not 12 but 30410?

The hard-line cornucopian view also has champions in Dennis T. Avery of the Hudson Institute and author of *Saving the World with Pesticides and Plastic* (1995) and Thomas Lambert of the Center for the Study of American Business (CSAB). Lambert writes that, "natural resources are not limited in any meaningful sense" because resources are really best understood as services. It is, after all, "the particular services a material provides—not its physical composition—that makes a material a resource" (Lambert 1996, 5).

While appealing in their reasonableness (unlike Simon's), Lambert's and Avery's visions deny the implications of the environment's being an envelope around the economy. Yet, the environment provides inputs to economic production, and the environment receives not only the useful but also the waste products of economic activity. As put by economist Herman Daly, "The economy is a wholly-owned subsidiary of the environment."

Ecologists and certain economists—for example, Daly (1990, 1991; Cobb and Daly 1990)—point out that technology can employ (or alter or discover) one resource to make up for shortfalls in another, and use assorted strategies to minimize pollution, but these expedients only change the pressure point. One cannot avoid the risk of shortfalls or bottlenecks developing in the substitutes and during the transformation process. Difficulty is compounded if the real world has a propensity to develop problems in multiples, not one at a time. In times of stress, anything that can go wrong might go wrong. How does technology cope with the snowball effect? "With difficulty," answers an ecologist or old-fashioned conservative. And, "Why take the risk?"

THE ENERGY CONSTRAINT. Since mid-century (Cottrell 1955), growing numbers of scientists have tried to make the public aware that the large increase in carrying capacity has been possible only because of readily available fossil fuels, especially oil. Walter Youngquist (1997), Colin Campbell, L. F. Ivanhoe, Richard Duncan, and others suggest that a peak in oil production approximately in the vicinity of AD 2005–2015 will be followed by steady decline. Natural gas is expected to be plentiful for about forty years after the peak in oil production, and new processes are likely to increase its versatility. Without fossil fuels, it would probably be impossible to farm the vast acreage that has made possible the present population size.

In November 2000, economist Richard Duncan addressed a Geological Society of America "summit," showing that world energy production per capita grew by 3.45 percent annually between 1945 and 1973; growth slowed to 0.64 percent annually from 1973 to 1979; then growth ended and began to decline at the rate of 0.33 annually from 1979 to 1999. Fitting a mathematical equation to data points on this curve, Duncan derives projections which suggest that, by 2030, energy production per capita will fall back to its 1930 value. This scenario envisions rolling, then permanent, blackouts of high-voltage electric power networks, worldwide.

INDUSTRY. Industry geologists are sanguine regarding the quantity and substitution possibilities for natural gas and other energy sources and do not yet state publicly that a peak in oil production is imminent. Nevertheless, more pessimistic forecasts are gaining ground (Banks 1998), and the Paris-based International Energy Agency (IEA) of the Organization for Economic Cooperation and Development (OECD) stated in 1998, for the first time, that "the peak of world oil production is in sight" (Kerr 1998). Were the majority to adopt the views of Campbell and others, entrepreneurial assumptions about limits might be readily reversed.

The habit of inductive reasoning makes entrepreneurs open to new perspectives. Sustained sharp price increases for essential commodities, rising public costs (higher taxes) associated with a rapidly growing population, and fees for the formerly free services of nature would be persuasive to those of the entrepreneurial bent. Many who reject ecological statistics would be weaned from the conviction that wealth is both abundant and renewable by market and financial signals.

Romanticists. Contrasting with the pragmatism of the entrepreneurial sector, the romanticist tradition appears to be driven by ideology. Denying limits in all realms, romanticists assert an unlimited human moral capacity to do right. While conceding that some people go wrong, romanticists explain that humans are not expected to reach their full moral potential under impoverished or mean social conditions.

The development of true altruism—not mere reciprocal altruism or mutual reciprocity—is the highest moral trait in the romantic pantheon, but it requires nurturing love and a sufficiency of goods. Thus, the theoretical perfectibility of humanity and human society carries a caveat regarding requirements for a supportive social and economic milieu. These presumptions are the source of advocacy for social reform and government activities aimed at overcoming deprivation through redistributing wealth.

Romanticists trust that nature can provide without limit because, if the goal that all humans should have access to sufficient resources is to be realized, that is clearly necessary. In the romanticist formulation, therefore, the ecologists' concept of carrying capacity is irrelevant, if not malevolent, because it sets an upper limit to the resources that ever can become available to humanity.

Lest moral potentials not be fulfilled, social reformers are constrained to believe in boundless wealth that need only be equitably distributed in order to create the perfect society. Given the romanticists' view that society has an obligation to rehabilitate the less fortunate so that every potential for human perfectibility is actualized, it becomes axiomatic that society can do it. The means exist.

Independently, Garret Hardin arrived at a similar analysis of the romanticist worldview. He cites in evidence Karl Marx's unprovoked ad hominem attacks on Malthus (in the vein of "'superficial,' 'a professional plagiarist'"). Hardin suggests that "a single overarching view accounts for these and many other invectives put forward by Marxists and liberals during the past century and a half: this is their tightly held denial of limits in the supply of terrestrial resources. Friedrich Engels, Marx's collaborator and financial supporter, baldly asserted that 'The productivity of the land can be infinitely increased by the application of capital, labour [sic], and science'" (Hardin 1998b, 182).

The romanticist tradition is manifest in modern times among those who strive to advance internationalist and collectivist agendas. They believe in breaking down national boundaries because nation-states perpetuate disparities in wealth. University of Chicago professor Martha Nussbaum exemplifies the tradition in her teaching that "the concept of national citizenship is too exclusive and 'morally dangerous.' Justice and equality, she claims, require 'allegiance to the worldwide community of human beings'" (Erasing Self-Rule 1998, 16). Romanticists support behavior and international institutions that tend to erode sovereignty.

Some who appear to favor world government try to deflect objections by asserting its inevitability. Joe De Courcy observes that, "On 17 February 1930, for instance, a leading member of the Council on Foreign Relations, James P. Warburg, told a U.S. Senate Committee: 'We shall have world government whether we like it or not . . . by consent or by conquest.' In 1976, Professor Saul Mendlovitz, director of the World Order Models Project, said there is '. . . no longer a question of whether or not there will be a world government by the year 2000.'" The stealth strategy is preferred by former Senator Alan Cranston (D–California), past president of United World Federalists. He "told Transition, a publication of the Institute for World Order, that: 'The more talk about world government, the less chance of achieving it, because it frightens people who would accept the concept of world laws'" (de Courcy 1998, 34–35).

Ecologists. The ecological tradition is in almost all respects the opposite of the romantic-internationalist. Ecologists are strongly influenced by biology, and many emerge from this academic discipline. Their views are formed from observation of natural systems, including behavior; that is, their method of reasoning is inductive, like the entrepreneur, although the two traditions attend to different data sets.

PHYSICAL LIMITS. Ecologists accept the concept of carrying capacity as essentially self-evident. The Earth is round and finite; so, therefore, must be its resources and its capacity to cope with pollution (Bartlett 1996; Pimentel and Pimentel 1991, 1996). Further, they see the imminence of carrying capacity limits in the deterioration of countless natural systems. Signs include the fifteen out of seventeen world fisheries that have crashed; falling water tables in aquifers; topsoil loss; annual oil production greater than discoveries (therefore, declining real reserves); mass extinction of species; and compromised capacity to cope with atmospheric and water pollution (Pimentel and Pimentel 1996, 1997).

Carrying capacity has greatest relevance to policy when viewed in local terms, because it often is not possible to affect the destiny of units larger than the local community or, at the outside limit, the nation. Information about the environment, including resources and vulnerabilities, is often best at regional or smaller levels. Further, cooperation is more easily mobilized at the neighborhood, state, or at least national level because it often depends upon kinship or friendship—a sense of identity and shared interests that facilitates the exchange of favors over periods sometimes longer than a generation. In addition, the presence of a competitor is an incentive to cooperate. Communities that are vying with an opponent will be more likely to cooperate internally, but this motive cannot coexist with the ethos that all belong to one world.

Finally, ecologists apply the lesson of the "tragedy of the commons." In 1968 Garrett Hardin illuminated the essential characteristic of a commons, defining it as a resource from which no one can be excluded. Everyone has access to a commons.

The fact of universal access has major implications for the motivation to conserve because conservation depends upon self-restraint, saving a resource in order to enjoy or use it in the future. No one has the incentive to conserve a resource to which no one can be denied access, for the reason that those making the effort, or their descendants, are very unlikely to have much of the future benefit from their present sacrifices.

In a commons, in fact, the better individual strategy is to use the resource as intensively and fast as one can. The maxim is, "Use it or lose it," with a vengeance.

Organizations with the appearance of a commons have successfully conserved or even improved a resource, at times. But delving deeper into instances of this type invariably reveals a mechanism for excluding users. This holds true whether the resource is a forest, a fishing ground, or a village green for pasturing sheep. Informal mechanisms for regulating use can be effective, if often rough on transgressors, and the penalty gradient may escalate. But regulation that lacks enforceable and meaningful sanctions is unlikely to protect a resource (Leal 1998; Ruttan 1998).

MORAL LIMITS. Ecologists tend to conclude that the physical capabilities of Earth and the moral capabilities of mankind are equally constrained by natural law. Humans are not so unlike other species that the principles of evolutionary biology would not apply to human behavior (Trivers 1971; Dawkins 1976; Wilson 1975). Survival and reproduction of one's genes is the de facto evolutionary test of success. Through natural selection, behavior is shaped to increase the probability of survival.

By extension, moral codes are subject to the possibilities inherent in a physically limited Earth. Ecologists take into account that humans are not generally altruistic, because altruism like other behavioral traits is to some extent heritable, and altruists are less likely than others to leave offspring (Hamilton 1964; Trivers 1971; Wilson 1975).

Behavior and culture that lead to the extinction of those who practice them cannot be moral, by definition. For example, if wastefulness in the use of resources leads to extinction, then it cannot be moral. Nor can altruism including the sharing of resources, if it leads to extinction, be moral (Elliott 1997).

Altruism is particularly self-destructive when applied internationally. Those who advocate altruism must necessarily believe that nature is a cornucopia of unlimited means.

Accepting limits in principle and in fact, ecologists advocate not only prudence in the use of resources but also discovery of motives which induce intrinsically self-interested humans to conserve. The moral hazard of the commons is the ultimate, logical reason why one-world, a world without borders, will not get one very far into a peaceful and prosperous future. If no person, region, or country can say, "Keep out; it's mine," then no person, community, or country has the incentive to conserve. And that, simply, is because conservationists would have almost no realistic hope of future benefit in proportion to their effort and self-restraint.

To sum up the ecologist perspective: given the probability of coming scarcity, a multiplicity of logistic problems in increasing efficiency, and the realities of human nature—including political and ethnic loyalties—many ecologists suspect that the only practicable solutions to most environmental problems will be local.

A Collision of Worldviews

The romanticist assumption that humankind and society are potentially perfectible, needing for fulfillment only that the planet's abundant resources should be equitably distributed, entails a surprising array of corollary axioms. The heirs of Rousseau and Marx advocate a world without borders: one-world. They reject the competitive efforts of one country or region to thrive beyond the realistic aspirations of any other. They espouse submerging national interests.

Applied to the United States, the one-world ideology is expressed in advocacy for reducing consumption to the average of world levels (substantially lower than present European levels of consumption) and for open borders. Offering a rationale for the latter goal, one-worlders say that the United States is unlike any other nation. It is a nation of immigrants having no history of a citizenry who feel united as a people, and therefore it has no legitimate territorial integrity. In short, the United States is not a nation-state like other countries of the world but is, rather, "an idea," appropriately stripped of sovereignty.

In the cultural and social realms, this description of America justifies accelerated immigration of peoples as unlike to existing Americans as possible, and advocacy of multiculturalism. Already a feature of public school (embodied in new, government-sponsored history standards) and many private school curricula, multiculturalism teaches that all cultures are equally relevant to America.

Remarkably (and illogically within the terms of multiculturalism's own worldview) one culture is presented as illegitimate—destined to be overcome by others. That is the culture of the founders based on

European and particularly Anglo-Saxon principles of ethics, government, religion, and Euro-American history.

Others think differently on each of these dimensions. Ecologists and entrepreneurs are converging on the view that humans are not altruists—the opposite of the romanticist credo. A factual basis for rejecting the myth of the "noble savage" is well developed. The current view is that altruism manifested in a conservation ethic is no more present in traditional than modern society (Williams 1966; Ruttan 1998).

Further, ecologists and entrepreneurs think differently than romanticists on the legitimacy of the nation and the sense of patriotism and kinship in being American. It seems likely that the majority of ecologists and entrepreneurs (with the exception of certain multinational corporations) assume that the United States is a nation-state, like others, with territorial integrity and its own culture. Culture is taken to mean the values and assumptions, history, language, and technology that are largely shared by all members of the society. The government has its primary responsibility to the nation, the United States, and a corollary obligation to protect the nation's people: all Americans. It would not put the matter too strongly to assert that the government of the United States is obliged to put the well-being of Americans above all others, just as the governments of all other countries are expected to do for their people.

Ecologists and entrepreneurs also have in common the habit of using inductive reasoning, although they focus on different data. Different data predict opposed conclusions. At present, entrepreneurs assert that the greatest good derives from free trade and minimal impediments to the movement of labor. Attentive to natural systems, the ecologists' view—one also having policy implications— is based on the limits of nature in general, and of human nature in particular.

Ecologists emphasize the inviolability of carrying capacity if the nation is to survive. Preservation of carrying capacity, which is inherently limited, is fundamental for the present and future well-being of any nation. Overtaxing the carrying capacity destroys, sometimes irremediably, the long-term ability of the resource base to sustain those who depend on it.

Population growth indubitably increases the pressure on the environment—even romanticists admit this so long as their focus is the rest of the world rather than the United States (see, for example, former Vice-President Albert Gore's *Earth in the Balance* [1992]).

Concern about US population growth pushes ecologists to protest present US immigration policy which allows the addition of over one million persons annually (net of emigration), as well as the subsequent growth from descendants of current immigrants. Immigration and the children of post-1970 immigrant families, together, accounted for over 70 percent of US population growth in 1990s (Camarota 1999). That share rises continuously as the stock of recent immigrants and their descendants grows and the native-born fertility rate remains low.

Ecologists see not only the direct threat to carrying capacity from increasing population size through immigration, but also the indirect effect arising from immigration's effect on the incentive system. Americans are disposed to conserve land that they own or control, to stabilize population through self-restraint in childbearing (the native-born fertility rate is below replacement level), to tax themselves for environmental rehabilitation efforts, and to mitigate ongoing environmental destruction. However, immigration makes the United States into an effective "commons," a condition conducive to using resources as fast as possible lest one lose out on one's share.

A rational person who sees no prospect of stabilizing population so long as immigration continues might well resist any sacrifice made on behalf of the environment or society at large (Abernethy 1993). If efforts to protect the carrying capacity are doomed to fail, anyway, because of continuing population growth, why conserve, why do without today, why support an environmental ethic? A case in point, to protest continuing immigration, some Californians responded to water use restrictions during the 1980s drought with the bumper sticker, "Flush Twice."

Unless reasonably assured that present and future benefit will accrue to themselves or their posterity, few persons will forego present consumption or childbearing for the purpose of conserving the environment. Americans' incentive to conserve the environment can probably be maintained only by offering hope that their efforts will not be in vain. Accordingly, ecologists conclude that reducing immigration to the number compatible with stabilizing population size, or even allowing population decline should that prove necessary, is the only sustainable course.

A Policy Collision

Translating worldviews into policy initiatives, partisans of the three distinct traditions find themselves joined in surprising coalitions. When the focus is on protecting a particular resource (a forest, a river, public lands), romanticists work together with ecologists.

Romanticists and entrepreneurs (the latter desiring access to the cheaper world labor market without moving production operations abroad) readily work together to defeat legislation that would reduce immigration numbers to a level compatible with US population stabilization. An instance of the serendipitous romanticist-entrepreneurial coalition was their mobilization to block a proposed reduction in numbers of legal immigrants in spring 1996. The proimmigration National Immigration Forum headed by Frank Sharry and the liberal Urban League as well as the National Association of Manufacturers and the National Trial Lawyers Association argued in concert—and successfully—for continuing high levels of legal immigration (Davidson 1995, 34; Chavez 1996; Levine 1996; Jacobs 1995; Freedburg 1996; Tech Firms 1996).

However, this coalition fragments on conservation issues. Divisions can be found within the entrepreneurial community itself. For example, Fred Charles Iklé, himself a conservative, takes neoconservatives to task for their idealization of nonstop economic and population growth: "The fabulous success of conservative economic policies has seduced many in our midst into taking economic growth as the defining attribute of conservatism. These brethren now believe that . . . good growth can and must continue indefinitely. They act as if conservative thought were nothing but the philosophy of perpetual growth" (Iklé 1994, 36).

Warning against immigration-driven growth, conservatives might cite Lester Thurow, former dean of MIT's Sloane School of Business Administration, who postulates that "No country can become rich without a century of good economic performance and a century of very slow population growth" (cited in Lind 1995). In other contexts, Paul Krugman (1994) observes that "Economic growth that is based on expansion of inputs, rather than on growth in output per unit of input, is inevitably subject to diminishing returns." Robert Stein in *Investor's Business Daily*, states that immigration dilutes the amount of capital available per job and thus undercuts the mechanism for raising labor productivity and noninflationary wage increases (Stein 1995).

Ecologists attempt to appeal to the business community by pointing out that population growth makes more environmental regulation necessary and adds dramatically to the fiscal burden of local and state governments. The more general arguments, that population growth threatens the carrying capacity, and immigration depresses the wages of American labor (very often the least skilled, already disadvantaged, are hurt most) seem more attuned to classical liberal thinking.

The competing rationales and outcomes appear reasonable or not depending upon one's perspective. Entrepreneurs hear restrictions on immigration as interference with free markets and the economies of low-wage labor. However, an imported labor force displaces Americans who may then go on the public dole. Moreover, low-skill immigrants and their families are very likely to depend on public assistance (especially during months of slack employment), lack health care insurance, and have children who are educated at public expense (Matloff 1998; Huddle 1998). Calls for government programs to correct poverty—anathema to entrepreneurs—are an almost inevitable result of importing poverty.

The radical-left element of the romanticist school hears immigration restriction as racist (Political Ecology Group 1998). Racism is inferred because reduced immigration would inevitably cut most from the largest streams of immigrants, which are from the third world and the former USSR. Further, one-world romanticists cast the attempt to conserve a unique American culture as illegitimate—although all nations, as a matter of course, intend to conserve their own language, history, traditions, and values. The charge of "racism" has successfully intimidated large numbers of Americans whose goals are conservation-ist and certainly not racist. I observe that the term "Nazism" is being substituted as "racism" loses credibility and punch.

Conservationists place a high priority on the quality of life in their communities, and their goals encompass preserving good opportunity for coming generations of Americans. Most Americans look to the future. In the present, wishing to protect American workers from having their wages competed down to third world standards, citizens seek a healthful, open environment and minimization of government intrusion into their lives. The majority sees no need to reject the traditional culture, which is not only their birthright but also the safeguard of democratic government and constitutionally guaranteed freedoms from government overreach.

Every country has its interests and its culture. The culture evolves from within as most citizens wish it to do. Such has been the course of history. In a healthful state, the culture promotes a rate of growth, or stasis, where the natural environment sustainably supports the associated society at a level that is expected and acceptable to its citizens.

But romanticists deny the importance of both limits and Western culture and, for the sake of a one-world internationalist chimera in which everyone is equal, would see everyone poor. This cannot be right. The moral high ground must have a basis in environmental and human

61

possibilities. Disrespect for the carrying capacity is destabilizing. It exacts, ultimately, a devastating toll.

A State Shows the Way*

An impressive roster of scientists warns that the United States lacks coherent water management and policy planning. Criteria guiding such activities "are ambiguous at a time when degradation of water supplies and aquatic resources is accelerating" (Naiman et al. 1995, 584). The authors think that the issues "promised to become increasingly complex, contentious, and strategic for the United States as demographic patterns, resource consumption, environmental quality, social and institutional organization, and technologies change" (p. 585). To cope with these multiple, looming crises, the authors recommend a research agenda.

Is anyone else laughing?

Just study it! For a while longer, deny how much of the problem is understood, and that the policies to address what we know of the problem may be politically incorrect but must be part of the plan for remediating and protecting fresh water supplies. Contrary to what these scientists imply, strategies to avoid worsening the crisis exist. They lie in the political realm, and to imply that science holds solutions is irresponsible. Science can at best mitigate. Science can avoid overselling itself by identifying the political choices a society faces.

For example, the United States is not a passive recipient of changing "demographic patterns." The primary change is growth, which can be experienced at the level of community, suburb, city, or nation. Growth can be curbed. One semiarid, drought-prone, water-short State is trying to do it.

On September 15, 1995, California Senate Bill 901 passed by a vote of 28 to 6. The Assembly had previously approved the measure by 66 to 0. California Governor Pete Wilson lost no time in signing. The bill adds a new requirement to the approval process for real estate developments of 500 or more houses or hotel rooms, or businesses employing 1,000 or more people. An environmental impact statement must now include a report from the local water supplier which identifies "sources of water for the new project—plus existing customers—for the next twenty years." Because water is scarce, this stipulation is expected to crimp the virtual overnight establishment of new towns. Of the 110

*Editorial in *Population and Environment* 17(6) pp. 445–46.

projects under construction or in the planning stage in 1995, "nearly half ... identify the State Water Project as their source, which is California dreamin' because that water is spoken for" (Common Sense 1995).

This legislation is a tribute to hard work and dedication. The initiative began with Dr. Wendell Peart and Placer County Board of Supervisors member Dr. Philip Ozenick.

They developed the concept of Drought Safety Standards: "The theme was that available water, not land, should be the determinant factor as to the number of structures to be built. [In a 1991 address to the State Water Resource Board,] Peart also pointed out that part of the problem was population growth, and one solution was to restrict immigration to the U.S." (Peart 1995). Limiting immigration is a federal government responsibility.

At the State level, in Peart's own words, the Water Bill passed the Legislature with Assemblyman Dominic Cortese "as the pitcher who tirelessly carried the game for six innings. Then [Assemblyman Jim Costa relieved Dominic in the seventh, and carried the game to the bottom of the ninth. At this point our team was behind, there were two outs, the bases were loaded and [Senator] Quentin Kopp came to bat. When you arose that day and took on the opposition in the arena call the State Senate, you hit the ball out of the [park]" (Peart 1995).

In California, the majority knows that its principal source of problems is population growth. Within the constitutional rights reserved to the States and the people, they are casting about for solutions. The Congress should help by addressing squarely, on environmental, economic, and social grounds, the population policy which can best serve the interests of the citizens of this nation.

Population Problems*

The abiding risk is that people needing jobs, needing housing, needing heating oil, or needing whatever—all needs that entail the throughput of more resources—can overwhelm the constituency for protecting the environment. Moreover, human needs are easily transposed into humanitarian claims. Good-hearted people are persuaded of the gravity of the humanitarian claim and do not reflect that many uses of resources and most new jobs and housing degrade the environment.

---

*In *The Wild Earth*, pp. 89–90 [Summer, 1997].

Humanitarian claims are compelling. They become more compelling when attached to persons residing within one's own country, but the asserted "right" of economic migrants to move across international borders also counts on good will. Yet, by adding to urban density and swelling the labor force, newcomers drive expansion and transformation of wild and agricultural lands to commercial or residential uses. Each person added to the population results in utilizing one acre of land for urbanization and road building (Pimentel 1996).

It is worth recalling that species diversity outside of zoos depends on adequate natural habitat; and that habitat is altered or destroyed by land transformations, as from wild to agricultural to residential. Such land transformations are significantly related to human encroachment secondary to population growth.

Population growth makes harder the already excruciating choices between the nation's people and conservation. The ethical dilemma is sharpened by humankind being entrusted with stewardship as an inescapable corollary of having dominion over Nature. As we fail in our responsibility, native species become extinct and the nation's natural life-support systems diminish.

But, one might counter, more people could be accommodated were all less wasteful. True, but this returns one to the problem of active environmentalism. Why is this constituency small and vulnerable to defections? What obstacles stand in the way of enlarging the active environmental constituency? In the words of John Cairns, "Benefits to society and maintenance and restoration of ecological quality must be more closely coupled" (1994, 12, 14). But how?

Here we focus on (1) education, teaching why it is important to all that each of us conserves; and (2) predispositions of human nature identified by behavioral ecologists. The latter divide into why natural selection operates against altruism (Trivers 1985; Low and Heinen 1993) and the higher cost of altruism in the particular context of a "commons" (Hardin 1968).

Education on the necessity of conservation is widely believed to be an effective and usually sufficient way to promote environmentally correct behavior. We "commonly think of ourselves as ethical individuals, giving value to the common good; thus, because none of us wishes to cause destruction of resources, each of us will accept some level of personal cost" (Low and Heinen 1993, p.8).

This said, Low and Heinen's review of the literature suggests, to the contrary, that both in preindustrial societies and modern industrial nations, conservation schemes "based solely on information are arguably less successful than those incorporating individual cost-benefit leverage" (Low and Heinen 1993, 31). This conclusion is congruent with sociobiological theory.

Sociobiology's premise is that individuals of all species including humans are genetically predisposed to act in ways that maximize their "inclusive fitness," that is, the chances that duplicates of their genes appear in successive generations. Axiomatically, every living individual had ancestors who succeeded in this realm through reproduction, so most of us carry genes impelling us toward similar goals and behavior.

Nevertheless, some individuals sometimes act in ways that enhance the success of unrelated others at a likely cost to their own fitness. Sociobiologists call this "altruism." By definition, altruists face an increased probability that their genes, including those predisposing them to altruism, will disappear from the future gene pool; i.e., these genes are selected against. For this reason, in no population can the prevalence of a genetically based predisposition to act altruistically be large; bearers of such traits are outcompeted, on average, by those predisposed to maximize their own and their relatives' reproductive success. Low and Heinen observe that, "Selection cannot favor individuals who act for the benefit of a group of nonrelatives at the expense of their own inclusive fitness. Situations in which the costs are paid by individuals other than those gaining the rewards are unstable" (1993, 13).

The relevance to environmentalism is this: conservation behaviors often burden the actor with most of the cost, but the return is imperceptible; the benefits are widely disseminated, whereas the cost is concentrated. That is to say, most voluntary environmentalism is altruistic, and education may be too weak to overcome the powerful genetic loading against altruism.

In this context, note that *deception* is a common social strategy. Individuals tend to understand their culture and act in socially approved ways. Many perceive that the *appearance* of altruism can lead to influence or higher status within a community. At the same time, no actual loss of fitness is entailed so long as seemingly altruistic sacrifices are made on behalf of kin (individuals likely to bear duplicate genes) or in the context of a fairly closed, long-lasting community where favors are likely to be returned. These instances are not true altruism because they involve a gain calculated to be roughly equal to or greater than its cost.

The final element in this conservation calculus is "the commons." A commons is a resource treated as though it belongs to all. When anyone can claim a resource simply on the grounds that he wants or needs to use it, one has a commons.

Disincentives to conservation inhere in common property because a resource both limited and accessible to all is disproportionately utilized by fast and prodigal users. A conservative approach to the resource is punished by losing out on one's fair share. A commons may function when a population is stable and social pressure prevents any individual from abusing the resource. However, if the population using the commons grows from within, or if nonnatives cannot be barred, conservation breaks down.

Neighborhoods, cities, and states are commons in the sense that no one is denied entry. The defining characteristic is that anyone may enter and, by entering, lay claim on its resources. Educational opportunity, the social safety net, the infrastructure, clean water, clean air—these are among the community's resources. A country becomes a commons to the extent that it allows immigration and that new residents are treated nearly equally with citizens.

A commons amplifies the genetically programmed resistance to altruism. As the individual costs of conservation rise, and to the extent that the benefits cannot be captured by kin or local community, selfish behavior inevitably becomes more advantageous and, therefore, ever more pronounced.

It follows that those who are disposed to use a resource modestly and sustainably must also have the means to protect it. If not, all efforts to conserve are futile. Ability to protect resources is the antithesis of the commons.

The United States is in some respects a "commons." Its population—the sum of potential claimants on its wealth—is growing rapidly and is projected to reach half a billion by the middle of the next century. The growth comes from both within and without. Accounting for 50 percent of US population growth already, immigration and children born to recent immigrants increasingly dominate America's demographic future. Over five million net new settlers between January 1, 1990, and March 1, 1995 (Census Bureau 1995) continue the transformation of America into a commons. Particularly in those States where immigrants concentrate, ordinary citizens find it increasingly difficult to capture the benefits of personal sacrifices made on behalf of the environment, the construction of infrastructure, investment in public education, or spending on other public projects. The mounting disincentives worsen, in my judgment, the prospects for developing a "constituency for preserving the ecosystems."

I forsee adjustments as individuals recognize the elements of a commons and inevitably attempt to protect themselves. Mechanisms may include regionalization (a fulminating scenario worldwide and as close as Quebec), regional control of immigration policy (which California has attempted with its constitutionally- in-limbo proposition 187), privatization of infrastructure (e.g., Hong Kong's privately owned transportation arteries between the island and the mainland, and privately funded toll roads (which are increasingly seen in the United States), privatization of education, health care, and conservation lands, and walled residential communities protected by private security forces.

These adjustments are not "solutions" because they do not optimize the well-being of all Americans in the spirit of unity we have traditionally treasured. But Congress and the president have not yet taken meaningful steps to protect our national home.

Who will be the environmental altruist in this context? How many will be found tomorrow?

References

Abernethy, Virginia Deane. 1993. *Population Politics: The Choices that Shape Our Future.* New York: Plenum Press.

Ahlburg, Dennis A., and James W. Vaupel. 1990. "500 Million Americans by 2050?" *Demography 27* (4): 639–47.

Avery, Dennis T. 1995. *Saving the Planet with Pesticides and Plastic.* Indianapolis, IN: Hudson Institute.

Banks, Howard. 1998. "Cheap Oil: Enjoy It While It Lasts." *Forbes,* June 15, 84–86.

Barnett, Don. February 26, 1996. "A Refuge of Lies." *National Review,* 46.

Bartlett, Albert A. 1996. "The Exponential Function, XI: The New Flat Earth Society." *The Physics Teacher* 34, September, pp. 1–2.

Benedetto, Richard. May 22, 1996. "Poll Points Toward Conservative Electorate." *USA Today,* 8A.

Bordering on Disaster. May 20, 1996. *National Review,* 16, 18.

Borjas, G. 1996. "The New Economics of Immigration." *The Atlantic Monthly,* November, 72–80.

Borjas, G., and R. Freeman. 1997. "Findings We Never Found." *The New York Times,* December 10, Op-Ed.

Cairns, John Jr. 1994. "The Study of Ecology and Environmental Management: Reflections on the Implications of Ecological History." *Environmental Management and Health* 5 (4): 7–15.

Camarota, Steven A. 1999. *Immigrants in the United States—1998.* Washington, DC: Center for Immigration Studies.

Carrying Capacity Network. 1995. *Polls Show Most Americans Want Immigration Levels Reduced.* Washington, DC: Author.

Census Bureau. March 1995. *Current Population Survey.* Washington, DC: U.S. Govt. Printing Office.

Chavez, Linda 1996. *USA Today*, 1.

Cobb, J. B. Jr. and H. E. Daly. 1990. "Free Trade versus Community: Social and Environmental Consequence of Free Trade in a World with Capital Mobility and Overpopulated Regions." *Population and Environment* 11 (3): 175–92.

Common Sense on Water Sources. October 5, 1995. *Los Angeles Times*, editorial page.

Cottrell, Fred 1955. *Energy and Society.* New York: McGraw-Hill.

Daly, Herman 1990. Toward Some Operational Principles of Sustainable Development. *Ecological Economics* 2:1–6.

Daly, Herman 1991. "Population and Economics: A Bioeconomic Analysis." *Population and Environment* 12 (3): 257–8.

Davidson, J. 1995. *Wall Street Journal*, June 9, 34.

Dawkins, R. 1976. *The Selfish Gene.* Oxford: Oxford University Press.

De Courcy, Joe 1997. "Globalists v. the Nation State." *The St. Croix Review* 31 (2): 34–38.

Dorf, Matthew. March 16, 1995. "Welfare Cuts Scary for Immigrant Jews." *Washington Jewish Week*, 18.

Dorf, Matthew. March 28, 1996. "Doors Stay Open." *Washington Jewish Week*, 25.

Elliott, Herschel 1997. "A General Statement of the Tragedy of the Commons." *Population and Environment* 18 (6): 515–31.

Erasing Self-Rule 1998. *Middle American News*, June, p.16.

Ferguson, Andrew 1998. *World Carrying Capacities.* Manchester, England: Optimum Population Trust.

Freedburg 1996. Few Visas. *San Francisco Chronicle*, March 11, p. 1.

Gever, J., R. Kaufman, D. Skole, and C. Vorosmarty. 1986. *Beyond Oil: The Threat to Food and Fuel in Coming Decades.* Cambridge: Ballinger.

Gore, A. 1992. *Earth in the Balance: Ecology and the Human Spirit.* Boston, MA: Houghton Mifflin.

Hamilton, W.D. 1964. "The Genetical Evolution of Social Behavior." *Journal of Theoretical Biology* 7:1–16.

Hardin, Garrett. 1968. "The Tragedy of the Commons." *Science* 162:1243–8.

Hardin, Garrett. 1998a. "The Number of Cars will Increase to Fill Six Lanes." *Social Contract* January 18, p. 4.

Hardin, Garrett. 1998b. "The Feast of Malthus." *Social Contract* 8 (3): 181–7.

Heim, Mary, and Austin, Nancy. 1996. "Fertility of Immigrant Women in California." *Population and Environment* 17 (5): 391–408.

Holdren, J. P. 1991. "Population and the Energy Problem." *Population and Environment* 12 (3): 231–56.

Huddle, Donald. 1995. *The Net National Costs of Immigration.* Washington, DC: Carrying Capacity Network.

Huddle, Donald 1998. *Executive Summary, Immigration's Costs Keep Rising.* Washington, DC: Carrying Capacity Network.

Iklé, Fred Charles. 1994. "Growth Without End, Amen?" *National Review*, March 7, pp. 36–44.

Jacobs, Margaret A. 1995. "U.S. Businesses Fight a Cutback of Green Cards." *Wall Street Journal*, Legal beat, July 11, pp. B1, 2.

Keyfitz, Nathan. 1993. "Thirty Years of Demography." *Demography* 30:533–49.

Kinsley, Michael J., and Lovins, L. Hunter. 1995. *Paying for Growth, Prospering from Development.* Snowmass, CO: Rocky Mountain Institute.

Lambert, Thomas 1996. Defusing the "Population Bomb" with Free Markets. *Policy Study* 129. Center for Study of American Business, February. Washington University, St.Louis.

Leal, Donald R. 1998. "Community-Run Fisheries: Avoiding the 'Tragedy of the Commons'." *Population and Environment* 19 (3): 225–46.

Levine, F. J. 1996. *Science* 271, March 22, 1649.

Lind, Michael 1995. America by Invitation. *The New Yorker*, April 24, pp. 107–12.

Long, John. March 21, 1995. Personal communication.

Low, Bobbi S., and Heinen, Joel, T. 1993. "Population, Resources and Environment. Implications of Human Behavioral Ecology for Conservation." *Population and Environment* 15 (1): 7–41

Malthus, Thomas Robert. 1789. *An Essay on the Principle of Population.* Edition (1976) with sources and criticism edited by Philip Adelman. New York: W.W. Norton & Co.

Matloff, Norman 1998. "Visa Program for High Tech Workers." *Wall Street Journal*, June 5, Letters.

Mittelstadt, Michelle. February 18, 1996. "Poll: Let in Fewer Immigrants." *San Francisco Examiner.*

Naiman, R. J., John J. Magnuson, Diane M. McKnight, Jack A. Stanford, and James R. Karr. (Oct. 27, 1995. "Freshwater Ecosystems and their Management: A National Initiative." *Science* 270:584–5.

National Research Council 1997. *The New Americans.* Washington, DC: The National Academy of Sciences.

Peart, Wendell G. October 2, 1995. Letter to Senator Quentin Kopp.

Pimentel, D., and Pimentel, M. 1991. *The Constraints Governing Ideal U.S. Population Size.* Teaneck, NJ: Negative Population Growth.

Pimentel, David, and Mario Giampietro. 1994. *Food, Land, Population and the U.S. Economy.* Washington, DC: Carrying Capacity Network.

Pimentel, David, and Pimentel, Marcia, eds. 1996. *Food, Energy and Society.* Niwot, CO: University Press of Colorado.

Pimentel, David and Pimentel, Marcia 1997. *Land, Energy, and Water.* Revised edition. Boulder, CO: University of Colorado.

Pimentel, David, C. Harvey, P. Resosudarmo, K. Sinclair, D. Kurz, M. McNair, S. Crist, L. Shpritz, L. Fitton, R. Saffouri, and R. Blair. 1995. "Environmental and Economic Costs of Soil Erosion and Conservation Benefits." *Science* 267, February 24, 1117–23.

Pimentel, David, C. Harvey, P. Resosudarmo, K. Sinclair, D. Kurz, M. McNair, S. Crist, L. Shpritz, L. Fitton, R. Saffouri, and R. Blair. February 24, 1995. "Environmental and Economic Costs of Soil Erosion and Conservation Benefits." *Science* 267:1117–23.

Pimentel, David. February 19, 1996. Paper, AAAS annual meetings, Baltimore, MD.

Political Ecology Group 1998. *Wooing the Sierra Club: Hate Groups Make Unlikely Suitors.* San Francisco, March 6, PEG, California.

Puente, Maria. April 25, 1996. "Immigration Numbers to Surge." *USA Today*, 3A.

Rough Road Ahead. Spring 1996. *Immigration Review* 25:3.

Ruttan, Lore M. 1998. "Closing the Commons: Cooperation for Gain or Restraint." *Human Ecology* 6 (1): 43–66.

Scares 1997. *The Economist,* December 20, pp. 19, 20.

Simon, Julian. 1995. "The State of Humanity: Steadily Improving." *Cato Policy Report* 17 (5), September/October, 131. Washington, DC: Cato Institute.

Steadman, David W. February 24, 1995. "Prehistoric Extinctions of Pacific Island Birds: Biodiversity Meets Zooarchaeology." *Science* 267:1123–7.

Stein, Robert. 1995. "Should We Still Welcome the Huddled Masses?" *Investors Business Daily*, September 11, p. B1. 17 ESEP 2001, 9–18

Stevens, William K. February 14, 1995. "Entire Ecosystems on Endangered List." *San Francisco Chronicle*, 2.

Tech Firms 1996. *USA Today*, February 28, p. 1.

Trivers, R. L. 1971. "The Evolution of Reciprocal Altruism." *Quarterly Review of Biology* 46:35–57.

Trivers, R. L. 1985. *Social Evolution.* Menlo Park, CA: Benjamin Cummings.

Ventura, Stephanie, Joyce A. Martin, T. J. Mathews, and Sally C. Clarke. 1996. Advance Report of Final Natality Statistics, 1994. *Supplement* 44 (11), June, Tables 10 and 11 (pp. 41–42). National Center for Health Statistics, Division of Vital Statistics, Bethesda, MD.

Williams, G. C. 1966. *Adaptation and Natural Selection: A Critique of Some Current Evolutionary Thought.* Princeton, NJ: Princeton University Press.

Williams, G. C. 1975. *Sex and Evolution.* Princeton, NJ: Princeton University Press.

Wilson, E. O. 1975. *Sociobiology.* Cambridge, MA: Harvard University Press

Wolf, Charles Jr. 1994. "The New Mercantilism." *The Public Interest* 116:96–106.

Youngquist, Walter. 1997. *GeoDestinies.* Portland, OR: National Book Company 18.

3

Explaining Fertility Rates: The Search for Causality

Introduction

A spirited dispute in Harvard's 1960s Social Relations/Anthropology doctoral program centered on whether a society's language, beliefs, values, traditions, and technology—its culture—derive from accidental and historical factors, or from adaptation to particular conditions. One of the materials presented was Ester Boserup's *Conditions of Agricultural Growth* (1965). This book sparked my fascination with demography—although I am in no way a demographer—and gives one an appreciation for adaptation as an explanation of change.

Adaptation is a dynamic process. Individuals, families, and ultimately the society adapt—change their beliefs and behavior—not only in response to the availability of natural and man-made resources but also to political, cultural, and even demographic conditions. Exceptional conditions such as a genocidal threat create exceptional responses: for example, a community feeling threatened may see population growth as its best means of resistance, regardless of resources. However, the decoupling of fertility rates from perceived plenty or scarcity is rare.

Population dynamics is a recurrent theme in my writing. G. Olin's 1961 quotation from "The Pre-industrial Tables of the Births and Funerals of the City of Breslaw" summarizes a cause-and-effect relationship that one sees repeatedly: "The growth and Encrease of Mankind is not so much stinted by anything in the nature of the Species, as it is from the cautious difficulty most People make to adventure on the state of marriage, from the prospect of the Trouble and Charge of providing for a family."

Foreword to Aldine-Transaction Edition of Ester Boserup's
*The Conditions of Agricultural Growth**

Ester Boserup's ground-breaking analysis of the dynamics of agricultural development was one of the highlights of my graduate school reading. I encountered it shortly after its 1965 publication date, in the midst of a controversy at Harvard's Department of Social Relations (Anthropology) that centered on historical, even accidental versus functional, i.e. causal, explanation of social systems. Boserup's thesis seemed to confirm the value of exploring causality.

Her focus is on technologies in primitive and developing societies where the more "developed" technologies yield less per man-hour of labor, but more total food because more of the available land is under cultivation. Her analysis is not intended to be relevant where fossil fuel largely replaces human labor, as in the mechanized agriculture of modern societies.

Whether Boserup correctly identified the causal factors in agricultural development is almost a secondary question. Her breakthrough was seeing that particular technologies do not develop, and are not adopted, in a social or environmental vacuum. Local conditions have to be right before agriculturalists will adopt more productive technologies, even if they are perfectly aware and able to adopt them.

Boserup assumes that people resist labor. Therefore, they resist agricultural practices that entail more labor. Necessity drives the invention or adoption of these more labor-intensive technologies. The driver, in Boserup's view, is the increasing demand for food that comes from population growth.

She takes agriculture from its most primitive stage—gardening, which relies on fire to clear forest patches that are cultivated for only a few years and then abandoned. The earth is so friable, fertile, and weed-free in this kind of shifting agriculture that seeds and root-crop eyes can be inserted with a digging stick and left to mature on their own. But maintenance of this quality of soil requires returning a patch to forest after just a few years' use, and then letting it fallow for twenty or more years. The system works well so long as population density is low enough for forests always to hold virgin or well-regenerated plots.

If population grows so that plot rotation is limited, each clearing must be worked longer, fallow periods are shortened, and gardening

*Transaction Publishers, Piscataway, NJ [2005].

becomes more difficult because weeds flourish, fertility declines, and the ground may harden. Plants need to be cultivated. Fertilizers such as fish may be added to enhance soil quality. Hoes replace digging sticks. Labor intensifies.

The next step is from shortened fallow periods to permanently cleared and enlarged plots. The land is now divided into fields and cannot be gardened with a hoe. A primitive plow and draught animals must help, requiring considerable strength and much human labor.

If land is insufficient to provide year-round graze for draught animals, the farmer (shifting agriculturalist and gardener no longer) must also contrive to plant forage and add the chore of feeding livestock. A legume crop may be introduced, both as feed and to restore soil fertility. Irrigation and terracing to maximize land-use may also develop.

Pretty soon the farmer and his family work during all daylight hours, twelve months a year. He is producing much more food than formerly because more of the available land is cultivated, but the trade-off is less leisure. Also, farm families live near neighbors, some also engaged in agriculture but others specializing in crafts. If the household becomes less self-sufficient in its various requirements, enough food—now often grains—must be grown to provide a cash crop.

Again, the trade-off is not ideal because the grains laboriously cultivated in plow agriculture yield fewer calories per acre than the root crops grown in long-fallow forest plots.

The transition to intensive agriculture may sound grim. Boserup's point, indeed, is that the added work requirements are a serious deterrent to making the switch from less to more productive technologies. She suggests that farmers often endure reduction in their food consumption before abandoning the less labor-intensive alternative. Making the point, she presents examples showing that people often revert to the less labor-intensive technology when population pressure eases.

Boserup's great contribution is drawing attention to causal relationships and motivation. Yet, she unnecessarily, in my opinion, sets up a Malthusian straw man. Challenging a simplistic version of Malthus' hypothesis, namely, food supply governs "the rate of population growth" (p. 11), she sets out to show that population growth, itself, drives people to increase the production of food. She never acknowledges that perceived scarcity could change demographic outcomes.

Moreover, Boserup's world knows no environmental limit other than arable land. She would be quite at home with certain economists' cornucopian views that scarcity is always a short-term phenomenon because higher prices, signaling scarcity, drive both/either substitution and/or enhanced technology. One can accept almost all of Boserup's conclusions, I think, but this one.

Observation of the world around forces an acknowledgment, in my opinion, that humans inevitably encounter limits in some essential resource, not necessarily land. Therefore, there are limits to what human ingenuity and work can do.

For example, Boserup points out that the transition from long-fallow forest gardening to cleared and plowed fields often dries out the soil. She never, however, looks at the possibility that erosion or climate change including desertification can be induced by human attempts to maximize agricultural production in marginally dry climates. She never examines fresh water as an ultimate limiting resource.

Boserup also gives short shrift to values other than leisure that are given up in the quest to feed a larger and larger population. She makes no mention of the diverse plant and animal species that exist in the forest and its margins but die out when their habitat is destroyed. What, further, of the value that some people place on wilderness, space, mobility, and other intangibles that lose out to crowding and population growth? What of the value that makes settlers move on when neighbors get so close that you can smell their smoke?

I think that the most fundamental criticism is that Boserup limits herself unnecessarily in seeing only one causal direction: population growth driving an increase in agricultural intensification in order to increase food production. A complete picture of population dynamics would include the possibility of a feedback loop. That is, Boserup does not consider that perceived scarcity of food—or that scarcity of some other valued resource—might retard, stop, and even reverse population growth.

The intervening demographic variable that Boserup does not consider is the fertility rate. Leaving aside possible changes in mortality, population growth is mediated by the number of children per woman, largely an effect of desired family size and reproductive behavior. Longitudinal studies show that fertility rates often vary dramatically within a single society and may pulse up or down depending upon perceived economic conditions.

My research suggests that perception of resource availability influences desired family size. Thus, perceived need for more food may drive changes in demographic variables, rather than population pressure simply driving food production. The causal pathway can run in either direction.

The idea that the perception of scarcity depresses fertility rates is not new. Malthus' Second Essay comes to this conclusion, similar to my explanation now usually called the *fertility opportunity hypothesis*. This hypothesis proposes that couples who perceive narrowing opportunity tend to limit family size by whatever means is available. If the sense of scarcity persists, mechanisms that limit reproductive opportunity may evolve beyond individual control to become more or less mandatory patterns of social behavior. For example, in eighteenth-century Switzerland and certain German principalities, a general understanding that couples should delay marriage until having a relatively assured financial future evolved into rules that a prospective groom prove an income—such as two years of gainful employment and not having been on the public dole.

On the other hand, people who see expanding opportunity tend to abandon reproductive self-restraint. They are more likely to marry young and welcome new additions to the family. Social or physical mechanisms for limiting fertility are likely to be ignored. Thus, attempts to introduce modern contraception in developing societies are largely unsuccessful so long as people think that the opportunity structure favors large families.

Perception may not be reality. The perception of growing prosperity is what, in my view, propelled rapid population growth in parts of the world where promised redistribution of wealth, or foreign aid, or introduced technologies, or new markets made formerly poor people much better off. Uniformly, these populations raised their fertility rate—or maintained a high rate even as modern medicine was reducing infant and child mortality.

Almost uniformly, however, the apparent prosperity of developing countries (and European countries through the nineteenth century) has been short-lived because rapid population growth quickly reduces per capita income and wealth. The cycles of building optimism, rising fertility rates, and an exploding population followed by disillusionment, rediscovered self-restraint, and declining fertility rates repeat themselves without end.

The choices available to those who see their livelihood disappearing are limited. Barring outside intervention or the possibility of emigration, choices narrow to (1) what Boserup describes and (2) what I describe as the fertility opportunity hypothesis. Both responses are adaptive and, in my experience, often coexist. People work harder, and people also avoid adding to their responsibilities through marriage and childbearing.

Two illustrations of the hypothesis fall within the spectrum of agricultural societies that interest Boserup. I recount here short histories of Malawi and Rwanda presented from the perspective of the fertility opportunity hypothesis.

Malawi is on the Southeast coast of Africa. Its first, 1966, census revealed a population of four million. By 1995, the population was ten million, from which is calculated an annual population growth rate of 3.5 percent. Confronted with a rising population and limited arable land, the 85 percent of Malawians who derive their livelihood from subsistence farming have three options for maintaining a viable ecological niche. Ezekiel Kalipeni (1996) concludes that they can (1) work harder on existing holdings, that is, practice agricultural intensification—the Boserup hypothesis; (2) migrate to available but less good, in fact, marginal lands; or (3) limit family size to avoid adding to existing pressure on the land—the fertility opportunity hypothesis.

Kalipeni suggests that the hard work of agricultural intensification held greatest promise when land scarcity first began to seem problematic but, in the long run, could not keep ahead of the momentum of population growth. Migration to infertile marginal land was unattractive, leaving only the option of limiting family size.

In comparison with other sub-Saharan Africans, rural Malawians began treating fertility control as a real choice relatively early. Between 1977 and 1987, crude birth rates declined from 48 to 41 births per 1,000 persons in the population. Kalipeni tested a number of academic explanations—call them demography's "received wisdom"—for declining fertility but found no significant relationships. He found that the fertility rate was not significantly related to education, infant mortality, or urbanization in either 1977 or 1987 data.

However, a 1987 regression (correlation) revealed a statistically significant inverse relationship between the fertility rate and population density ($r = -0.40$). That is, the denser the population, the lower the fertility rate. Drawing together his data, Kalipeni infers that land hunger was the central stimulus in the onset of Malawi's fertility decline. He writes: "Correlation does not prove causality. Nevertheless, variation in the rate at which fertility is declining within regions suggests that land hunger does, indeed, drive the more cautious approach to childbearing: specifically, the fastest fertility decline is occurring in the region of highest population density. . . . areas that are experiencing intense environmental pressure are also beginning to go through a fertility transition" (Kalipeni 1996, 299–300).

Rwanda, in Central Africa, is one of the most densely populated countries of the continent. The colonial power, Belgium, and successor indigenous governments (beginning in 1962) recognized growing population pressure but, avers demographer John May, projected an image of expansionary opportunity until the 1980s. The governments' principal responses to population pressure after World War II were agricultural intensification and "extensification." Extensification entailed dispersing the Rwandan population to empty *paysannats* within Rwanda and to less congested territories in neighboring countries (Zaire, now the Democratic Republic of Congo, Uganda, and Tanzania). These strategies, especially relocation, became "by far the most important policy response ever adopted in Rwanda to cope with rapid population growth" (May 1995, 329).

May speculates that agricultural extensification created a frontier mentality—an image of opportunity—and that these expansive expectations may have raised the fertility rate: "In fact, the relative availability of land . . . might have been conducive to higher fertility levels" (May 1995, 329). The mid-1980s fertility rate was 8.5 births per woman. By the 1990s, Rwanda was "the most densely populated country of continental sub-Saharan Africa" (May 1995, 333). States demographer Leon Bouvier, "Largely because of extremely high fertility, [the population] quadrupled between 1950 and 1993" (Bouvier 1995, 1).

Belatedly in 1981, donors of international aid forced the initiation of a national family planning effort. Fertility began to decline in 1985. Within five years, fertility had declined by more than two children per woman, to an average completed family size of 6.2 children. One could easily infer that offering women modern contraception caused the fertility decline. That inference, however, would overlook a contrary fact: by 1992, only 12.9 percent of married, reproductive-age women used modern contraceptive methods. *Later marriage*, May observes, was the most visible contributor to the Rwandan fertility decline (May 1995).

Independent of contraception, any couple can choose to postpone marriage, and any society can develop social or cultural institutions that encourage it. Delayed marriage is just one of many adjustments that can be made in any society—rural or not, deeply illiterate or not, patriarchal or not. Delayed marriage in response to hard times has been observed in many European countries as well as African countries and may be a pan-human response to adversity.

For example, Yoruba villagers in Nigeria explicitly ascribe decisions to delay marriage to "hard economic times" (Caldwell et al. 1992, 237). Nineteenth-century Irish, well before the 1845 famine, responded to the decreasing size of inherited plots in each generation with very late marriage or celibacy in a very large fraction of the population (Connell 1968). More examples are in *Population Politics* (Abernethy 1993 [1999]).

John May reasons that Rwandans began to delay marriage by the late 1980s because the incentive structure had changed. Gains from intensifying agriculture had run their course. Land productivity decreased as marginal soils brought into cultivation twenty years earlier steadily deteriorated. Droughts appeared to worsen, and the competition among alternate uses for land (e.g., cultivation, pastureland, forests, and domestic woodlots for fuel) intensified. Political realities ruled out further population dispersal, so family plots were subdivided to accommodate each maturing generation. Many farms reached a size that barely supports a family. By 1984, 57 percent of family holdings were less than one hectare in size (May, 1995).

The shrinking opportunity structure apparently forced itself into Rwandan calculations by the mid-1980s and accounted for delaying marriages and first births. The new availability of modern contraception no doubt helped by making it easier to space and limit births within marriage.

The beginning and course of population cycles are sometimes shrouded in history. One may conclude, nevertheless, that the Malawian and Rwandan stories illustrate the effects of contrasting expectations. Relatively early, the Malawians accepted a theory of limits on arable land. Rwandans farmers, on the contrary, were encouraged to believe that the settlement of fertile new lands would be a continuing option. Both cases illustrate how societies cast about for the adaptation most suited to their particular circumstances. The Rwandan case, with the preference for moving to empty lands rather than intensifying agriculture locally, strongly supports Boserup's contentions that the easier, "least work" alternative is usually preferred. Both the Rwandan and Malawian cases also support the fertility opportunity hypothesis—when no better alternative exists, perceptions of scarcity drive reproductive self-restraint. People reduce family size when they see that it enhances future opportunities for a better life.

Boserup provides a model for exploring causality, and she was one of the first to include a demographic variable in a functional analysis of economic development. We will not say that she got it backward. Rather, her model is one of at least two possible models for explaining how the economy and population are linked. Readers who seek to see how "everything is related to everything else" will find this volume both enjoyable and enlightening.

Population Planning in a Premodern Context*

Introduction

The human biological potential for childbearing is probably about ten or eleven births per woman. But a far lower fertility rate typically occurs, whether in historical, contemporary, modern, or premodern societies. Averaging nearly ten children per woman, early Hutterite settlers in the open, productive lands of the northwestern United States stand out as exceptional. Fertility rates lower than the biological potential suggest that a voluntaristic, purposive motive or a cultural adaptation operates universally.

An analysis of traditional, undisturbed societies reveals numerous cultural as well as biological strategies for keeping fertility low. Populations have remained stable over long periods of time, and not because of inordinately high adult mortality, but because cultures have evolved to maintain population size within the carrying capacity of local environments. While some of the strategies used may seem repellent to contemporary, Western observers, their efficacy is well established.

The prevalence of strategies for limiting fertility has major theoretical significance. It means that birth control does not depend upon modernization. Birth control is a long-standing human adaptation that allows individual families to exist over the long term more or less in balance with the carrying capacity of their environment. So long as perceptions about carrying capacity are accurate, huge oscillations in population size are usually avoided. Societies where timely feedback from the local environment influences family-size preference seldom see either rapid population growth or periodic collapses.

Cultural Brakes on Fertility

Within biological limits, children are born or not as the result of particular human actions. Abstinence, mating, contraception, and

---

* In *Wild Earth*, Winter 1997/98, pp. 71–77 [1997/98].

induced abortion are voluntary behaviors that determine whether a woman will be exposed to pregnancy and, if pregnant, whether she will carry to term.

People in every society know that sexual relations between a man and woman can lead to pregnancy. People in some cultures do believe that it takes repeated acts of intercourse to make a baby. In other cultures, a woman is thought to be impregnated by totemic spirits that reside in sacred places. But everyone also understands that reproduction takes a man and a woman. Magic alone will not do it.

Men, women, and sometimes their families make the decisions affecting pregnancy and birth. A woman may have many more children than she wants, but that usually means someone else is in control. Wanting more children is a principal reason that some people have large families, while others have small ones or voluntarily forgo child-bearing altogether. The idea that family-size preference is the most likely determinant of how many children a woman has is not new. The surprise is how much preferences matter. Wanting fewer or more children matters so much that access to modern contraception seems to make little difference. Lant Pritchett (1994) of the World Bank suggests that preferences account for 85 percent of completed family size.

Perhaps because Westerners are used to distinguishing between recreational and procreational sex, and to a pattern in which almost every young person is sexually active, we can hardly envision ways to limit births that do not rely on contraception. Overreliance on modern biological methods results in overlooking cultural and social patterns that affect a threshold factor: exposure to the risk of pregnancy.

This Western blind spot can have serious consequences. For example, it encourages the assumption that modernizing will help third world countries to control their population growth. Traditional beliefs and behaviors may be attacked simply because they are not modern. The possibility that they have helped limit population growth is generally overlooked.

Undisturbed, intact societies usually do well on their own; without modern contraception, they still manage to keep fertility rates low and population size in balance with available resources. Traditional societies do not have natural fertility, that is, all the children that every woman can bear in her natural lifetime. Anthropologists have noted many beliefs, rules, and behaviors that depress fertility. Most of them involve limiting women's exposure to pregnancy, rather than birth control or abortion. A woman who is prevented from being sexually active during all, or even most, of her adult life will not have a large family.

Delayed Childbearing. Delaying age of first birth, the traditional European pattern, is, in fact, quite common. First, emphasis on virginity before marriage limits young women's chances of becoming pregnant. Then, if marriage is delayed into the late twenties, or if some women never marry, average fertility remains low even if a few women have very large families.

Various African and Muslim societies have particularly harsh ways of enforcing premarital virginity. Some do not flinch at documenting virginity by hanging out bloody sheets from the marriage bed. Other societies, including nomadic Somali clans and some in North Africa, leave little to chance: a girl is infibulated; the labia of the vagina are sewn together when she reaches puberty. In European countries as recently as the nineteenth century, a premaritally pregnant woman would be disowned by her family, condemned to a life of destitution and probable early death.

Delaying marriage is another major strategy for limiting fertility. One way to delay marriage is to require property accumulation or a demonstration of economic stability before marriage. A vestige of this tradition exists in a suitor explaining his financial prospects to the prospective bride's father. Bride-price and dowry serve the same purpose. Another brake on marriage is having complex rules about who can marry whom. Such rules are effective where populations are small because it is difficult to find an eligible partner.

Child Spacing. Even after marriage, exposure to pregnancy can be limited by physiological or behavioral mechanisms. Breastfeeding, for example, delays the return of ovulatory cycles for an average of thirteen months after delivery. The full contraceptive effectiveness of nursing depends on several factors, however. The most important is frequency because suckling depresses the hormones which trigger ovulation. The mother's nutritional status and whether the baby gets supplementary feeding also make a difference. Nursing on demand, and often, is most likely when the baby is carried everywhere during the day and sleeps beside its mother at night—common in polygynous marriages because the husband is not present.

Long postpartum sex taboos are a very effective way of avoiding closely bunched pregnancies. The taboo is often reinforced by beliefs that a malevolent magical influence is triggered by resuming sexual relations too soon, or that the mother's milk will be poisoned by another pregnancy, causing the nursling to die. Polygyny—popularly called polygamy— the practice of one male having multiple wives—is often associated with a post-partum sex taboo.

Both prostitution and polygyny make it easier to observe long post-partum sex taboos. The pressure on women to resume sexual relations after childbirth is less, simply put, if men have more than one wife or sexual partner. Wife-sharing among traditional Eskimo has the same effect. In societies that infibulate, a woman may be reinfibulated for a time after each birth.

Celibacy and Polyandry. The mirror image of polygyny is polyandry. Practiced in Tibet, polyandry depresses fertility because many women cannot find a husband when it is common for several brothers to share a wife. The paternity of children is attributed sequentially; brothers "pass the arrow." In pre-Communist times, up to 30 percent of Tibetan women remained unmarried and childless because a large proportion of the marriageable men were either in polyandrous unions or dedicated to the celibate Buddhist priesthood.

Other ways of limiting women's exposure to pregnancy are not benign. Divorce or widowhood can end both a woman's marriage and her life, socially or in fact. Rules prohibiting female remarriage are the least onerous of this set. Many subcultures still depersonalize widows even where discrimination against women is officially illegal.

High-caste Hindus in India carried women's marital monogamy to an extreme; suttee, voluntary or not, meant immolation on the husband's funeral pyre. Suttee in India was outlawed in the 1920s under British colonial influence. Nevertheless, it persisted in remote areas until at least 1960, and rumblings about it are still heard (Chaudry 1990). A primitive New Guinea tribe, the Enga, had a similar custom: Within twenty-four hours of becoming a widow, a woman was strangled by her husband's brother. (Meggitt 1964; Abernethy 1979).

The reproductive effect of not letting women remarry varies. If a woman is divorced or widowed very young and cannot remarry, she is unlikely to have many children. A young girl married to a very old man might not even reach puberty before being widowed. Anthropologist Mahinder Chaudry (1990) states that during the 1960s, the average age of Indian women being widowed was thirty-five, whereas earlier, in the 1930s, women were widowed by age twenty-nine. The six extra years let the 1960s woman have two or three more children than her counterpart would have had thirty years earlier. Thus, the ethos of modernization, which challenges arranged marriage, contributes to population growth.

Voluntary behavior that limits women's exposure to pregnancy can have various rationales. People may accept prohibitions on sex during festive and ritual occasions. Planting, harvesting, expeditions for fishing, hunting, war, and certain lunar phases are all reasons, in one society or another, to avoid sex. In the extreme case, where sex is taboo more often than it is permitted, the likelihood of pregnancy is probably cut by about two-thirds. Accounts of some traditional societies, e.g., the Yap, suggest that coital frequency averages as little as once every six or seven weeks.

Whether or not a cultural belief system encourages fairness in reproductive opportunity, individuals can be counted upon to act in their own perceived best interest. Thus, a fisherman avoids sex because he believes this behavior will improve the catch, or perhaps make waves less likely to swamp his boat. Sexual self-restraint is bolstered by a whole constellation of beliefs, which are usually part of the male, rather than the female, culture.

For example, a devout member of the Brahman (Hindu) caste would ideally sleep once with his wife and would on that occasion father a son. His main incentives are belief that abstinence in life increases the chances of reaching Nirvana, and fear of losing his health by succumbing too often to sex. Many Asian and Pacific cultures contain beliefs that blood and semen are interchangeable body fluids: both are thought to be finite in quantity and nonrenewable. A man could shrivel up and turn black when his supply is gone, so he should not call on his reserve too often.

Nonprocreational Sex. Impediments to sexual intercourse are the principal, but not the only, ways of avoiding reproduction in premodern cultures. Coitus interruptus (withdrawal) is used for birth control in many societies and was known by the time of Augustus Caesar, the first Roman Emperor. Pessaries, plugs placed against the cervix to block sperm from the uterus, are another widely known device. Sometimes, pessaries are used with ointments that supposedly have spermicidal properties. Intrauterine devices have a long history and may have been tried as well.

Abortion. Abortion is known and used by women essentially everywhere. The most common methods are mechanical, including internal probes, blows to the stomach, jumping from heights, and violent exercise. In some societies—including those of American Indian and

Pacific peoples—women moved into a separate house on a monthly basis, supposedly for menstruation. So-called menstrual huts are known as a way to protect other members of a society at a time when women are ritually unclean. But retirement for the menstrual period is far from being a burden to women; it is an opportunity for rest and sociability and, if need be, creates an opportunity for discreet abortion. Menstrual huts provided privacy, help from other women, and time to recuperate.

Prescriptions and potions to induce abortion are also common, but not many have proven to be both effective and safe. Most concoctions that would cause elimination of the fetus also poison the mother. Indeed, the British penal code first mentioned abortion in 1803 in connection with the Poison Laws.

Occasionally, a chemical method turns out to be both effective and safe. A lush creeping plant of the family Asclepiadaceae is known to women in Bangladesh. A twig, inserted through the cervical canal and left protruding into the uterus, brings on cramping and abortion within seventy-two hours. The method was tested by Dr. A. F. M. Burhan-Ud-Din, then with the United Nations, in trials with 108 women who wished to terminate pregnancies ensuing from rape during the 1972 Pakistan-Bangladesh War. Burhan-Ud-Din reported successful abortion in all cases, although the procedure was accompanied by severe abdominal cramps, elevated temperature, and bleeding. Without treatment by ergometrine and broad-spectrum antibiotics, some women might have died from excessive bleeding.

An overview of traditional abortion practices suggests that they are usually on par with the crude midwifery or quack medicine practiced in countries where abortion remains illegal. The chances of complicating infections are high, so sterility and mortality are severe risks.

Infanticide. Infanticide is an extreme means of changing reproductive outcomes. No society relies on it, but in periods of stress or in certain individual circumstances, it is a last resort. Unwed mothers are perhaps the most likely to commit infanticide, both in traditional societies and in the United States. Neglect of prenatal care as well as of the infant is common and increases the risk of infant mortality.

Infanticide may be tacitly approved but still practiced surreptitiously. Bugos and McCarthy (1984) state that although the unwed Ayoreo (South American Indian) woman is not punished, she still tries to keep infanticide a secret. Sometimes infanticide is ignored even if illegal. Although classed as murder in Great Britain and Continental Europe, infanticide was relatively common up through the nineteenth century. Dead babies could be found on the garbage heaps of every large European city through the nineteenth century, but no mother was ever convicted of murder. The greater part of official action in Europe was to outlaw taking a baby into an adult's bed. The law was meant to eliminate the excuse "I rolled over and smothered him—by accident."

Infanticide may also be condoned. For example, Early and Peters' ethnography (1990) of the Mucajai Yanomama (South American Indians) reveals that 43.6 percent of all infant mortality is due to deliberate parental behavior. Twinning (among the Australian Aborigines) or a congenital anomaly often triggers infanticide, which may be a parental or paternal right, or even a duty, in some societies.

Nomads who walk and carry all their possessions over vast territories have no alternative to infanticide if the physiological suppression of ovulation induced by breastfeeding fails them. Aborigine mothers in their traditional habitats carried their young on long desert treks, and two at once were too much to handle. The African !Kung of the Kalahari Desert used infanticide as a backup method for spacing children, but abandoned the practice when they stopped their nomadic migrations and became settled agriculturalists.

Netsilik Eskimo, another people who needed to cope with an unusually harsh environment, practiced infanticide as necessary. The link to poverty (effective overpopulation) is strong: groups with the lowest sled-dog-to-human ratio—meaning that they led a near-marginal existence—had the highest ratio of men to women. More boys than girls are born as a rule, but Eskimo men had high occupational mortality so, all else equal, one would expect more females to survive into adulthood. A strong indication of female infanticide among the Netsilik is that the observed sex ratio of adults favored males.

Female infanticide is the most common type in third world countries. Sons tend to be valued because their lifelong labor is usually available to their family of birth, and they often have ritual funerary responsibility to parents. On the contrary, daughters tend to leave home, and marrying them off can ruin—literally ruin—a family in societies where dowries must be large.

The fact is, traditional societies limit reproduction in ways that may be bitter: women and babies are often victims. Men are luckier. Some religious vocations demand temporary (Buddhist) or lifelong (Roman Catholic) celibacy, but only a fraction of men take the cloth

85

when celibacy is lifelong. Their cost is suppression of sexual drives, and even that can be mitigated, sometimes, by redirecting energy to non-procreative contexts, including use of prostitutes and homosexuality.

Male Methods

With an exception for vasectomy, culturally sanctioned physical impairments of men's ability to procreate are rare, but present nonetheless. Eunuchs formed a class of professional bureaucrats in the Ottoman Empire. Castration so that choirboys did not lose the falsetto singing voice was practiced up to the nineteenth century in Italy. And certain Australian Aborigine tribes practiced subincision. Subincision was part of the rite of passage from puberty to full manhood. A stone knife laid open the underside of the penis, lengthwise from base to tip. The urethra was allowed to heal so that an opening remained near the base; henceforth, urine and semen discharged through this orifice. Physiologist S. J. Segal (1972) suggests that such anatomical rearrangement would result in low conception rates because "the semen flow, mainly, is diverted and lost."

Aborigine men explain subincision as (1) making them more like their totem, the kangaroo, which has a bifid penis; and (2) making themselves more attractive to women. Women are said to prefer subincised men because the plateau and ejaculation phases in sex last longer. Each of these explanations is supported by evidence, and the rationales are not mutually exclusive. But the birth control function of subincision may explain why it was rigorously practiced in the desert interior of Australia—where the population carrying capacity is extremely low— and was merely an option available to men in the rich coastal regions of the continent.

Subincision illustrates the point that behaviors which lead to low fertility are often built into the culture as tastes and conventions. They usually do not require specific decisions about family size but depend on beliefs and rules that are rationalized in ways other than by conscious reproductive goals. Since a successful society (one that lasts) has adjusted over time to the limits and opportunities of a particular environment, the fertility level actually realized is likely to be adaptive to local conditions.

Conclusions

Culture has put, is putting, the brakes on population growth in many settings. Anthropology and history do not justify the belief that out-of-control population growth is a necessary human condition. Those who think it is, or believe that modernization is the best corrective, see only a tiny slice of human experience.

The rapid population growth that occurred worldwide during the twentieth century can be attributed to several factors. Most often noticed is the control of disease and premature mortality by public health measures and modern medicine. But fertility rates also rose.

The rise in fertility was caused in part by the disruption of traditional cultures that had built-in control mechanisms. But, in addition, preferred family size increased. In case after case, one sees that families began to believe in a richer resource base or more productive technology that would allow them to afford and successfully raise more children.

More realistic perceptions of carrying capacity are returning as, worldwide, per capita grain production declines and potable water is in ever shorter supply. Moreover, societies that are successfully industrializing are beset by an unforeseen accompaniment of modernization: the consumer culture. Consumerism means that, however much one has, it is insufficient.

The ironic, redeeming feature of consumerism is that it fosters— however artificially—the sense of scarcity. My work suggests that the single feature of modernization that reliably depresses family size is this sense of not having enough, i.e., scarcity. The desire for goods impels people to postpone and limit childbearing, because children compete for available resources.

Carrying capacity means more than some person-to-resource ratio. It includes intangibles such as standards and desired quality of life. Sensitivity to carrying capacity appears ubiquitous among humans and, I think, to perceptions about the resources to which one has access. Perception about the adequacy of resources is universally, I think, the regulator of desired family size.

The Shipibo: Modernity Begets Fertility*

Some tribes of the Peruvian and Brazilian Amazon became extinct in the centuries after contact with Western civilization. The survivors, however, are experiencing very rapid population growth even as their traditional lands are destroyed by roads, deforestation, and development.

The Peruvian Shipibo and the Brazilian Bororo, Xavante, and Yanomama, like many other Brazilian tribes, traditionally practiced abortion, infanticide, and sororal polygyny (a man married to sisters).

---

* In *Wild Earth*, Winter 1997/98, pp. 72–73 [1997/98].

As many as 50 percent of all marriages were polygynous in traditional Yanomama villages, but it is much less common in more acculturated groups. In the 1970s, only about 10 percent of reproductive-age Shipibo women were in polygynous marriages, and the practice was declining.

Epidemiologist Warren Hern (1991) makes a strong case that polygyny is one of the key mechanisms for limiting fertility in traditional cultures. He found that Shipibo women in polygynous unions have longer intervals between births—4.5 months longer—than monogamously married women. The traditional Yanomama average forty months between births, at least partly because of widespread polygyny.

The length of birth intervals affects total fertility. Hern sees "an almost straight line negative relationship" between village fertility rates and the length of birth intervals. The greater the fraction of women whose childbearing occurred in a polygynous context, the lower the fertility rate. Polygynously married women that Hern studied averaged one to two fewer births than their monogamous counterparts.

Postpartum sex taboos and breastfeeding are both likely to last longer in polygynous marriages. Breastfeeding itself delays the return of ovulatory menstrual cycles, adding to the effect of limiting women's exposure to pregnancy. Emphasis on the sexual taboo may also increase abortion and infanticide, because children conceived in illicit sexual activity are not wanted.

All these practices are abandoned as South American Indians become more attuned to Western values. Shipibo fertility has soared, edging close to ten live births per woman in some villages. Hern estimates that villages are growing at about 4 percent annually, which suggests that populations are doubling every seventeen years. The increase seems entirely due to changes which come about as Shipibo and other Indians' jungle homes become the fringe, and then are absorbed by modern settlements.

Bereft of traditional folkways, Shipibo women take desperate measures to avoid closely spaced pregnancies. Some use a caustic substance for contraceptive purposes which, says Hern, contributes to their very high mortality from cervical cancer.

One fairly concludes that Shipibo women would be receptive to modern contraception. Whether the family power structure and/or a husband's approval would allow it to be used, if available, is a separate question, one that can be answered only by experience.

First steps into a more modern world have not brought much good to the Shipibo. Modernity intruded on them. It did not seduce them. The development process itself probably fueled fertility. Hern concludes, "From this and other studies, I think one should expect higher fertility in tribal societies making the transition from traditional to peasant, to urban societies, and it appears unlikely that native Amazonians will be able to escape the process" (p. 43).

References

Abernethy, Virginia Deane. 1979. *Population Pressure and Cultural Adjustment.* New York: Human Sciences Press (Reprinted 2005, Transaction Publishers).

Abernethy, Virginia Deane 1993. *Population Politics.* New York: Plenum Press.

Abernethy, Virginia Deane 1993. *Population Politics.* New York: Plenum Press (Reprinted 1999, Transaction Publishers).

Bugoss, P. E., Jr., and McCarthy, L. M. 1984. *Ayoreo Infanticide: A Case Study.* G. Hausfater and S. Hrdy, eds. New York: Wenner-Gren Foundation for Anthropological Research Inc.

Chaudry, M. 1990. "Role of the Social and Cultural Factors in Human Fertility in India." *Population and Environment* 12 (2): 117–38.

Early, J. D. and Peters, J. F. 1990. *The Population Dynamics of the Mucajai Yanomama.* San Diego, CA: Academic Press.

Hern, Warren. 1991. "Effects of Cultural Change on Fertility in Amazonian Indian Societies: Recent Research and Projections." *Population and Environment* 13 (1): 23–44.

Kalipeni, Ezekiel. 1996. "Demographic Response to Environmental Pressure in Malawi." *Population and Environment* 17 (4): 285–308.

May, John F. 1995. "Policies on Population, Land Use, and Environment in Rwanda." *Population and Environment* 16 (4): 321–34.

Meggitt, M. J. 1964. "Male-female Relationships in the Highlands of Australian New Guinea." *American Anthropologist Special Publication* (pt2) 66:204.

Pritchett, Lant. 1994. "Desired Fertility and the Impact of Population Policies." *Population and Development Review* 20 (1): 1–55.

Riddle, J. M. and Estes, J. W. 1992. "Oral Contraceptives in Ancient and Medieval Times." *American Scientist* 80:226–33.

Segal, S. J. 1972. "Contraception Research: A Male Chauvinist Plot?" *Family Planning Perspectives* 4 (3): 21–25.

4

Surprised by Sex: The Fertility Opportunity Hypothesis

Introduction

Writing in 1997 on sustainable societies, prominent University of Colorado physicist Albert A. Bartlett summarized my idea on why people want fewer—or more—children and named it the "economic opportunity theory of fertility." Economics is the study of the allocation of scarce resources among alternate and competing ends. I propose that the motive for wanting a smaller- or larger-size family is perceived scarcity, or abundance, of resources. The fertility opportunity hypothesis, by any name, was well received by ecologist Garrett Hardin, sociobiologists, numerous physical scientists, and mathematicians.

However, the centrality of perceived resource availability in decision making is not universally accepted. Consultants on third world development bear enmity toward the fertility opportunity hypothesis because it challenges the iconic "demographic transition" model on which many build careers. That model became, and still is, the basis for allocating much international aid. However, it is not science because its postulated cause-and-effect relationships are not testable.

My article, "Fertility Decline No Mystery," reflects large increases in data supporting the fertility opportunity hypothesis. Sources range from academic case studies to the media. Reporters do not have most demographers' biases; the best faithfully report what interviewees tell them, including that couples delay marriage and childbearing because times are tough and apparently worsening.

Christian Science Monitor reporter George Moffett's 1994 book, *Critical Masses*, is illustrative. His material includes interviews with a Cairo slumdweller who said, "We're just surviving . . . Certain days we don't eat . . . I don't understand how people with seven or eight children survive." Also, responses from an Ethiopian mother of five who says, "If I were wealthy, say if I had horses and a better house, I'd have more children"; and a Russian mother of two who used abortion to avoid other births and says, "I would have had more children if life were better."

News accounts of national fertility and marriage rates remain straight forward. The cover story of the May 30–June 5, 2015, issue of *The Economist* includes the observation, "men without work find it hard to attract a permanent mate." A report on low fertility rates in Iran cites a professor who says that improving young people's "attitude" will not reverse their avoidance of marriage so long as economic factors discourage them from marrying (http://www.al-monitor.com/pulse/originals/2015/06/iran-birth-rate-marriage-decline-divorce.html?utm_source=Al-Monitor+Newsletter+%5BEnglish%5D&utm_campaign=fc19adc49b-June_03_2015&utm_medium=email&utm_term=0_28264b27a0-fc19adc49b-102432577, June 2, 2015, in *Tehran Posted*). A June 17, 2015, *Wall Street Journal* article (p. 6) titled, "U.S. Birthrate Exits Postrecession Funk," includes the line, "Demographers have forecast a recovery in births as the economy picks up and more young couples have families." Does the phrase, "demographers have forecast a recovery" hint that the academic argument about what causes change in fertility rates is won?

The article, "Population Dynamics: Why We Can Sit Back and Watch Fertility Fall," flags a difficulty with scenarios that would drive fertility reduction actually playing out. Conditions that militate against wanting a large family may be harsh, so international humanitarian efforts are marshalled to mitigate them. Unfortunately, confirming a people's belief in rescue encourages the continuation of explosive population growth and sets the stage for greater tragedy.

Human societies cannot be manipulated in controlled settings, but final articles indicate that the fertility opportunity hypothesis is testable. The Netsilik Eskimo excerpt is a modest controlled comparison, but a better testable occasion arose in summer, 1997, with the financial collapse in nine Asian countries then-called "Asian tigers." My prediction, that fertility rates in these countries would fall faster than trend line, appeared in print in 1998. Results were reported in 2002. Babies, or the absence thereof, seldom appear in less than nine months, and getting into print takes longer.

Fertility Decline No Mystery*

Abstract

The economic opportunity hypothesis states that perceived shrinkage of opportunity discourages women or couples from embarking on marriage or reproduction. On the contrary, the sense that opportunity is expanding encourages couples to raise their family-size target. The hypothesis assumes that humans are genetically programmed to maximize successful reproduction by having more offspring when environmental/economic conditions appear favorable, but exercise restraint—waiting or limiting the total number of offspring—if the latter strategy promises greater longrun reproductive success.

Introduction

The March 8, 2002, UN report (Crossette 2000, 3; Francis 2002) on declining fertility rates is pleasant reading, especially because a *New York Times* summary states that, "The decline in birthrates in nations where poverty and illiteracy are still widespread defies almost all conventional wisdom. Planners once argued—and some still do—that a falling birthrate can only follow improved living standards and more educational opportunities, not outrun them. It now seems that women are not waiting for that day" (Crosette 2002).

For women's rights advocates the response is triumphalist—given any power at all to control their own reproduction, women have opted for smaller family size. For environmentalists, the lower fertility rates are a relief—fewer people means less pressure on the carrying capacity and less degradation of natural resources. Only some professional demographers are bemused; they have long maintained that a decline in poverty and illiteracy are preconditions for smaller family size, a hypothesis that is manifestly inadequate.

For an anthropologist, that is, myself, the UN report is a great vindication. Over several decades I have explored the effects of economic opportunity (Abernethy 1979, 1993), concluding that a sense of expanding opportunity encourages people to raise their family-size targets. Conversely, falling expectations and the perception of heightened competition for limited goods bring about reproductive and marital caution. I call this the economic opportunity hypothesis.

---

* *Ethics in Science and Environmental Politics*/ESEP, pp. 1–11. [May 24, 2002].

Fertility rates are now falling almost worldwide because maintaining a culturally defined good standard of living is becoming more difficult in most settings. Despite over $1 trillion dollars in foreign aid given by the United States alone since World War II (Poverty Lobby II, 2002, p.18) and globalized trade, increasing numbers live in poverty or must compete harder to stay in the middle class. "Most people in Latin America, the Middle East and Central Asia are poorer than at the cold war's close, despite the fast economic integration of the 1990's" (Kahn and Weiner 2002).

In today's poorer countries, clean fresh water is scarce for a growing number of people. Worldwide, grain production per capita has not risen since the mid-1980s, and an enormous gap between the infant mortality rates in developed and developing countries—the difference between 8 and 67 deaths per 1,000—persists (World Population Data Sheet 2001).

Explosive population growth is a principal contributor to many of these negative developments. Optimistically, some would say, the economic opportunity (EO) hypothesis implies that runaway population growth is self-correcting in the long run, because reproductive caution is triggered by the tougher economic, social, and environmental conditions associated with rapid population growth.

That "long run" appears to have arrived. Can the title of an article published several years ago, "Population Dynamics: Why We can Sit Back and Watch Fertility Fall" (Abernethy 2002), be more explicit?

The EO hypothesis is a simple and comprehensive explanation of declining fertility rates. It is equally applicable in developed or less-developed countries and in urban or rural settings. But to say that it does not disturb certain experts of the international development cabal would be to ignore such comments as, "She's a nut" (Lant Pritchett of the World Bank) and "Her ideas are ignored by the demographic community. I'd say that's justified" (John Bongaarts of the Population Institute). Both statements appeared in a *Wall Street Journal* feature story on the EO hypothesis (Zachary 1998, B1, p.2).

Testing the Hypothesis in the Wake of Economic Collapse

The economic collapse of former Asian tigers (Hong Kong, Indonesia, Japan, Malaysia, The Philippines, Singapore, South Korea, Taiwan, and Thailand) in late summer, 1997, presented the opportunity for a prospective test of the economic opportunity hypothesis. In 1998, I predicted in print (Abernethy 2002, pp.46–47) that the tigers' collapsing economies would cause their fertility rates to decline at a faster rate during the 1997–1999 interval than observed in preceding two-year intervals. Fertility had been declining in each of these countries for varying numbers of years, but now that decline was expected to accelerate.

The nine economies of the former Asian tigers are modern in at least one primary sector of the society and, until 1997, this sector was relatively affluent. The economies vary greatly, however, in the pervasiveness of modernizing influences. The Philippines might have been excluded because it never achieved independent economic take-off and remained heavily reliant on the presence of US naval bases for nearly a century, until the early 1990s. Other observers would exclude Japan from the sample because of the length of time that its economy has been modernizing. Japan began to invest in technology and education before the turn of the twentieth century, and to modernize other facets of society immediately after World War II. Taiwan and Hong Kong embarked on extensive modernization within a decade of the ending of World War II (Abernethy and Penaloza 2002, 245–66).

Whatever their differences and pace of change, some generalizations apply. By 1997, each country had experienced improvements in standard of living, the value of education was increasingly appreciated as the high road to economic success, and the prospect of entering the middle class was influencing an increasing proportion of the population (Abernethy and Penaloza 2002).

Then, within a matter of months after late summer, 1997, the nine economic tigers faced collapsing asset values including currency devaluation of up to 40 percent. The downward spiral was initiated by a sharp devaluation of the Thai baht and quickly spread. In Japan, the unemployment rates in 1998 and 1999 rose to a level higher than at any time since 1953. Personal bankruptcies in 1999 were 50 percent higher than in 1997 and, a further sign of falling incomes, Japanese retail sales declined from 1997 through 1999. In 1998, the Japanese suicide rate was the highest recorded. Contemplating an uncertain future, a majority of university students expressed a preference for government as opposed to private sector employment (Abernethy and Penaloza 2002).

The EO hypothesis suggests that effort to adjust to uncertainty, unemployment, and negative wealth effects is likely to entail the derailment of marital and reproductive plans. Further decline from already low fertility rates in most Asian tiger economies seemed possible. Under similarly difficult circumstances, fertility rates in East Germany temporarily declined to a level where, if maintained over women's entire lifetimes, would have led to an average completed family size of as little as 0.6 children per woman (Conrad, Lechner, and Werner 1996, 331–58).

Illustrations of the Economic Opportunity Hypothesis

South Asia. Timothy Dyson's analysis of a century of major famines in the Indian subcontinent connects the fertility rate to fluctuations in the natural and socioeconomic environment. He shows that small price increases for staple foods—typically the first response to a drought and a warning of possible famine—resulted in significantly lower fertility rates.

The mechanism was a series of behavioral adjustments. Dowries, for example, are more difficult to accumulate when crops are failing, so marriages and therefore births were delayed. Reproduction within marriage was also often delayed because married men left home to seek work in less affected areas.

Such marital and reproductive responses to price-mediated signs of shortage, coming well before the full force of famine materialized, effectively reduced the total fertility rate because a birth delayed is often a birth avoided. All to the good, these adaptations seem also to have largely forestalled significant, famine-induced increases in mortality. Mortality appeared actually to fall among reproductive-age women, perhaps because of lower exposure to the perils of childbirth (Dyson 1991a, 1991b).

Morocco. The Moroccan fertility rate rose in the wake of independence (1957), strong world prices for a principal export (phosphates), and the government's use of export profits to subsidize social programs. The total fertility rate (TFR) was approximately 7 in 1960, and by 1973 had risen to 7.4 children per woman (Courbage 1995).

Late 1974 and 1975 were watershed years, however, because phosphate prices collapsed. Declining revenues forced the government to both raise personal income taxes and scale back subsidies for health care, education, food subsidies, and housing. The new role of government was not giver but taker of incomes, and it drove a renewed imperative: family self-reliance. Families cast back onto their own resources sought to satisfy basic needs as well as recently acquired tastes (for example, education and health care). Many women entered the workforce for the first time in order to supplement family income.

Youssef Courbage suggests that these unanticipated pressures on family lifestyles were the major cause of a fertility decline beginning in 1975. "The sudden reversal of the economic and fiscal condition of Moroccan households is related to the sharp drop in fertility, which diminished by 20 percent from 7.3 to 5.9 children in just four years" (Courbage 1995, 89). Socioeconomic pressures have been unrelenting and, by 1997, the Moroccan TFR was 3.3 children per woman.

Egypt. Among all other Muslim countries, Egypt has the longest history of concern over its expanding population. Coinciding with consolidation of President Gamal Abdel Nasser's socialist regime in the 1960s, family planning advocates expanded their political base, programs became active, and, by 1970, fertility had declined from 6.7 to a new low of 5.0 children per woman.

Philippe Fargue nevertheless rejects the conclusion that programmatic family planning efforts caused the fertility decline. He cites, instead, the economic recession through which Egypt floundered until the death of President Nasser in 1970 (Fargues 1997).

Nasser left a political void that soon was filled by the economically progressive Anwar el-Sadat (1973–1985). President El Sadat encouraged domestic entrepreneurial activity as well as emigration, welcomed foreign investment, and signed a formal peace treaty with Israel (the 1981 Camp David accords) guaranteed by the United States.

The Camp David accords promise Egypt $2.5 billion in aid, annually, from the United States. This aid supplemented by oil revenues and fees for foreign shipping through the Suez Canal allowed serious expansion of the government's education, health care, food, and housing subsidies and other social programs that benefited broad segments of society. Such freshening breezes from windfall government revenues entailed, "At the household level . . . a substantial increase in the standard of living." Government largesse was augmented by remittances from overseas Egyptians that flowed directly to relatives, which by the early 1980s amounted to US$5 billion a year, the equivalent of 90 percent of Egypt's annual export revenues (Fargues1995, p.183; 1997). The broadly distributed new wealth was enjoyed nationwide.

Fargue observes that "Now better off, families could more easily satisfy an unchanged desire to have numerous offspring" (p.124). The fertility rate did indeed spike higher, rising 30 percent from 1970 to a high of 6.5 births per woman in the early 1980s (Fargues 1997, 124).

Another economic reversal was evident by the mid-1980s. Indeed, the standard of living had noticeably eroded because falling oil prices, population growth, and tougher World Bank and other international lending criteria forced rollbacks in government spending. President Hosni Mubarak, successor to the murdered El Sadat, had no choice but to scale back social programs and subsidies at the same time that the historically huge population was producing massive underemployment.

In addition, Egypt was no longer self-sufficient in food production. Much of Egypt's "breadbasket" outside of Cairo and along the Nile had been converted from agricultural to commercial and residential use. Shortage of water as well as arable land, and increasing dependence on imported food, contributed to the sense of foreboding that comes with growing unemployment and underemployment (Fargues 1995, 1997; Courbage 1995). Riots erupted when the government announced a higher price (lower subsidy) on bread. The price hike on bread was rescinded, but the government's next moves were introduction of a larger, higher-priced loaf followed by erosion of the size of both loaves, until the original loaf, price unchanged, was materially smaller.

Seen in 1987, Cairo's schools had become so crowded that children were divided into three shifts and attended classes for only a few hours daily. Port Said was able to hold the line at just two shifts. Everywhere, the relative scarcity of more-coveted professional jobs forced job-sharing: schoolteachers teach one shift and eke out income as waiters or bazaar peddlers, and university professors drive cabs. Low wages forced many into home crafts that are peddled on street corners, some earn tips from doling out single sheets of toilet paper in public-access bathrooms, and tens of thousands make their living from rag-picking in the smoldering garbage dumps that ring Cairo. By 1988, the government was unable to honor its pledge of a job for every university graduate and offered title to a five-acre desert tract as a substitute for the job.

Such indicators (Abernethy 1993) presaged a renewed, rapid decline in the fertility rate. The Egyptian TFR declined from 5.0 in 1988 to 3.6 by 1997 (World Population Data Sheet 1997). The decline appeared to accelerate at the same time that ground was being lost in measures of social welfare including literacy. Whereas, 60 percent of women were literate in the late 1970s, the total adult literacy rate in 1997 was just 50 percent.

Trends in socioeconomic indicators and the fertility rate support Fargues's contention that, "Egypt's demographic transition has been driven not so much by economic development as by its hiccups" (Fargues 1997, p.131).

Morocco Compared to Egypt and Other Muslim, Arab Countries. Youssef Courbage and Philippe Fargue concur that fertility rates in Middle Eastern Muslim countries do not correlate with the modernization variables that many demographers see as fundamental. Reductions in infant mortality, better health care, and education—especially for women—and rising standards of living are not even correlated, and clearly are not causally related, to declining fertility rates (Fargues 1995, 1997).

For example, modernization indicators in Morocco compared to other Muslim, Arab countries would not have predicted that Morocco would attain one of the first sustained fertility rate declines in the region. Moroccan women lagged others in both literacy and achieved educational level. Fewer than 40 percent of Moroccan women of childbearing age were literate when its fertility decline began, compared to approximately 60 percent in Egypt. Within each social stratum, moreover, Egyptian women were attaining a higher educational level (Courbage 1995). By the late 1970s, nevertheless, Moroccan fertility was lower than Egypt's. Writes Courbage:

> No one could have foreseen the slower fertility decline in Egypt and its relative acceleration in Morocco, because the evidence suggested exactly the opposite. . . . Egyptian economic growth has been particularly rapid without bringing down fertility, while in Morocco slow economic growth and a decrease in fertility have gone hand in hand. (Courbage 1995, p.85)

The comparison is still more striking with rich countries such as Kuwait and Saudi Arabia, where all sectors of the population have had access to education, excellent health care, and other social subsidies for many decades. Arab oil kingdoms have much lower infant mortality and proportionately more literate and better-educated women than Morocco but their fertility rates remained at very high levels until approximately 1990 (Courbage1995).

Only in the past decade has extremely rapid population growth begun to overtake Mid East oil wealth. Per capita income and subsidies have declined; young men are seeking but not always finding employment; and, at last, Iranian, Saudi, and Kuwaiti fertility rates have begun to fall.

Fertility Rates Reflect Perceived Changes in Economic Prospects

The Malaysian Example. Before withdrawing from their Malaysian colony in 1957, the British instituted democratic reforms that left the more numerous Malays politically dominant. In addition, Great Britain affirmed the special position of the Malays, "reserving for them four-fifths of all jobs in the civil service, three-fourths of university scholar-ships and training programs offered by the federal government, and a majority of license permits from the operation of trade and business" (Govindasamy 1992, 247).

The Malay gained at the expense of the Indians and Chinese—Malaysia's two other principal ethnic groups. As the Malays consolidated their economic and cultural advantage, both Indians and Chinese were progressively discriminated against in access to education, jobs, and public office. Many Chinese fled to Singapore after race riots and a switch in the official language from English to Malay in the early 1960s. In 1965, Singapore became a separate political entity.

Demographers Govindasamy and DaVanzo trace the culmination of Malay bureaucratic and legislative power through the passage of a twenty-year blueprint for development (1971–1990) known as the New Economic Policy. By 1983, "the Malay language was used as a medium of instruction at all levels of education" (Govindasamy and DaVanzo 1992, p.248) and competency in Malay became a criterion for graduation and civil service jobs.

The reversals in Malaysia's power structure after 1957 foretold demographic trends. In 1957, when Malays still were the least educated and poorest as well as the most rural population, they had the lowest total fertility rate. When they acquired political power at the expense of other ethnic groups, the pattern reversed.

Indian and Chinese fertility rates declined, respectively, from nearly 8 children per woman in 1957 to about 3 in 1987; and from more than 7 to 2.5 children over the same period. The Malay fertility rate, in contrast, increased by 12 percent. Thus, by 1987, after the Malays had consolidated power, their fertility rate stood "twice as high as the Chinese and 63 percent higher than that of the Indians" (Govindasamy and DaVanzo 1992, 243). Differential ethnic fertility has been persistent except for a brief period when trend lines crossed. By 1988, the Malays were a solid majority of the population.

Persistently high Malay fertility—despite increasing urbanization, economic expansion, and better education and health care—has been variously attributed to the pronatalism of Muslim religious forces as well as to the reversal in the opportunity structures, particularly after 1971 (Govindasamy and DaVanzo 1992). They offer the interpretation that the differential access to political and economic advantage "is consistent with the arrested decline in total fertility rates for Malays in the mid-1970s, in the face of continuing decline for Chinese and Indians" (Govindasamy and DaVanzo 1992, p.250).

Differential fertility among groups which gain (or lose) access to political levers and the spoils of victory may be a common phenomenon. Shifting political arrangements offer a promising setting in which to test the fertility opportunity model.

Cycles of Rising and Falling Fertility

Peru. A boom-and-bust psychology has long been associated with Peru's exports of natural resources. Peru became a prosperous exporter of guano (fertilizer) in the 1850s, but the boom psychology was damped by timely recognition of the limited nature of the resource. By the 1940s, guano mining was being managed frugally, with exports limited to the equivalent of the 255,000 tons of guano deposited in a normal year.

To supplement guano, President Manuel Odria, newly elected in 1948, began encouraging development of anchoveta exports. Anchovetas appeared inexhaustible and Peru again prospered from fishing and associated industries. The growth phase of anchoveta fishing lasted for over a decade, and harvests remained strong until the El Nino Southern Oscillation (ENSO) event of 1972–1973 decimated the haul (Pauly and Tsukayama 1987; Golnaraghi and Kaul 1995).

Beginning around 1972, the anchoveta industry and the Peruvian economy went into steep decline (*The Dark Side of the Boom*, 1995, 21–23). Successive Socialist governments nationalized key food producing sectors including fishing, with disastrous results for productivity. Natural disasters such as drought and recurrent ENSO events further undermined yields. Worsening hyperinflation and unemployment contributed to popular support for insurgent revolutionary groups that ultimately threatened Peru's political as well as economic viability. The terrorist force, El Sendero Luminoso, appeared on the verge of destabilizing Lima until reigned in by President Alberto Fujimori after his election in August 1990.

With these facts in hand as of February, 1995, I expected that the fast-growing anchoveta industry would have spurred fertility right up to the 1972–1973 episode of El Nino, but that subsequent to this natural event and to political developments, fertility rates would decline. I asked several demographers for help in locating Peruvian fertility statistics. Most helpfully, John F. May of the Futures Group (Washington, DC) unearthed a paper from the Peruvian Instituto de Estudios en Población y Desarrollo.

As expected, the fertility rate did rise following the growth period of anchoveta fishing and its supporting industry. Whereas from 1876 through the early 1940s, Peru's total fertility rate remained in the range of 5.6–5.8 ("la fecundidad permanecio mas o menos constante"), it then rose by more than 1 child per woman, to 6.85 ("Hacia 1950 . . . llegó a 6.85 hijos per mujer") (Montenegro and de Muente 1990, pp.70–71).

Historically high levels of fertility were maintained for some fifteen years after 1950. Then, coinciding with the plateau of the anchoveta industry began a slow decline. The fertility decline accelerated after the ENSO-related fishery collapse in 1972. The TFR tracked the economy, still hovering at 6.85 in 1965; then declining to 6.56 by 1970; 6.00 by 1975; 5.38 by 1980; and 4.59 by 1985 (Ferrando and Ponce 1983). The 1995 Population Data Sheet of the Population Reference Bureau shows Peru with a fertility rate of 3.5 children per woman.

The EO hypothesis accounts for oscillations in Peru's fertility rate: profits and employment in the anchoveta industry led fertility up then down. This, however, is not the interpretation put upon the data by Peruvian demographers Montenegro and de Muente. They suggest that women's better health and survival rates account for the fertility increase in 1950, and that classic modernization variables caused the post-1965 decline (Montenegro and de Muente 1990, 70–71).

But congruent with the EO hypothesis, Delicia Ferrando and Carlos Aramburu (1996) explain the fertility decline by way of varying economic prospects. They write, "even though the process of economic and cultural modernization created favourable conditions for the beginning of the decline, it was the economic crisis that accelerated the process, causing it to extend to the lower classes in both urban and rural areas in the 1970s." They cite structural conditions in Peruvian society, both the great and growing inequalities and, second, the "central" factor which is "the profound and prolonged economic crisis suffered by Peru, which continues with variable intensity and has become more acute in the past two years" (Ferrando and Aramburu 1996, p. 415).

The United States. Demographic studies of the United States span the earliest English settlements to the present. Several points are significant.

First, colonists in the New World—whether Roman Catholic French in Quebec or English Protestants in New England—averaged much higher fertility rates than were usual in the societies from which they came. The colonists' high rates have been attributed to seemingly boundless natural resources which could absorb almost any amount of labor and, indeed, could not be transformed into wealth without human labor.

Second, the transition from the frontier to established agricultural community meant that free land vanished and good land became expensive. Land prices became an obstacle to setting up families on farms of the expected size and quality, delaying marriage. Economist Richard Easterlin (1971) shows that denser settlement, with or without industrialization, was linked to declining fertility (Easterlin 1971, 1976).

Third, economic cycles are superimposed on other factors almost from the beginning of colonial settlement. For example, prosperity in Concord, an offshoot of the Massachusetts Bay colony settled by Puritans in 1630, varied with earnings from lumber and agricultural exports. The export trade relied upon backloading, the return trip of ships that had brought new colonists, as well as on strong demand for raw products in England.

The first hiatus in Concord's export trade occurred around 1642, when Puritans temporarily ceased immigrating to the colony so no ships were available to carry back lumber and other colonial products. Subsequent interruptions in revenue from exports followed economic recessions and collapsing demand in England.

Each dislocation in the colony's export market, including 1642, the 1680s, the 1740s, and the 1790s, affected the fertility rate. Political scientist Brian Berry observes that, in every case, the contracting export market was followed by decline in the fertility rate (Berry 1996).

Easterlin traces the later history of the colonies and the United States, showing how the domestic economy drove fertility rates. For example, the 1920 break in farm prices followed by the 1929–1939 Great Depression was reflected in declining fertility first in rural and then in urban areas (Easterlin 1962).

The economy revived during World War II and, particularly after the war, was characterized by low inflation, growth in labor productivity, and a labor force that was sufficiently small and stable to drive up entry-level wages and accelerate promotions. Easterlin concludes that the expansive opportunities available to (young) entry-level workers account for the rapid increase in family formation and family size that became known as the 1947–1962 baby boom (Easterlin 1962).

Not to belabor the contrast, but US fertility rates had declined in the 1930s when educational opportunity, wealth, and infant mortality indexes were at depression-era levels. However, the fertility rate was high in the 1950s and early 1960s, when young families benefitted from favorable educational and employment opportunities and national health statistics looked better than ever, conditions that would have the demographic transition model predicting lower fertility.

Fertility drifted lower during the later 1960s as after-tax, inflation-adjusted income failed to rise at the pace to which labor had become accustomed. The 1973–1974 oil shock began the "quiet depression" with productivity and wage increases much below those of the previous three decades. Fertility followed economic trends, declining to 1.7 children per woman in 1976 (Macunovich and Easterlin1990).

The fertility rate of native-born Americans as the United States enters the twenty-first century is 1.9, which is below replacement level. At least two forces seem responsible. First, consumerism puts the goal of acquiring things into competition with the value of extra children, both because of the time value of childrearing and the actual expense associated with raising children in the United States (Macunovich and Easterlin 1990). Second, earnings have deteriorated for men, especially young white men who entered the labor market starting in the early 1980s.

Rapid growth in the supply of labor goes far to explain declining wages. Historically, rapid growth in the labor supply leads to decline in the value of labor, so that workers are obliged to accept lower wages and less desirable conditions (Lee 1980; *Social Security and the Future of U.S. Fertility* 1997). Approximately since 1980, several factors including mass immigration have caused rapid and continuing expansion in the labor supply and significantly negative effects for workers (Borjas, Freeman, and Katz 1996).

A study released in spring, 2002, by the liberal-leaning Russell Sage Foundation finds that 90 percent of young white male workers, specifically, can expect to have lower lifetime wage growth than the previous generation (Bernhardt et al. 2002). A reviewer cites the four sociologist and statistician authors' conclusion that the "change is significant and permanent, comprising 'a massive downshift in earnings standards'" (Roberts 2002). Fertility in this sector will almost certainly remain below replacement level so long as their disadvantage in the labor market—relative to their expectations and, perhaps, relative to other groups—persists.

Thus, both consumerism and competition in the labor market heighten the sense that acquisition of desirable, limited goods is an unremitting struggle. The EO hypothesis suggests that this perception, or worldview, makes people cautious in embarking on marriage and childbearing.

Persuaded by history, the Advisory Council on Social Security has generalized to the future. Their 1994–1995 Report, excerpted in the journal *Population and Development Review*, argues that low fertility will result in a small birth cohort whose members are likely to encounter ample job opportunities relative to their number, will command high wages, see rapid career advancement and, therefore, have relatively large families (*Social Security and the Future of U.S. Fertility* 1997).

The Advisory Council reckoned without the effect of mass immigration and immigrants' large average family size. Although the fertility rate of native-born Americans remains at about 1.9 children per woman, the total fertility rate of the United States had risen to replacement level, 2.1 births per woman, by 2000, because it blends native-born and foreign-born rates.

Economic immigrants in the United States usually encounter conditions better than those left behind, so their perceptions of opportunity probably differ materially from those of native-born Americans. Although less than 10 percent of the population, the foreign-born already in 1994 accounted for 18 percent of all US births (Ventura, Martin, Mathews, and Clark 1996), proportions that have since risen.

Discussion

These brief histories linking economic and fertility variables include single-society vignettes, comparisons between countries, and cyclic patterns over time as well as one prospective, statistical test of the economic opportunity hypothesis. Much more data is available, becomes available on an almost daily basis, and some have been collected in my previous publications.

How many illustrations and statistical tests constitute proof of a scientific proposition? Outside of mathematics, perhaps nothing is ever proved because science operates, famously, through putting its hypotheses in jeopardy. Social science hypotheses are perhaps hardest to prove because only trivialities can be tested under controlled laboratory conditions. Theories about important relationships usually await testing through opportune circumstances that arise in nature, or by an accumulation of examples that almost always leave room for alternate explanations. The economic opportunity hypothesis is easily mired in such objections.

Nevertheless, readers who plan their own families with one eye on a budget may easily absorb the EO hypothesis because it seems like common sense. Others, whose family history includes suffering through the Great Depression and, perhaps, whispered tales of an aunt who aborted a third or fourth pregnancy, acknowledge that small families are imposed by a sense of limited resources, whereas larger families would be wanted if their means of support were no object. Finally, biologists who recognize a common, large-animal-species pattern of adjusting reproduction to available resources tend to accept the hypothesis as a true account of reality.

The economic opportunity hypothesis suggests that a sense of contracting opportunity promotes low or declining fertility whereas the perception of expanding opportunity allows people to raise family-size targets. Mechanisms associated with small family size include delaying marriage or interrupting marital relations, abstinence before marriage, or protected sex. Social, cultural, and behavioral adjustments as well as intentional contraception can limit childbearing.

The hypothesis has its roots in biology, anthropology, economics, and psychology. The incentive structure and the innate motive to maximize one's chances for successful reproduction are assumed to underlie the relationship between perception of economic prospects and fertility.

The EO hypothesis, the women's empowerment lobby, and the "just provide contraception" school do not have mutually exclusive interests. The questions of why women want fewer children than most currently have, and how avoiding pregnancy can be made easier, link these perspectives to the economic opportunity hypothesis.

In fact, women today want fewer children because raising children in a culturally acceptable manner is hard and possibly getting harder. Depending upon gender roles and family structure, women may feel the constraints earlier and more acutely than men. And easily used contraception is clearly helpful in avoiding pregnancy where privacy, stability, and hygienic conditions are in short supply.

The implication of the EO hypothesis is that most humanitarian policies are self-defeating because they neutralize the subtle, or direr, signals of economic and resource emergency that ordinarily lead to reproductive caution. That is, large-scale international interventions are unlikely to help and may harm. Exceptions are assistance with family planning and micro-loans that link small amounts of start-up capital to large measures of self-help. These types of assistance tend to be offered in small scale, face-to-face settings.

Thus, the EO hypothesis does not militate against helping. But its message is to be aware that assistance may change the incentive structure. One ought not risk giving the impression that wealth and assistance are limitless, or even so much as enough for all. Think before offering an outstretched hand.

Crowd Control. Review of George M. Moffett's *Critical Masses: The Global Population Challenge**

The author's journalistic background is the touchstone of this in-depth exploration of the perils of overpopulation. George Moffett's skillful weaving of facts and anecdotes vividly convey the population-driven environmental, social, political, and economic disintegration that is occurring worldwide; unfortunately, he also credulously repeats some of the bankrupt conventional wisdom about how to confront the current situation. The book's greatest strength derives from the extensive interviews he has conducted with men and women from all walks of life. These quotes and paraphrases open a window on the calculus underlying survival strategies and family-size decisions in diverse settings ranging from Cairo to Thailand to Guatemala.

The comments elicited by Moffett support my own findings that a sense of limited environmental resources and deteriorating economic opportunity strongly encourages people to exercise reproductive caution. In Cairo, he writes, "housing shortages have forced thousands of couples to delay marriage, sometimes for years." In Thailand, "Sam Ruang would like to have one more child, but he understands that that is beyond his means"; In Mexico, a thirty-two-year-old mother of two defends her use of contraceptives to the village priest, saying that "things are difficult here. A majority of people are having hard times. Jobs are hard to come by."

---

*In *Scientific American* 273(1) p. 83 [July, 1995].

A further brake on fertility comes from the new pattern of international lending, in which loans are tied to the important contingency that the recipient governments implement austerity measures. Moffett observes that the Mexican government "has turned adversity to good account, communicating the message that because of the country's protracted economic crisis, more children means less for everyone." When the Kenyan government eliminated subsidies for education, "faced with the need to shoulder the costs of education alone, many parents have responded by embracing family planning and having fewer children."

Drawing on his own extensive research and scientific background, Moffett writes that "the inverse relationship between living costs and childbearing is found throughout the developing world." That conclusion is congruent with a recent report on the acceptance rates of contraceptives among the Yoruba in Nigeria. John Caldwell, a respected demographer, stated that "two-thirds of all respondents claimed that the major force behind marriage postponement and the use of contraception to achieve it was the present hard economic conditions" (Caldwell et al. 1992, 220). Many of Caldwell's informants also perceived that as local crowding increased, children seem more susceptible to dying; they viewed this result—higher infant mortality—as a deterrent to frequent childbearing, counter to what the demographic transition model predicts.

The policy implications are not arcane. On the contrary, they are all too clear but do not sit well with the interventionist-internationalists (a cabal well represented in the media), who espouse the fifty-year-old demographic transition model that justifies blanket foreign aid aimed at increasing personal wealth.

Unfortunately, Moffett quickly retreats from his rich data in favor of the conventional tenets. He is soon laying out the need for economic development and reporting that half of a successful family planning policy entails "continuing efforts to alleviate poverty and raise living standards." Yet by Moffett's own account, it is perception of the fact and threat of declining living standards that have induced countless people to limit family size.

Indeed, the data suggest—but well-meaning people are loath to state—that past government subsidies of food, housing, health care, and education (made possible by international development aid) were counterproductive precisely because they fostered images of abundance and prosperity. I have found that fertility stays high and may in fact rise under such circumstances. History provides numerous examples of fertility rising in response to expansion of the ecological niche, whether as a result of innovative technology, improved crops, new sources of income, escape through emigration, or a populist political change that promises to redistribute wealth.

Tellingly, those few of Moffett's informants who remain comfortable with large family size are the very ones who still perceive a frontier of opportunity. Guatemalan Lopez Alala, for example, was a pioneer logger in the Peten region, a virgin forest opened to settlement in the early 1970s. He and his fellow pioneer families average nearly eight children each. Lopez anticipates that his children's families will be of similar size and expects also that "the forest will be there for them to clear." Who but the willfully blind would not speculate that Lopez's grand procreative strategy might be linked to his optimism?

Every time Moffett mentions the "demographic transition model" as a prescription for slowing population growth, it chills the blood because cash infusions that subsidize consumption seem only to fuel high fertility. The larger part of his recommendations are sound, however. In the excellent chapter called "A World Plan of Action," he describes the importance of getting contraceptive services to impoverished peoples and hard-to-reach constituencies, a challenge that often involves overcoming the concerted objections of entrenched religious entities. Moffett rightly cites improved employment opportunities for women as another promising strategy for limiting family size. Case studies show that women who work in the cash economy, however menially, recognize the cost of time spent raising children and so are more willing to limit the number of offspring.

But Moffett and others are also ready—too ready, in my opinion— to spend resources on women's education and health care. Although these services are desirable in themselves, the little evidence linking them to lower fertility is correlational and open to multiple interpretations. Nevertheless, health and education were part of the mainstream credo of the 1994 International Conference on Population and Development held in Cairo last September. With the caveats mentioned, Moffett's book can be recommended for those who want a lively and provocative introduction to the world population crisis. It is a challenge for the reader to sort out real data from rote repetition of demographic transition theory. The problem is important enough, one hopes, to spur policymakers and informed citizens to consult a wider reference list.

Population Dynamics: Why We Can Sit Back and Watch Fertility Fall*

Introduction

Worldwide, the resource, pollution, socioeconomic and political news is not cheering. Environments are degrading, climatic change perturbs seasonal rainfall, per capita food production is falling, and the disparity between the rich and poor within countries is growing even as total gross domestic product (GDP) rises. These developments make hopes for international rescue of third world countries decreasingly credible.

The good news is that awareness of limits causes marital and reproductive caution. As the perception of limits revives in parts of the third world where it had been temporarily allayed, fertility rates will fall. Declining fertility rates and population stabilization two or three generations later seem increasingly likely. With good fortune, technology will stretch resources so that collapse—in most countries—can be averted.

Population boom and bust cycles are neither novel nor unique. Historically, for example, China's principal dynasties established order that facilitated communication, rising productivity and trade, and prosperity; the good times led to population growth, overuse, and degradation of the environment, famine, and, invariably, political turmoil with dynastic reconsolidation at a new, lower population base. Easter Island society followed a grimmer path: the pristine, natural-resource-rich island colonized by Polynesian migrants fostered a complex civilization, but population growth and ensuing degradation of the environment led, in less than 1,000 years, to total collapse. Similarly, the ancient Mesopotamian civilization in the "fertile crescent" of the Tigris and Euphrates Rivers prospered, grew, developed irrigation to expand the agricultural base, and ended by irreparably salinizing the soil antecedent to population collapse.

A recognizable pattern still today, a society prospers, population grows as a result of both lower mortality and higher fertility, technology is applied to support the additional people, newer technology expands opportunity and often stimulates further population growth, gradually the environment degrades, eventually population collapses. The challenge is to deploy sustainable technology which supports the existing population without creating a stimulus for continued multiplication

---

* In *Population Problems: Topical Issues*, J. Rose {Ed.} Gordon and Breach Science Publishers, Amsterdam [2000].

of humanity. The objective is to let population stabilize—or better yet recede—in some relatively humane manner. Few births per woman so that annual births are no greater than deaths will stabilize a population in the span of about seventy years—a lifetime. Sustained low fertility is obviously preferable to cataclysmic increases in mortality. One hopes to avoid great suffering while reaching a plateau (perhaps but not inevitably a staging area for further advances) where the population is within the (sustainable) carrying capacity of the environment.

Many decades of fallacious population theory have contributed to the present tenuous balance. The demographic transition model—instructing policymakers that certain attributes of development lead to fertility *decline*—has been our nemesis. The modernization envisioned in this model is benign: prosperity and an improved quality of life for all, declining infant mortality, better education, opportunity for women, and urbanization. In short, enlightened, Utopian, environmentally friendly, global cooperation at a high standard of living.

The flaw is that, when people perceive expanding economic opportunity and the possibility of successfully raising more children, they increase their family-size target and, in fact, have larger families. Therefore, the very programs designed to improve health, education, and welfare inadvertently prevent fertility decline even when child mortality is declining. Without a reduction in fertility to compensate for declining mortality rates, populations explode. As population size exceeds the long-term environmental carrying capacity, persons are condemned to lives of unmitigated poverty.

Perception is subjective. Lester Thurow (1993), dean of MIT's Sloane School, suggests that a 10 percent change in income is sufficient to trigger the perception of improving or worsening opportunity. People measure well-being against expectations formed from a reference group or reference period.

Testing the Hypothesis: The Rise and Fall of Fertility in Modern Times

The perfect case history provides data on both perceived economic opportunity and fertility rates and includes the authors' views on causality. For example, Díaz-Briquets and Pérez (1981, p. 15) explain the baby boom which occurred in Cuba after the 1959 Castro revolution as an effect of "the real income rise among the most disadvantaged groups brought about by the redistributionist measures of the revolutionary government. The fertility rise in almost every age group suggests that couples viewed the future as more promising and felt they could now afford more children." Also comprehensive, Ezekiel Kalipeni (1996) attributes recent declines in Malawi's fertility rate to "lack of resources to grow enough food to feed a large family" and to disappearance by the early 1980s of "the international migratory safety valve"; regions experiencing the most intense environmental pressure are leading the decline (pp. 300–1).

Data for testing the economic opportunity hypothesis are rarely so well organized. Typically, inferences about the economy come from one source and fertility data from another. Fertility rates before 1970 are often difficult to reconstruct, and this work has had low priority because, compared to declining mortality rates, possible rises in fertility were thought to contribute little to the modern population increase (Bongaarts 1994).

Cycles of Boom and Bust

Peru. A discussion of booms and busts in Peru's export economy and its corresponding fertility cycles is above, in Fertility Decline No Mystery [published in *Ethics in Science and Environmental Politics*/ESEP, pp. 1–11. [May 24, 2002]].

As predicted by the economic opportunity hypothesis , fertility did increase during Peru's periodic export booms, and did decline during periods of recession: guano and then anchoveta exports, accompanied by good employment prospects, led fertility up. Stable or declining fertility rates followed political instability and contraction in these key industries.

The Population Reference Bureau 1995 Data Sheet shows Peru with a TFR of 3.5, significantly lower than in previous decades. Rivera and Espenshade (1995) predict that the decline will stall temporarily because Peru's new political stability, declining inflation, and improved economic outlook are again raising expectations.

Nevertheless, I prefer to hedge. The prospering upper middle class shares the US consumerist culture in which *perceived* scarcity and insecurity tend to depress fertility. Moreover, the austerity of President Fujimori's policies precludes unrealistic optimism: most subsidies on food and housing for the poor have been eliminated, government jobs have been slashed, the private sector is newly allowed to fire workers, two-thirds of the work force is underemployed, and "in per capita terms, Peru's national income is no more than it was in the 1960s" (*The Economist* 1995, 22). Droughts periodically threaten the potato crop (although foreign research and development money still go into potatoes), and Peru remains the most densely populated country in South America (*Nashville Banner* 1990). Entrepreneurial activity increases total wealth but, as in the Asian tigers adds mainly to the concentration of wealth. The economic freefall has been arrested but the average Peruvian remains in dire straits; so fertility is likely to keep falling.

The CARICOM Countries. Thirteen English-speaking Caribbean countries are collectively known as the CARICOM countries. All have been characterized by rapidly worsening population densities—growth of up to 3 percent per year—high unemployment, and few economic resources. Opportunity expanded after World War II with the development of tourism, "massive emigration" (Guengant 1985, 3), and with the planning around the 1960s for transition from colonial to independent status. The rising fertility rates that transpired would have been predicted by the economic opportunity hypothesis.

Fertility rates rose after 1945 in every CARICOM country except the Bahamas (where an expanding tourism industry and the fertility increase occurred earlier). In nine of the thirteen countries, fertility increased by at least one child per woman. Dominica and Grenada saw increases of approximately 1.5 births per woman; St. Lucia and St. Vincent registered increases of over 2 births per woman (Guengant 1985).

Most rates peaked between 1955 and 1965. Better maternal health may account adequately for the increases, but the timing appears somewhat late: antibiotics and public health measures, given that these were British colonies, might have made an earlier mark. Thus, economic development, the emigration option, and anticipation of independence remain likely contributors to the baby boom.

Independence, achieved by all CARICOM countries between 1962 and 1981, did not yield the looked-for prosperity. Opportunity to immigrate to Great Britain ended, and per capita incomes sagged because of population growth. Trinidad is a sad example: "since 1982, real GNP has dropped by one-third," pay for government employees has been cut, and "real wages have fallen each year since 1984" (*The Economist* 1990, 31). The Trinidadian fertility rate peaked in 1965 at about 5.2 (Guengant 1985); by 1991, it had declined to 2.4 births per woman (PRB 1980–1995).

Rwanda. Rwanda is the most densely populated country in continental sub-Saharan Africa. Population pressure was recognized during the colonial period and by the indigenous government which succeeded from Belgian rule in 1962. The policy response developed by the Belgians and continued under self-rule was dispersal of the population to less congested territories, through both immigration to neighboring countries (e.g., to Zaire after World War II) and relocation into formerly empty (and agriculturally marginal) lands.

These policies partially relieved land hunger but were not constructive in the long run: "The relative availability of land during the agricultural colonization and intensification processes might have been conducive to higher fertility levels" (May 1995, 329) concludes John May. The population did, in fact, quadruple between 1950 and 1993, "largely because of extremely high fertility" (Bouvier 1995).

Fertility rates are now declining. The reason is that, as in almost all countries, people perceive that their situation is worsening. This mirrors reality in many poverty-stricken regions where per capita income is insufficient to provide life's necessities. Entire regions are in absolute want.

Perceptions of scarcity are also growing in regions making the transition to becoming powerful industrial economies. This perception springs from factors which are far from benign and were not anticipated in the demographic transition model's vision of modernity.

Increasingly obvious as part of the modernization pattern is the consumer ethos. Consumerism fosters the sense of not having enough. Whatever one has, it could be more! The sense of scarcity, albeit artificial, is psychologically real enough to depress fertility. It appears that consumerism is an incentive to limit family size in the growing middle class of South and Central America, North Africa, and the former Asian tigers, that is, in countries where average income is relatively high and economic growth has set records. Consumer-driven scarcity has long had this effect on fertility in the United States (Abernethy 1979).

Real poverty, however, also affects many persons within rapidly industrializing societies. This comes as the aftermath of rapid population growth and the enormous supply of labor which drives down wages (the price of labor); concurrently, the return to owners of capital increases. Inevitably, the society includes both a mass of poorly paid, underemployed workers, and a wealthy, elite few. This polarization into rich and poor has been cited as a further, unexpected and unwanted corollary of modernization. But modernization is irrelevant. An oversupply of labor drives down its price in any kind of economy; Ronald Lee (1980, 1987) documents the effect in late-medieval England (Lee 1987).

Perceived scarcity, reality-based or artificial, will, in every case, depress the family-size target. Cases which illustrate fertility decline are discussed in this paper.

Whether or not modern contraception is available—witness Burma and the Sudan—perceived worsening of economic opportunity leads to fertility decline or continuing low fertility. Traditional methods for curtailing family size are discussed in the anthropological literature (Abernethy 1993; Nag 1968). That said, modern contraception is the most humane means for limiting fertility and it seems likely to increase the speed of responding to perceptions that additional children are unaffordable.

Illustrating the Economic Opportunity Model

Examples of declining fertility from agricultural, industrial, premodern, and modern societies illustrate the effect of perceived scarcity. In any setting, a decline in relative wages or their equivalent, increasingly dense settlement, higher cost of land, smaller farm size, or withdrawal of subsidies to which people have become accustomed are observed to precede falling fertility rates. In Kenya, for example, fertility began to decline in the 1990s after the government announced that education would no longer be publicly subsidized (Martha Campbell, personal communication, 1997). In Morocco and Algeria, fertility declined sharply (in 1975 and the early 1980s, respectively) after collapse of the market for their principal export products. The loss of revenue led to the withdrawal of major government subsidies so that families had to rely on themselves for both staples and social goods (Courbage 1995; Fargues 1995).

Concord, an outpost of the Puritan, Massachusetts Bay Company established in Boston in 1630, also illustrates that collapse of an export market depresses the fertility rate. Like other new world settlements, the Concord fertility rate hovered around a level much higher than seen in any European country of the period. Numerous observers have attributed the typical large family size to the North American continent's seemingly limitless resource base, where children's on-farm labor produced a large net return. But Brian Berry (1996) shows that even before 1787—the colonial period—the fertility rate fluctuated.

Specifically, fertility in colonial Concord declined each time that export earnings were interrupted by political or economic events in England. A fertility decline first occurred when exports ceased in 1642 (while the Puritans, or Roundheads, were preoccupied with wresting control from King Charles I by refusing to adjourn Parliament) and then "again during the 1680s as both the British and Colonial economies sagged toward the financial crisis of the 1690s" (1996, 212–13). Berry summarizes his analysis of Concord's preindustrial period: "These bad times of plummeting commodity prices and falling real incomes came in the 1640s, the 1690s, the 1740s, and the 1790s, and are clearly identifiable in the Concord birth record" (Berry 1996, 215).

Historical demography contributes the further examples of five nineteenth- and twentieth-century South Asian famines. Here, slight increases in the price of staple foods were followed almost immediately by behavioral adjustments which reduced the likelihood of pregnancy (Dyson 1991, 1991b).

Rising prices for staple foods and falling wages also account, in part, for the recent dramatic fertility declines in the former republics of the USSR, especially Russia. In all Eastern-bloc countries, economic restructuring, dissipation of government consumption subsidies, and public perception of rising infant mortality have promoted lower fertility rates and created a demand for the avoidance of pregnancy (Haub 1994; Conrad, Lechner, and Werner 1996).

In Hungary, a birth dearth is following government austerity programs and real deterioration in the standard of living (Abernethy 1997). From nearly 2.0 births per woman in 1980, fertility declined to 1.8 in 1989, to 1.7 in 1994, to 1.6 in 1996. This decline is modest compared to the startling fertility bust seen after the demise of Communism in East Germany. Nicholas Eberstadt observes that East Germany's 1989 shift from central planning to markets "entailed enormous dislocations in its economy" (Eberstadt 1994, 150). Christoph Conrad et al. (1996) show that the economic shock of reunification into one Germany was a precursor to a 45 percent fertility decline in 1991–1992 alone. This was part of a 50 percent decline in five years which left East Germany with a total fertility rate of 0.77 births per woman in 1994 (Conrad, Lechner, and Werner 1996).

Twentieth-century US fertility has also been responsive to economic opportunity—boom or bust. Some demographic work showed that the 1947–1962 baby boom could be traced to the very strong labor market beginning shortly after World War II (Easterlin 1962). The reasons underlying cohort fertility are a matter for economic inquiry because funding of US Social Security (the retirement pension system) depends on the ongoing contributions of the workforce. Congruent with the economic opportunity hypothesis, the independent report of the 1994–1996 Advisory Council on Social Security links income and fertility: "large birth cohorts meet unfavorable labor market circumstances that cause them to delay/forgo family formation." That is, the US baby boom cohort flooded the labor market beginning in the late 1960s, opportunity appeared relatively tight, and, concludes the report, this cohort lowered "their desired family sizes in light of poor labor market experiences" (Social Security 1997, 211).

The other half of the Abernethy economic opportunity hypothesis is that a sense of expanding economic opportunity leads to higher family-size targets. Therefore, the second part of the commission's conclusion comes as no surprise. Small cohorts ("like the baby-bust cohort of the 1930s") (Social Security 1997) have favorable labor market experiences and go on to achieve higher fertility levels: the baby boom.

Within the pattern of generational oscillation, those who feel relatively affluent also may have higher fertility. A newstory headline notes, "Older more Educated Couples Feel Two Kids Are No Longer Enough". In 1980, college graduates had 22 percent of third births to women in their 40s according to the National Center for Health Statistics. By 1993, that had shot up to 40 percent (Blumenthal 1996, 1).

College-educated women are likely candidates for being both professionally successful and married to college-educated, successful men. The college-educated are approximately 23 percent of the US population and are likely to be among that upper 20 percent which prospered disproportionately in the late 1980s and 1990s (partly as employers profiting from low-wage services including the household services of immigrants). Their accounting for 40 percent of third births to older women, when the total fertility rate of the native-born sector is under two children per woman, appears to support the economic opportunity hypothesis.

Wealthy Chinese businessmen particularly in southern China exhibit a related pattern. They reportedly form liaisons with several women in order to maximize their progeny despite rules allowing only one child per woman (*New York Times* 1997).

Although the United States is affluent overall, it exemplifies the pressures—consumerism and growing disparity between rich and poor—which have as their principal redeeming feature the downward pressure on fertility. The consumer-driven sense of scarcity is amplified by real threats to the standard of living in most sectors: inflation-adjusted wages received by approximately 80 percent of the working force have been stagnant since the mid-1970s. The relatively lower return to labor is driven by the population growth which has been unremitting since World War II. Population grew because the initially strong labor market was an inducement to raise fertility—the baby boom. Subsequently, native-born fertility declined to as low as 1.7 children per woman, but flows of immigrants, mostly from the third world and Russia, have swollen the labor force and kept population growth at over 1 percent annually, the highest of any Western country. (Wealth disparities are also greater in the United States than in any other Western society.)

The low return to labor is probably a factor depressing the fertility rate of the native-born middle class, as has already been suggested. On the other hand, immigrants, who find good economic opportunity relative to their former experience, appear to have higher fertility than do counterparts in their country of origin (Landale and Hauan 1996).

Immigration and the children of immigrants account for over 60 percent of US population growth and their share is growing. The foreign-born are 10 percent of the US population but accounted for over 18 percent of 1994 births.

Overview

Examples of the relationship sketched here can be multiplied. Fertility rates rise in response to perceived opportunity, and fall when ordinary persons perceive that competition is increasingly harsh or conditions are deteriorating. I have not found true exceptions, including the constellation of declining fertility and economic growth in countries known as Asia's "economic tigers."

In Japan and Taiwan, population pressure increased sharply due to immigration: Japan because of the post–World War II repatriation of citizens who had colonized territory conquered in the expansionist years after 1920 (by 1940, about 6 percent of the population was expatriate); Taiwan, because of the Nationalist Chinese retreat to this island from the mainland in 1949. In both countries, the fertility decline was on track before the advent of economic growth and modernization. The Taiwanese government was a leader in promoting small family size and modern contraception. But in Japan the government was relatively passive, if not obstructionist; the "pill" remained illegal until recently.

In most Asian tigers including Korea, Thailand, Indonesia, and now China, growth in the gross domestic product (GDP) overlies a pattern of some entrepreneurs becoming extremely wealthy while the majority of the population remains poor or has a tenuous hold on middle-class status. That is, the distribution of wealth lets most people feel that their personal needs are unsatisfied. Moreover, wants multiply as consumer goods are introduced into the society. Even those whose incomes rise substantially acquire a sense of needing more, i.e. scarcity. Consumption sops up personal resources. Competition intensifies. Large families are viewed as unaffordable by most of the lower and middle class.

International Interventions

In light of these remarks, international aid should be limited to programs which do not convey a sense of vastly expanding resources and opportunity. Family planning assistance and microloan programs along the model of the Grameen Bank in Bangladesh are appropriate.

International agencies would seem well advised to continue efforts to promote family planning because it offers a humane means to limit fertility and is inexpensive to provide. But one ought not depend on contraceptive availability to overcome the contrary, reproductive imperative. Especially when family planning assistance is paired with well-funded development programs which signal a windfall of opportunity and the option to emigrate, the incentive to limit family size may be nil. Nathan Keyfitz writes that "if there is no economic or cultural incentive to population control, then sponsored programs providing contraception will do little" (Keyfitz 1993).

Immigration policy in industrialized countries is seldom analyzed from the perspective of its effect on fertility rates in the third world. Nevertheless, much data suggests that a safety valve for excess population delays the fertility decline in countries that emigrants leave. That was first suggested by Kingsley Davis and is congruent with conclusions from subsequent work (Davis 1963; Brittain 1990, 1991). Davis shows that couples married young and fertility remained high in Japan through the early 1930s just so long as substantial emigration continued in connection with the Asian Co-prosperity Sphere. He shows also that Irish fertility fluctuated after the 1845–1854 potato famine, but did not descend crashingly so long as emigration to the colonies and the United States remained attractive options. Anne Brittain's studies of matched Caribbean island communities during the 1970s and 1980s suggest a similar pattern: fertility remained high in communities that many people left, but declined rapidly in stable communities where emigration was not used, apparently, as an escape valve.

Not only the economic space that becomes available when someone departs, but also remittances, create a perception of expanding opportunity. Egyptian migrants to Saudi Arabia remitted $5 billion annually in the late 1970s, a cash flow said to be a factor in Egypt's stalled fertility decline (Fargues 1997); Mexican migrants to the United States are said to remit $3.5 billion annually.

Reiterating, many forces are now at work to reduce fertility rates worldwide. Real poverty is afflicting not only large regions of the world but also significant sectors within developed and rapidly industrializing societies. Moreover, many who live well above subsistence levels have adopted the ethos of consumerism, making their perceived needs far greater than their resources. Whatever the source, perceptions of scarcity drive down fertility.

It remains only to avoid counterproductive international and national policies. Without the possibility of emigrating and without transfers of wealth that prop up social programs, world fertility rates would go into free fall. Every form of assistance, therefore, should be weighed against the capacity of Earth to support extra births.

Eskimo Adaptation to a Harsh Environment*

The harshness of the Eskimo environment has been emphasized both by early explorers and by anthropologists. Particularly among the northernmost groups, hardships routinely borne by a hunter testify to the extreme rigors of subsistence.

For example, to kill a seal, a hunter sits immobile by a "breathing hole" in the ice waiting for the animal to surface. Any slight motion warns the seal away, and a full day's literally frozen attention may still go unrewarded by meat. When the ice breaks up in spring, hunters go to sea in their skin boats. The prey may be large walrus; the undertaking is dangerous and casualties not infrequent. On land, the hunter is equally threatened: he stalks polar bear with stone-age weapons; in addition, he is often threatened by starvation, subsisting on little more than tea for several days of solitary hunting.

It seems hardly surprising that Knud Rasmussen would write of the Pelly Bay area, home of the Netsilik, "There is scarcely any country on earth that presents conditions more severe and inclement for man ... for it lies waste and bare of all that is otherwise necessary to life."(cited in Jenness 1968). Several factors should be considered in evaluating the total force of environmental pressure borne by the Eskimo. First,

---

* In *Population Pressure and Cultural Adjustment*, pp. 74–81. Human Sciences Press (1979) and Transaction Publishers (2005).

hunting and fishing are almost their sole source of food, whereas in every other hunting group in the world, gathering of plant foods makes a measurable and usually the major contribution to subsistence. Second, the unusually large amplitude in seasonal variation means that peak ecological pressure may be a more severely limiting factor than subsistence viewed over most parts of the year would imply. Finally, and of major significance for Freeman's thesis of the adaptive value of infanticide, the Arctic ecosystem is intrinsically unstable because of its limited number of species. Thus, overcropping of food sources can have particularly catastrophic consequences. A corollary of all this is that there is little opportunity for food accumulation, so the provision for subsistence needs over prolonged periods can rarely be planned.

Infanticide

Given these harsh, environmentally imposed constraints, the Eskimo adaptation for achieving population balance operates with small tolerance for error. Obviously, groups cannot be allowed to dwindle to the point of extinction, but either a population increase or a high dependency ratio (the number of young and aged compared to productive members of the society) are equally a threat to survival.

Alone among societies known to me, the Eskimo depend almost exclusively upon mortality for the limitation of their number. Much mortality is accidental, but both the suicide of an old person and infanticide represent premeditated acts which have the effect of eliminating nonproductive members of the group. Freeman suggests that infanticide is a strategic choice given harsh Eskimo ecology because reproductive decisions are thereby delayed as long as possible, and thus are based on the maximum amount of information, i.e., sex of baby and the latest subsistence outlook.

Apparently, Eskimo methods were successful. Diamond Jenness is among those who consider that the traditional Eskimo achieved population resource equilibrium: "In prehistoric times, and right down to the present day in the Central Canadian Arctic, the toll of famines, sickness, accidents, blood feuds, infanticides [particularly of girl babies), and suicides of the aged and infirm restricted the size of their bands to the number of mouths their hunters could feed from the daily catch" (p. 40). Similarly, Freeman suggests that the combined mortality from natural causes and purposive acts apparently served as an absolute brake on growth in that, "the Netsilik population has probably remained stable at around 450–500 individuals throughout the last 100 years of their aboriginal existence" (p. 1013).

So effective a check was mortality that population stationarity apparently occurred despite uncontrolled fertility. Early marriage and high fertility within marriage was the norm. For example, one ethnographer reports that the ten postmenopausal Nesilik women for whom he was able to collect data averaged 8.3 live births (cited by Freeman). Ironically, infanticide appears to have been one reason for the high completed fertility because conception is hastened by cutting short lactation. The Eskimo themselves contend that reestablishment of menses and reproductive capacity is the primary objective in practicing female infanticide, particularly of first children. A father desired sons to be partners in his fishing boat but, so long as a woman nursed a daughter, the birth of sons was that much more delayed.

David Riches undertook to test the hypothesis that female infanticide is a response to subsistence pressure. He predicted that most female infanticide occurs precisely where environmental conditions are harshest and, presumably, where population control must be most stringent. In designing his study, Riches devised ingenious proxy measures for relative scarcity (or prosperity) as well as for female infanticide, the hypothesized dependent variable. His prosperity measure is the sled dog/nuclear family ratio, chosen because huskies are essential to the Eskimo economy: not only are dogs used in hunting and transportation, but they also have great symbolic value as an index of wealth. Thus, the fewer dogs per family, the less the prosperity.

Riches' estimate of female infanticide builds on the expectation of finding more adult females than males because males are selectively exposed to a high rate of accidental death in the Arctic hunting economy. Sex ratio refers to the number of males per female and, without female infanticide, would usually be less than 1.0. The higher the sex ratio among adults, the greater the likelihood that female infanticide had been practiced in the past.

Riches' findings, from four tribes of between 200 and 800 persons each, support the environmental-determination-of-infanticide hypothesis: environmental pressure as assessed either by the dog/family ratio or from impressionistic measures is correlated with sex ratio, in the predicted direction. Specifically, the Netsilik, who are placed at the harshest end of the environmental continuum both by consensual impressionistic data and from having just 1.5 sled dogs per family, also had the highest adult sex ratio, 1.38 males per female.

Environmentally intermediate societies showed intermediate sex ratios. At the environmentally most benign-seeming end or the continuum, evidence of prosperity was confirmed by the average of twelve sled dogs per family, and this appeared simultaneously with a low (or nonexistent) rate of female infanticide as indicated by a ratio of .91 males to each female.

Before leaving the Eskimo, one may note that within the last decades their culture and society have changed. Subsistence is now guaranteed by the US and Canadian governments. There is no more infanticide (although newborn babies may still be given away—mailed direct, on one occasion, to innocent anthropologist Sergei Bogojavalensky). There is no more exposure of the aged, fewer hunting accidents because of much less hunting, and a major reduction in disease. Missionaries have exhorted and been heeded; physicians have prevented and cured. Mortality is down, the population is up. Not until 1965 was any family planning assistance offered by government health agencies. And the success of such programs will depend anyway on Eskimo resilience in assimilating still another facet of Western culture because, as we have seen, limitation of conception is not within the range of their traditional options.

Although poverty among the Eskimo often appears to be great, poor circumstances are now more often due to greatly increased needs per person and to population growth, rather than to the Eskimo not having been the recipients of vastly more than was ever available from traditional subsistence activities. If they were again thrown upon their own resources, not only would it become evident in the short run that their numbers have multiplied beyond any hope of being in balance with what the environment can provide, but it might transpire that they have lost the cultural knack for maintaining appropriate population size within the exceedingly narrow tolerance of this most hostile inhabited region in the world.

It appears that their former success depended upon (1) maintaining very low population density; (2) rigidly limiting the costs of supporting unproductive members of the society; (3) maximizing flexibility by delaying as long as possible the decision to add an extra mouth, i.e., infanticide rather than birth control; (4) raising fewer females because even their potential contribution to subsistence was less than that of the male; and (5) making the most of the reproductive potential of each woman who survived to maturity.

It may be that reliance on mortality as the primary population-limiting mechanism is the only way to achieve the Eskimo's exquisite titration between slow decline to extinction and calamitous overpopulation. Fortunately, it appears that only in Arctic environment is the margin for error so small.

Why Asian Population Growth Is Grinding Down*

Asia's currencies will not be the only thing plummeting in 1998. Look next for a decline in fertility rates (the number of births per woman) in the countries affected by Asia's financial meltdown. Most people want children, but not more than can be raised well given family standards. Caution about childbearing is widespread when resources and opportunity contract or seem severely limited. A 40 percent decline in assets probably makes a lot of people feel poor enough to postpone marriage or parenthood.

A fertility rate of 2.1 just replaces parents (with an allowance for child mortality), so this number leads, in the long run, to stable population. Some Asian countries already have fertility rates below the replacement level. States such as Hong Kong (1.2 births per woman), Japan (1.5), South Korea (1.7), Singapore (1.8), China (1.8), and Taiwan (1.8) expect to see the end to population growth in twenty–sixty years, depending on when replacement-level fertility, or lower, took root. If fertility rates fall very low, population growth stops sooner.

East Germany's experience with reunification suggests that the fertility rate can fall below one child per woman. Live births declined 46 percent between 1989 and 1991, a drop that Nicholas Eberstadt attributes to "enormous dislocations in the economy." By 1994, the fertility rate was 0.77 births per woman, down 50.9 percent in five years due to the combined effects of a 60 percent decline in the number of marriages and delayed childbearing: first-time mothers averaged 22.9 years of age in 1989 compared to 26.2 years by 1993. These marital and fertility changes have been described as part of a "rational adaptation process."

The Thai fertility rate, 2.2 children per woman in 1996, hovers already on the brink of replacement and will probably fall more during

---

* In *Chronicles*, Rockford, Illinois, pp. 46–47 [October,1998].

124

the present financial convulsion. Two pressures have long pinched optimism (and family-size targets) in Thailand: population growth has shrunk per capita land holdings, so the rural population foresees farms being divided into plots too small to support a large family; in cities, economic security is hindered by a large disparity between rich and poor and by the precariousness of middle-class status in an economy where the fast-growing labor force threatens to overwhelm the creation of net new good jobs.

The situation in Malaysia differs slightly because of diversity and affirmative action. Ethnic Malays are nearly 60 percent of the population and, since independence in 1957, have benefited from many educational and employment opportunities available only to them, while the Chinese and Indian minorities have been progressively discriminated against. The latters' economic woes are reflected in declining fertility rates, from 7 births per woman before independence to 2.5 in 1987 for Chinese, and from approximately 8 down to 3 births per woman for Indians. At the same time, the Malay rate declined little. The 1996 national statistic—dominated by the more numerous Malays—was 3.3 births per woman, a rate sure to decline because not even privileged Malays will be able to avoid economic meltdown.

India began 1996 with a rate of 3.4 births per woman, and larger family size is reportedly in vogue. Both the loosening of bureaucratic barriers to entrepreneurial activity and high emigration would account for increased income and greater family security. Domestic prosperity is likely to be dashed, however, by regional financial events, and this should renew the decline in fertility.

The highest fertility rates in South, East, and Southeast Asia occur where significant proportions of the population have emigrated, and immigration to the United States offers continuing opportunity. Many immigrants remit funds to relatives back home, a source of income which is widely distributed among poor and middle-class families— precisely where most decisions about family size are made. Filipino women average 4.1 births. Similarly, Laotians (6.1 births per woman), Cambodians (5.8), and Vietnamese (3.7) are partially insulated from regional economic cycles by emigration and their ongoing refugee entitlements in the United States. Therefore, no sharp fertility decline should be expected soon.

These predictions grow out of the fertility opportunity explanation of family size. Some observers still argue that fertility falls because infant mortality rates fall or because women are educated (the UN's favorite). But the commonsensical idea that people have as many children as seem affordable, given their childbearing and living standards, is gaining adherents. This rationale explains rising as well as declining fertility. Moreover, it builds on the theory of natural selection, which links evolutionary success to having the maximum number of offspring who survive and reproduce in turn.

Although deriving from biology and anthropology, the fertility opportunity hypothesis converges with economic theory. In fact, America's history of low fertility in times of meager economic opportunity (e.g., the Depression) and high fertility rates during times of economic expansion (e.g., the baby boom years) has convinced the Advisory Council on Social Security that a small birth cohort, whose members are likely to encounter ample job opportunities relative to their number, will command high wages and see rapid career advancement and, therefore, have big families; it says so in its 1994 report. On the other hand, a large birth cohort tends to flood the labor market, causing wages and benefits to stagnate or fall and leading to decline in desired family size.

Both labor market opportunities and asset values subject to financial gyrations change the gleam in a father's eye. Knowing recent economic events and the distribution of wealth in any society, it is possible to predict the likely trajectory of fertility rates. When the middle class—not just the wealthy few—feels secure and rich, fertility rates turn up. That could happen in America. In Asia, however, expect decline.

Fertility Decline in Former "Asian Tigers"*

Abstract

The fertility opportunity hypothesis suggests that individuals and couples adjust family size in response to their perception that economic opportunity is increasing—or diminishing. A sense that opportunities are expanding encourages a relatively high, even rising, family size target. On the contrary, the perception that opportunities and resources will fall short of satisfying the aspirations of oneself or family lead to lowering family size targets. The literature suggests that family size target translates into completed family size on the order of 85 to 90

---

* Virginia Abernethy and Roberto V. Penaloza. Excerpted from *Population and Environment* 23 (3): 245–66 [January, 2002].

percent. The economic collapse of former "Asian tigers" in late summer, 1997, offered a chance to test the hypothesis prospectively. In 1998, an author (Abernethy) predicted that fertility rates in the nine Asian tiger countries would fall during the 1997–1999 interval at a faster rate than had been observed in immediately preceding two-year intervals. This paper reports the results of tests of the hypothesis with respect to the Asian tigers and several other country clusters for which no particular prediction was made. Findings appear to support the fertility opportunity hypothesis.

Introduction

The economic collapse in former Asian tigers presents an opportunity to test, prospectively, the fertility opportunity hypothesis (Abernethy 1979, 1993 [1999], 1994). The hypothesis claims to predict country or regional trends in the fertility rate.

The rationale for the fertility opportunity hypothesis derives from sociobiology's assumption that the desire for descendants is the result of evolutionary selection and is innate. The preeminent strategy of natural selection is successful reproduction, which is distinct from maximum reproduction. The motive to reproduce is tempered by judgments about how many children can be raised well given expectations, aspirations that entail alternate uses for resources, and subjective perceptions about resource availability. Thus, the motive to reproduce is balanced by restraint.

The hypothesis also has roots in, or is congruent with, the economic literature that relates fertility to resources (for example, Becker 1960, 1974; Easterlin 1962, 1971, 1976; Macunovitch 1996.) The hypothesis differs slightly, however, in suggesting that individuals, either consciously or subliminally, size up the economic and social climate. Apparently good or improving conditions are seized upon as a reproductive opportunity, whereas a perception that conditions are deteriorating and resources, scarce, leads to reducing family size targets and, hence, to a declining fertility rate.

In addition to its links with sociobiology and economic models, the fertility opportunity hypothesis derives from the study of whole human societies by anthropologists. Both anthropology and sociobiology (including studies of nonhuman species) are rich in case studies that can be interpreted as meaning, or are explicitly presented as evidence, that individuals seek to avoid (ameliorate) hardship through reproductive restraint. Limiting the total number of young, and/or optimizing the timing and spacing of births, tends to improve the quality of offspring and their chance of survival until they, too, reproduce.

The leap from family size targets to total fertility rate (TFR) relies upon the cross-cultural finding that the number of children wanted accounts for 85–90 percent of completed family size (Pritchett 1994). This finding challenges the school of thought that sees provision of family planning services as the sufficient condition for reducing family size (Robey 1993). Exclusive reliance upon contraceptive availability as the road to fertility decline denies motivational factors. The fertility opportunity hypothesis integrates psychological variables including both motivation and perception.

The fertility opportunity hypothesis poses a problem for certain popular demographic theories that explain a transition to low fertility through the mechanisms of modernization and declining infant mortality (Thompson 1929; Davis 1945; Notestein 1945) or merely cultural diffusion (Coale and Watkins 1986). Historical demography, on the contrary, is replete with studies that support and expand the opportunity hypothesis (Davis 1963; Demeny 1968; Diaz-Briquets and Perez 1981; Lee 1980, 1987.)

A scenario for prospectively testing part of the opportunity explanation of changing fertility patterns presented itself in summer, 1997, the beginning of the economic meltdown, or "Asian contagion," that was to afflict the nine countries which had come to be known, informally, as the "Asian tigers." Rapidly collapsing asset and currency values, with losses of up to 40 percent, weighed on most sectors of these societies (Abernethy 1998).

The nine countries of this sample are characterized by modernization in at least one primary sector of the society and, until 1997, by this sector being relatively affluent. The countries vary greatly, however, in the pervasiveness of modernizing influences. Some observers would exclude the Philippines because it never achieved independent economic take-off and remained heavily reliant on the presence of the US naval bases for nearly a century, until the early 1990s. Others would exclude Japan from the list of former "tigers" because of the length of time that its economy has been modernizing. Japan began to invest in technology and education near the turn of the twentieth century, and to modernize other facets of society immediately after World War II. Taiwan and Hong Kong embarked on extensive modernization within a decade of the ending of World War II.

Whatever their differences and pace of change, however, some generalizations apply. By 1997, each country had experienced improvements in standard of living, the value of education was increasingly appreciated as the high road to economic success, and the prospect of entering the middle class was influencing an increasing proportion of the population.

For all countries in the group, economic prospects changed radically in the summer of 1997, a downward spiral initiated by a sharp devaluation of the Thai baht. In Japan, the unemployment rates in 1998 and 1999 rose to a level higher than at any time since 1953 (Much 1999). Personal bankruptcies in 1999 were 50 percent higher than in 1997 and, a further sign of falling incomes, Japanese retail sales declined from 1997 through 1999 (Bonner 2000). In 1998, the Japanese suicide rate was the highest recorded. Contemplating an uncertain future, a majority of university students expressed a preference for government as opposed to private sector employment (Rogers 1999).

The 1997 economic collapse occurred not only in Thailand and Japan but was area-wide. This development presented an opportunity for hypothesis testing. So far as is known to the authors, this is the first prospective test of the fertility opportunity hypothesis.

If the hypothesis is correct, the general economic deterioration would be expected to produce a declining fertility rate. Insofar as fertility decline is a secular trend that has been observed in the Asian tigers for a number of years (since the end of World War II, in the case of Japan), *the specific prediction is for an increasing rate of decline in the period after 1997* (Abernethy 1998). That is, the fertility decline from 1997 to 1999 was expected to be significantly faster than the decline observed in preceding two-year intervals. The year, 1998, may be seen as a transition period during which women who had conceived prior to the economic collapse gave birth.

The data, all derived from Population Reference Bureau (PRB) Population Data Sheets, are far from ideal. If annual census data are not available, PRB reports and adjusts findings from the closest year. They are the most recent data available but are not necessarily the figures for the date in question. Further, the quality of census data varies by country.

These difficulties have not deterred us from testing the hypothesis because the errors in data are expected to be random. It is commonly said that random errors easily obscure a significant relationship but

129

are unlikely to create the appearance of a relationship that does not, in fact, exist.

Data and Preliminary Findings

Fertility rates and percentage change for the Asian tigers are shown in Tables 1 and 2. The relevant comparison is between the two-year interval from 1997 to 1999, and earlier two-year intervals.

Parallel data for South and Central America and the Caribbean appear in Tables 3 and 4. Since no comparable watershed economic event occurred in these countries during the study period, the fertility opportunity hypothesis predicts that the rate of change from 1997 to 1999 will be no different from the change rates observed in preceding intervals.

The comparison groups, while not ideal, appear on their face to be the best available. Many countries and sectors within each country have made gains toward modernization and industrialization. Nevertheless, the regions as a whole would be considered as "developing" or "underdeveloped" by most observers, and, with few exceptions, have begun the transition to smaller family size relatively recently. No other continent or coherent grouping of countries seems as suitable as a control group.

Nevertheless, future studies will entertain the possibilities for a better control group and, in addition, for the quantification of independent variables. Preliminary considerations suggest that fluctuations in the exchange rate could be a useful proxy for a societal and individual perception of improving or deteriorating economic opportunity.

Table 1 shows the (former) Asian tigers' total fertility rate (TFR) by country, by two-year intervals, from 1991 through 1999. Table 2 shows the percentage change in TFR between each interval, both by country and by average for all countries in the sample. In every one of the former Asian tigers except Thailand, the percentage decline between 1997 and 1999 was greater than the decline in the previous interval.

The average decline in the fertility rate between 1997 and 1999, including Thailand, was 6.6 percent. The largest average decline in any other interval was 1.6 percent between 1991 and 1993, due largely to a shift in Malay fertility. That is, the average fertility decline from 1997 to 1999 is four times as large as the decline in the next most salient two-year interval.

Table 1. The Total Fertility Rate (TFR) by economy by year.

	1991	**1993**	**1995**	**1997**	**1999**
Hong Kong	1.2	1.2	1.2	1.2*	1.1
Indonesia	3.03	3.03	2.8	2.9	2.8
Japan	1.5	1.5	1.5	1.5	1.4
Malaysia	4.1	3.6	3.3	3.3	3.2
Philippines	4.1	4.1	4.1	4.1	3.7
Singapore	1.8	1.7	1.8	1.7	1.6
South Korea	1.6	1.6	1.6	1.7	1.6
Taiwan	1.7	1.6	1.8	1.8	1.4
Thailand	2.2	2.4	2.2	1.9	2.0

Source: World Population Data Sheets, 1991–1999. Washington, DC: Population Reference Bureau.

* Estimated. Hong Kong's changed administrative status—reversion to Mainland China—is responsible for gap in PRB data.

In Thailand, the fertility rates had declined fast in the two, two-year intervals that preceded the 1997–1999 interval (8.3 percent and 13.6 percent decline, respectively). One might surmise that such rates of decline could not reasonably be expected to persist. Moreover, an ex post facto search reveals a possible explanation for the unexpectedly early decline. The timing of the Thai fertility rate decline may possibly be explained as a serendipitous effect of the government's energetic efforts to head off an HIV/AIDS epidemic.

In the late 1980s, the Royal Thai Army recognized HIV/AIDS as an emerging epidemic among its "roughly 60,000 annual military conscripts, selected by lottery from 21-year-old Thai males." The rate increased steadily from 0.5 percent in 1989 to 3.7 percent in 1993, when it appeared to level off. Sero-surveillance of pregnant women showed similarly rising rates of infection, a pattern of rising incidence reminiscent of the early years of HIV/AIDS infection in the worst affected regions of sub-Saharan Africa.

In response to the 1989 alert, the Thai government made the control of HIV/AIDS infection a national priority. Education and warning ads aired through all types of media channels as well as the promotion of condom use in government-sponsored sexually transmitted disease (STD) clinics were in full swing by 1990. "The '100% condom program'enlisted the cooperation of sex establishment owners and sex

Table 2. Percentage change in Total Fertility Rate, by economy, in two-year intervals.

	1991–1993	1993–1995	1995–1997	1997–1999
Hong Kong	0.0	0.0	0.0	−8.3
Indonesia	0.0	−7.6	+3.6	−3.4
Japan	0.0	0.0	0.0	−6.7
Malaysia	−12.2	−8.3	0.0	−3.0
Philippines	0.0	0.0	0.0	−9.8
Singapore	−5.6	+5.9	−5.6	−5.9
South Korea	0.0	0.0	+6.3	−5.9
Taiwan	−5.9	+12.5	0.0	−22.2
Thailand	+9.1	−8.3	−13.6	+5.3
Average Decline	−1.6	−0.6	−1.0	−6.6

workers to encourage all clients to use condoms when obtaining sex. The government supplied almost 60 million free condoms a year to support this activity" (Phoolcharoen 1998).

Targeting the approximately 100,000 sex workers in Thailand began in 1991 after an initial, successful pilot project in Ratchaburi province (WHO Regional Office 2000). Thai men as well as foreigners are known to use brothels on a regular basis, so it seems probable that men fearing exposure to HIV would import condom use into their own homes. Responding to the national education campaign, wives may also have demanded the precaution. In addition, "life skills empowerment" was fostered among Thai youth, with the object of encouraging "safer sex behavior" (Phoolcharoen 1998, 1873).

It seems probable that the combination of widespread use of condoms in Thailand, and perhaps abstinence, resulted in the rapidly declining fertility rates observed in the 1991 through 1997 intervals. This additional factor, preceding and unrelated to the economic dislocation of 1997, could be seen to justify excluding Thailand from the analysis, as was done in several unpublished iterations .

Methods

If the fertility opportunity hypothesis is correct, the fertility rate for the Asian tigers should decline at a faster rate after the 1997 economic collapse than in previous years. To present a formal test of this hypothesis, the mean percentage changes in TFR for periods 1991–1993,

Table 3. The Total Fertility Rate (TFR) by country by year, Latin America*.

Central America	1991	1993	1995	1997	1999
Costa Rica	3.3	3.3	3.1	2.8	2.7
El Salvador	4.6	4.6	3.8	3.9	3.6
Guatemala	5.3	5.2	5.4	5.1	5.1
Honduras	5.3	5.6	5.2	5.2	4.4
Mexico	3.8	3.4	3.1	3.1	3.0
Nicaragua	5.5	4.8	4.6	4.6	3.9
Panama	3.0	2.9	3.0	2.8	2.7
Caribbean					
Cuba	1.9	1.8	1.8	1.5	1.6
Dominican Republic	3.6	3.3	3.3	3.2	3.2
Haiti	6.4	6.0	4.8	4.8	4.8
Jamaica	2.6	2.4	2.4	2.6	2.8
Puerto Rico	2.2	2.2	2.2	2.1	2.1
Trinidad and Tobago	2.4	2.4	2.7	2.0	1.7
South America					
Argentina	2.7	2.9	2.8	2.8	2.6
Bolivia	4.9	4.9	4.8	4.8	4.2
Brazil	3.3	2.6	2.9	2.5	2.3
Chile	2.7	2.6	2.5	2.4	2.4
Colombia	2.9	2.8	2.7	3.0	3.0
Ecuador	3.8	3.8	3.5	3.6	3.3
Paraguay	4.5	4.4	4.3	4.5	4.4
Peru	4.0	3.5	3.5	3.5	3.5
Uruguay	2.4	2.5	2.3	2.3	2.4
Venezuela	3.3	3.7	3.6	3.1	2.9

*Fourteen countries with population of less than one million each were excluded from the sample. These are Antigua and Barbuda, Bahamas, Barbados, Belize, Dominica, Grenada, Guadaloupe, Guyana, Martinique, The Netherland Antilles, St Kitts-Nevis, Saint Lucia, St. Vincent and the Grenadines, and Suriname.

Source: World Population Data Sheets, 1991–1999. Washington, DC: Population Reference Bureau.

Table 4. Percentage change in Total Fertility Rate, by country, in two-year intervals: Latin America.

	1991–1993	1993–1995	1995–1997	1997–1999
Central America				
Costa Rica	0.0	−6.1	−9.7	−3.6
El Salvador	0.0	−17.4	+2.6	−7.7
Guatemala	−1.9	+3.8	−5.6	0.0
Honduras	+5.7	−7.1	0.0	−15.4
Mexico	−10.5	−8.8	0.0	−3.2
Nicaragua	−12.7	−4.2	0.0	−15.2
Panama	−3.3	+3.4	−6.7	−3.6
Average Decline	−3.2	−5.2	−2.8	−7.0
Caribbean				
Cuba	−5.3	0.0	−16.7	+6.7
Dominican Republic	−8.3	0.0	−3.0	0.0
Haiti	−6.3	−20.0	0.0	0.0
Jamaica	−7.7	0.0	+8.3	+7.7
Puerto Rico	0.0	0.0	−4.5	0.0
Trinidad and Tobago	0.0	+12.5	−25.9	−15.0
Average Decline	−4.6	−1.3	−7.0	−0.1
South America				
Argentina	+7.4	−3.4	0.0	−7.1
Bolivia	0.0	−2.0	0.0	−12.5
Brazil	−21.2	+11.5	−13.8	−8.0
Chile	−3.7	−3.8	−4.0	0.0
Colombia	−3.4	−3.6	+11.1	0.0
Ecuador	0.0	−7.9	+2.9	−8.3
Paraguay	−2.2	−2.3	+4.7	−2.2
Peru	−12.5	0.0	0.0	0.0
Uruguay	+4.2	−8.0	0.0	+4.3
Venezuela	+12.1	−2.7	−13.9	−6.5
Average Decline	−1.9	−2.2	−1.3	−4.0
Average Decline (For Full Table)	−3.0	−4.0	−3.2	−3.9

1993–1995, and 1995–1997 are compared to the mean percentage change for period 1997–1999 for the sample of Asian tigers. For the three comparisons, the test is of the form.

Ho: $\mu a,i \leq \mu b$
Ha: $\mu a,i] \mu b$

where $\mu a,i$ is the mean of the period i population of percentage changes in TFR, with i = 1991–1993, 1993–1995, and 1995–1997; and μb is the mean of the period 1997–1999 population of percentage changes in TFR. The test is one-tail because we expect to see a greater decline in TFR percentage change in period 1997–1999. The comparison signs are in the direction shown because declines in the percentage change have a negative sign. If the null hypothesis is rejected we conclude that the population of percentage changes in TFR in period 1997–1999 has a lower mean than that in the previous period i, implying either a slower increase or a faster decline in TFR percentage change relative to the previous periods. Because we have the same sample of countries in all periods, the appropriate test for each comparison is a paired test. A t-test is performed in each case, but because the normality assumption for the percentage changes in TFRs may be too strong, the results of nonparametric sign tests were also considered.

For comparison purposes, three other groups of countries—Central America, Caribbean, and South America—which did not suffer the economic collapse that started in 1997 for the Asian tigers, are also included in the analysis, and the same tests are performed with their data. For these "comparison" groups of countries, we expect not to reject the null hypothesis, while for the Asian tigers we expect to reject it. Considering the small sample sizes in all cases, the power of the tests is low, and so the null hypothesis is never accepted.

The analysis with individual tests concentrates on the behavior of the percentage change in TFR for each group of countries separately. That is, we are able to make comparisons between period 1997–1999 and previous periods within groups of countries. Regression analysis provides a means to make cross-group comparisons. The objective is to try to determine for which group of countries the decrease in 1997–1999 TFR percentage change is greater. The main limitation of the two regression analyses used in this study lies in the classical OLS assumptions, which we do not challenge. (OLS refers to "ordinary least squares", as in a regression model.)

As a first attempt we model the TFR growth for the "average country" in each group of countries. To get the average country's TFR we average the TFR for all the countries in the group per year. We assume that between 1991 and 1997, the TFR for the average country in a group grows exponentially at an instantaneous constant rate r1 (in two-year intervals) but between 1997 and 1999 this growth rate changes to r2. That is, making t = 1, 2, 3, 4, and 5 for years 1991, 1993, 1995, 1997, and 1999, respectively, for average country i, the TFR grows according to

$TFR_{i,t} = TFR_{i,1} \exp(r_{i,1} t)$, for t = 1, 2, 3, and 4, and
$TFR_{i,t} = TFR_{i,4} \exp(r_{i,2} t)$, between t = 4 and 5,

which gives rise to the following econometric model

$Log(TFR_{i,t}) = \beta1 + \beta2\ Central_{i,t} + \beta3\ South_{i,t} + \beta4\ Tiger_{i,t} + (\beta5 + \beta6\ Central_{i,t} + \beta7\ South_{i,t} + \beta8\ Tiger_{i,t}) t + (\beta9 + \beta10\ Central_{i,t} + \beta11\ South_{i,t} + \beta12\ Tiger_{i,t}) Year99_{i,t} + \epsilon_{i,t}$

where Central, South, and Tiger are dummy variables for Central America, South America, and the Asian tigers, respectively; t is for the years, and Year99 is a dummy variable for year 1999. Rate r1 is calculated as $\beta5$ for the Caribbean, $\beta5 + \beta6$ for Central America, $\beta5 + \beta7$ for South America, and $\beta5 + \beta8$ for the Asian tigers. Rate r2 is calculated as $\beta5 + \beta9$ for the Caribbean, $\beta5 + \beta6 + \beta9 + \beta I10$ for Central America, $\beta5 + \beta7 + \beta9 + \beta11$ for South America, and $\beta5 + \beta8 + \beta9 + \beta12$ for the Asian tigers. For the Asian tigers' average country we expect the percentage change from r2 to r1 to be larger than that for the other groups' average countries, an expectation that was met.

A limitation of modeling the TFR for the "average country" of each group is that we completely ignore the variability of TFR values among the countries within the groups. Working with averages, our sample size becomes only twenty—four groups of countries and five years of data. To take country variability into account we use a different approach. Our second regression analysis models the TFR percentage change, TFRG—for TFR growth—for each country over the periods. We assume that, for each group of countries, the TFRG remains at a constant average value during periods 1991–1993, 1993–1995, and 1995–1997, but that it suddenly changes to in period 1997–1999. With data on TFRG for 32 countries and four periods we get 128 usable observations. Our second econometric model is:

$TFRG_{i,t} = \alpha1 + \alpha2\ Central_{i,t} + \alpha3\ South_{i,t} + \alpha4\ Tiger_{i,t} + (\alpha5 + \alpha6\ Central_{i,t} + \alpha7\ South_{i,t} + \alpha8\ Tiger_{i,t}) P9799_{i,t} + \epsilon_{i,t}$

where Central, South, and Tiger are dummy variables for Central America, South America, and the Asian tigers, respectively, and P9799 is a dummy variable for period 1997–1999. Subscript i is for the countries, and subscript t is for the periods. Rate rave,1, is calculated as $\alpha 1$ for the Caribbean, $\alpha 1 + \alpha 2$ for Central America, $\alpha 1 + \alpha 3$ for South America, and $\alpha 1 + \alpha 4$ for the Asian tigers. Rate rave $\alpha 2$ is calculated as $\alpha 1 + \alpha 5$ for the Caribbean, $\alpha 1 + \alpha 2 + \alpha 5 + \alpha 6$ for Central America, $\alpha 1 + \alpha 3 + \alpha 5 + \alpha 7$ for South America, and $\alpha 1 + \alpha 4 + \alpha 5 + \alpha 8$ for the Asian tigers.

Results

Comparison 1 corresponds to the test for period 1991–1993 with 1997–1999, comparison 2 corresponds to 1993–1995 with 1997–1999, and comparison 3 corresponds to 1995–1997 with 1997–1999. If the p-value is less than 0.05 we conclude that there has been a statistically significant decline in the percentage change in TFR when comparing the previous period with period 1997–1999. This happens in the first comparison for the Asian tigers only. The table also reports the tests for the Asian tigers excluding Thailand—which could be considered an outlier. Without Thailand, the null hypothesis is rejected for the Asian tigers in all three comparisons. For the non-Asian groups, the null hypothesis is never rejected. These results support the fertility opportunity hypothesis.

A special case among the groups of non-Asian, comparison countries is the Caribbean. Contrary to the other groups, the Caribbean's decline in TFR becomes apparently slower on average in the period 1997–1999 relative to the previous periods. For this group only, all the tests were performed to test if the percentage change in 1997–1999 is slower rather than faster for the previous periods. The results show that statistically the percentage change in TFRs in all the periods is more or less similar.

Results for the sign tests are as follows. Comparison 1 corresponds to the test for period 1991–1993 with 1997–1999, comparison 2 corresponds to 1993–1995 with 1997–1999, and comparison 3 corresponds to 1995–1997 with 1997–1999. With the sign test, the test statistic produced follows a binomial distribution. The numbers in the table are the tests statistics and they show the number of times the percentage change in the previous period was greater than the percentage change for 1997–1999. For each group, the 90 percent confidence interval is reported, and if the test statistic falls outside this interval we reject the null hypothesis. For the Asian tigers only, we reject the null hypothesis in comparisons 1 and 3. The null hypothesis is rejected in all instances when Thailand is excluded from the group. Therefore, we conclude that the rate of decline in 1997–1999 TFR is statistically significantly higher only for the Asian tigers, supporting the fertility opportunity hypothesis.

Regression models show all p-values at less than 0.05. These results are used to produce estimated r1 and r2 values. One sees that during years 1991, 1993, 1995, and 1997, the average country's two-year TFR rate of decline is 5.42 percent for the Caribbean, 3.94 percent for Central America, 2.03 percent for South America, and 1.88 percent for the Asian tigers. From 1997 to 1999, these rates of decline became greater for all groups except the Caribbean. For this last period, the average country's two-year TFR declines at a rate that is greater by 3.55 percent for Central America, 2.35 percent for South America, and 4.32 percent for the Asian Tigers. For the Caribbean, this rate of decline becomes smaller by 5.13 percent. We notice that the decline from r1 to r2 is the greatest for the Asian tigers, representing an over 200 percent change, compared to lower than 120 percent changes for Central and South America. Excluding Thailand from the group of Asian tigers simply strengthens our results.

Results for a second regression model show that p-values for the country-group dummy variables are in no case less than 0.05. This indicates that—the average percentage change in TFR for the periods before 1997–1999—is roughly the same across the four groups of countries. Looking at the coefficients for Central*P9799 and South*P9799, and considering that the coefficient for P*9799 is not significant, we notice that—the average percentage change in TFR for period 1997–1999—for Central American countries appears to be 7.38 percent lower on average than for the Caribbean; for South American countries, it appears to be 6.59 percent lower on average than the Caribbean. However, in these two cases the p-values indicate that those differences are not statistically significant.

The case is different for the Asian tigers. For this group of countries, the percentage change in TFR is on average statistically significantly lower, that is, 9.72 percent lower than for the Caribbean. That is, the results of our second regression model imply that in period 1997–1999, the Asian tigers experienced on average the fastest decline in TFR among all the groups of countries considered. As with our first regression model, the exclusion of Thailand from the Asian tigers group just strengthens the conclusions.

Implications of the two regression analyses complement the conclusion drawn from the previous independent test analyses, that the Asian tigers were the only group of countries that showed an average faster decline in TFR in period 1997–1999 relative to the previous periods analyzed. Although these results supporting the fertility opportunity hypothesis are suggestive, an appropriate follow-up would include in-depth studies of individual countries and within-country sectors. Other factors that could be driving our findings should be ruled out before generalizing our conclusions.

Limitations

The main methodological limitation of this study lies in the implicit assumption that we make that the group of Asian tigers and the chosen comparison groups are essentially similar, and that the only difference is on the former suffering an important economic collapse. There are known techniques that we could use to classify the countries before testing, but the main problem is to come up with the best variables or characteristics we could comfortably use to decide if a country is similar enough to another. We could also make our regression models more complicated by adding variables that control for inherent country differences—income level, education level, political, economic, financial, and currency stability, for example—but then we would need to decide on the way these variables would enter the model.

Another limitation is that our approach is not direct. It assumes that the fact that a country suffers economic hardship implies that its citizens have a net negative perception about their future. That is, we are not using a direct measure of citizens' confidence about what their future would be. A more direct approach to measuring effects on the fertility rate would use an independent indicator of citizens' perceptions. We would still need to control for inherent differences among countries.

Despite its limitations, this study serves its purpose of presenting preliminary evidence in support of the fertility opportunity hypothesis. A more definitive answer would have to address the limitations mentioned. (Note: This version of the article abbreviates the Methods section, with apologies to co-author Roberto Penaloza. V.A.)

Discussion

The Asian tiger data and comparison with regions unaffected by an extraordinary economic shift add to the picture of fertility responding to economic opportunity. The predicted and observed rapid fertility decline in eight of the nine Asian countries is congruent with the expectation that couples and individuals who perceive a contraction in economic opportunity will lower family-size targets and, indeed, have fewer births. If the stimulus is exogenous to natural demographic cycles (such as change in the size of cohorts entering the labor market), the response can be rapid.

This is a first attempt at quantification in any test of the fertility opportunity hypothesis. Many refinements are possible, especially those responsive to the limitations noted above, and should be encouraged.

In addition, one variant might include separate tests for subsets of populations where distinct patterns of declining (or rising) fertility might be expected. The model is Malaysia before 1990. A thumbnail sketch begins in 1957, with Malaysia gaining independence from Great Britain. Subsequently, the majority Malaysian population voted themselves numerous educational and employment opportunities, benefits available only to them and progressively discriminating against the country's Chinese and Indian minorities.

Malaysia's affirmative action policies that favored the majority created conditions that apparently delayed fertility decline among the favored 60 percent of the population. The Malay fertility rate (which in 1957 was about five children per woman—the lowest among Malaysia's three main ethnic groups) declined little after independence and by 1987 was significantly higher than that of other ethnic groups (Govindasamy and DaVanzo 1992.) Thus, educational opportunity and improved health care and survival rates among Malays became well established without having, for decades, a discernible effect in lowering their fertility rate.

After 1957, the newly disadvantaged Chinese and Indian sectors experienced not only economic and cultural discrimination but also sharply declining fertility rates. Chinese fertility declined from seven births per woman before independence to two and a half in 1987. Indian fertility declined from approximately eight to three births per woman in the same period (Govindasamy and DaVanzo 1992).

The fertility opportunity hypothesis explains both effects. Fertility remained high among Malays, who for thirty years enjoyed unprecedented opportunity and prosperity. In the same period, the economic woes experienced by Malaysia's Chinese and Indian populations could account for the rapid decline in their fertility rates.

140

Inevitably, the Malay's relative share of the population increased rapidly, to about 60 percent in the 1980s. By 1990, competition within the large cohort of young Malays just entering the labor market meant that, despite their politically guaranteed, preferential access, opportunities were significantly diminished in comparison with expectations (Abernethy 1998, and see Macunovich 1996, 1999). This relatively sudden competitive shock may explain the decline in the Malay TFR from 4.1 to 3.6 during the 1991–1993 interval.

The period of depressed oil prices (from about 1994 through 1999) suggest a further opportunity to test the fertility opportunity hypothesis. Mid-Eastern oil-producing countries, although modernized in terms of education, urbanization, and health care, have had persistently high fertility rates. Some attribute the high rates to the still-limited public role for women. It also may be that fertility remained high because families bore few of the costs of raising children: government health care, education, and housing programs and subsidies for infrastructure were generous, not to say lavish. The decline in oil revenues forced governments to scale back on benefits to which citizens had become accustomed. The hypothesis predicts that citizens would hesitate to assume the burden of an additional child under the newly more difficult circumstances.

Other opportunities for testing will inevitably present themselves over time, perhaps with renewed attention to the other arm of the fertility opportunity hypothesis, namely, that a sense of expanding opportunity—all else equal—causes an increase in fertility.

The literature suggests that a sense of rapidly expanding opportunity, especially if it is unrelated to individual effort or an ethic of saving in order to further improve one's standard of living, runs the risk of stimulating fertility. Perceived windfalls of opportunity from either political or economic sources have, in the past, preceded baby booms (Abernethy 1979, 1999 [1993], 1994; Diaz-Briquet and Perez 1981; Easterlin 1962; Lee 1980, 1987).

One situation that might be watched is the unfolding policy of land redistribution in Zimbabwe. By August 2000, over 3,000 commercial farms had been promised to landless veterans, or taken over by squatters (Zimbabwe 2000). The redistributed plots of land, though individually small, will probably be perceived as wealth, and certainly as windfalls, by recipients. Formerly landless families, assessing their good fortune, are likely to raise their preferred family size. Unless other factors such as civil war or an epidemic intervene, Zimbabwe has the earmarks of a baby boom in the making.

Conclusion

Understanding conditions that alter the fertility rate is clearly important. World population will stabilize when the rate of child survival is two per woman, and this rate has been maintained for two–three generations. Population would stabilize sooner if women averaged fewer than two surviving children. High premature mortality is an undesirable mechanism for stabilizing population, whereas low fertility not only stabilizes population size but also helps protect the health of the mother and children.

Despite unique histories and within-country variation, eight of nine former Asian tiger countries' fertility declines support fertility opportunity hypothesis predictions. The sharp decline in fertility rates in the interval between 1997 and 1999, compared to declines within other intervals, strongly suggests that families adapted to contracting economic opportunity by trying to minimize additional child-raising obligations. The average decline in the fertility rate of the nine Asian tiger countries studied was 6.6 percent in the 1997–1999 interval, compared to an average decline of 1.6 percent in the next most changed interval.

Hypothesis testing in other countries and regions is needed. Part of the strength of the present study is that it apparently confirms a prediction. Nevertheless, not all tests can be prospective. Historical studies have many advantages. They lend themselves to careful specification as well as finer selection of control countries. Comparisons among specifiable, distinctly different sectors within countries, such as within Malaysia, are also likely to be rewarding.

The sensitivity of the linkage between economic or political opportunity and fertility rates should be confirmed or refined through further historical and prospective studies. The present findings may be sufficient to suggest, however, that domestic and international interventions into a nation's economy may alter demographic outcomes in hitherto unexpected ways.

References

Abernethy, Virginia Deane 1979. *Population Pressure and Cultural Adjustment.* New York: Human Sciences Press.

Abernethy, Virginia Deane 1993. *Populations Politics.* New Brunswick, NJ: Transactions Publishers.

Abernethy, Virginia Deane 1993. *Population Politics: The Choices that Shape Our Future.* New York: Plenum Press/Insight Books. Reprinted by Transaction Publishers 1990.

Abernethy, Virginia Deane. 1994. "Optimism and Overpopulation." *The Atlantic Monthly*, December, 84–91.

Abernethy, Virginia Deane March 1997. "The Fickle Finger of Fate: Hungary and Austria." *Population and Environment* 18 (4): 333–8.

Abernethy, Virginia Deane. 1998. Why Asian Population Growth Is Winding Down. *Chronicles*, October, 46–47.

Abernethy, Virginia Deane. 1999 [1993]. *Population Politics. Reprinted with New Foreword*. New Brunswick, NJ: Transaction Publications.

Abernethy, Virginia Deane 2000. "Population Dynamics: Why We can Sit Back and Watch Fertility Fall." Population Problems: Topical Issues. Canada.

Abernethy, V. 2002. "Why Asian Population Growth Is Winding Down." *Chronicles*.

Abernethy, Virginia Deane, and Penaloza, Roberto V. 2002. "Fertility Decline in Former Asian Tigers." *Population and Environment* 23 (3): 245–66.

Becker, G.S. 1960. "An Economic Analysis of Fertility." In *Demographic and Economic Change in Developed Countries*, edited by National Bureau of Economic Research, 209–31. Princeton, NJ: Princeton University Press.

Becker, Gary, and H. Gregg Lewis. 1974. "Interaction between Quantity and Quality of Children." In *Economics of the Family: Marriage, Children and Human Capital*, edited by T. W. Schultz, 81–90. NBER Conference Report. Chicago, IL: University of Chicago Press.

Bernhardt, Annette, Martina Morris, Mark S. Handcock, and Marc A. Scott. 2002. *Divergent Paths: Economic Mobility in the New American Labor Market*. New York: Russell Sage Foundation.

Berry, B. J. L. June 1996. "From Malthusian Frontier to Demographic Steady State in Concord, 1635–1993." *Population and Development Review* 22 (2): 207–30.

Berry, Brian J. L. 1996. "From Malthusian Frontier to Demographic Steady State in Concord, 1635–1993." *Population and Development Review* 22 (2): 207–30.

Blumenthal, R. G. 1996. "Midlife Brooding: Some Parents Find Third Time a Charm." *Wall Street Journal*, 1, March 29, 1996.

Bongaarts, J. 1994. "Population Policy Options in the Developing World." *Science* 263:771–6.

Bonner, William. January 27, 2000. The High Priestess Speaks. Daily Reckoning, on-line @agora-inc.com

Borjas, G., R. Freeman, and L. Katz. 1996. "Searching for the Labor Market Effects of Immigration." *American Economic Review* 86:246–51.

Bouvier, L. 1995. "More African Famines in the Future?" *Clearing House Bulletin* 5 (2): 1–3.

Brittain, A. W. 1990. "Migration and the Demographic Transition: A West Indian Example." *Social and Economic Studies* 39 (3): 39–64.

Brittain, Anne W. 1991. "Anticipated Child Loss to Migration and Sustained High Fertility in an East Caribbean Population." *Social Biology* 38 (1–2): 94–112;

Caldwell, John C., I.O. Orubuloye, and P. Caldwell. 1992. "Fertility Decline in Africa: A New Type of Transition?" *Population and Development Review* 18 (2): 211–43.

Coale, A., and S. Watkins, eds. 1986. *The Decline of Fertility in Europe*. Princeton, NJ: Princeton University Press.

Connell, K. H. 1968. *The Population of Ireland, 1750–1845*. Oxford: Clarendon Press.

Conrad, C., M. Lechner, and W. Werner. June 1996. "East German fertility after Unification: Crisis or Adaptation?" *Population and Development Review* 22 (2): 331–58.

Conrad, Cristoph, M. Lechner, and Welf Werner. 1996. "East German Fertility after Unification: Crisis or Adaptation?" *Population and Development Review* 22 (2): 331–58.

Courbage, Y. 1995. "Fertility Transition in the Mashriq and Maghrib" In *Family, Gender, and Population in the Middle East*, edited by Carla M. Obermeyer). Cairo: The American University in Cairo Press.

Courbage, Youssef. 1995. "Fertility Transition in the Mashriq and Maghrib." In *Family, Gender and Population in the Middle East*, edited by Carla M. Obermeyer. Cairo: The American University in Cairo Press.

Crossette, Barbara. 2002. "Population Estimates Fall as Poor Women Assert Control." *New York Times*, 3.

Davis, K. 1963. "The Theory of Change and Response in the Modern Demographic History." *Population Index* 29 (4): 345–65.

Davis, Kingsley. 1945. "The World Demographic Transition." *Annals of the American Academy of Political and Social Science* 237:11–18.

Davis, Kingsley. 1963. "The Theory of Change and Response in the Modern Demographic History." *Population Index* 29 (4): 345–65.

Diaz-Briquets, S. and L. Perez. 1981. *Cuba: The Demography of Revolution*. Washington, D.C: Population Reference Bureau.

Diaz-Briquets, S. and L. Pérez. 1981. *Cuba: The Demography of Revolution*. Washington, DC: Population Reference Bureau.

Dyson, T. 1991b. "On the Demography of South Asian Famines. Part II." *Population Studies* 45:279–97.

Dyson, Tim. 1991a. "On the Demography of South Asian Famines. Part I." *Population Studies* 45:5–25.

Dyson, Tim. 1991b. "On the Demography of South Asian Famines. Part II." *Population Studies* 45:279–97.

Dyson, Timothy. 1991a. "On the Demography of South Asian Famines. Part I." *Population Studies* 45:5–25.

Easterlin, R. 1962. "*The American Baby Boom in Historical perspective*" Occasional Paper #79. New York: National Bureau of Economic Research.

Easterlin, R. 1971. "Does Human Fertility Adjust to the Environment?" *American Economic Review* 61 (2): 399–407.

Easterlin, R. 1976. "Population change and farm settlement in the Northern United States." *Journal of Economic History* 36:45–75.

Easterlin, Richard. 1962. *The American Baby Boom in Historical Perspective*. Occasional Paper #79. New York: National Bureau of Economic Research.

Easterlin, Richard. 1971. "Does Human Fertility Adjust to the Environment?" *American Economic Review* 61 (2): 399–407.

Easterlin, Richard. 1976. "Population Change and Farm Settlement in the Northern United States." *Journal of Economic History* 36:45–75.

Eberstadt, N. March 1994. "Demographic Shocks after Communism: Eastern Germany 1989–93." *Population and Development Review* 20 (1): 137–52.

Fargues, P. 1995. "Changing Hierarchies of Gender and Generation in the Arab World" In *Family, Gender, and Population in the Middle East*, edited by C. M. Obermeyer, 80–104. Cairo: The American University in Cairo Press, Cairo.

Fargues, P. 1997. "State Policies and the Birth Rate in Egypt: From Socialism to Liberalism." *Population and Development Review* 23 (1): 115–38.

Fargues, Philippe. 1995. "Changing Hierarchies of Gender and Generation in the Arab World." In *Family, Gender and Population in the Middle East*, edited by Carla Maklouf Obermeyer. Cairo: The American University in Cairo Press.

Fargues, Philippe. 1997. "State Policies and the Birth Rate in Egypt: From Socialism to Liberalism." *Population and Development Review* 23 (1): 115–38.

Ferrando and Ponce. 1983. cited in Montenegro, Alberto Varillas & de Muente, Patricia Mopstajo. 1990. *La situación poplacional Peruviana: Balance y perspectivas.* Lima, Peru: Instituto Andino de Estudios en Población y Desarrollo (INANDEP).

Ferrando, Delicia, and Aramburu, Carlos. 1996. "The Fertility Transition in Peru." In *The Fertility Transition in Latin America*, edited by Jose Miguel Guzman, S. Singh, G. Rodriguez, E. A. Pantelides. Oxford: Clarendon Press.

Francis, David R. 2002. "New Global Forecast: Population Decline in Sight." *Christian Science Monitor*, from World, Global Issues online.

Freeman, Milton R. 1971. "A Social and Ecological Analysis of Systematic Female Infanticide Among the Netsilik Eskimo." *American Anthropologist* 73:1011–18.

Golnaraghi, M., and R. Kaul. 1995. *Environment* 37 (1): 17–44.

Govindasamy, P., and J. DaVanzo. 1992. "Policy Impact on Fertility Differentials in Peninsular Malaysia." *Population and Development Review* 18 (2): 243–67.

Guengant, J. -P. 1985. *Population and Development in the Caribbean: A Demographic Survey.* New York: Inter-American Parliamentary Group on Population and Development.

Haub, C. 1994. "Population Change in the Former Soviet Republics." *Population Bulletin* 49 (4). Washington DC: Population Reference Bureau.

Jenness, Diamond. 1968. *Eskimo Administration: V. Analysis and Reflections*, 40. Technical Paper #21. Arlington, VA: Institute of North America.

Kahn, Joseph, and Tim Weiner. 2002. "World Leaders to Discuss Strategy for Aid to Poor." *New York Times*, March 18.

Kalipeni, Ezekel. 1996. "Demographic Response to Environmental Pressure in Malawi." *Population and Environment* 17 (4): 285–308.

Keyfitz, N. 1993. "Thirty Years of Demography." *Demography* 30:533–49.

Landale, N. S., and S. M. Hauan. November 1996. "Migration and Premarital Childbearing among Puerto Rican Women." *Demography* 33:429–42.

Lee, R. D. 1980. "A Historical Perspective on Economic Aspects of the Population Explosion: The Case of a Pre-Industrial England." In *Population and Economic Change in Developing Countries*, edited by Richard A. Easterlin, 517–56. Chicago, IL: University of Chicago Press.

Lee, R. D. 1980. "A Historical Perspective on Economic Aspects of the Population Explosion: The Case of Pre-Industrial England" In *Population and Economic Change in Developing Countries*, edited by R. E. Easterlin, 517–56. Chicago, IL: University of Chicago Press, Chicago.

Lee, R. D. November 1987. "Population Dynamics of Humans and Other Animals." *Demography* 24 (4): 443–65.

Lee, Ronald D. 1980. "A Historical Perspective on Economic Aspects of the Population Explosion: The Case of Pre-Industrial England." In *Population and Economic Change in Developing Countries*, edited by R.E. Easterlin, 517–56. Chicago, IL: University of Chicago Press.

Lee, Ronald D. 1987. "Population Dynamics of Humans and Other Animals." *Demography* 24 (4): 443–65.

Macunovich, D. J., and R. A. Easterlin. 1990. "How Parents Have Coped: The Effect of Life-Cycle Demographic Decisions on the Economic Status of Preschool Children." *Population and Development Review* 16 (2): 301–25.

Macunovich, Diane J. 1996. "A Review of Recent Developments in the Economics of Fertility." In *Household and Family Economics*, edited by Paul Menchik, 91–150. Boston, MA: Kluwer Academic Publishers.

Macunovich, Diane J. 1999. "The Role of Cohort Size and Relative Income in the Demographic Transition." *Population and Environment* 21 (2): 155–92.

May, John F. 1995. "Policies on Population, Land Use, and Environment in Rwanda." *Population and Environment* 16 (4): 321–34.

Moffet, George D. 1994. *Critical Masses*. New York: Viking.

Montenegro, A. V., and P. M. de Muente. 1990. *La Situación Poplacional Pervana: Balance y Perspectivas*. Lima, Peru: Instituto Andino de Estudios en Población y Desarrollo, INANDEP.

Montenegro, Alberto Varillas, and Patricia Mopstajao de Meunte. *La situación poplacional Peruviana: Balance y perspectivas*. Lima, Peru: Instituto Andino de Estudios en Población y Desarrollo (INANDEP).

Much, Marilyn. September 29, 1999. "Japan's New Labor Scene Creates Opportunities." *Investors' Business Daily*, A10.

Nag, Moni. 1968. *Factors Affecting Human Fertility in Nonindustrial Societies: A Cross Cultural Study*. New Haven, CN: Human Relations Area Files.

Notestein, F. 1945. Population: The Long View. In *Food for Thought*, edited by T.W. Schultz, Norman Wait Harris Memorial Lectures.

Pauly, D., and L. Tsukayama, eds. 1987. *The Peruvian Anchoveta and Its Upwelling Ecosystem: Three Decades of Change*. Manila: International Center for Living Aquatic Resources Management Studies and Reviews.

"Peruvian Austerity Program Brings State of Emergency." *Nashville Banner*, A5, August 10, 1990.

Phoolcharoen, Wiput. June 19, 1998. "HIV/AIDS Prevention in Thailand: Success and Challenges." *Science* 280:1873–4.

Population Reference Bureau, 1980 through 1995, Population Data Sheets (Washington, DC).

Poverty Lobby II. 2002. *Investors' Business Daily*, 18.

Pritchett, Lant A. 1994. "Desired Fertility and the Impact of Population Policies." *Population and Development Review* 20 (1): 1–55.

Riches, David. 1974. "The Netsilik Eskimo: A Special Case of Selective Female Infanticide." *Ethnology* 13 (4): 351–62.

Rivera, M. N., and T. J. Espenshade. 1995. "Peru's Coming Baby Boomlet." *Population and Environment* 16 (5): 399–414.

Roberts, Paul Craig. 2002. "Abolishing America: The Economic Eviction of White Men." VDARE, online.

Rogers, James. 1999. "The Pitiful, Helpless Giant." *Real Asset Investor*, October, 2–3.

Social Security and the Future of U.S. Fertility. 1997. "Documents." *Population and Development Review* 23 (1): 208–13.

Social Security and the Future of U.S. Fertility, Excerpted Documents. *Population and Development Review* 23 (1): 208–13 (1997).

Statistics. 1994. Supplement 44 (11), Tables 10 & 11 (pp. 41–42). National Center for Health Statistics, Division of Vital Statistics.

"The Dark Side of the Boom." *The Economist*, 21–23, August 5, 1995.

Thompson, Warren S. 1929. "Population." *American Sociological Review* 34(6): 959–75.

Thurow, L. 1993. Address (Annual Meetings of the American Association for the Advancement of Science, Boston, MA, February 12, 1993).

Trinidad. *The Economist*, 30–31, August 4, 1990.

Ventura, Stephanie, Joyce A. Martin, T. J. Mathews, Sally C Clarke. 1996. Advance Report of Final Natality.

"Wealthy Chinese Men Skirt One-Child Family Rules." *New York Times*, August 17, 1997.

World Population Data Sheet. 1997. Population Reference Bureau, Washington, DC.

World Population Data Sheet. 2001. Population Reference Bureau, Washington, DC.

Zachary, G. Paschal. 1998. "Unconventional Academic Sounds Population Alarm." *Wall Street Journal*, B1, 2.

Zimbabwe: More Farm Takeovers. August 19, 2000. *New York Times*, 4.

5

The Unintended Consequences of Redistributed Wealth

Introduction

The second half of the twentieth century was unique in the quantity of aid flowing internationally. Prosperous industrial countries saw it as their responsibility to lift third world countries out of poverty, illiteracy, and premature mortality. Explosive population growth was identified as one cause of third world misery. Increasingly after World War II, aid was justified as a contribution toward lowering the fertility rate (births per woman) and thus halting population growth. Unfortunately, interventionists relied on the wrong model.

During the 1930s, demographers compared industrialized and third world countries and drew conclusions that morphed into a cause-and-effect model that guided development aid. Known as the demographic transition (DT) model, the idea was to make poor people in the third world more like the average person in industrialized societies. Demographers asserted, and both the public and policymakers believed, that making poor people prosperous, literate, and healthier as well as lowering the child mortality rate would lower the fertility rate.

For good reason, certain more analytically minded demographers soon became skeptical of the DT model. However, it retained its appeal to the international aid industry for a very long time. Typical is a 1994 statement by Shaukut Hassan: "Population growth is an effect of underdevelopment arising from the conflict between the demand for social security and the skewed development process. Such a conflict can be resolved only be economic growth and social development" (Hassan 1994).

Sophisticated language, but are the asserted cause-and-effect relationships real? Do declining child mortality, higher literacy rates for men and women, and greater economic opportunity promote lower fertility rates? Articles in this chapter critique the model that has guided much international aid over the previous six or more decades. Data suggest that interventions inspired by the DT model are useless at best, counterproductive, at worst.

Fertility rates have fallen almost worldwide. But improving child survival rates, access to education, and greater economic opportunity do not appear to be the relevant causal factors. On the contrary, widespread perception of *contracting* economic opportunity, of more women needing as well as choosing to work in the paid labor force, and of poorer health outcomes for children appear to drive the decline in fertility rates. That relationship is worldwide, in industrialized and developing countries alike. And, it is congruent with historical data.

The first article in this section was published in the Atlantic. Facts are declared without reference, but be assured that factual statements can be documented; months-long grilling by Atlantic "fact-checkers" is an author's nightmare. More documentation is in my books *Population Pressure* (1979, 2005) and *Population Politics* (1993, 2000) and throughout this volume. Interpretations, of course, are mine.

Optimism and Overpopulation*

Well, yes, the West must pay attention to the population problems of the third world. But what sort of attention? The conventional wisdom holds that economic development—and thus economic aid from the West—is the key to curbing population growth in poor nations. Not true, says the author [Ed. *Atlantic*].

Overpopulation afflicts most countries but remains primarily a local problem—an idea that this article will seek to explain. Reproductive restraint, the solution, is also primarily local; it grows out of a sense that resources are shrinking. Under these circumstances individuals and couples often see limitation of family size as the most likely path to success.

Many scholars, ancient and modern, have known that actual family size is very closely linked to the number of children people want. Paul Demeny, of The Population Council, is exceptionally clear on this, and World Bank economist Lant Pritchett asserts that 85–95 percent of actual fertility rates are explained by parents' desires—not by mere

---

*In *The Atlantic Monthly*, pp. 84–91 [December, 1994].

availability of contraceptives. Pritchett writes that "the impressive declines in fertility observed in the contemporary world are due almost entirely to equally impressive declines in desired fertility." Of Paul Kennedy's contention, in his book *Preparing for the Twenty-First Century,* that "the only practical way to ensure a decrease in fertility rates, and thus in population growth, is to introduce cheap and reliable forms of birth control," Pritchett says, "We could not have invented a clearer and more articulate statement of the view we argue is wrong." (Pritchett 1994)

Progress and Population

Cross-cultural and historical data suggest that people have usually limited their families to a size consistent with living comfortably in stable communities. If left undisturbed, traditional societies survive over long periods in balance with local resources. A society lasts in part because it maintains itself within the carrying capacity of its environment.

However, the perception of limits that derive from the local environment is easily neutralized by signals that promise prosperity. Quoting the late Georg Borgstrom, a renowned food scientist and a much-decorated specialist in third world economies, a 1971 Population Reference Bureau publication explains, "A number of civilizations, including India and Indonesia, 'had a clear picture of the limitations of their villages or communities' before foreign intervention disrupted the traditional patterns. Technical aid programs 'made them believe that the adoption of certain technical advances [was] going to free them of this bondage and of dependence on such restrictions'" (Population Reference Bureau 1991).

Economic expansion, especially if it is introduced from outside the society and is also broad-based, encourages the belief that formerly recognized limits can be discounted, that everyone can look forward to prosperity and, as in recent instances, that the West can be counted upon to provide assistance, rescue, and an escape valve for excess population.

The perception of new opportunity, whether due to technological advance, expanded trade, political change, foreign aid, moving to a richer land, or the disappearance of competitors (who move away or die), encourages larger family size. Families eagerly fill any apparently larger niche, and the extra births and consequent population growth often overshoot actual opportunity.

Increase beyond a sustainable number is an ever-present threat, because human beings take their cue from the opportunity that is apparent today and are easily fooled by change. Relying on what is near in space or time, we calculate with difficulty the long-term momentum of population growth, the limits to future technological advance, and the inexorable progression of resource depletion.

The appearance (and short-term reality) of expanding opportunity takes various guises. In the 1950s, land redistribution in Turkey led formerly landless peasants to increase significantly the size of their families. Among African Sahel pastoralists, deep-water wells drilled by donor countries in the 1950s and 1960s prompted larger herds of cattle and goats, earlier marriage (because bride-prices are paid in animals and the required number became easier to accumulate), and higher fertility. Similarly, Ireland's widespread cultivation of the potato in the early eighteenth century increased agricultural productivity and encouraged peasants to subdivide portions of their farms into plots for their sons, which in turn promoted younger marriage and a baby boom. Still earlier, between the sixth and ninth centuries, the introduction in Europe of the stirrup, the rigid-collar harness, and nailed horseshoes greatly enhanced the agricultural output of Europe's northern plains. Better nutrition helped lead Europe out of the Dark Ages to economic recovery and thence, from about 1050 to 1350, to a tripling of population size in countries such as England and France.

India offers another example. Its population was nearly stable from 400 BC to about AD 1600. After the end of the Mogul invasions, and with the advent of new trade opportunities, the population began to grow (at about half the European rate). Later, European trade offered India further opportunity, and population growth accelerated. It took off for the skies shortly after the country shed its colonial status in 1947; assistance from the USSR, the World Bank, and the International Monetary Fund bolstered perceptions of a prosperous future, and the rate of population growth accelerated until approximately 1980.

Successful independence movements and populist coups are prominent among the kinds of changes that carry the message that times are good and getting better. China commenced its euphoric interlude with the expulsion of the Nationalists, in 1949. Communism triumphed, and its philosophy held that a greater nation required more people. The fertility rate and population size rocketed upward. A Mainland China population that was estimated to be 559 million in 1949 grew to 654 million by 1959, whereas in the preceding 100 years of political turmoil and war the average growth rate of the Chinese population had been just 0.3 percent a year. Both lower mortality and higher fertility contributed to the increase.

Judith Banister (1987) writes in *China's Changing Population*, "Fertility began rising in the late 1940s, and was near or above 6 births per woman during the years 1952–57, higher fertility than had been customary" in prior decades. Banister attributes China's baby boom to war's end and to government policy: "Land reform of 1950–51 redistributed land to landless peasants and tenant farmers."

Cuba experienced a baby boom when Fidel Castro displaced Fulgencio Batista, in 1959. Castro explicitly promised a redistribution of wealth and, according to the demographers S. Diaz-Briquets and L. Perez, fertility rose in response. Diaz-Briquets and Perez write, "The main factor was the real income rise among the most disadvantaged groups brought about by the redistribution measures of the revolutionary government. The fertility rises in almost every age group suggest that couples viewed the future as more promising and felt they could now afford more children" (Díaz-Briquets and Pérez 1981).

The populations of Algeria, Zimbabwe, and Rwanda grew rapidly around the time colonial powers left. Algeria, for example, achieved independence in 1962, and thirty years later 70 percent of its population was under thirty years of age. Zimbabwe gained independence in 1980, and soon achieved one of the highest population-growth rates in the world; the growth was encouraged by the health minister, who attacked family planning as a "white colonialist plot" to limit black power.

Because of their effect on family size, development programs entailing large transfers of technology and funds to the third world have been especially pernicious. This kind of aid is inappropriate because it sends the signal that wealth and opportunity can grow without effort and without limit. That rapid population growth ensues should surprise no one. Africa, which in recent decades has received three times as much foreign aid per capita as any other continent, now also has the highest fertility rates. During the 1950s and 1960s the African fertility rate rose—to almost seven children per woman—at the same time that infant mortality was dramatically reduced, health care availability grew, literacy for women and men became more widespread, and economic optimism pervaded more and more sectors of society. Extraordinarily high rates of population growth were new to Africa; during the 1950s the Latin American rate had been higher.

Even migration can affect total world population. Studies of nine-teenth-century England and Wales and modem Caribbean societies show that in communities already in the throes of rapid population growth, fertility stays high as long as the option to emigrate exists, whereas fertility falls rapidly in communities that lack such an escape valve. And while fertility rates are falling in most African countries, the rate remains high in Ghana (6.2 births per woman in 1993), perhaps because an established pattern of emigration (1 per 1,000 in the population) provides a safety valve for excess numbers. This effect on fertility is consistent with independent reports that emigration raises incomes both among emigrants and among those they leave behind.

In sum, it is true, if awkward, that efforts to alleviate poverty often spur population growth, as does leaving open the door to immigration. Subsidies, windfalls, and the prospect of economic opportunity remove the immediacy of needing to conserve. The mantras of democracy, redistribution, and economic development raise expectations and fertility rates, fostering population growth and thereby steepening a downward environmental and economic spiral.

Despite this sequence, certain experts and the public they inform wish to believe that fertility rates have traditionally been high worldwide and have declined only in industrialized countries or in countries where modern contraception is available; further, that the post–Second World War population explosion is explained mostly by better health and nutrition which led to rapidly declining mortality rates. The possibility that larger family size resulted from wanting more children—voluntary increases in fertility—continues to be denied.

Experts in population studies were the first to be fooled. In the 1930s many demographers predicted a steady decline in population because the low fertility of Western industrialized countries was attributed to development and modernization, rather than to the endemic pessimism brought on by the Great Depression. Still missing the point, many failed to see that the high fertility after the Second World War was a response to the perception of expanding economic opportunity. The US baby boom (1947–1961) and the slightly later booms in Western Europe took most demographers by surprise.

The Message of Scarcity

As it happens, encounters with scarcity that are currently being forced upon literally billions of people by the natural limits of their environment

154

are beginning to correct the consequences of decades of misperception. The rhetoric of modernization, international development, and egalitarianism is losing its power to mislead. As Europe is revealed to be incapable of alleviating the suffering of the former Yugoslavia, as rich countries in general prove nearly powerless to help the countless distant multitudes, it becomes difficult to believe in rescue. Now, as it has done many times in human history, the rediscovery of limits is awakening the motivation to limit family size.

In Ireland, land became scarce relative to the rapidly growing population in the early nineteenth century, whereupon fertility began a retreat to its low, prepotato farming level. By 1830, about two-thirds of women married before age twenty-five. Ten percent married this young in 1851—a drastic postponement of marriage in response to the 1846–1851 potato famine. Following a brief recovery, as few as 12 percent married before age twenty-five. The pattern of late marriage persisted from about 1890 through the Second World War.

In the United States, the baby boom ended at about the time the job pipeline began to fill (1962); the fertility rate dropped below replacement level after the 1973 oil shock occurred and many Americans' real income stopped rising. In postrevolutionary China, population momentum built until famine unrelieved by Western aid forced a confrontation with limits. In 1979, mindful of severe food shortages, the government instituted a one-child-per-family policy, thus completing the evolution of incentives and controls that returned the country to the pre-Communist pattern of marital and reproductive restraint. In Cuba, the Castro-inspired baby boom gave way to below-replacement-level fertility when Communism's inability to deliver prosperity became manifest. In Eastern-bloc countries, including Russia, economic restructuring, the dissipation of government consumption subsidies, and the public perception of rising infant mortality promoted lower fertility rates and created demand for the avoidance of pregnancy.

In Zimbabwe, prodded by the international economic retrenchment of the late 1980s, the government began to support family planning. According to *The Economist*, "The hefty cost of supporting a large family has helped persuade some men of the value of limiting its size." The fertility rate is falling among the Yoruba in Nigeria, owing to a combination of delayed marriage and increasing acceptance of modem contraception. Two-thirds of the women who responded to a recent survey said that "the major force behind marriage postponement and

155

the use of contraception to achieve it was the present hard economic conditions."

Elsewhere the demand for modern contraception is also rising, and again the reason seems to be that couples view early marriage and large families as unaffordable. The point is made, repeatedly, in journalist George D. Moffett's book, *Critical Masses.* Quoting interviewees in half a dozen less developed countries, Moffet illustrates the caution which motivates people to avoid larger family size.

Without the motivation to limit family size, access to modern contraception is nearly irrelevant. For six years in the 1950s, a project directed by the British physician John Wyon provided several villages in northern India with family planning education, access to contraception, and medical care. The villagers had positive attitudes toward the health care providers and toward family planning; and infant mortality fell way down. But the fertility rate stayed way up. Wyon's group soon figured out why: the villagers liked large families. They were delighted that now, with lower infant mortality, they could have the six surviving children they had always wanted. The well-funded Wyon project may even have reinforced the preference for large families by playing a part in making extra children affordable.

Think Locally

Miscalculation about the cause of the population explosion has led to irrelevant and even counterproductive strategies for helping the third world to balance its population size and its resources. In the late 1940s and the heady decades that followed, trade, independence movements, populist revolutions, foreign aid, and new technology made people in all walks of life believe in abundance and an end to the natural limits imposed by environments with which they were familiar.

More recently, it is a step forward for industrial nations, their wealth much diminished, to be retrenching and targeting aid more narrowly. Their remaining wealth must not be squandered on arming opposing factions, reckless foreign assistance, or support for international migrations that rob and ultimately enrage—to the point of violence and possibly civil war—resident populations. This retrenchment saddens many, but the former liberality did a disservice to every country targeted for development.

With a new, informed understanding of human responses, certain kinds of aid remain appropriate: microloans that foster grassroots enterprise, where success is substantially related to effort; and

156

assistance with family planning services, not because contraception is a solution in and of itself but because modern contraception is a humane way of achieving small family size when small family size is desired. This modest agenda remains within the means of industrialized countries even as they look to the needs of the growing ranks of their own poor. And it does not mislead and unintentionally harm intended beneficiaries.

The idea that economic development is the key to curbing world population growth rests on assumptions and assertions that have influenced international aid policy for some fifty years. These assumptions do not stand up to historical or anthropological scrutiny, however, and the policies they spawned have contributed to runaway population growth.

The human capacity for adaptive response evolved in face-to-face interactions. Humanity's strong suit is quick response to environmental cues—a response more likely to be appropriate when the relevant environment is immediate and local. The mind's horizon is here and now. Our ancestors evolved and had to succeed in small groups that moved within relatively small territories. They had to succeed one day at a time—or not be anyone's ancestors. So, unsurprisingly, signals that come from the local environment are powerfully motivating.

Let the globalists step aside. One-world solutions do not work. Local solutions will. Everywhere people act in accord with their perception of their best interests. People are adept at interpreting local signs to find the next move needed. In many countries and communities today, where social, economic, and environmental conditions are indubitably worsening, the demand for modern contraception is rising, marriage and sexual initiation are delayed, and family size is contracting. Individuals responding with low fertility to signs of limits are the local solution. One prays that the hucksters of inappropriate development do not mess this up.

The Demographic Transition Revisited: Lessons for Foreign Aid and US Immigration Policy*

Abstract

The completed demographic transitions in industrialized countries inspired a model what underlies many well-meant policies affecting the Third World. However, the model's postulate—modernization and

---

In Ecological Economics 8, pp. 235–52 [1993].

prosperity will lower fertility rates—has exacerbated rather than helped control worldwide population growth and the associated environmental degradation. Here we show that perceived economic opportunity leads to raising family size targets and to discarding elements of traditional cultures that formerly held fertility rate in check. Conversely, fertility rates fall when limits are recognized. These observations imply that a liberal immigration policy and large-scale foreign aid are counterproductive for restoring balance between population size and carrying capacity.

Introduction

Environmentalists, economists, and ethicists cannot afford to ignore population growth. In poorer countries, high fertility rates have created a momentum for growth which will last through the foreseeable future. As more people try to subsist, their efforts progressively deplete resources and strain the environment's capacity to cope with pollution. Problems differ in rich and poor countries. In any setting, however, a growing population exacerbates the already-daunting difficulty of conserving the carrying capacity, preserving (restoring) environmental quality, and offering opportunity to all citizens (Benedick 1988; Keyfitz 1989; Ehrlich and Ehrlich 1990; Pimentel and Pimentel 1990; Atiyah and Press 1992).

Historically, undisturbed traditional societies survived over long periods of time through balancing their population size with what the environment could support over the long term, i.e., without damage to the carrying capacity. Experts are confounded that exponential population growth could be occurring today, particularly in the face of international technological assistance, modernization and urbanization, improved health care which greatly reduced infant mortality, increased literacy for women as well as men, democratization of governments, and thirty years of liberal immigration, asylee and refugee policies which favor nationals of the third world. Proponents of development programs postulated that positive movement on one or more of these factors would control the population explosion (Notestein 1945).

In the words of Garrett Hardin, "In the search for easy solutions to overpopulation, demographers in the 1930s produced their own *deus ex machina*, which they called the 'demographic transition' (DT). Inherent ambiguity conferred long life on this verbal invention. Sometimes the term stands for the merely descriptive assertion that fertility and prosperity are inversely related. Unfortunately it is more often taken to mean that excessive fertility cures itself whenever prosperity is conferred on a population" (Hardin 1993, Foreword to *Population Politics*). This paper addresses flaws in the second of the two meanings of demographic transition that Hardin identifies. Failures can be shown for every postulate of causal sequence, i.e., a condition which supposedly leads to lower fertility.

Between the end of World War II and 1970, fertility rates rose virtually everywhere in the third world. The demographic transition model bears a share of responsibility for this overpopulation debacle because the policies it spawned raised worldwide expectations. The greatest damage was done by aid and the rhetoric of development and prosperity because they undermine the rationale for limiting family size. Africa, which has received more in foreign aid per capita than any other continent, has the highest fertility rate in the world—about six children per woman. It was not always so. In the 1950s, fertility in Africa averaged about one-half child less per woman than in South America.

What changed? Could it be that Africans got three times as much aid per capita as South Americans? Admittedly, Africa has among the highest illiteracy and mortality rates in the world. But these conditions were not new; indeed, illiteracy and mortality rates were both declining even as fertility rose! Moreover, anthropologist and development specialist Penn Handwerker (1991) says that, in Africa, educating women barely changes completed family size; at best it delays the first birth for a few extra years while girls remain in school.

Multinational aid and liberal immigration policies work at cross-purposes with their stated goals because they dispel motivation to exercise caution and restraint. Family-size targets stay high or rise when people think that environmental limits which formerly operated have been relieved; so a perceived windfall of resources or emigration opportunity frequently results in a population explosion in the region supposedly being helped. Conversely, declining fertility—where it has occurred—is linked to deteriorating expectations and to the absence of an emigration option.

Nevertheless, the demographic transition model still inspires well-meant words and deeds. As recently as spring, 1990, the president of the National Academy of Engineering, Robert M. White, editorialized, "History shows that without economic development there is no hope of changing the population patterns that are the root cause of global pressures." Senator and 1992 vice-presidential candidate Albert Gore (D-TN) is another who repeats the prevailing wisdom. See his 1992 book, *Earth in the Balance*.

The present analysis (1) is in accord with modern and classical scholars who state that fertility is a response to the perceived costs and benefits associated with children; (2) illustrates conditions which raise family-size targets (and others which lower them); (3) exposes a historical fallacy underlying the demographic transition model; and (4) examines recent aid, emigration, and fertility in countries which have a significant proportion of their nationals residing in the United States.

Motivation Is Key to Family Size

Within biological limits, fertility is a function of individual behavior (mating, contraception, or abortion). In the short term, women or their husbands and families make decisions regarding family size. Over the longer term, culture adapts in ways that facilitate, or not, early and universal marriage, spacing between children, and nonreproductive roles for women. Through these individual and cultural processes runs the thread of purposive and/or adaptive behavior.

Paul Demeny of the Population Council points out that the drop to replacement-level fertility in much of the US urban population by the late nineteenth century is not explained by "people's access to some superior contraceptive technology—'modern' methods were yet to be invented—but was the result of individual motivation to keep fertility low. The experience of Western demographic history resoundingly demonstrated that, compared to micro-level interest in limiting fertility, 'really suitable technology' was of second-order importance for determining birth rates. Lacking such technology, the Mayor of Peipei [in China] still could have been confidently advised to get fertility incentives right and then sit back and watch the birth rate fall" (1988, 458). Motivation to have fewer or more children, says Demeny in effect, is the major determinant of childbearing and population dynamics.

Charles Westoff (1988) also concludes (ruefully) that the family planning concept is widely implemented. His study of the nonuse of modern contraception shows that "by and large, contraceptive behavior—at least in the four developing countries for which data are examined—is not grossly inconsistent with reproductive intention" (p. 226). In Brazil, the Dominican Republic, Peru, and Liberia only 1–2 percent of women were not using or intending[3] to use contraception in a manner consistent with their completed family size preference; the gap approaches zero when contraception is considered as means of spacing children. That is, nonuse of contraception in countries where fertility is high is not explained by informational or attitudinal obstacles. Westoff concludes, "The overwhelming majority of women who want no more children or who want to postpone fertility, at least in the four countries discussed here, are behaving in a manner consistent with that goal" (Westoff 1988, 232). That is, fertility corresponds to family-size preferences.

Historically as well, the net costs and benefits of childbearing appear to have been closely calculated. Malthus' observations suggested to him that women or couples adjust their reproductive strategy to the perceived advantage of children given prevailing economic conditions ([1789] 1967, 1803). G. Ohlin cites another early scholar's analysis of the "curious Tables of the Births and Funerals of the City of Breslaw": "That the growth and Encrease of Mankind is not so much stinted by anything in the nature of the Species, as it is from the cautious difficulty most People make to adventure on the state of marriage, from the prospect of the Trouble and Charge of providing for a family" (1961, 190).

Anthropologist P. W. Turke (1989) notes that adequate subsistence is the prior condition for successful reproduction. He suggests, therefore, that humans have been "selected" in the evolutionary sense to plan childbearing around economic and material conditions. The purposiveness of reproductive behavior can also be inferred from the ineffectiveness of authorities in imposing family-size policy. When families are determined either to have children or restrict fertility, they do so despite opposite official targets.

Low fertility in the face of official pronatalist policy occurs repeatedly. The native-born American population maintains a below-replacement-level fertility rate (1.7 in 1991)[4] despite tax incentives for additional children, transfer payments for child support, and gradual erosion of access to abortion. The effect is also discernible in the Augustan and later periods of the Roman Empire (Abernethy 1979) and recently in Romania. Although Nikolae Ceausescu's Communist government criminalized both contraceptive use and abortion by married women with fewer than five children, the Population Reference Bureaus 1989 Data Sheet reports the Romanian crude birth rate as 16 per 1,000 persons in the population, identical to that in the United States. (Compare with 29 per 1,000 in Peru, 30 in Mexico, 31 in the Dominican Republic, and 43 in Nicaragua).

Conversely, rural Chinese enjoyed new prosperity in the 1980s because of partial privatization of the agricultural sector. Fertility rose, in keeping with Malthusian expectations, and was hidden by

161

shifting children between villages as necessary to avoid detection by central government authorities attempting to enforce a two-child-per-family policy. A rural population explosion and migration into cities in search of jobs ensued. As of 1990, the Chinese government had curtailed migration from the hinterland into the larger cities. Thus, the small-family-size policy was reinforced with a changed incentive structure. Each sector will now bear the burden of its own reproduction because the cities no longer will act as a safety valve for excess rural population. Farmers may still profit from cheap child labor, but will have to absorb the future cost of supporting young adults who wish to found families of their own. One expects that rural fertility will fall, but this is as yet unverified.

Historical and cross-cultural data confirm that motivation (rather than differential access to modern contraception) is the primary determinant of fertility. A variety of behaviors, usually buttressed by beliefs and values, limit or encourage reproduction. The following section suggests that individuals respond to scarcity by having fewer children, and to perceived opportunity by having more children. Greater detail and additional cases appear in *Population Politics*. Contrary to the demographic transition model, the data show that economic development does not cause family size to shrink; rather, at every point where serious economic opportunity beckons, family size preferences expand.

Getting the Incentives Right

The demographic transition model postulates a number of conditions that lead to lower fertility. This section presents a selection of examples which, together, begin to constitute a test. Cases include effects of perceived opportunity in Western and non-Western societies, diachronic comparisons, and tracings of single societies over time. Test each one against the predictions of the demographic transition model. The predictions are:

- modernization lowers fertility
- urbanization lowers fertility
- prosperity lowers fertility
- education lowers fertility
- declining infant mortality lowers fertility.

Where one or more of the antecedents changes, fertility should change, too. A positive antecedent predicts declining fertility if the demographic transition model is right. But, instead, one finds the opposite sequence: deteriorating conditions precede fertility decline.

Prosperity, Urbanization, Modernization

Some African countries that had historically high fertility in the 1960s and 1970s are now seeing declines. For example, East Africa's buoyant optimism wrought by the 1960s' expanding, urbanizing economy gave way in the 1980s to a deteriorating environment, curtailment of foreign aid, and the AIDS epidemic. Against this backdrop of devastated morale, fertility fell between 14 and 20 percent in every country of the region.

Likewise in Egypt, the Aswan Dam's hydroelectric power, oil, and Suez Canal revenues, plus $2.5 million annual United States' aid from the 1980 Camp David accord (Egypt's share for Egypt-Israeli peace-making) promoted rapid urbanization, expansion of health care and education, and modernization through the early 1980s. All of this was supposed—according to demographic transition theorists—to lower fertility. But it did not work out that way. After slight declines in the early 1970s, fertility stalled for over a decade at about six births per woman. By the mid-1980s it became impossible for the average Egyptian to ignore signals that their situation was getting rapidly worse. Population growth was staying ahead of gains in wealth so that per capita income actually shrank. A historically rich land is home to seventy-five million very poor people, nearly forty million more than in 1974. *The London Economist* (1990) calls Egypt "the Mediterranean's Bangladesh." This scenario is heralding a now-rapid fertility decline. Egyptian women averaged 4.5 children in 1991. The decline cannot be traced to improving education or improving anything else, and it cannot come too soon. The population already almost certainly exceeds the long-term carrying capacity of Egypt's lands and resources.

Similarly, Sudan's fertility rate dropped by 17 percent (to 5.0 births per woman) during the late 1980s. This trend could have many explanations, but prosperity and modern family planning are nonstarters. A Newsletter ("Fertility Declining," 1991) of the Demographic and Health Surveys states: "The use of contraception, although increasing, is still very low (6 percent of couples) and probably has had little impact on fertility." Instead, the decline is attributed mainly to later ages for marriage and first birth among the predominantly Moslem population. Believers in a benign, orderly demographic transition would have one look for socioeconomic development and modernization as the underlying causes of this later childbearing. But in reality, the Sudanese economy deteriorated markedly during the 1980s, the government remained authoritarian, people lost hope, and famine was widespread.

Also in Brazil, the worsening conditions of the 1980s coincided with a 50 percent drop in the fertility rate. Observers attribute the freefall to economic stagnation and rising infant mortality. And Indonesia saw fertility decline most among people on the most crowded islands and farmers who live on the most eroded slopes, i.e., the most impoverished.

So much for needing development and prosperity in order to lower fertility! Instead one sees declines in family size developing only as times get significantly harder. The Indonesian example also shows, a conclusion supported by European history, that farming is not necessarily associated with high fertility.

Only the enrichment of farmers relative to their expectations—as seen in China in the early 1980s—stimulates high fertility. In Ireland as well, farmers became suddenly prosperous from adoption of potato farming after 1745, and fertility skyrocketed (Abernethy 1979). Land distribution to Turkish sharecroppers in the middle of the twentieth century provides a similar, unambiguous insight into cause and effect: Aswad (1981) states that the new wealth was very quickly followed by a baby boom. Some who received land had so many children born after the land redistribution that their family size rose to twice the usual number for that part of Turkey. The new, higher average was 6.4 children per family. Sudden windfalls raise fertility.

Child Mortality

Change in child mortality is another sign of the times. Falling infant mortality is a joyous trend and one wishes that achieving it would lower fertility. Nevertheless, Dr. John Wyon's project in Khanna, India, showed the futility of changing family size preferences with even the most inclusive health care programs. For six years, Wyon's group provided a whole village with education, nutritional supplements, public health, and direct medical care; and infant mortality declined. (Wyon 1971). But the fertility rate was unchanged. The reason, it became clear, was that the Khanna people liked large families. Maurice King (1990) summarizes the international data on infant mortality this way: "The view that, if the child death rate declines sufficiently, the birth rate must decline also, and that there is a causal link between them is untenable if the data are examined closely. Indeed the opposite can occur."

Insights into the process are all around us. In Haiti, Save the Children Fund set out to learn if women who had lost children compensated by increasing their total number of births. The exactly opposite effect was found: women who had never lost children had the most births; women who had an infant die were least likely to continue childbearing. Indeed, studies in several continents fail to find that high child mortality leads to more births. Comparison of Indian women who had lost young children with those whose family was intact showed no increased childbearing among the former. Research in Guatemala yielded similar results: women who had lost children did not desire additional births as replacements. Cross-cultural data implicate infanticide in some deaths (Abernethy 1979; Hern 1991). Women do not set out to replace an infant which they had felt unable to raise.

Historical data shed further light on the sequence of declining fertility and infant mortality. Fertility, it seems, often declines even while infant mortality stays high or rises. The Population Reference Bureau (1990) quotes an analysis of declining fertility in the first and second German Reichs. Reviewing the records from 1871 onward of the Reich's 71 administrative areas, John Knodel (1974) states that "'[T]he decline in infant mortality could not have been an initiating cause of the fertility decline in most areas,' because fertility began to fall before, or at the same time as infant mortality."

Still stronger evidence that declining child mortality is not a cause of lower fertility comes from France, the country which led Europe into the fertility transition. Catherine Rollet-Echalier (1990) finds that small family size was established by 1850, but the decline in infant mortality was not detectable until the twentieth century.

Reader take note that even in Europe, the model for the demographic transition, a sequence of urbanization, modernization, declining infant mortality, and increasing prosperity followed by falling fertility is not real, but imagined. One should look for a continuing stream of new data that document a different sequence. Expect to see that parents want more children when they believe that opportunity is expanding. The expected sequence is exactly opposite to what writers on the demographic transition have taught a generation of policymakers to believe.

Optimism Is the Human Condition

Any number of developments create a perception of economic opportunity. New trading partners, cheap land, improved technology, popular revolutions that are expected to redistribute resources, and emigration in pursuit of a higher standard of living have each been perceived as a way to escape environmental/economic constraints; each such development also appears to stimulate fertility. "Ecological release" is the term for fortuitous conditions which lift pressures that would otherwise inspire reproductive caution.

For example, cheap land consequent to the depopulation of Europe in the Dark Ages followed by the introduction of the stirrup, horse-power, and beans—which provided a new protein source and facil-itated double-cropping—created a condition of ecological release and set the stage for the tripling of population size in medieval Europe. The Industrial Revolution and raw materials from colonial outposts stimulated further population growth in seventeenth- and eighteenth-century Europe. Superior technology introduced into the Americas let settlers take possession of cheap land and raise as many as ten or eleven children per family. Trade with Arabs and Europeans and new job opportunities freed Pacific, Asian, and African peoples from the limitations of traditional agriculture, hunting, or fishing and coincided with the start of their population explosions. And upticks in the business cycle set off fertility in the industrial world, e.g., the baby boom in the United States and post–World War II Germany. Most people seem ready to believe in lasting prosperity. They adjust family-size targets accordingly.

Trade

India's experience illustrates the effect of both trade and the popular movement which culminated in independence from Great Britain. Her population was nearly stable from 400 BC to about AD 1500, but commenced growing, to a rate of 0.6 percent a year,[5] with restoration of peace from Mogul invasions and the stimulus of new trade opportu-nities. South India enjoyed particular prosperity under the Vijayanagar kings. The strongest of these, Krishna Deva Raya (1509–1530), is described by Spaeth (1991) "as an early advocate of free trade. He im-ported velvets and damasks from Aden and China, horses from Arabia, elephants from Ceylon, gold, silver—and precious gems." European trade offered further opportunity and population growth accelerated after 1900. The real take-off came with independence, in 1947; the rate of growth accelerated in the following decades, ultimately reaching 2.3 percent annually.

Revolution

Political change linked to lifting repression or to expectations of prosperity has often raised fertility. Cuba, for example, experienced a baby boom when Fidel Castro replaced the unpopular dictator, Batista, in 1959. Díaz-Briquets and Pérez (1981) say the explanation is "straightforward . . . The main factor was the real income rise among the most disadvantaged groups brought about by the redistribution measures of the revolutionary government. The fertility rises in almost every age group suggest that couples viewed the future as more promising and felt they could now afford more children."

Algerian independence from France in 1962 had a similar effect on fertility. Thirty years later, 70 percent of the population is under thirty years of age. The growth rate in 1991 was 2.7 percent per year. Unsurprisingly, 7.5 million of Algeria's 25 million inhabitants are unemployed; the disparity between rich and poor is rapidly increasing; and religious fundamentalism threatens to negate women's hard-won civil rights (Lemsine 1992). Impoverishment and religiosity are likely to usher in swiftly declining fertility—as they did beginning several decades prior to Ireland's 1845 potato famine—so long as the international community refrains from undercutting local perceptions of scarcity with premature policies which promise relief.

Aid

Christianity has spread the ideal of the unreciprocated gift. Indeed, the United States is often misunderstood because giving is a tenet of its foreign policy. When governments proclaim an intention to give—expecting nothing back—it means one of three things in most parts of the world: (1) the givers are fools; (2) they are very devious and plan to entrap recipients in a web of obligations; (3) they have so much wealth as to have stopped counting. But for the salutary developments of Western banks demanding repayment of their loans and international agencies attaching political as well as economic conditions to new loans, the third world would still be settled on one of these interpretations.

The most dangerous conclusion that any country could draw is that wealth is abundant and renewable. Nevertheless, that unfounded view is widespread and encouraged by the international rhetoric of aid. Promises overwhelm the reality that Earth is finite; resources, limited; and that population growth is outrunning every possibility of providing sustenance to all.

The scale of the global effort to help the third world (and the deception it fosters) can hardly be overstated. Harper's Index 1989 reports that forty countries rely on foreign aid for at least a quarter of their national budget. Direct US government aid had climbed to fourteen billion dollars by 1990, and much more is masked within unlikely sounding programs in the Departments of State, Defense, Commerce, Health and Human Services, and Education. Easy borrowing from private banks ended only when Mexico defaulted on its debt in the summer of 1982. By then, Latin America, alone, had received $500 billion. The May, 1989, issue of *The World Monitor* recalls that "donations from foreign countries averaged about $20 per person in Africa . . . $7 per person in Latin America and $5 per person in Asia" (p. 34).

Such transfers of wealth cannot but perpetuate trust in one-world rhetoric—a belief that the community of nations can be relied upon to help, just like family. A sense of security grows along with the felt entitlement to share in the world's resources on the basis of need. Behind it all is the fantasy of abundance. Efforts to plan for one's own future do not thrive in this climate. Neither do private birth control nor national population control policies advance in the purposive mode essential for avoiding the looming tragedy.

Conversely, countries which are self-reliant either by choice or historical accident are more determined to stop population growth. Isolation, beginning before 1949 and reinforced under Mao Tse T'ung, made self-reliance a core tenet of Chinese national policy. Indeed, news of a serious famine which ran from 1958 through much of the 1960s barely penetrated China's borders to reach the Western world. The famine was formative. No international assistance blurred China's perception of reality, and Mao's subsequent policy shows that he acquired a crystal clear grasp of the finitude of resources and the need to cut demand. Reduction of population pressure became a central part of the long-term solution. Before the famine, official policy was aggressively pronatalist: more children meant a greater nation. By famine's end, the policy had reversed. The one-child-per-family goal was in place by 1970.

Myanmar (Burma) also makes self-reliance a tenet of national policy. The trade-off for doing without international aid is "isolation and lack of a full-fledged national family planning program." Nevertheless, without benefit of technical assistance or funds for deploying modern contraception, fertility has dropped. In 1983, women averaged 5.2 children. In 1990, the fertility rate was below 4.0, a significant decline. The

Population Reference Bureau (1991) admits that professional demographers are bemused: how the Myanmarians did it "is unclear." But it is not unclear. Limits to resources were widely apparent, and never in fact or fantasy did illusions of being bailed out of their predicament enter into calculation.

Assumptions and values give form to behavior. When ideas are realistic, the behavior they promote is likely to be realistic and adaptive, too. Conversely, countries' beliefs that others have the capacity and will to take care of them for the long haul put them at risk. A greatly underestimated danger is that such trust will undermine incentives for third world countries to limit fertility while there is time to avoid worse tragedy.

Emigration

Incentives related to migration opportunities—or conversely, the need to absorb one's own youth—are insufficiently studied. However, it seems likely that the opportunity to emigrate is functionally equivalent in its effect on fertility to foreign aid, new trading opportunities, and popular revolutions. Emigration relieves population pressure in the sending country and often reflects anticipation of opportunity elsewhere. It is a form of ecological release. Thus, one expects that it encourages preference for large family size.

Two studies supporting this prediction have come to my attention. Anthropologist Anne Brittain (1991) reports a positive relationship between marital fertility and emigration, by district, in present-day St. Vincent and the Grenadines. She concludes that the "anticipated loss of children to migration may be an important factor in maintaining high reproductive rates." Brittain cites Friedlander's (1983) similar conclusion drawn from a comparative study, by district, of nineteenth-century England and Wales. Those districts which had high rates of emigration showed much less reduction in marital fertility . . . than would have been predicted."

Studies modeled on Britain and the Caribbean are sorely needed in Mexico, Guatemala, The Philippines, El Salvador, Nicaragua, and Haiti. Good census data in Mexico suggest that it would be feasible to compare fertility rates in the villages from which California's and the southwest's Mexican immigrants predominantly come with rates in areas which send out fewer emigrants.

Opportunity to immigrate to the United States as well as large-scale international aid are probable factors contributing to high fertility in third world countries. No matter the local poverty and unemployment, wealth may seem within reach. Appraisal of environmental limits seems likely to be distorted because of opportunity apparently available elsewhere.

US Aid and Immigration Policy

Present US immigration law was enacted in 1965. It replaced the national-origin quota system and encouraged persons from regions that appeared underrepresented in the US population to immigrate; family reunification became the basis of visa "preference categories." Subsequent modifications of preference categories, the 1980 Refugee Act, and the 1990 Immigration Reform Act result in 90 percent of immigration visas being awarded to family reunification immigrants, and under 10 percent to skills-based immigration.

Total legal immigration, including refugees and asylees, runs at one million annually. Illegal immigration by those who come to stay is estimated at between 200,000 and 800,000 persons annually. Former commissioner of the Immigration and Naturalization Service, Alan Nelson, estimates that one million enter the United States illegally each year, with a total of three–six million in the United States on any given day (Nelson, 1990). An indication of the magnitude is that over 3.1 million persons took advantage of amnesty provisions in the 1986 Immigration Reform and Control Act (IRCA). IRCA's effectiveness in controlling further illegal immigration is doubtful: although sanctions are designed to discourage hiring illegal aliens, employers meet statutory requirements by merely inspecting an applicant's documents. Seventeen types of identification are acceptable; employers are not responsible for the authenticity of documents; and there is a market for rented documents (Skerry, 1989).

Both the push factor of overpopulation and the pull factor of jobs and other benefits in the United States maintain the demand for immigration. Rewards from having offspring who emigrate include receiving remittances. In some rural areas of Mexico, "remittances constitute over 80 percent of monthly cash incomes" (Sullivan, 1988, 1059; Wiarda and Wiarda, 1986; Hong Kong Women, 1989). Similarly, "Economists often say El Salvador's best export is its residents. In fact, the estimated $700 million that Salvadorans living abroad send back each year is more than the country earns from coffee, sugar and all its other exports combined" (Johnson, 1992, 9A). Families in these and like communities may rationally calculate that the chances of having at least one child emigrate improve with the total number of children they have. Children may seem a good investment as parents conclude that scarcity within their own country, which would otherwise encourage reproductive restraint, is outweighed by opportunities for their children to move.

Although the number of legal and illegal immigrants continues to rise, their distribution as to country of origin appears remarkably stable. Stability is in part a function of chain migration of relatives exempt from the statutory ceiling on visas. It also reflects the greater ease of immigrating when information on US procedures, employment, housing, and social/educational/medical services is readily available within a network where some members already are established. A Mexican campesino making his decision to migrate considers Los Angeles, San Antonio, Houston, or Chicago as much of an urban option for him as Mexico City, Guadalajara, Tijuana, or Monterey.

Wayne Cornelius (1989) concludes that, "The Immigration Reform and Control Act of 1986 has not eliminated the basic economic incentive to migrate clandestinely to the United States, nor has it undermined the powerful social mechanisms that facilitate such movement. In Mexican communities that have long depended on income earned in the United States, our data show that most people continue to have an essentially positive view of the U.S. opportunity structure: not as wide-open as before, but still accessible to those with determination, perhaps assisted by bogus documents and, even more importantly, by family contacts" (p. 703).

Country-of-birth tables published by the Immigration and Naturalization Service (INS) show that 601,708 persons immigrated legally into the United States in 1986. Countries with the largest legal contingents were Mexico, 66,533; The Philippines, 52,558; Korea, 35,776; Cuba, 33,1147; India, 26,227; the Dominican Republic, 26,175; and China, 25,106. Several small countries had fewer immigrants, but cumulatively their numbers represent a significant proportion of these countries' total populations. About 15 percent of Haitians and 20 percent of El Salvadorans are estimated to be in the United States.

Fertility in these high-immigration countries has been slow to decline. Countries with high immigration to the United States (in proportion to their total population size) have also received substantial US aid. Persistent, above-replacement-level fertility in every country seems unsurprising. Only Cuba and two tiny island societies have fertility levels that will stabilize population in the foreseeable future.

Historically, Cuba had low fertility except for the blip associated with the Castro revolution and, apart from an exodus of the upper class immediately after the revolution and the 1980 Mariel boatload, emigration does not act as a safety valve for excess numbers. Antigua-Barbuda, Barbados, and Jamaica have become tourist destinations; hotel jobs opening up for women help control fertility because child-care requires an opportunity cost when women work outside the home.

Such observations suggest that, in most countries, precisely the wrong incentive structure is in place, because perception that children have a net economic cost appears to be a necessary condition for overcoming large-family-size norms. Nevertheless, there is no sign as yet that US immigration policy will be weighed in terms of its effect on countries from which immigrants come. The 1990 Immigration Reform Act raised legal immigration by 40 percent, and bills to relax enforcement provisions of IRCA [which legislates penalties on employers of illegal aliens] have been introduced in every recent session of Congress. Policymakers err by not recognizing that US immigration policy, to the extent that it helps dispel realistic appraisal of signs that population size is exceeding carrying capacity, contributes to maladaptive responses in third world countries and thus almost certainly will increase suffering in the long run.

Inducements for continued high fertility are ill-afforded in South and Central America, Africa, and many Pacific Rim countries. Central America (including Mexico) and The Caribbean have about 150 million people (vs. 250 million in the United States), and their numbers double every eighteen to twenty-six years. Growing populations may doom them. The United States hastens the day by neutralizing local signals of scarcity. The United States would help, not harm, by encouraging an appreciation of limits sooner rather than later. A relatively closed US border would create most vividly an image of limits and be an incentive to restrict family size.

The scale of the third world population problem will be—may be already—beyond the power of the community of nations to resolve. The United States cannot help all who live and may die in misery, but only the relatively few luckiest. The so-called help will be outweighed by the suffering of the extra millions who will be born if our policies, under the spell of the demographic transition model, retard correct appraisal of environmental limits. Often, allowing ourselves to be ruled by good-hearted but wrong-headed humanitarian impulses, we encourage ecologically disastrous responses among ourselves and our less fortunate neighbors. Impulses, which seem in the short run to do good, but which lead ultimately to worldwide disaster—and most quickly to disaster in the countries we wish to help—are not in fact humanitarian.

Immigration Reduction Offers Chance for Softer Landing*

Overview

Stakeholders to consider when evaluating mass immigration include the immigrants themselves, various socioeconomic sectors in the receiving countries, and those remaining in the developing countries that migrants leave. This paper suggests that those remaining will be harmed because emigration stimulates fertility. Continuing high fertility is an obstacle to the saving and investment that are needed for even modest rises in the standard of living. The fertility opportunity hypothesis suggests that perceptions of economic opportunity control fertility rates.

Fertility rises or stays high if people perceive that opportunity is expanding. If the emigration option creates the impression of vast opportunity, fertility is likely to stay high in countries that emigrants leave. This result is detrimental in the long run, and overwhelms the immediate benefit of remittances and opportunities enjoyed by immigrants themselves.

Introduction

Immigrants themselves usually benefit from immigration. Both the numbers that choose to escape from their native country and studies showing benefits (often inversely related to the costs borne by residents of destination countries) reveal the attractiveness of immigration. In fact, mass immigration results in very large wealth transfers to immigrants from the poor and middle class of immigrant-receiving countries (Rubenstein 2004). A remaining component in evaluating costs and benefits is the effect of emigration from undeveloped countries on those who remain at home. The vast number of those who might like to emigrate will never have that opportunity. How do global mass flows of migrants affect them?

---

*In Ecological Economics 59(2) pp. 226–30 [September 12, 2006].

Answers build on the premise that rapid population growth retards saving and capital accumulation and, therefore, perpetuates poverty. I further suggest that emigration has counterintuitive effects, actually perpetuating population pressure in the long run. By acting as an escape valve for excess population, emigration contributes to perception of rising economic opportunity, thus tending to raise the fertility rate or, at the least, prevent it from falling. Those last clauses are controversial. Although the fertility opportunity hypothesis is empirical (Abernethy 1979, 1993) and has been significantly supported in a prospective, controlled test (Abernethy and Penaloza 2002), it contradicts received wisdom.

The fertility opportunity hypothesis is a bitter pill. It states that couples relax their vigilance and allow additional births when opportunity appears to be expanding. The departure of a fraction of the population opens up employment niches. And immigrants often send relatives a significant fraction of their pay, confirming the signal that prosperity is literally over the horizon. In 2004, remittances from the United States to Latin America reached $30 billion, (IADB 2004). Even when perceptions are shortsighted or misguided, they are key to behavior.

Emigration Prolongs High Fertility Rates

Historical records from Great Britain and, recently, the Caribbean show that the prospect of emigration tends to spur childbearing. Ann Brittain reports a positive correlation, by district, between emigration and marital fertility rates in present-day St. Vincent/Grenadines. The more emigration, the higher the fertility rates (1991). Brittain cites supportive studies, including Friedlander (1983), who compared economically depressed, nineteenth-century English and Welsh districts. Those with high rates of emigration showed prolonged, high marital fertility, whereas fertility declined rapidly in communities where the young were absorbed, painfully, into the local economy. The question arises: would Mexican fertility rates, 2.8 children per woman in 2004 (PRB 2004), be falling faster if an estimated 10 percent of the Mexican population were not in the United States?

Frontier Mentality Prolongs High Fertility Rates

Even after the 1990s massacre of its Tutsi population, Rwanda, in Central Africa, remains one of the most densely populated countries of the continent. Belgium, a colonial power until 1962, and successor indigenous governments recognized population pressure as early as the 1960s but, states demographer John May, projected an image of expansionary opportunity until the 1980s.

The governments' principal responses to population pressure after World War II were agricultural intensification and population dispersal. Relocation became "by far the most important policy response ever adopted in Rwanda to cope with rapid population growth" (May 1995, 329).

May speculates that dispersing the population to relatively empty lands created a frontier mentality—an image of opportunity.

Parenthetically, the early 1970s Guatemalan decision to open virgin forests to "settlement and exploitation" also created a frontier mentality. Unsurprisingly, average family size among the pioneers soared to nearly eight children per woman (Moffett 1994).

The mid-1980s Rwandan fertility rate was 8.5 births per woman, soon making Rwanda "the most densely populated country of continental sub-Saharan Africa" (May 1995, 333), quadrupling between 1950 and 1993 (Bouvier 1995). Belatedly, international aid became contingent on the government's encouraging family planning. Fertility began to decline and, by 1990, arrived at 6.2 children per woman. The declining fertility rate could be attributed to the new availability of modern contraception except that, by 1992, only 12.9 percent of married, reproductive-age women used modern methods. May states that the most visible contributor to the Rwandan fertility decline was later marriage. Expecting a difficult future, couples very commonly delay marriage—enough to move the average age of marriage by three, four, or a dozen years. See historic Irish (Drake 1963–1964; Connell 1968), Indian (Dyson 1991a, 1991b), and more recent German (Conrad 1996; Eberstadt 1994) and Yoruba (Caldwell 1992) data for congruent examples.

Unlike Rwanda, Malawi, on Africa's Southeast coast, moved quickly after World War II to stop rapid population growth. The disproportionate number of young people created momentum, nevertheless, which more than doubled the population between 1966, the first census, and 1995.

Anthropologist Ezekiel Kalipeni suggests that the 85 percent of Malawians who are subsistence farmers had three options for dealing with population pressure on limited arable land. They could work harder on existing holdings; migrate to available but marginal lands; or limit family size to avoid having to further subdivide already small farms (1996). The hard work of agricultural intensification on existing plots seemed most promising in the early stages of land scarcity but did not keep ahead of the momentum of population growth. Migration to infertile marginal land was unattractive, leaving only the option of limiting family size.

Kalipeni found that the fertility rate was not significantly related to education, infant mortality, or urbanization in either 1977 or 1987 data. However, regression of 1987 data revealed a statistically significant *inverse* relationship between the fertility rate and population density: the denser this rural population, the lower the fertility rate. Observing that "the fastest fertility decline is occurring in the region of highest population density . . . [and] areas that are experiencing intense environmental pressure are also beginning to go through a fertility transition," Kalipeni suggests that land hunger was the central stimulus driving a more cautious approach to childbearing (1966, 299–300). Parenthetically again, economist Richard Easterlin found that population density explained declining fertility in the United States during the nineteenth and early twentieth centuries, whereas education made little difference (1971).

Redistribution Accelerates Population Growth

In both China and Cuba, revolution and the redistribution of wealth to people who had formerly been among the poorest in the society blasted fertility rates into a higher orbit.

From the traditional four births per woman (not much above replacement in high mortality regimes), China's fertility rate reached approximately six births per woman during the 1952–1957 heyday of Communism. Judith Banister attributes China's baby boom to war's end and the 1950–1951 government policy of redistributing land to poor peasants and tenant farmers (1987).

Cuba's 1959 revolution had strikingly similar demographic results. Demographers Diaz-Briquets and Perez explain that fertility rose from moderate to significantly higher levels after Fidel Castro expropriated wealthy landowners, promising to redistribute plots to the masses. They write that the cause of the fertility increase is "straightforward. . . . The main factor was the real income rise among the most disadvantaged groups brought about by the redistribution measures of the revolutionary government. The fertility rises in almost every age group suggest that couples viewed the future as more promising and felt they could now afford more children" (1981, 17).

Fertility Up on Perceived Opportunity; Down on Deteriorating Future

Demographers Youssef Courbage (1995) and Philippe Fargues (1995, 1997) suggest that fluctuations in the household economy drive changes in the fertility rate. In both Morocco and Egypt, flows of new, broadly distributed wealth were followed by rising fertility. Conversely, economic retrenchment marked by increasing disparity between aspirations and reality was linked to falling fertility.

Morocco's demographic experience after 1957 paralleled that of other countries in the region. Fertility rose in the wake of achieving independence from a colonial power, strong world prices for its principal export (phosphates), and the government's use of export profits to subsidize social programs. The total fertility rate [TFR] reached approximately 7 by 1960, and 7.4 children per woman by 1973. Late 1974 and 1975 were watershed years, however. Phosphate prices collapsed and declining revenues forced the government to both scale back subsidies for health care, education, and other social spending and raise personal income taxes. Government now took more than it gave. As family self-reliance became a renewed imperative, many women—although mostly illiterate—entered the workforce. The sudden reversal in family economics was immediately followed by a "sharp drop in fertility, which diminished by 20 percent from 7.3 to 5.9 children in just four years" (Courbage 1995, 89). By 1997, the Moroccan TFR was 3.3 children per woman (WPDS 1997).

Whereas Moroccans were cast on their own resources after 1974, Egyptian families received significant subsidies until approximately 1985 (Fargues 1995). After being stuck at upward of 6 children per woman for decades, the Egyptian TFR sank to approximately 5.0 in 1988, and had declined by 1997 to 3.6 (WPDS 1997). In both Moroccan and Egyptian examples, the fertility decline tracked families' increasing need to make do with their own resources.

Courbage notes that the fertility rate in Middle Eastern Muslim countries has never been reliably associated with women's education, infant mortality rates, health care, or other "traditional explanations of the demographic transition" (1995, 84, 1996). Fewer than 40 percent of Moroccan women of childbearing age were literate when that country's fertility decline started. In Egypt, female literacy had reached approximately 60 percent, but was decling at the very time that the fertility decline was accelerating. And rich countries like Kuwait and Saudi Arabia had very high fertility rates through 1990 although most women were educated; social benefits including health care were generous; and infant mortality rates were low.

Ethnic Group Fertility Rates Track Opportunity

Fertility rates by ethnic group closely tracked access to resources after the British exited Malaysia in 1957. In the beginning of the period, Malays were rural, least educated, and at the bottom of the income pyramid; and they had the lowest fertility rate. Thirty years later, Malays had voted themselves both economic and political power, gains made at the expense of Indian and Chinese minorities. Newly empowered and well-educated Malays now had the highest fertility rate (5–6 children per woman) whereas Indian fertility declined steadily from nearly eight children per woman in 1957 to about three in 1987. In the same period, the Chinese rate fell from over 7 to 2.5 children.

Demographers Govindasamy and DaVanzo suggest that a sense of relative deprivation among Chinese and Indian citizens contributed to the decline in their family size (1992, 250). The disproportionate obstacles in the way of their own and their children's advancement appeared to explain reproductive caution. This divergence among ethnic groups that have been differentially impacted politically and economically is entirely congruent with the fertility opportunity model.

Hearing from the Grassroots

Readers who prefer prospective, statistical tests are referred to my 2002 publication with Roberto Penaloza. But here, I turn to the micro level. First person statements consonant with the fertility opportunity hypothesis are ubiquitous. See these examples:

Journalist George D. Moffett interviewed dozens of persons in developing countries and repeatedly heard informants link their avoidance of childbearing to resource limitations. Similarly, the Caldwell team found that the NigerianYoruba began to avoid childbearing in the aftermath of five years of a faltering economy and diminishing international aid. Interviews revealed that "Two-thirds of all respondents claimed that the major force behind marriage postponement and the use of contraception to achieve it was the present hard economic conditions." Most also "believed that child mortality had risen over the previous five years of economic difficulty" (Caldwell et al. 1992, 226, 229).

Motives do not change. Historian Michael Drake quotes an early-nineteenth-century visitor to Norway who questioned a peasant about the discrepancy in ages between himself and his wife: "'Tell me, Nils, how was it possible that such an active boy as you could go out and take such an old person as a wife?' . . . Nils replies, 'I thought that when I took such an old woman the crowd of young ones would not be so great, for it is difficult for one who is in small circumstances to feed so many'" (1969, 140).

Conclusion

Much of the developing world is mired in poverty. Prosperity proves elusive so long as population growth outruns resources and investment. Thus, a challenge—met with painstaking effort in much of Asia and South America—is matching new entrants into the labor force with opportunities for productive work. If fertility rates decline, job creation gradually whittles away the army of unemployed. By means of a few examples (of the many documented), I have tried to show that letting the population bear the weight of a contracting economy, so that they perceive that opportunity has diminished, is the path to rapid fertility decline and eventual population stabilization. The present may be painful, but the future is not hopeless because prosperity can build from a platform of demographic stability.

Fertility rates fall where children are perceived as a burden. But humanitarians everywhere struggle with the moral dilemma of watching as the economy does its work upon the human psyche.

If developed countries act as safety valves for excess population in high-fertility countries, the expected fertility response will not operate efficiently. Several examples cited earlier show how fertility rates stay high when people perceive that emigration is the solution to local pressures.

In conclusion are brief observations about immigration's effect on the receiving country. First note that the low US fertility rates suggest that most Americans do not view the future as holding great opportunity for themselves or their children. White Americans have had substantially below-replacement-level fertility since the 1970s. Black Americans have recently experienced a rapid fertility decline to almost exactly replacement level. Only recent immigrants, particularly Hispanics, maintain high fertility rates (Camarota 2005).

The perceptions apparently correspond with reality. Scholars including George Borjas (1999, 2004), Stephen Camarota (2000, 2004), Donald Huddle (1994, 1997), John Attarian (2003), and others show how mass immigration from less-developed countries undermines the job market, disposable income, social services including health care and educational opportunity, and the Social Security prospects of most persons in immigrant-receiving countries. Average native-born Americans have been losing real, inflation-adjusted income since approximately the first oil embargo of 1974–1975, and immigration accounts for much of the continuing decline. Economist George Borjas observes that immigration depresses wages and displaces Americans from jobs, costing native-born working Americans $195 billion annually (1999, 2004).

Steven Camarota analyzes Census Bureau data, finding that "between March 2000 and March 2004, the number of adults working actually increased, but all of the net change went to immigrant workers" (2004). Andrew Sum and his colleagues at Northeastern University concur. Since 2000, immigrants have taken more than 100 percent of new jobs, that is, both capturing new jobs and displacing Americans from existing jobs (Sum 2004).

Borjas and Freeman find that the loss is borne disproportionately by poorest Americans (1996). As political scientist Frank Morris, then dean of Graduate Studies and Urban Research at Morgan State University, testified before Congress, "It is clear that America's black population is bearing a disproportionate share of immigrants' competition for jobs, housing and social services" (1990). Immigration harms America and harms most those who are in greatest need of their countrymen's compassion (Rubenstein 1997).

Only now are losses creeping up from the most disadvantaged Americans into the middle class. It appears that the introduction of H1-B visa programs added computer analysts, engineers, and medical researchers to the losers' column (Zibel 2003, 1). In summary, immigration mainly helps the immigrants themselves and employers who profit from cheap labor. As a driver of continuing high fertility rates, immigration harms people remaining in countries from which immigrants come. Perhaps immigration should be taken in small doses. Mass immigration is a dangerous phenomenon, one that should be seen as a threat to the well-being of societies worldwide.

The "One-World" Thesis as an Obstacle to Environmental Preservation*

In its modern form, the ethic of international redistribution is expressed in such terms as "one-world." Although one-world has primarily an ecological meaning, the phrase also calls upon industrialized countries to assist countries of the third world; in some

---

In Resources, Environment, and Population: Present Knowledge, Future Options, Edited by Kinglsley Davis and Mikhail S. Berstam based on a conference held at the Hoover Institution, Stanford University, 1–3 February 1989 and published as a Supplement to Volume 16, Population and Development Review, pp. 323–28. Oxford University Press [1991].

contexts, one-world implies an attack on the legitimacy of unevenly distributed wealth. So construed, it may in fact be incompatible with conservation goals.

The idea that conservation depends upon appropriate incentives is not new. Garrett Hardin (1968), in "The Tragedy of the Commons," develops the insight that a scarce resource is inevitably consumed when those who use it most intensively get the largest share. In an unregulated commons, the admonition to "use it or lose it" takes on new meaning.

Any idea or practice that treats a resource as belonging to all or as claimable on the basis of need would appear to create a commons, and thus, except perhaps under conditions of low population density, creates the possibility if not the probability, of a tragedy of the commons. An ethic of equity that entails *involuntary* redistribution undermines the legitimacy of ownership and undercuts the incentive to save. Since saving entails self-denial and postponement of consumption to some future date, it must overcome an initial handicap. A further burden, insecurity over rights to enjoy future benefits, can be overwhelming. A resource must, therefore, be conveyed with as much certainty as social institutions can muster, namely, through ownership. When tenure is not secure, individual strategies of rapid consumption defeat efforts at conservation.

Nations, like individuals, have less motivation to forgo present benefits if they doubt they will reap future rewards from their saving. One-world ideology, which implies a commitment to sustaining the needy wherever they may be, creates ambiguity over the ownership of resources. As with most "commons," it fosters a preference for short-term consumption over long-term saving.

The redistribution ethic not only undercuts incentives to conserve, but in a vastly overpopulated world may be impracticable. Uneven distribution seems a requisite of conservation under conditions where many are absolutely destitute and cannot afford to forgo consumption of their capital stock.

With respect to land, continuing redistribution produces smaller and smaller units to the point where subsistence needs overwhelm all possibility of protecting long-term viability. The threat of famine is a quite sufficient inducement for a family to plant every last hectare in food crops, which in many instances results in deforestation and the degradation of marginal lands.

Thus, ethicists need to reexamine equity issues in terms of a system that encompasses global conservation. A conservation ethic may require a renewed acceptance of uneven distribution. Conservation in the sense of future-oriented protection of the carrying capacity is *preferred* by those who anticipate long-term tenure and is *affordable* only by those nations, institutions, and individuals who are not compelled to consume their wealth, including natural capital, as a last-ditch survival strategy.

No simple formula for conservation can be drawn, however, from such observations, which suggest only that the prospect for environmental preservation depends upon characteristics of the entity that owns, uses, or otherwise controls a resource. In other words, destruction of resources may result not only from entitlements and unregulated use of those that are held in a commons, but also from numerous functional equivalents.

Affluent individuals or entities will be motivated to protect the Earth's natural resources only insofar as it is in their interest to do so. The wealthy should be prevented from despoiling one niche and moving on to another: for example, lumbering off the Brazilian rain forest, selling the denuded land, and depositing profits in a foreign bank (Cohen 1989). In the first quarter of 1989, nationals of the third world's fifteen largest debtor nations were holding US$340 billion in foreign banks, up from less than $100 billion in 1980 (*Business Week* 1989). Given the mobility of monetized capital, it is difficult to envision a sufficient incentive, or workable enforcement mechanism, to tie wealthy individuals to land or any particular natural resource so that they would have a stake in conserving its long-term productivity. Yet, this must eventually be part of a solution.

Nor is government a reliable repository of resources. The Brazilian government regards international efforts to protect the rain forest as intrusive; conservation is secondary to its seeing forest lands as "resources to be exploited and as space for its fast-growing population" (Cohen 1989, p. A6). Government control of the entire productive enterprise can be similarly wasteful of natural resources and long-term carrying capacity and without corresponding benefit to those governed in terms of useful outputs (see *Resources, Environment, and Population: Present Knowledge, Future Options*, edited by Kinglsley Davis and Mikhail S. Berstam 1991).

The essential factor in every situation is the irrevocable linkage of individual long-term benefit to a particular piece of land, resource, community, or nation. The key appears to be accountability to one's own future and that of one's children in terms of preserving carrying capacity within a niche that one can control. Without control, or with the possibility of moving on, conservation becomes unlikely if not impossible.

The variety of tenure arrangements congruent with conservation of trees could become a model for policy research. Bruce and Fortmann (1989) confirm that the expectation of enjoying a long-term benefit is a common factor in all successful conservation efforts. They show that maintaining secure, private ownership of land on which trees grow and establishing rights to land by planting trees are both conducive to conservation. Under very limited circumstances they find that a commons may be a workable arrangement; but commons seem virtually impossible to establish programmatically, and they function only if use is regulated by strong conservation traditions. Moreover, conservation traditions governing use of forest products do not survive pressure from growing populations (Bruce and Fortmann 1989). The gradual movement toward more intensive and ultimately destructive use resembles the shortening of fallow periods in shifting-agriculture economies beset by overpopulation (see Russell 1988).

A final criticism of the redistributive aspect of one-world ideology is that it may undermine population control efforts within the very countries that could most benefit from such efforts. Forty countries are estimated to rely on foreign aid for at least a quarter of their national budget (Harper's Index 1989), no doubt reinforcing both belief in the one-world rhetoric and felt entitlement to a share in the world's resources. The resulting sense of security, although false, can only neutralize signals of local scarcity that should be warnings against further population growth.

Local scarcity within a global, one-world frame of reference, when others are richer, must seem both unfair and artificial. Any shortfalls in supply tend to be interpreted as a problem of distribution and equity rather than as a signal of limits that inevitably impinge on all. Scarcity does not act as an inducement to curtail demand if one feels entitled to a share of someone else's property. This response is especially pernicious when those others (because of their generosity) are perceived to have unlimited and renewable wealth. One-world thinking, I suggest, is a stimulus to increase, not reduce, demands. It is probably a deterrent as well to decreasing desired family size.

Diversion of international development capital to support third world consumption has been common (Brooks 1989) and, unfortunately, probably confirms the widespread sense of entitlement and global wealth. Moreover, even if international aid results, as intended, in economic development, recent research suggests that the fertility reduction predicted by demographic transition theory may not materialize.

I have suggested elsewhere (Abernethy 1979) that expectations of scarcity or of unfulfilled wants may facilitate demographic change. Consider, for example, China's 1958 famine that preceded a decade of fertility control measures as severe as any recorded in modern times. Famine would probably not have inspired such draconian measures had China been linked with the world community at the time. By its own choice, China remained isolated. News of famine barely penetrated into the Western world. Certainly no assistance was asked for or proffered. One-world thinking did not blur reality: appreciation of the scarcity of China's own resources could not have been more stark.

By contrast, one-world redistributive ideology obscures the reality that resources are finite. By encouraging overpopulated countries to tolerate further growth, it may seal their fate.

There is a similar effect when one nation is perceived to have open borders, welcoming all migrants. A country that allows itself to be used as a safety valve for others' excess population gives a counterproductive signal. If people who cannot find jobs in their own country are welcome to migrate across national boundaries, a reasonable interpretation is that resources at the destination are abundant. Such, of course, is the message sent by the very open, kinship-driven immigration policy of the United States (McConnell 1988). This policy probably contributes to neutralizing what would otherwise be alarming signals of scarcity and overpopulation in Central America (Willis 1984) and elsewhere (Haub 1988). The incorrect reading defeats many other inducements to reduce fertility.

Thus, much-reduced, time-limited international aid and restrictive immigration policies in wealthier countries are responsible and ethical approaches on several grounds. Not only would correct signals about scarcity and population growth be sent to high-fertility regions, but also the dissipation of wealth and the impact of population growth on a wealthier nation's natural resources would be avoided (costs that almost always are disproportionately borne by their own poor).

Most Western countries now adhere to restrictive immigration policies. France, known as the refugee capital of Europe, rejects 67 percent of asylum applications: "French officials claim these are economic refugees rather than victims of political persecution" (Marlow 1989, 19). The United States alone has raised both immigration and refugee admissions in response to advocacy group pressures. For example, recent legislation waives the usual test for refugee status—"having a well-founded fear of persecution"—for nationals of the Soviet Union and Indochina; if fully funded, the program would admit such persons in unlimited numbers on the basis of being "presumed" to be refugees. This legislation traveled at high speed despite its potential billion dollar annual cost: introduced by Congressmen Morrison, Frank, Schumer, Berman, and Fish on April 18, 1989, it passed both the House of Representatives and Senate before the summer recess.

Although a restrictive immigration policy has not yet been adopted by either the executive branch or the US Congress, it may be one of the stronger means available in the short run for impressing upon third world countries the unsustainability of their population growth rates. Moreover, limiting immigration into the United States to "replacement level" would both help protect the domestic environment and accurately reflect the average American's concern over world population growth and immigration (Pittsburgh Press 1988; Hernandez and Braun 1988). Replacement-level immigration, an all-inclusive inflow of about 200,000 annually, would slightly more than balance those entering with the number estimated to be voluntarily leaving. Complementing the below-replacement fertility level already achieved in the United States, it would lead eventually to a stationary population and at a much lower level of population than is currently assumed with, say, 600,000 immigrants per year.

I have suggested that unequal distribution, both within and among nations, is a sine qua non of conservation in a world of growing populations. Waste and degradation of natural resources seem likely to become normal practice when the private, local incentive to conserve the carrying capacity disappears. If everyone owns or uses the resource, who is going to conserve it? And who will believe in scarcity (overpopulation) so long as anyone, anywhere, is better off and professes a commitment to share?

When ownership of a natural resource is ambiguous, or the resource is inadequate, the consumption and loss of natural capital are inevitable. Thus in an overpopulated world, a redistribution ethic is inappropriate.

The challenge is to develop a policy and ethic which recognizes that a modicum of distributional equity is probably a luxury sustainable only within relatively rich nations that have stationary populations. Given the speed of global environmental deterioration, hard thinking seems in order.

Notes

1. This paper contains excerpts from a book in press, *Population Politics: choices That Shape Our Future* (New York: Plenum Press/Insight Books, 1993 Reprinted by Transaction Publishers 1990).
2. Intention is relevant for women who are not at risk for pregnancy either because of postpartum amenorrhea or abstinence, or because they already are pregnant.
3. The overall rate 2.1 is a blend of the native-born and the immigrant sectors.
4. Population doubling times are computed by dividing a growth rate into 70. Thus $70/0.6 = 117$ years.
5. Doubling time $= 70/2.3 = 30.4$ years.

References

Abernethy, Virginia Deane. 1979. *Population Pressure and Cultural Adjustment.* New York: Human Sciences Press.

Abernethy, Virginia Deane 1979. *Population Pressure and Cultural Adjustment.* New York: Human Sciences Press/Plenum Press.

Abernethy, Virginia Deane 1979. *Population Pressure and Cultural Adjustment.* New York: Human Sciences Press. [Second edition, Transactions Publications 2005].

Abernethy, Virginia Deane, and Roberto V. Penaloza. 2002. "Fertility Decline in Former Asian Tigers." *Population and Environment* 23 (3): 245–66.

Abernethy, Virginia Deane. 1993a. *Population Politics: The Choices that Shape Our Future.* New York: Plenum Press (Reprinted 2000, Transaction Publishers).

Abernethy, Virginia Deane. 1994. "Asclepian Perspective on Immigration: First Do No Harm." *National Geographic Research and Exploration* 10 (4): 379–83.

Abernethy, Virginia Deane. 1996. "Ethics, Migration, and Global Stewardship." *International Migration Review* 30 (1): 132–50.

Abernethy, Virginia Deane. 1997. "Allowing Fertility Decline: 200 Years after Malthus's Essay on Population." *Environmental Law* 27 (4): 1097–110.

Abernethy, Virginia Deane. 1999. "A Darwinian Account of the Fertility Opportunity Hypothesis." *Population and Environment* 21 (2): 119–48.

Abernethy, Virginia Deane. 2000. "Population and Environment: Assumptions, Interpretation, and Other Reasons for Confusion." In *Where Next: Reflections on the Human Future,* edited by Duncan Poore. Kew (London): Board of Trustees: Royal Botanic Gardens.

Abernethy, Virginia Deane. 2000. "Population Dynamics: Why We can Sit Back and Watch Fertility Fall." In *Population Problems: Topical Issues,* edited by J. Rose, 35–43. Amsterdam: Gordon and Breach Science Publishers.

Abernethy, Virginia Deane. 2002. "Fertility Decline; No Mystery." Published Electronically in Ethics in Science and Environmental Politics (ESEP), 1–11, May 24, 2002. Accessed January 12, 2016. http://www.esep.de/articles/esep/2002/article1.pdf

Abernethy, Virginia Deane. 2002. "Population Dynamics: Poverty, Inequality, and Self-Regulating Fertility Rates." *Population and Environment* 24 (1): 69–96.

Abernethy, Virginia Deane. December 1994. "Optimism and Overpopulation." *The Atlantic Monthly*, 84–91.

Aswad, B. 1981. *And the Poor Get Children: Radical Perspectives on Population Dynamics.* Edited by K. L. Michaelson. New York: Monthly Review Press.

Atiyah, M., and Press, F. February. 1992. *Population Growth, Resource Consumption, and a Sustainable World.* Washington, DC: Royal Society of London and U.S. National Academy of Sciences.

Attarian, John. 2003. *Immigration: Wrong Answer for Social Security.* Raleigh, NC: American Control Press.

Ayres, R. 1983. *Banking on the Poor: The World Bank and World Poverty.* Cambridge, MA: MIT Press.

Banister, Judith. 1987. *China's Changing Population.* Stanford, CA: Stanford University Press.

Benedick, R. E. 1988. "Population-environment Linkages and Sustainable Development." *Populi* 15 (3): 15–21.

Borjas, George, R. Freeman, and L. Katz. May 1996. "Searching for the Labor Market Effects of Immigration." *American Economic Review* 86:246–51.

Borjas, George. 1999. *Heaven's Door.* Princeton, NJ: Princeton University Press.

Borjas, George. 2004. "Increasing the Supply of Labor Through Immigration." CIS Backgrounder, May 2004.

Bouvier, Leon. 1995. "More African Famines in the Future?" *Clearing House Bulletin* 5 (2): 1–3. Washington, DC: Carrying Capacity Network.

Brittain, A. W. 1990. "Migration and the Demographic Transition: A West Indian Example." *Social and Economic Studies* 39 (3): 39–64.

Brittain, A. W. 1991. "Anticipated Child Loss to Migration and Sustained High Fertility in an East Caribbean Population." *Social Biology* 38 (1–2): 94–112.

Brooks, G. 1989. "Lavish U.S. Food Aid to Egypt Has Bought Peace but Little Else." *Wall Street Journal*, 3 April, pp. 1 and 8.

Bruce, J. W., and L. Fortmann. 1989. "Agroforestry: Tenure and incentives," Land Tenure Center Paper No. 35. Madison: Land Tenure Center, University of Wisconsin.

Business Week. 1989. "Can this Flight Be Grounded?," 10 April, p. 74.

Caldwell, John C., I. O. Orubuloye, and Pat Caldwell. June 1992. "Fertility Decline in Africa: A New Type of Transition?" *Population and Development Review* 18 (2): 211–43.

Camarota, Steven A. 2005. *Births to Immigrants in America, 1970 to 2002.* Washington, DC: Center for Immigration Studies.

Camarota, Steven A. *Immigrants in the United States—2000: A Snapshot of America's Foreign-Born Population.* Washington, D.C.: Center for Immigration Studies, January, 2001.

Camarota, Steven A. July 2005. *Births to Immigrants in America, 1970 to 2002.* Washington, DC: Backgrounder, Center for Immigration Studies.

Camarota, Steven A. October 2004. *A Jobless Recovery? Immigrant Gains and Native Losses.* Washington, DC: Center for Immigration Studies.

Cohen, R. 1989. "Amazon Tug-of-War Reaches Fever Pitch." *Wall Street Journal*, 7 April, p. A6.

Connell, K. H. 1968. *The Population of Ireland, 1750–1845*. Oxford: Clarendon Press.

Conrad, Cristoph, Lechner, M., and Werner, Welf. 1996. East German Fertility after Unification: Crisis or Adaptation? *Population and Development Review* 22 (2): 331–58.

Cornelius, W. A. 1989. "Impacts of the 1986 U.S. Immigration Law on Emigration from Rural Mexican Sending Communities." *Population and Development Review* 15 (4): 689–705.

Courbage, Youssef. 1995. "Fertility Transition in the Mashriq and Maghrib." In *Family, Gender, and Population in the Middle East*, edited by Carla M. Obermeyer. Cairo: The American University in Cairo Press.

Demeny, P. 1968. "Early Fertility Decline in Austria-Hungary: A Lesson in Demographic Transition." *Daedalus* 97 (2): 502–22.

Demeny, P. 1988. "Social Science and Population Policy." *Population and Development Review* 14 (3): 451–80.

Díaz-Briquets, S., and L. Pérez. 1981. *Cuba: The Demography of Revolution*. Washington, DC: Population Reference Bureau.

Drake, M. 1963–1964. "Marriage and Population Growth in Ireland, 1740–1845." *Economic History Review*, 2nd series 16:303–5.

Drake, M. 1969. *Population and Society in Norway 1735–1865*. Cambridge: Cambridge University Press.

Dyson, Tim. 1991a. "On the Demography of South Asian Famines. Part I." *Population Studies* 45:5–25.

Dyson, Tim. 1991b. "On the Demography of South Asian Famines. Part II." *Population Studies* 45:279–97.

Easterlin, R. 1962. *The American Baby Boom in Historical Perspective*. Occasional paper #79. New York: National Bureau of Economic Research.

Easterlin, R. 1971. "Does Human Fertility Adjust to the Environment?" *American Economic Review* 61 (2): 399–407.

Eberstadt, Nicholas. 1994. "Demographic Shocks after Communism: Eastern Germany 1989–93." *Population and Development Review* 20 (1): 137–52.

Ehrlich, P. and A. Ehrlich. 1990. *The Population Explosion*. New York: Simon and Schuster.

Fargues, Philippe. 1995. "Changing Hierarchies of Gender and Generation in the Arab World." In *Family, Gender, and Population in the Middle East*, edited by Carla Maklouf Obermeyer. Cairo: The American University in Cairo Press.

Fargues, Philippe. 1997. "State Policies and the Birth Rate in Egypt: From Socialism to Liberalism." *Population and Development Review* 23 (1): 115–38.

"Fertility Declining Among Younger Women in Sudan," 1991. Newsletter 4 (1): 5, Demographic and Health Surveys, IRD/Maco, Columbia, MD.

Fletcher, J. 1976. "Feeding the Hungry: An Ethical Appraisal." In *Lifeboat Ethics: The Moral Dilemmas of World Hunger*, edited by George L. Lucas, Jr. and Thomas W. Ogletree. New York: Harper and Row.

Freidlander, D. 1983. "Demographic Responses and Socioeconomic Structure: Population Processes in England and Wales in the Nineteenth Century." *Demography* 20:249–72.

Gore, A. 1992. *Earth in the Balance: Ecology and the Human Spirit.* Boston, MA: Houghton Mifflin.

Govindasamy, P., and J. DaVanzo. 1992. "Policy Impact on Fertility Differentials in Peninsular Malaysia." *Population and Development Review* 18 (2): 243–67.

Handwerker, W. P. 1991. "Women's Power and Fertility Transition: The Cases of Africa and the West Indies." *Population and Environment* 13 (1): 55–78.

Hardin, G. 1968. "The Tragedy of the Commons." *Science* 162 (13 December): 1243–8.

Hardin, G. 1993. "Foreword to Abernethy, V." *Population Politics: Choices That Shape our Future.* New York: Plenum Press.

Harper's Index. 1989. *Harper's Magazine,* March, p. 17.

Hassan, S. "After UNCED: The Population Issue Revisited." Conference: Tufts University May 31–June 4, 1994.

Haub, C. 1988. "A Billion More each Decade: The Population Crisis Lives." *International Herald Tribune,* 29 July.

Heilig, G., T. Buttner, and W. Lutz. 1990. *Germany's Population: Turbulent Past, Uncertain Future.* Washington, DC: Population Reference Bureau.

Hern, W. M. 1991. "Book review of *The Population Dynamics of the Mucajai Yanomama* by J.D. Early and J.F. Peters." *Population Studies* 45:359.

Hernandez, M., and S. Braun. 1988. "Negatives Cited in Times Poll on Immigrants." *Los Angeles Times,* 19 September.

"Hong Kong Women Flying to U.S. to Have Their Babies." March 27, 1989. *San Francisco Chronicle,* 1, 12.

Huddle, D. L. 1997. *The Net Fiscal Costs of Immigration 1996.* Washington, DC: Carrying Capacity Network.

Huddle, D. L., and D. Simcox. 1994. "The Impact of Immigration on the Social Security System." *Population and Environment* 16 (1): 91–98.

Inter-American Development Bank Web (IADB). 2004. *Sending Money Home: Remittances to Latin America from the US, 2004.* [http:/iadb.org] Author, 2004.

Johnson, T. January 27, 1992. "Kin in U.S. Keep Salvador Afloat in Cash." *Miami Herald,* 1, 9A.

Kalipeni, Ezekiel. 1996. "Demographic Response to Environmental Pressure in Malawi." *Population and Environment* 17 (4): 285–308.

Keyfitz, N. September, 1989. "The Growing Human Population." *Scientific American,* 119–26.

King, M. 1990. "Health Is a Sustainable State." *The Lancet* 336:664–7.

Knodel, J. E. 1974. *The Decline of Fertility in Germany, 1871–1939.* Princeton, NJ: Princeton University Press.

Lappe, F. M. 1980. *Aid as Obstacle: Twenty Questions, Foreign Aid and The Hungry.* San Francisco, CA: Institute for Food and Development.

Lemsine, A. March, 1992. *God Guard Islam from the Islamists.* The Washington Report on Middle Eastern Affairs, 14, 16.

Malthus, T. R. [1798] 1967. *Population: The First Essay.* Ann Arbor, MI: University of Michigan Press.

Malthus, T. R. 1803. *Essays on Population,* "New Edition." Privately printed, London.

Marlowe, L. 1989. "A Five-star Exit." *This World,* 2 April, 18–19.

May, John F. 1995. "Policies on Population, Land Use, and Environment in Rwanda." *Population and Environment* 16 (4): 321–34.

McConnell, S. 1988. "The New Battle Over Immigration." *Fortune,* 9 May, 89–102.

Micklin, P. O. 1988. "Dessication of the Aral Sea: A Water Management Disaster in the Soviet Union." *Science* 241:1170–76.

Moffett, George D. 1994. *The Global Population Challenge: Critical Masses*. New York: Viking Press.

Morris, Frank. 1990. "Testimony before the US House of Representatives Judiciary Committee Subcommittee on Immigration, Refugees, and International Law." Congressional Record, March 13, 1990.

Nelson, A. January 20, 1990. Personal communication. Washington, D.C.

Notestein, F. 1945. "Population: The Long View." In *Food For Thought*, edited by T.W. Schultz. Norman Wait Harris Memorial Lectures.

Ohlin, G. 1961. "Mortality, Marriage and Growth in Pre-industrial Populations." *Population Studies* 14 (3): 190–7.

Pimentel, D. and M. Pimentel. 1990. *Land, Energy and Water: The Constraints Governing Ideal U.S. Population Size*. Teaneck, NJ: Negative Population Growth.

Pittsburgh Press. 1988. "Poll Reveals U.S. Fear of Global Population." 19 September, p. 2.

Population Reference Bureau, "Man's Population Predicament." *Population Today*, Dec. 4, 1991, Washington, DC.

Population Reference Bureau. 1991. Spot Light: Myanmar. *Population Today* 12:4, PRB, Washington, DC.

Population Reference Bureau. *2004 World Population Data Sheet*. Washington, DC: Author, various dates.

Pritchett, L. A. 1994. "Desired Fertility and the Impact of Population Policies." *Population and Development Review* 20 (l): 1–55.

Rollet-Echalier, C. 1990. *La Politique à l'Égard de la Petite Enfance sous la IIIe Republique*. Paris: Presses Universitaires de France.

Rubenstein, Edwin. 1997. "Right Data: Wealth Disparity Larger in High Immigration Impact Cities, 1980–1996." *National Review* December 22:12.

Rubenstein, Edwin. 2004. Immigration Impact on American Dropouts, College Grads, Increasing. www.VDARE.com August 17, 2004.

Russell, W. M. S. 1988. "Population, Swidden Farming and the Tropical Environment." *Population and Environment* 10 (2): 77–94.

Shepherd, J. April 1985, "When Foreign Aid Fails." *Atlantic Monthly*, 41–46.

Skerry, P. 1989. "Boarders and Quotas: Immigration and the Affirmative-action State." *The Public Interest* 96:86–102.

Spaeth, A. December 31, 1991. "An Indian Lawyer and His Ruby as Big as the Ritz," *Wall Street Journal, Arts and Leisure page*.

Steele, W.K.. August 5, 1989. Letter to the Hon. Tom Foley, U.S. House of Representatives, Washington, D.C..

Sullivan, T. 1988. "Immigration from Mexico. Review of Return to Aztlan by D.S. Massey, R. Alarcon, J. Durand, and H. Gonzalez." *Science* 240:1059–60.

Sum, Andrew, et al. 2004. *Foreign Immigration and the Labor Force of the United States*. Center for Labor Market Studies, Northeastern University, July, 2004.

Turke, P. W. 1989. "Evolution and the Demand for Children." *Population and Development Review* 15 (1): 61–90.

U.S. Immigration and Naturalization Service. 1987. Table: Immigrants admitted by country or region of birth, fiscal years 1945–1986. Statistical Analysis Branch, INS, Washington, DC.

Willis, D. K. 1984. "Overcrowding: The Impact and the Risks." *The Christian Science Monitor* 8 August: 21–22.

Zibel, Alan. 2003. "American Jobs in Jeopardy: High Tech, Low Security." *Oakland Tribune*, August 31, 2003, p. 1.

6

Population Growth Threatens Women and Children

Introduction

Sociobiology contributes to understanding male and female roles in large animal species as well as the distinction between mating and procreation.

The male role in procreation can be as little as transfer of sperm, implying that males can father multiple offspring within a very short time. On the contrary, females are committed to gestation time and, usually, nurturing the young after birth. Time constraints often limit females to one, or a brood of a few, at a time. Because of investing heavily in each birth, females tend to choose males whose qualities promise to make them the best bet for successfully raising the cherished few.

The time constraints involved in procreation and the relatively greater investment by females usually determines that they are "scarce" relative to males. The corollary is that males often compete for access to the relatively scarce females. Sociobiologists call the competition to mate "reproductive effort".

Seahorse procreative and mating patterns prove, at least to me, that investment in raising young determines which sex is scarcer, and which sex must compete for a mate. Almost uniquely among vertebrates, the female seahorse investment in procreation is minimal; her sole contribution is egg-laying. A male invests by both fertilizing the eggs and taking them into his pouch for maturation, so sociobiologists reckon that relative investment in procreation makes males the scarcer sex. Observation reveals the expected result: females compete hardest in the mating game.

Among humans, the scenario of males competing for females applies so long as births are wanted. Women are highly valued both sexually and as mothers when their community accommodates, comfortably, its resident population. However, females' procreative capacity becomes a liability if population grows beyond the point where couples can maintain a culturally defined good standard of living.

Women-as-mothers lose value, and the balance between men and women shifts, when males successful enough to provision a family become scarce. Women's and children's lives are cheapened; exploitation in work or sex is common. Health care and sometime food for women and girl children are skimped. Differential mortality rates for girls and boys suggest discrimination against girls.

Humanitarian aid to developing countries often has the explicit goal of improving the life chances and well-being of women and children. My view, that aid that stimulates population growth is ultimately harmful to women, puts me at loggerheads with interventionists and entrenched public opinion naturally sympathetic to humanitarian-sounding (albeit shortsighted) arguments.

Women face different challenges in third world and more developed countries. In industrialized regions, women are better able to adapt to population pressure because they often have options beyond motherhood. In the United States, the phenomenon of women working in the paid labor force during peacetime emerged almost in lockstep with rapid population growth. Feminism was invented (think, Simone de Beauvoir) in France prior to being widely adopted in the United States. Had rapid population growth not combined with the 1960s frantic geographic mobility, which made women's maternal roles less rewarding at the same time that families began to need income from two earners, feminism might have withered.

Initially, I adopted feminism's tenets. But early articles were too optimistic because feminism's ostensible goals triggered unforeseen consequences. The pendulum, responding to women's needs for career options other than being housewives, has swung too far. I now think of feminism as a well-scripted attack on traditional families, male self-esteem, and normally enterprising men. As a wedge in a broader attack on culture, feminism has been remarkably successful—and remarkably damaging to the society at large.

Yet, my suspicion may be wrong. Perhaps traditional American culture does not have enemies who set out to upend its values and tradition. Perhaps rapid population growth is itself the sole and only enemy of women, men, and families alike.

Speculation aside, the formula for computing the *doubling time* for a population (or bank account) requires knowing the *percentage growth rate per time period.* Then, divide the percentage rate into seventy. The result is Time to Double. Seventy is a mathematically-established constant. [Examples: a population growing by 2 percent annually doubles in thirty-five years, because seventy divided by 2 = thirty-five. Or, growing by 1 percent annually, doubles in seventy years.

Al Bartlett, in each of his several thousand speeches on population growth and the exponential function, would add that a second doubling results in quadruple the starting size of a population. The third doubling results in eight times the starting size: exponential growth.

Coverage of the 1994 International Conference on Population and Development*

Articles on the Cairo Conference outlined several key points in the population debate, including the value of modern contraception as a humane means of limiting family size, and the need for loans to start women's business enterprises. Were I to dwell on these areas of agreement, I would create less friction but shirk a duty to critique current policy. Indeed, I think Cairo's World Programme of Action misses important connections between women and population.

The much-ballyhooed shift of emphasis in Cairo from population control to giving "priority to reproductive health, women's empowerment, and reproductive rights" is ironic. It denies the reality that the greatest threat to women's well-being is overpopulation—because their reproductive role is devalued in overpopulated societies. A comparison of countries and historical periods shows that women have been especially honored and treated as equals in frontier situations where population growth is a goal. Women are abused and relegated to subordinate roles when a region's ability to support its human burden is strained.

Cairo's World Programme of Action's implicit support of additional resource transfers from North to South is also troublesome. Policies that promote openness to international immigration or more development aid will only be counterproductive to population concerns. Especially in less-developed counties with high emigration rates, these policies relieve the sense of limits in the local environment. Abundant evidence shows that a perception of expanding economic opportunities leads to larger families and higher fertility rates, whereas fertility rates

---

*In *Environment* 37(6), p. 4 [July/August, 1995].

fall, often quickly, in response to perceived resource constraints. The need to absorb one's own young, as opposed to their setting forth as emigrants, also exerts downward pressure on family size.

In addition, the role of education, especially for women, is imperfectly understood. Although education and lower fertility rates are correlated statistically, this proves nothing about cause and effect. Moreover, subsistence societies such as the Yapese and Labrador Inuit, with little or no formal education, have been able to drastically lower fertility rates, and others, such as the New Guinea Enga, certain Australian Aborigines, and peoples of the Amazonian blackwater ecosystem maintain small family size through a variety of behaviors that affect reproduction. I conclude that developments that signal a need to limit the number of one's dependents should be allowed to work unfettered. Correspondingly, incentives to maintain large family size should be avoided, because replacement level fertility or lower is a *sine qua non* of long-term sustainability.

The rub is getting from here to there, and the intervening years of slowing population growth may be a time of painful readjustment. Since perception of expansive economic opportunity leads to raising family-size targets, one should avoid sending false signals about the availability of resources or the North's ability to provide support. A virtue of helping women into the cash economy and fostering the spread of modern contraception is that these programs do not signal rescue and are not consumption subsidies. Thus, they do not undercut the sense of limits that is critical for promoting reproductive and marital caution. Microloans and contraception are simply ways to prevent the burden of scarcity from being disproportionately placed on women.

The World's Women: Fighting a Battle, Losing the War*

When population pressure against resources rises, women's reproductive capacity—the key to future population growth—is devalued. Women are themselves often treated as threats in overpopulated societies, and their rights and freedoms shrink. This cultural response to rising population pressure is adaptive insofar as its effect is to damp growth. Nevertheless, the process is often inhumane. Women are victimized in myriad ways that legislated efforts to protect women's rights and health status seem powerless to quell. Some family planning programs

---

*In *Journal of Women's Health* 2(1), pp. 7–16 [1993].

are being redirected to give highest priority to women's health and status. These are laudable goals but, unfortunately, divert resources from the more basic task of lowering fertility to limit population growth. Assistance with birth control, paid work for women, and fostering the motivation to plan for small family size are the most effective ways to address fertility. Any strategy that shifts resources away from birth control and job programs of proven effectiveness is ultimately self-defeating because population growth itself poses the greatest threat to women's and children's well-being.

Introduction

People can be co-opted, we know. Less obvious is that issues are co-optable. High-visibility issues are seized on and used to further peripheral agendas or agendas related only as symptoms of an underlying common cause. The issue becomes a politicized tool, and resulting policy may contribute little to real solutions.

An issue that currently has high visibility and appears particularly vulnerable to being co-opted is overpopulation. Inescapably one of the foremost problems of our time, affecting almost every dimension of human experience, overpopulation is being seized on as a vehicle for promoting projects that focus on women's health and status (Jacobson 1992).

Improving women's health and status is a laudable goal to be sure, valuable in its own right, so ought one demur? The answer is unequivocably "Yes" if the hope and intent is to effect long-term, real benefits for women. Overpopulation must be addressed directly—not relegated to second place—because growing population pressure against resources is a (probably the) underlying cause of deterioration in women's health and status.

A much touted theory, that fertility (Jacobson 1992) will decline if women are educated, employed, and empowered, puts most of the cart before the horse. Contrary to much current thinking, improving women's health, status, and education have not been shown to change fertility. Fertility does decline after women go to work in the money economy, but this causal relationship is specific. Advocacy—other than for employment opportunity—diverts population control efforts. Therefore, it risks unwise deployment of the limited resources for which all family planning and population control programs compete.

This article shows that population pressure against resources constitutes the greatest threat to women's well-being. Women are victims of both poverty and deliberate, culturally sanctioned patterns of community and familial discrimination. These developments are discussed in the context of a larger topic: cultural adaptations that promote lower fertility and militate against further population growth. A fuller account appears in *Population Politics: Choices that Shape Our Future* (Abernethy 1993).

Women Are Early Victims of Population Pressure

Women appear to suffer disproportionately from overpopulation. They experience both deprivations that are inevitable when population outruns resources, and mounting discrimination within the family and from society at large. Although profound ambivalence toward women exists in many cultures, it is regularly seen to be most vicious where population threatens to grow beyond the carrying capacity of the environment. Childbearing is a uniquely female function, and when a family's standard of living is threatened by more mouths, the value of women's reproductive capacity plummets. Girl children are negatively regarded, particularly in families that have accumulated some wealth, because they signify future childbearing and so are often expensive to marry off. The demand for boys makes every birth a performance crisis with potential to provoke punitive retaliation against the mother. The UN Development Report's "female human development index" encapsulates the negative association between population growth and women's well-being (*Economist* 1991). Country studies also consistently show that the status accorded to women, as well as the control women have over their bodies and lives, varies inversely with population pressure.

At one extreme, settlers in the American west contemplated apparently boundless opportunity, fertility was valued, and—not altogether coincidentally I suggest—Wyoming Territory was the first in the United States to extend voting rights to women. Contrast this respect for women with cultural patterns that evolved in a chronically overpopulated country, China (Tien et al. 1992), and are being transplanted, regrettably, into the United States. In 1989, a Chinese immigrant (Dong Lu Chen) received only five years' probation after being convicted of killing his wife. She confessed to adultery, he bashed in her skull with a clawhammer, and the defense successfully argued to a New York City judge that the husband's action was understandable within the context of his own culture and ethnic enclave (Young 1992).

Different historical roots do not explain the contrast. Women have been abused at times worldwide, including in Europe. In various periods, European women have had no choice over whom they married, have been kicked and reviled during childbirth, and in the twelfth and thirteenth centuries were locked into chastity belts (which sometimes caused abrasions, blood poisoning, and death) while their husbands followed the Crusades.

The medieval pattern can be understood as an adaptive response to an exploding population. Numbers had begun to build fast starting about AD 800. In England, France, and other European countries, population approximately tripled between the years 1000 and 1300, and by the early thirteenth century, overpopulation resulted in famines during which many Europeans and English died. The Crusades (which removed tens of thousands of men, women, and children from Europe), religious persecution of minorities in Spain, and the onset of the Hundred Years War between England and France, like the discrimination against women, are symptomatic of population pressure (Abernethy 1979).

Pathways leading from deteriorating economic opportunity to oppression of women are varied. One often sees females exploited for their most obvious economic value: sex. Another route leads through religious fundamentalism: "Fundamentalism seems to thrive alongside the spread of poverty and unemployment" (*Economist* 1989).

Algeria's history since independence from France in 1962 exemplifies a not atypical cycle. The euphoria associated with independence triggered very high fertility, so that today, after thirty years, 70 percent of the population is under thirty years of age, and the population growth rate in 1991 surged on at 2.7 percent per year. A result is that 7.5 million of Algeria's 25 million inhabitants are unemployed; the society increasingly polarizes into rich and poor; and women's recently-won civil rights are threatened by religious fundamentalism (Lemsine 1992).

The rise of the religious right and the still-present threat to women's reproductive choice in the United States also coincide with narrowing economic opportunity. The poor and middle class are especially hard hit because their job prospects have shrunk as a result of a swollen unskilled labor force and a rate of population growth—1.1 percent per year—which contrasts starkly with that of every other industrialized Western nation (Borjas and Freeman 1992; Francis 1991; Harrison 1992; Huddle 1992).

Japan experienced overpopulation in the past but has now turned a corner. Population growth was ushered in by political stability in the late seventeenth century and accelerated with the opening of international trade in the late nineteenth century. It culminated by the 1930s in population increases running at one million per year. One may assume that institutionalized prostitution (geishas), the subservient status of wives, and militarism were among the many consequences. Since 1950, however, the Japanese have had very low fertility and have prohibited immigration. The result is that their population growth is nearly halted. Women, now needed in the workforce, are seeing their status rise. Moves are underway that, by 1995, will allow married women to legally use their own names in business and official contexts (*Wall Street Journal* 1992).

Recent history contains few examples of rising female status. On the contrary, the crescendo of overpopulation in most regions of the world is accelerating the opposite trend.

India and Pakistan

India's 2 percent rate of natural increase (excess of births over deaths) means that the population doubles every thirty-five years (doubling times are easily computed by dividing a growth rate into seventy). Unsurprisingly, the sex ratio is slowly becoming more extreme, revealing more and more discrimination against women and female children. Bose (Bose 1991) finds that in just the decade from 1981 to 1991, a ratio of 934 females per 1,000 males changed to 929 per 1,000. Restating these data for comparison with Ansley Coale's numbers in the next paragraph: a ratio of 107 males to 100 females rose within one decade to nearly 108 males per 100 females.

Demographer Ansley Coale (Coale 1991) of Princeton University calculates that India would have just 102 males for every 100 females if the sexes were treated equally, which suggests that nearly 6 percent of India's women are missing! Comparing expected and actual sex ratios, demographers calculate that sixty million females are missing in Asia alone. Worldwide, the number may top a hundred million. Other countries with fewer females than expected are Afghanistan (despite military losses in their civil war), Bangladesh, Bhutan, Nepal, Pakistan, Papua New Guinea, China, Egypt, and Turkey.

Discrimination against widows perhaps even unto murder (suttee), abuse and murder of brides, female neglect and infanticide, abortion, and the caste system (which preordains who will go without when there is not enough) persist in India despite a constitution that discourages all and even prohibits most such practices. A Hindu fundamentalist revival, which may be occurring, would almost certainly bring back suttee, which was outlawed in 1920s under British colonial influence. Nevertheless, it occurred in remote areas until at least 1960, and rumors of its persistence continue (Chaudry 1990; Abernethy 1979).

A similar renewal of fundamentalism, in this case Muslim, threatens women in Pakistan.* Islamic sex laws were reintroduced in 1979, and the number of women in prison for alleged adultery (after an improperly registered divorce) rose from 70 in 1980 to 4,500 in 1990. Many of these women prefer prison to being released to the custody of their natal families, from whom they fear abuse if not death* (*Tennessean* 1992).

Even where illegal, abuse persists because it is supported, or at least tolerated, by secular and religious authority. For example, setting the scene for a domestic accident, a traditional Indian family struggles to arrange a daughter's marriage. Trying to avoid the shame of an unwed daughter, a father is likely to promise an obviously larger dowry than ever can be accumulated. Problems surface after a marriage is consummated and dowry installments come due but are not paid. The bridegroom's family becomes infuriated at being cheated, and the bride (who lives in her father-in-law's house) suffers. Stories crop up repeatedly in the Indian press of young women found in wells or accidentally burned to death. Even in notorious cases, though, the bridegroom and his family have not been convicted of crimes (Bumiller 1990; Freed and Freed 1989).

In most castes, females are the most frequent victims of both crime and neglect. Bajpai (1991) reports, "In Punjabi families where there is already a girl, the mortality rate for the next daughter is as high as 53 percent." Congruently, the sex ratio in one community in Rajasthan State is among the highest in the world, approximately 1,000 men per 550 women. Well-documented differential access to health care explains part of these findings (Booth and Verma 1992).

Bangladesh, Sri Lanka, and Thailand

Bairagi's observations (Bairagi 1986) in Bangladesh show an increasing disparity in the treatment of boys and girls during a famine. Boys remain better off in terms of both mortality and weight for age, and the greater a family's wealth, the more pronounced the male advantage becomes. In-laws in the household, which in most societies means women, are the first deprived during a famine and, after them, their daughters.

---

*With a 3 percent rate of natural increase, Pakistan's population doubles every twenty-three years (70/3 = 23.3).

Tien et al. (1992) approach disproportionate female mortality from the perspective of "the internationally 'normal' sex ratio among infant deaths" (pp. 16–17). Greater male vulnerability and data from countries without obvious discrimination by sex suggest that the expected ratio is 130 male to 100 female infant deaths. In China, however, the 1989 ratio was 100.3 male to 100 female deaths, and in the first three months of 1990 (the most current data), the ratio dropped further to 96.3 male to 100 female deaths.

Additionally, "A United Nations Agency reports that child labor has 'worsened' in many areas." Many children work and live at home, but "indentured servitude is widespread in such poor countries as Pakistan, Bangladesh and Sri Lanka. . . . Girls bear extra burdens in many countries that value male children more; girls work twice as many hours as boys in Nepal" (*Wall Street Journal* July 21, 1992)

Prostitution

Up to one million third world women and children are sold into slavery by their families or kidnapped each year, often for prostitution (Barry 1979). In 1992, Sri Lankan authorities exposed a baby-selling ring. Families, mothers as well as fathers, sell their daughters into prostitution (the Asian-Pacific euphemism is sex worker). Bangladeshi girls eight–ten years old are sold at auction. Thailand's Foundation for Children estimates that 800,000 children and a further 1.2 million women are engaged in prostitution in that country alone. Some put the total at just 200,000, but, continues *The Economist* (*Economist*, November 10, 1990), "Even this figure would mean that 1 in 40 of all women aged 13–29 are engaged in prostitution" and at high risk, therefore, for sexually transmitted diseases [STDs].

Voluntary prostitution by poverty-stricken people occurs under almost as bad conditions. Both boys and girls trade sex for food or money in the Philippines. Half of the seven million prostitutes in France are from the third world, mostly South America. Pimps smuggle them in, arrange a location, and collect weekly fees. Prostitutes contract disease. Male prostitution in Haiti may be the route by which AIDS entered the United States. In Asia, AIDS spreads through heterosexual prostitution, particularly along drug routes of the golden triangle: Thailand, Burma, and Southern China.

Prostitution takes women out of reproductive contexts and, on the scale seen in Asia, will inevitably depress fertility rates and slow population growth. In this sense, prostitution is an adaptive response to overpopulation, albeit one that comes at terrible human cost. Overpopulation is real, and pathologic responses appear inexorable.

Eskimo

Comparisons between traditional societies whose main point of difference is population pressure on resources illuminate the idea that scarcity drives culture. Consider that Eskimo groups varied widely with respect to access to resources and prevalence of female infanticide. Moreover, resources and infanticide were strongly correlated (Freeman 1971; Riches 1974). Groups with the lowest sled dog/human ratio—meaning that they led a near-marginal existence—had the highest ratio of men/women. The more the sex ratio favors males, the stronger the suggestion of female infanticide.

Enga and Fore

Both population pressure and treatment of women contrast in two New Guinea societies, the Enga and the Fore (Abernethy 1979; Lindenbaum 1972; Meggitt 1964). The Enga warred constantly over their insufficient land. Overpopulation was an unrelenting threat, and, here, women and their reproductive capacity were severely devalued. The Enga demanded premarital virginity of both men and women, made every agricultural, hunting, or warlike event an occasion for abstinence, and strangled widows within 24 hours of bereavement. Funerary rituals honored men and pigs but not women or children.

The Fore had the opposite constraint. They were chronically underpopulated and in need of manpower to defend their territory. Kuru, a fatal neurologic disorder (similar to Jakob-Creutzfeldt disease) transmitted through a virus present in infected organs, was endemic. Its greatest prevalence was among women and children because women were responsible for preparing relatives for burial, which included ritual tasting of brains. With replacement of their numbers continually threatened by kuru, the Fore intensely valued every person, equally mourned a man, woman, or child's death, encouraged premarital sex, used fertility rituals to encourage growth in their gardens, dramatized the reproductive role of women, and performed erotic music at festivals. Young girls and widows were enthusiastically courted.

Australian Aborigines

The differing ecologies to which coastal and interior (outback) Australian Aborigines had to adapt probably explain certain other cultural contrasts. Marriage rules, for example, were much more elaborate in the outback, which is desert, and has a very low carrying capacity. Kinship divided each outback Aborigine tribe into eight marriage classes, and a woman in one class was restricted to marrying a man from a specific other class or subdivision. That is, only one-eighth of opposite sex persons were even potential mates. The number of marriage classes dropped from eight to two with nearness to the coast, where more rainfall and availability of marine resources make subsistence easier—that is, the ease of finding eligible mates rose along with the carrying capacity of the environment (Abernethy 1979).

Ethnographies of the Australian outback also abound with anecdotes about the brutal treatment of wives. In contrast, the Tiwi on the rich north coast lived easily from gathering shellfish and fishing; wives were greatly valued; older women were deeply immersed and powerful in the politics of marriage; men killed each other over runaway wives; and even a repeatedly adulterous wife was eagerly sought after and reaccepted (albeit beaten) by the aggrieved husband (Hart and Pilling 1960).

Small Islands

Islanders may be particularly sensitive to population pressure because limits are brutally manifest. The population cannot easily disperse. Indeed, anthropologist Raymond Firth (1936) links elaborate rules regulating premarital sexuality, marriage, and food exchanges to a history of terrible famine on one small Pacific island, Tikopia.

The history of Yap, another Pacific island, is less well known but possibly more dramatic. Oral tradition and archeology suggest that Yapese population pressure climaxed in about 1850, some generations after first contacts with Western trading ships. Anthropologist E.E. Hunt et al. (1954) use evidence of abandoned dwelling sites to estimate that population peaked at 51,000 persons, or about 1,300 per square mile. Formal records begin in 1899, by which time the population had dropped to 7,808 persons. By 1946, it was down to 2,582, a decline of 2.3 percent per year, a rate at which many third world countries today are growing. Suffering in Yap must have been intense over at least a generation. Oral tradition has it that, "Yap was then so crowded that disinherited and destitute men and even their families lived miserably on rafts in the mangrove swamps . . . and that sometimes four hungry men had to make a meal from a single coconut" (Hunt et al. 1954).

Hunt visited the Yapese around 1950 and concluded that contraception, abortion, and periods of abstinence even within marriage were used to limit family size. All of these methods were probably present in early Yapese culture, but Hunt thinks that they were greatly elaborated in response to nineteenth-century population pressure. Values and behaviors conducive to low fertility are too prominent to be random. The Yapese define "too much sex" as more than two or three times a month and, writes Hunt, "The usual jibe at a man who is weak or unwilling to work is that he has been copulating 'too much'" (Hunt et al. 1954). Weakness from sexual excess was caused by loss of vital body fluids. It also made one vulnerable to supernatural vengeance or fatal bites from poisonous fish. Hunt questioned native informants (presumably male) about sexual frequency and found only four of sixteen who would admit to having had sexual intercourse within the preceding ten–fifteen days. An additional six reported coitus within the preceding eight months.

Yapese women were at least as motivated as men to avoid reproduction. Ritual age-grading greatly multiplied married women's work in a large family, because sex age groups ate separately and at different times and had to be fed from separate garden plots. Their food had to be cooked in separate utensils and transported in separate trips from gardens that lay on top of steep mountain slopes. All this entailed more work for women.

Pregnancy was avoided by long postpartum sex taboos (up to seven years), contraception (bathing with concentrated ocean water after coitus and insertion of grass plugs to obstruct the cervix), and secret abortion. A few days' monthly retirement to a menstrual hut was available for abortion. Techniques included drinking salt water and insertion of rolled hibiscus leaves into the cervix.

Hunt et al. (1954) report finding no reference to infanticide or female neglect. However, they fail to make obvious connections. Births reported in the years 1946–1951 showed sex ratios ranging between 109 to 160 males per 100 females. Moreover, girls were three times as likely as boys to die in their first year.

The Yapese, forced to live within their island confines, devised a culture that motivated everyone to avoid childbearing. Much in their system seems harsh, and the harshest elements affected women, e.g., the household work associated with age-grading, a double bind that combined opportunity for premarital sex with shame being attached to premarital pregnancy, and female infanticide. Especially in the disproportionate burden falling on the female sex, these remnants of a cultural response to an overpopulation crisis recall worldwide developments today.

This cause-and-effect relationship, where discrimination against females both reflects devaluation of their reproductive role and appears, frequently, to limit successful reproduction, creates a profound dilemma. Campaigns against traditional practices seem humane on the surface but become problematic if one considers the role of culture in depressing fertility. The dilemma cannot be underestimated. Even when fertility-limiting practices are not defensible within the Western value system, can one ethically disturb them, in full knowledge that a society keeps population size and resources in balance by resort to such mechanisms? What if a country cannot otherwise avoid a cataclysmic imbalance of population and resources?

Trading Modern Contraception for Tradition

Traditional practices could be discarded without raising fertility if modern contraception were swiftly accepted as a substitute. However, customs that depress fertility are often lost faster than modern contraception becomes available or is accepted. Countries in flux, such as India, let us catch a glimpse of the process. Anthropologist Mahinder Chaudry (1990) expects that, in India, the transition from a partially traditional society to one where couples take responsibility for small family size will take twenty years. In the meantime, Chaudry expects progressive loss of indigenous cultures to enhance fertility more than the spread of contraceptive use depresses it. His prediction is congruent with a headline in a 1976 issue of the International Family Planning Digest: "Development alone may spur population growth."

Kingsley Davis (1951) suggests that traditional ways probably accounted for significantly lower fertility in India even as late as World War II, compared to what developed later. Perhaps independence from Great Britain, accomplished in 1947, triggered the surge in fertility because it promoted exuberant faith in the future. Moreover, people who had clung to traditional practices as a nationalistic statement might have become inclined to abandon them. By 1950, six to eight children (about three children more than formerly) was average for continuously married Indian women.

Today, the decline in Indian fertility seems stalled at just below four children per woman, although deteriorating economic conditions could prod it further down. However, it is not good news that Chaudry expects new contraceptive acceptance to have a weaker effect on fertility than the offsetting effect from modernization, that is, from abandoning traditional practices. The behaviors being lost are often not consistent with modern Western values, which is a principal reason they have been attacked and are disappearing. Nevertheless, those mechanisms were effective. Before contact, they probably were fully effective in keeping population size about constant, except for invasions and periods of exuberant trade.

Traditional Practices That Limit Successful Reproduction

Given normal fecundity, particular human actions including abstinence, mating, contraception, and induced abortion determine whether a woman will be exposed to pregnancy and, if pregnant, whether she will carry to term. The idea that family size preference is the likeliest determinant of how many children a women has is not new. Wanting fewer, or more, children matters so much that access to modern contraception seems to make little difference.

In fact, undisturbed, intact societies usually do well on their own. Without modern contraception, they still manage to keep fertility rates low and population size in balance with available resources. Traditional societies do not have natural fertility—all the children that every woman can bear in her natural lifetime. Moni Nag (1968), Davis (1951), and other students of culture have identified many beliefs, rules, and behaviors that depress fertility. Most of them involve limiting women's exposure to pregnancy rather than birth control or abortion. A woman who is prevented from being sexually active during most, or even all, of her adult life will not have a large family.

1. Delayed Childbearing. Delaying age of first birth, the traditional European pattern, is, in fact, quite common (Low 1990; Ohlin 1961). First, emphasis on virginity before marriage limits young women's chances of becoming pregnant. Then, if marriage is delayed into the late twenties or if some women never marry, average fertility remains low even if a few women have very large families (Abernethy 1979).

   Some African and Muslim societies have particularly harsh ways of enforcing premarital virginity. Some do not flinch at documenting virginity by hanging out bloody sheets from the marriage bed. A chicken may have to make the supreme sacrifice to uphold family honor. Other societies, including nomadic Somali clans and some North Africans, leave little to chance. A girl is infibulated, that is, the labia of the vagina are sewn together when she reaches puberty. The practice is entrenched in the culture so that the population control function, which may at one time have been explicit, is submerged in the intent to protect virginity. Infibulation and its frequent rider, clitoridectomy, are sometimes performed on Muslim girls even after immigrating with their families to Western Europe or the United States (Catchpole 1992; Hansen and Scroggins 1992).

A requirement to accumulate property (e.g., a dowry, paid by the bride's family) or demonstrate economic stability (e.g., steady employment or bride-price, paid by the groom) can delay marriage for all but the richest sector of a society. In an agricultural economy, inheriting land is often made a condition of marriage. Where all of a family's land devolves on one heir, as in the European patterns of primogeniture and ultimogeniture (inheritance by the youngest), only one son can easily support a family, and he alone is likely to marry. Many women marry very late or not at all, so the fertility rate stays low even if ideal family size and some families are large (Abernethy 1979; Demeny 1968; Low 1990; Ohlin 1961).

Polyandry, practiced in Tibet, depresses fertility because many women are unable to find a husband. In pre-Communist times, up to 30 percent of Tibetan women remained childless spinsters because a large proportion of the marriageable men were either in polyandrous unions or dedicated to the celibate Buddhist priesthood (Abernethy 1981; Beall and Goldstein 1981). Polyandry, primogeniture, and ultimogeniture have the same effect: many women remain unmarried.

2. Child Spacing. Even after marriage, exposure to pregnancy can be limited by physiologic or behavioral mechanisms. In societies that infibulate, a woman may be reinfibulated for a time after each birth. Breastfeeding is more benign, albeit less certain, delaying the return of ovulatory cycles for an average of thirteen months after delivery. The full contraceptive effectiveness of nursing depends on several factors. The most important are nursing frequency, because suckling depresses the hormones that trigger ovulation, and avoidance of supplementary feeding. Nursing on demand, and often, is most likely when the baby is carried everywhere in the day and sleeps beside its mother at night—common in polygynous marriages because the husband is not present.

Polygyny, popularly called polygamy, is often associated with long postpartum sex taboos, an obvious way to space pregnancies (Abernethy 1979; Early and Peters 1990; Hern 1991). Prostitution as well as polygyny make the taboo easier to observe because men potentially have access to more than one sexual partner. Wife-sharing among traditional Eskimo has the same effect. The postpartum sex taboo is often reinforced by magical beliefs, e.g., that a malevolent magical influence will be triggered by resuming sexual relations too soon or that mother's milk will be poisoned by another pregnancy. Yoruba women (in Nigeria) use polygyny to space children, even taking the initiative to provide their husband with an extra wife. They are the traditional traders of the society, and their choice to continue market activities sometimes takes them away from their village (Abernethy 1979).

3. The End Game. Rules prohibiting female remarriage are common, particularly in Asia, but their reproductive effect varies. If a woman is divorced or widowed very young and cannot remarry, she is unlikely ever to have many children. A young girl married by arrangement to a very old man might not even reach puberty before being widowed. Chaudry (1990) states that during the 1960s the average age of Indian

women being widowed was thirty-five, whereas earlier, in the 1930s, women were widowed by age twenty-nine. The six extra years let the culturally more modern 1960s woman have several children more than her counterpart would have had thirty years earlier.

4. Nonprocreational Sex. Impediments to sexual intercourse are the principal, but not the only, ways of avoiding reproduction in premodern cultures. Coitus interruptus (withdrawal) is used for birth control in many societies and was known by the time of Augustus Caesar, the first Roman Emperor. Pessaries, plugs placed against the cervix to block sperm away from the uterus, are another widely known device and are sometimes used with ointments that supposedly have spermicidal properties. Intrauterine devices have a long history, but premodern use by women is not documented. Sixteenth-century Arab drovers used intrauterine plugs on camels because pregnant camels are irritable beasts, suffering extremely from nausea and vomiting. Desert travelers cannot afford unreliable mounts, so stakes for camel contraception are high (Abernethy 1979).

5. Abortion. Abortion is known and used by women essentially everywhere. The most common methods are mechanical, including internal probes, blows to the stomach, jumping from heights, and violent exercise. Prescriptions and potions to induce abortion are also common, but not many have proven to be both effective and safe (Abernethy 1979). Riddle and Estes review traditional medicinal contraceptive and abortion agents but warn of their dangers (Riddle and Estes 1992).

6. Sterility. An overview of traditional abortion practices suggests that they are usually on par with the crude midwifery or quack medicine practiced in any country where abortion remains illegal. The chances of complicating infections are high, so that sterility and mortality are severe risks. Whenever premarital sex is more or less allowed (ignored) but premarital pregnancy is cause for scandal, women get pregnant and then have to hide it. The United States would still be putting women in this double bind except for relief available through *Roe v Wade* (1973).

   In contrast to industrialized countries, sterility rates as high as 50 percent have been reported in third world countries where STDs are widespread. A public health approach, both prophylactic and clinical, can reduce sterility secondary to STDs in less than a generation. The prevalence of STDs is probably increasing rather than decreasing, however, because prostitution is a major cause of spread.

7. Infanticide. Infanticide is another extreme means for changing reproductive outcomes. Rarely do societies relay on it, but in periods of stress or in certain individual circumstances, it is a last resort. Unwed mothers are perhaps the most likely candidates for committing infanticide, in both traditional and modern societies (Abernethy 1979; Bugos and McCarthy 1984). Early and Peters' ethnography of the (South American) Mucajai Yanomama (Early and Peters. 1990) reveals that 43.6 percent of all infant mortality is due to deliberate parental behavior. Twinning (among the Australian Aborigines) or a congenital anomaly often triggers infanticide Nomads who walk and carry their whole possessions

over vast territories have no alternative to infanticide if several years' suppression of ovulation induced by breastfeeding fails them (Hausfater and Hrdy 1984).

Female infanticide is the most common type in third world countries. Economic and ritual explanations for the sexual disparity are usually offered, but as shown, females are routinely devalued when overpopulation looms. Evolutionary selection for facultative, differential discrimination against females, except in the lowest strata of society, cannot be ruled out (Abernethy and Yip 1990; Betzig, Mulder, and Turke 1988; Boone 1986; Dickemann 1975),

Contraceptive Acceptance

Anthropology and history suggest that out-of-control population growth is an infrequent human condition. And rather than acting as a corrective to overpopulation, modernization and other interventions seem likely to trigger explosive population growth.

Even where large families are idealized, behavior patterns in undisturbed societies often limit fertility. Traditions and beliefs almost inadvertently limit successful reproduction, so that in many cultures, the explicit intention to limit family size is irrelevant as well as alien. This dysjunction between the cultures of some third world countries and developed countries explains, in part, why introducing modern contraception has been difficult. Low levels of contraceptive acceptance, even when access is easy, continue to frustrate family planning specialists.

Some two decades ago, Wyon and Gordon (1971) found that lavishly laying on resources did not induce people in Khanna, India, to limit family size. Health care, reducing infant mortality, education, and access to the technology of modern contraception did not lead to contraceptive use while family size was still small. Six children remained the preferred number. Motivational factors are as great impediments as any to adoption of modern contraception (Demeny 1968, 1988; Westoff 1988).

Family size targets stay high or rise when people think that limits that formerly operated have been relieved; so a windfall, real or perceived, encourages population growth. Perception of diminishing opportunity leads to behavioral and cultural modifications that depress fertility and eventually halt population growth (Abernethy 1979; Population Reference Bureau 1971).

In *Population Politics*, I reach the conclusion that rising expectations associated with modernization initially raise fertility rates. Modernization promises affluence—the new ways will make lives easier and better—so the first exposed generation has little reason to limit reproduction. Even emigration opportunity, which temporarily relieves population pressure for those who remain, appears to contribute to continuing high fertility (Brittain 1991; Friedlander 1983). Thus, well-meant programs and policies work at cross-purposes with their stated goals when they appear to signal rising prosperity and easily accessed wealth. Such beliefs dispel motivation to exercise caution and restraint. Large family size ideals persist and result in high fertility when extra children seem affordable.

So long as childbearing carries little opportunity cost to the family members who make fertility decisions, modern contraception is accepted only after the birth of many children—more than might formerly have been desired. A woman is seldom the sole decision maker. When male preferences prevail, fertility may remain high because men in third world countries bear much the lesser cost of childrearing, and many dislike both the idea and the mechanics of contraception (Draper 1989). Fertility declines, however, when women contribute to household cash flow. If women can earn money, child care has an opportunity cost in terms of economic benefits foregone, and both women and families who depend on their income are motivated to delay and space childbearing.

Anthropologist W. Penn Handwerker (Handwerker 1991) and others, going back at least twenty years, have found that fertility declines when women get job opportunities. Handwerker shows that even uneducated women reduce fertility below replacement level when they become financially independent of boyfriends and husbands. On several Caribbean islands, for example, menial hotel jobs became the harbingers of change.

The relationship between women's work and fertility holds true in many settings. Textile manufacture (employing women) in nineteenth-century Europe evolved from a cottage to a factory setting, and fertility rates fell sharply. In recent Taiwanese and Korean experience, women went to work, and fertility rates plummeted. In the 1960s and 1970s, American and European women went to work in very large numbers, and fertility also fell.

Save the Children Fund is a leader in creating economic opportunity for women. In Bangladesh, they have addressed women's needs with projects that are small scale and build on local efforts. Savings cooperatives help women invest in simple technology, such as mechanically operated sewing machines. Sometimes sewing results in financial independence, sometimes not. Men also see the advantage of putting women to work. Reportedly, one Muslim man has married the four allowable wives and has got them all sewing commercially. Exploitative? Probably, yes. But for Bangladesh and, arguably, the women themselves, that is better than getting pregnant.

The connection is clear, and the rationale is compelling. Fertility falls when women, or others who control them, can profit from woman's work outside the agricultural sector or home. A woman with independent income does not have to marry young or barter sex or childbearing for support. Husbands also have an incentive to limit family size when the family standard of living depends partly on women's earnings. Women's increased labor force participation reliably lowers fertility.

Unlike the proven effectiveness of jobs in lowering fertility, educating women per se is problematic. Studies linking women's education to declining fertility are largely correlational, and one learns to distrust those. Education is more a result than a cause of delayed childbearing. In some parts of Africa, even highly educated women who are unemployed or marginally employed continue to bear many children. Handwerker (1991) suggests that, at best, the first birth is delayed by the few years beyond puberty that a young woman remains in school. He shows that when women get resources only through men, as is the pattern in parts of Africa* where fertility remained high or was rising through 1987, women's best economic strategy is to have serial sexual relationships—that is, they forge ties with as many men as possible by bearing their children.

Educated but without independent access to jobs, women tend to be viewed as sex objects. At St. Kizito's boarding school, Kenya, seventy-one girls were raped and nineteen others died when a group of boys raided the girls' dormitory. The deputy principal was prompted to observe, "The boys never meant any harm against the girls. They just wanted to rape" (Kithira Joyce 1991).

In short, women badly need opportunities other than prostitution to acquire economic worth through work. An improved quality of life gained through one's own efforts fosters responsibility as well as escape from having no alternative to childbearing. Simple tasks (repetitively assembling electronic parts, operating a sewing machine, working as

---

*Benin, Burkina Faso, Burundi, Cameroon, the Central African Republic, Chad, the Congo Ethiopia, Gabon, the Gambia, Guinea-Bissau, Lesotho, Liberia, Mali, Mauritania, Nigeria, Niger, Rwanda, Sierra Leone, Somalia, Tanzania, Uganda, Zaire, and Zambia.

a chambermaid) do not have the obvious health risk of prostitution, do not constitute a windfall that can be misunderstood as a signal of easily accessed wealth, and do not depend on literacy; but such jobs are associated with declining fertility.

Freedom from childbearing and higher status cannot be conferred by fiat alone. Indian and Thai women have countless constitutional and legal protections, but the quality of their lives is dismal and probably worsening.

Health status deteriorates rapidly as population grows. Where it has been growing more rapidly than jobs, as in parts of Africa, Asia, the Pacific, South and Central America, and even the United States, women's meager alternatives to prostitution or sexual availability create a condition of extreme vulnerability to contracting the HIV virus (Obbo 1993). From the perspective of women's health alone, the third world would be well advised to defer education and use the money to both create jobs and improve access to modern birth control methods. No evidence supports the hope that addressing women's educational and health needs (other than what is intrinsic to birth control) would result in declining fertility.

Cultural Perspectives on the Impact of Women's Changing Roles on Psychiatry*

Abstract

The author examines sex role stereotypes in the United States and their impact on the self-concept of women. She suggests that the fact that women's roles are changing may have a positive impact on general mental health because both men and women will profit from increased flexibility in gender role specifications. She points out that therapists as well as their patients have been socialized into accepting the values and assumptions of our society; there is thus a high probability that not only the presenting complaints but also the treatment goals for women in therapy are culturally determined.

Although the ideas of the women's movement are still difficult to understand and alien to many, the social pattern embodied in renewed agitation for women's rights can be seen as a fundamentally creative effort to innovate and grow that is in harmony with the underlying tenets of the mental health professions. The objectives of this paper are

*In *American Journal of Psychiatry* 133(6), pp. 657–61 [June, 1976].

to show ways in which the new directions taken by women today are constructive and, in view of the charges of sexist bias that have been leveled against some mental health professionals, to suggest that the source of conflict is culture change rather than a war of patients against therapists or, still more destructive, women against men.

Cultural Determinism

A premise of anthropology is that all of us are bound by our culture. The deeply held ideas, values, or beliefs of our society inevitably represent our reality. This phenomenological sense of authenticity may be so great that we remain unconscious of the extent to which our cultural assumptions are mental constructs. Moreover, as long as we remain within a single stable culture, our certainty of its assumptions is continually reinforced because culture is the shared contents of minds. Both therapists and patients are products of our culture; therefore, they are similarly determined, or bound, by our society's attitudes and behavior patterns.

When there is no free choice, responsibility and recrimination are irrelevant. However, freedom from responsibility coupled with absence of free will is not a condition in which many might wish to remain. Just as psychoanalysis has the goal of exposing and thereby freeing an individual from the determinations of his or her developmental history, so an awareness of cultural forces can enlarge an individual's range of free choice.

Awareness of how women are constrained by our culture can be focused by considering sex-role stereotypes. Research suggests that sex-role stereotypes in our culture are pervasive, that they exert a major influence on self-concept and behavior, and that they may present an obstacle to the growth and mental health of both men and women (although they are more particularly damaging to women). Health care professionals necessarily share the stereotypes of their culture. Therefore, therapeutic goals are sometimes limited by culture-bound preconceptions of what is ideal or adaptive male or female behavior.

Sex-Role Stereotypes

A number of research teams in the United States have reported congruent findings on ideas of what is archetypically male and female (Abramowitz, Abramowitz, Jackson et al 1973; Alper 1974; Horner 1970; Levine, Kamin, and Levine 1974; Haan and Livson 1973). Especially impressive is the work of Broverman and associates (Broverman 1972), who developed a sex-role questionnaire consisting of forty-one empirically derived items that distinguish, at highly significant levels, between popular conceptions of the average man and the average woman. Broverman and associates tested nearly 1,000 subjects in samples that covered a broad spectrum of religious, socioeconomic, sex, and age categories; they were consistently able to replicate their findings. The stereotypically masculine traits they identified clustered around the concept of competency; the stereotypically female traits clustered around the dimensions of warmth and expressiveness.

Social Desirability

The isolation of sex-role stereotypes is in itself not so striking as Broverman and associates' discovery that the masculine cluster of attributes was more socially desirable than the female cluster: twenty-nine of the forty-one stereotypic traits at the masculine pole of the scale were judged to be not only more desirable but also more descriptive of a healthy adult; by comparison, only twelve of the forty-one traits at the feminine pole were judged to be more desirable and part of the healthy adult profile.

A sampling of the socially desirable items that clustered at the masculine pole follows: aggressive, independent, not emotional, hides emotions, objective, not easily influenced, dominant, active, competitive, logical, and worldly. The complete list of the socially desirable items that clustered at the feminine pole is as follows: doesn't use harsh language, talkative, tactful, gentle, aware of feelings of others, religious, interested in own appearance, neat, quiet, needs security, enjoys art and literature, and easily expresses tender feelings.

Self-Concept

The data of Broverman and associates further suggest that the skewed social desirability of the stereotypes impinges in a negative way on women's self-concept. Not only were there fewer positively valued feminine traits, but women, unlike men, appeared to incorporate the devalued characteristics attributed to their sex along with the positive characteristics. It appears that women saw themselves not only as sensitive, gentle, and expressive but also as subjective, easily influenced, passive, irrational, and not independent. Men, however, described themselves as possessing not only the positively valued competency attributes that were judged stereotypic for the average man, but also

215

the traits of the feminine cluster that were positively valued for the average woman.

It is not known to what extent poor self-concept may be crippling. It seems a reasonable hypothesis, however, that a woman's internalization of a negative evaluation of female capabilities promotes her withdrawal from competition. This would then be a factor in the well-known tendency for girls' school performances to begin to deteriorate around high school age, and in the associated downgrading of achievement goals among adolescent girls (Alper 1974; Horner 1970).

Innate or Learned?

Justification for the stereotypes usually hinges on the protest that they represent the natural order and, therefore, nothing can be done. Thus it is necessary to confront a different order of question, i.e., whether the stereotypes are in fact an accurate reflection of male and female potentials independent of socialization pressure. In other words, are the differences between men and women innate or learned? Furthermore, if they are innate, do they exist in a small degree or in the magnitude suggested by the stereotypes?

Some assert that innate differences in any of the stereotypic traits must be negligible because observable variations within a sex are of greater magnitude than the difference between the averages of each sex, i.e., there is enormous overlap of male and female distributions. Clearly, the evidence that will resolve this hard question is not and may never be in. However, the facts that girls perform academically at least as well as boys up to the age when career choices begin to be made, and that only after adolescence do discrepancies in male-female achievements favor the male (Horner 1970), must present a problem for those who believe in innate differences in competence.

Similarly, statistics on the prevalence of various mental disorders in childhood show that boys greatly outnumber girls in every category, be it learning difficulties, behavior disorders, or childhood psychoses. However, among adults the prevalence of almost all categories of mental illness is reversed: women are sicker than men (Levine, Kamin, and Levine 1974).

What causes this shift? Are adult, but not developing, women weaker than men? Is labeling applied differentially to men and women? Is the environment perhaps more pathogenic for women than for men? It is at least a plausible explanation of these related phenomena that the dawning realization of the culturally determined expectations for women and the choices closed to them causes young women to constrict their horizons, thus increasing their susceptibility to psychological disorders.

The issue of innate differences was directly addressed by Mead in *Sex and Temperament* (1963), which described a New Guinea society in which women assume responsibility for the management and productive functions of the economy. These women exhibit characteristics associated with what our society judges to be competence to a greater degree than men, who are passive, narcissistic, and, to the extent that they dwell on jealous intriguing for the women's attentions, could be seen as masochistic. These findings suggest that differences between men and women along the specific dimensions of our cultural stereotypes are not so great as to be immutable. Role reversal is possible.

Finally, although ongoing investigation of innate male and female behavior is identifying some differences in predispositions between the sexes, these appear to be tangential to the stereotypic attributes. The apparent differences are that the male's activity level is higher (Goy 1970; Money and Ehrhardt 1972) and that from the embryonic stage onward the female's tolerance for stress is greater (Lane 1969; Teitelbaum and Mantel 1971). In addition, the cyclicity of female hormonal production probably exaggerates and inhibits certain traits in a rhythmic way; there is some evidence that there is an increase in sexual drive and in sense of competence and well-being around the time of ovulation (Money and Ehrhardt 1972; Bardwick 1970; Udry and Morris 1968).

The feminist position is that the issue of innate differences is a red herring. Because it is indubitably true that socialization accounts for at least some of the differences between male and female personalities, is it not a truer form of justice and a straighter road to mental health to endeavor to equalize the self-concept, training, and opportunities available to men and women (Haan and Livson 1973; Asher 1975; Kronsky 1971)?

Psychotherapeutic Practice

The evidence is mixed as to whether the average mental health professional provides constructive and appropriate support to female patients. The findings of Haan and Livson (Haan and Livson 1973) suggest that female therapists are more critical of close adherence to sexual stereotypes by either male or female patients but that male therapists are

217

more concerned by deviance from sexual stereotypes. However, other data (Broverman 1972) suggest that both male and female therapists evaluate patients against an idealization of these stereotypes.

The Broverman team (Broverman 1972) found not only that male and female mental health professionals agreed with each other on descriptions of characteristic differences between men and women but also that a comparison of clinicians' profiles of the average man and the average woman revealed a negative evaluation of the female character:

> The clinicians' ratings of a healthy adult and a healthy man did not differ from each other. However, a significant difference did exist between the ratings of the healthy adult and the healthy woman. Our hypothesis that a double standard of health exists for men and women was thus confirmed: the general standard of health (adult, sex-unspecified) is actually applied to men only, while healthy women are perceived as significantly less healthy by adult standards (p. 71).

From these data it appears that some clinicians share the general cultural sex-role stereotypes. The further inference is that these stereotypes color their perception of patients, their clinical judgments about prognosis and, most vitally, their interactions with female patients. The net effect is probably that they promote women patients' choosing the traditional female roles and self-concept. The less healthy aspects of the feminine personality may be reinforced because so much of what is healthy is considered to be specifically masculine. It is difficult to allay the suspicion that in therapy just as in the culture generally a woman is rewarded for unaggressiveness, irrationality, dependence, passivity, and emotionality and that she may be attacked for exhibiting the opposite traits, which are judged by clinicians to be healthy in the socially competent adult person.

There are limits to inferences that can be drawn from therapists' responses to questionnaires or to hypothetical patient profiles. Clinical evidence that treatment varies systematically with the sex of therapist and patient is usually anecdotal. However, those who wish to be sensitized to this area of physician-patient interaction will find documentation in Asher's report on the American Psychological Association's casebook on sex bias and sex-role stereotyping in psychotherapeutic practice (Asher 1975).

According to Asher (1975), patients' complaints focused on the male therapist's tendency to view women's problems in terms of unfeminine assertiveness, lack of compliance, inattentiveness to a husband's emotional requirements, and failure to put the needs of the marriage above personal satisfactions. The patient's career or aspirations may be depreciated, and the therapeutic goals might be set in terms of acceptance and adjustment to the roles of wife and mother. In addition, a woman's assertiveness is not infrequently interpreted as penis envy, and her attitudes toward childbearing or childrearing may be used as indices of emotional maturity.

The Relevance of Psychotherapy

Value judgments based on our society's traditional view of men and women carry a therapist a vast distance from the currents of the present cultural trend, which is gradually legitimizing a broad range of roles for women. Many women no longer docilely accept the idea that their psychological difficulties lie within themselves and that they must therefore strive to adapt to difficult environmental situations. Instead of trying to change themselves, their newly legitimized objective is to change or reject the difficult social environments (Elias 1975).

Specifically, to view "feminine assertiveness as a neurotic phenomenon . . . aimed at overcompensation for and denial of the lack of a penis" (Kronsky 1971, 90) is beginning to conflict with the ideas of our culture. On the contrary, large numbers of women accept the idea that women envy men for their social power and for the cultural permission given them to be competitive, rational, competent, and sometimes just plain ornery. Moreover, many women are asking why a mature woman should want a penis as part of herself. Consider a contemporary feminist joke: a mother consoles her young daughter who feels outdone by a playmate's external anatomy, "Honey, with what you've got, you can get all you want of what he's got."

In order to be relevant to women today, therapists are asked to be creative, open, and nondirective. The fact that the therapist as an individual is a product of the traditional culture does not prevent him or her as a professional from recognizing that attitudes toward women have been culturally determined and do not necessarily represent truth. In the service of promoting mental health, a therapist can support a woman's endeavor to think and feel better about herself, to keep from becoming (in a self-fulfilling prophecy) a dependent, passive, and ineffective non-adult.

It should be recognized that some women find that the best adjustment for them lies within the dependent stereotypic role model; increasing numbers, however, are questioning, distressed, or raging at the confines in which their lifestyle places them. The constructive therapist can provide support or insight for the change compatible with each patient's strengths and wishes.

In this context, it may be useful to repeat that many patients are as unaware as any traditional therapist that their treatment goals might be culturally prescribed and sex specific. Because of gender stereotyping, which until recently virtually all women accepted, both patient and therapist may misinterpret the presenting complaints. Thus treatment may fall short of its potential to stimulate growth.

Marriage and Feminism

A further issue for the therapist is the impact of women's new attitudes and roles on a male-female relationship and, by extension, what the therapeutic goals for this dyad should be. This is an area in which there has been pessimism because of the prevailing view that a marriage necessarily suffers if a woman puts her own needs first. I wish to suggest the contrary, that the effect of the new trend is positive, and that this will be increasingly evident as equality is more fully accepted, and women who wish to expand their horizons are no longer pushed into positions of feminist militancy.

The basis for this healthier male-female relationship is that women who acquire social power for themselves in a career or professional setting are able to empathize in a new way with men who have always had this power and responsibility. Not only do the couple share new areas of common experience but the woman now has a sense of independence and competence and is therefore not threatened by the man's occasional needs to be passive, emotional, and taken care of.

The traditional culture denies men permission to express passivity and vulnerability. This is inevitable as long as husbands bear the sole responsibility for the security of dependent, stereotypically feminine wives. The artificial and rigid rules for masculine behavior can relax, however, as new rules for feminine behavior apply. A reprieve for women is a reprieve for men because, as the culture comes to allow women greater scope for exercise of competence, men will benefit from a complementary permission to be more expressive and less determinedly, exhaustingly invulnerable (Elias 1975).

The prediction that male and female stereotypes will become increasingly blurred, to the benefit of both men and women, does not carry the implication that there will be role reversal in intimate dyadic relationships. Logically, it should be clear that for a woman to have an independent power base because of her societal role in no way determines the balance of power between her and any particular man: an increase in the overall competence and independence of women carries no intrinsic threat to male control of individual intimate relationships.

There is no evidence that a marriage is well served by the husband's being the weaker partner, but there is evidence to the contrary (Abernethy 1974). Some have speculated that a cause of the currently high divorce rate is that, as the traditional marriage develops, the woman becomes the more powerful personality. The imbalance occurs because of the cultural obstacles put in the way of a young woman's realizing her potential at a reasonable age. In the present pattern, a woman limits her self-concept and marries what seems to be a paragon of strength relative to her culturally prescribed weakness; the woman's later, unanticipated growth upsets the balance of the marriage.

I suggest that the trend should be toward more careful mate selection and that marriage should be delayed until both men and women have found occupational identities for themselves and have come to terms with who they are and can be. It is worth noting, in this context, that fostering achievement goals in young women is compatible with delayed marriage. Indeed, it might be sufficient cause for development of a delayed marriage pattern.

Conclusions

There is inherent contradiction in a health care tradition that systematically forces women into a stereotypic role that is judged by both clinicians and public opinion to be inferior to a healthy adult level of functioning.

It also appears that our culture is changing: new expectations, behaviors, and choices are opening to women. If the medical and mental health professions are to remain relevant, they need to be open in dealing with the changes. Conflicts and problems will inevitably arise; the opportunity for creativity lies in viewing these as manifestations of culture change rather than as the wrongheadedness of men or women.

The greatest challenge and field for innovation may lie in developing a model for marriage that is habitable by two fully adult persons. Men as well as women can derive greater satisfaction from a marriage in which both partners are allowed a full range of human expression— from competence and rationality to passivity and tenderness. Both men and women are, by turns, tough and soft. By accepting these needs in each other, they can be friends.

Therapists are participants in and products of their culture. Therefore, when the evolution in sex roles is completed, that transition will have been made in the mental health professions as well. However, why proceed in lockstep with the culture? By understanding the forces that shape our minds, it is possible to be objective about the different and conflicting currents that are swirling around us today and to use our knowledge and self-knowledge creatively.

References

A crime in motherhood. *Tennessean*, September 11, 1992:10A.

A culture apart: Pakistani sex. *Tennessean*, July 12, 1992:A2.

Abernethy, Virginia Deane 1974. "Dominance and Sexual Behavior: A Hypothesis." *American Journal of Psychiatry* 131:813–17.

Abernethy, Virginia Deane 1979. *Population Pressure and Cultural Adjustment.* New York: Human Sciences Press.

Abernethy, Virginia Deane 1981. "Comments on Tibitan Fraternal Polyandry." *American Anthropologist* 83:895.

Abernethy, Virginia Deane 1993. "The Demographic Transition Revisited: Lessons for Foreign Aid and U.S. Immigration Policy." *Ecological Economics* 8 (3): 235–52.

Abernethy, Virginia Deane and R. Yip. 1990. "Parent Characteristics and Sex Differential Infant Mortality: The Case in Tennessee." *Human Biology* 62:279.

Abramowitz, S. I., C. V. Abramowitz, C. Jackson, et al. 1973. "The Politics of Clinical Judgment: What Nonliberal Examiners Infer about Women Who Do not Stifle Themselves." *Journal of Consulting and Clinical Psychology* 41:385–91.

Alper, T. G. 1974. *Achievement Motivation in College Women.* Wellesley, MA: Wellesley College Department of Psychology (unpublished paper).

Asher, J. 1975. "Sex Bias Found in Therapy." *American Psychological Association Monitor* April:1, 4.

Bairagi, R. 1986. "Food Crisis, Nutrition, and Female Children in Rural Bangladesh." *Population and Development Review* 12:307.

Bajpai, S. April 1991. *India's Lost Women.* New Delhi Indian Express, 1991. Reprinted in World Press Review, April 1991:49.

Bardwick, J. 1970. "Psychological Conflict and the Reproductive System." In *Feminine Personality and Conflict*, 3–30. Belmont, CA: Brooks/Cole Publishing Co.

Barry, K. 1979. *Female Sexual Slavery.* Englewood Cliffs, NJ: Prentice Hall.

Beall, C. M., and M. C. Goldstein. 1981. "Tibetan Fraternal Polyandry: A Test of Sociobiological Theory." *American Anthropologist* 83:5.

Betzig, L., M. B. Mulder, and P. Turke, eds. 1988. *Human Reproductive Behavior.* New York: Cambridge University Press.

Boone, J. L. III. 1986. "Parental Investment and Elite Family Structure in Preindustrial States: A Case Study of Late Medieval-early Portuguese Genealogies." *American Anthropologist* 88:859.

Booth, B. E., and M. Verma. 1992. "Decreased Access to Medical Care for Girls in Punjab, India: The Roles of Age, Religion, and Distance." *American Journal of Public Health* 82:1155.

Borjas, G., R. B. Freeman 1992. *The Economic Effects of Immigration in Source and Receiving Countries*. Chicago, IL: University of Chicago Press.

Bose, A. 1991. *Population of India: 1991 Census Results and Methodology*. Delhi: B.R. Publishing Co.

Brittain, A. W. 1991. "Anticipated Child Loss to Migration and Sustained High Fertility in an East Caribbean Population." *Social Biology* 38: 94.50.

Broverman, I. K., S. R. Vogel, D. M. Broverman, et al. 1972. "Sex-role Stereotypes: A Current Appraisal." *Journal of Social Issues* 28:59–78.

Bugos, P. E. Jr., and L. M. McCarthy. 1984. "Ayoreo Infanticide: A Case Study." In *Infanticide*, edited by G. Hausfater and S. Hrdy S.. New York: Aldine.

Bumiller, E. 1990. *May You Be the Mother of a Hundred Sons: A Journey among the Women of India*. New York: Random House.

Catchpole, S. 1992. "Fighting Against a Rite: Mali Woman Seeks French Asylum to Flee Custom of Sexual Excision." *Boston Globe*, February 26, 1992.

Center for Immigration Studies. 1992 "1990 Immigration Level Is the Highest in U.S. History." *Scope* 10:5.

Chaudry, M. 1990. "Role of the Social and Cultural Factors in Human Fertility in India." *Population and Environment* 12:117.

Child labor. *Wall Street Journal*, July 21, 1992:1A.

Coale, A. J. 1991. "Excess Female Mortality and the Balance of Sexes in the Population: An Estimate of Number of 'Missing Females.'" *Population and Development Review* 17:517.

Davis, K. 1951. *Population of India and Pakistan*. Princeton, NJ: Princeton University Press.

Demeny, P. 1968. "Early Fertility Decline in Austria-Hungary: A Lesson in Demographic Transition." *Daedalus* 97:502.

Demeny, P. 1988. "Social Science and Population Policy." *Population and Development Review* 14:451.

Demographic and Health Surveys: DHS documents major fertility declines. Newsletter. Columbia, MD: IRD/Maco, 1991;4:1.

Dickemann, M. 1975. "Demographic Consequences in Infanticide in Man." *Annual Review of Ecology and Systematics* 6:107.

Draper, P. 1989. "African Marriage Systems: Perspectives from Evolutionary Ecology." *Ethology and Sociobiology* 10:145.

Early, J. D., and J. F. Peters. 1990. *The Population Dynamics of the Mucajai Yanomama*. San Diego, CA: Academic Press.

Elias, M. 1975. "Sisterhood Therapy." *Human Behavior*, April:56–63.

Firth, R. 1936. *We, the Tikopia*. Boston, MA: Beacon Press.

Francis, D. R. 1991. "Imports, Immigrants Hurt the Unskilled." *Christian Science Monitor* September 6, 1991.

Freed, R. S., and S. A. Freed. 1989. "Beliefs and Practices Resulting in Female Deaths and Fewer Females than Males in India." *Population and Environment* 10:144.

Freeman, M. R. 1971. "A Social and Ecologic Analysis of Systematic Female Infanticide among the Netsilik Eskimo." *American Anthropologist* 73:1011.

Friedlander, D. 1983. "Demographic Responses and Socioeconomic Structure: Population Processes in England and Wales in the Nineteenth Century." *Demography* 20:249.

Goy, R. W. 1970. "Experimental Control of Psychosexuality." In *A Discussion of the Determination of Sex*. Philosophical Transactions of the Royal Society of

London, series B, vol 259, edited by G. W. Harris and R. G. Edwards, 149–60. London: Royal Society of London.

Haan, N., and N. Livson 1973. "Sex Differences in the Eyes of Expert Personality Assessors: Blind Spots?" *Journal of Personality Assessment* 37:486–92.

Handwerker, W. P. 1991. "Women's Power and Fertility Transition: The Cases of Africa and the West Indies." *Population and Environment* 13:55.

Hansen, J., and D. Scroggins. 1992. "Ancient Surgical Rite for Girls Poses Health, Cultural Dilemma." *Tennessean*, November 22, 1992:3D.

Harrison, L. E. 1992. "America and Its Immigrants." *National Interest*, Summer 1992:37.

Hart, C. W. M, and A. R. Pilling. 1960. *The Tiwi of North Australia*. New York: Holt, Rinehart and Winston.

Hausfater, G., and S. B. Hrdy, eds. 1984. *Infanticide*. New York: Aldine.

Hern, W. 1991. "Effects of Culture Change on Fertility in Amazonian Indian Societies: Recent Research and Projections." *Population and Environment* 13:23.

Horner, M. S. 1970. "Femininity and Successful Achievement: A Basic Inconsistency." In *Feminine Personality and Conflict*, 45–76. Belmont, CA: Brooks/Cole Publishing Co.

Huddle, D. L. 1992. *Immigration, Jobs, and Wages: The Misuses of Econometrics*. Teaneck, NJ: Negative Population Growth.

Hunt, E. E., N. R. Kidder, and D. Schneider. 1954. "The Depopulation of Yap." *Human Biology* 26:20.

Jacobson, J. L. 1992. *Gender Bias: Roadblock to Sustainable Development*. Worldwatch paper 110, Washington, DC: Worldwatch Institute.

Kithira Joyce, deputy principal, St. Kizito's boarding school. Quotation, 1991.

Kronsky, B. J. 1971. "Feminism and Psychotherapy." *Journal of Contemporary Psychotherapy* 3:89–98.

Lane, E. A. 1969. "The Sex Ratio of Children Born to Schizophrenics and a Theory of Stress." *Psychological Record* 19:579–84.

Lemsine, A. 1992. God guard Islam from the Islamists. Washington Report on Middle Eastern Affairs, March 1992:14.

Levine, S. V., L. E. Kamin, and E. L. Levine. 1974. "Sexism and Psychiatry." *American Journal of Orthopsychiatry* 44:327–36.

Lindenbaum, S. 1972. "Sorcerers, Ghosts, and Polluting Women: An Analysis of Religious Belief and Population Control." *Ethnology* 11:241.

Living standards declined in U.S. in '90, study finds. *Wall Street Journal*, July 10, 1991:1.

Low, B. S. 1990. "Occupational Status, Landownership, and Reproductive Behavior in 19th-Century Sweden: Tuna Parish." *American Anthropologist* 1990:92:457.

Math Ph.D.s: A bleak picture. *Science* 1991;252:502.

Mead, M. 1963. *Sex and Temperament in Three Primitive Societies*. New York: William Morrow & Co.

Meggitt, M. J. 1964. "Male-female Relationships in the Highlands of Australian New Guinea." *American Anthropologist Special Publication* (pt2) 66:204.

Money, J., and A. A. Ehrhardt 1972. *Man and Woman, Boy and Girl*. Baltimore, MD: Johns Hopkins University Press.

More Japanese women keep names for business use. *Wall Street Journal*, July 2, 1992:B1.

Nag, M. 1968. *Factors Affecting Human Fertility in Nonindustrial Societies: A Cross-cultural Study.* New Haven, CT: Human Relations Area Files.

Noah, T. 1991. "Number of Poor Americans is up 6%." *Wall Street Journal,* September 27, 1991:A2.

Obbo, C. 1993. "HIV Transmission: Men Are the Solution." *Population and Environment* 14:211–43.

Ohlin, G. 1961. "Mortality, Marriage and Growth in Pre-industrial Populations." *Population Studies* 14:190.

People doing better. *Economist,* May 25, 1991:48.

Population Reference Bureau. 1971. "Man's Population Predicament." *Population Bulletin* 27:1.

Population Reference Bureau: Spot light: Myanmar. *Population Today,* July/August 1991;12:4.

Repetto, R. 1989. "Soil Loss and Population Pressure in Java." In *Population and Resources in a Changing World,* edited by K. Davis, et al. Stanford, CA: Morrison Institute for Population and Resource Studies.

Riches, D. 1974. "The Nesilik Eskimo: A Special Case of Selective Female Infanticide." *Ethnology* 13:351.

Riddle, J. M., and J. W. Estes. 1992. "Oral Contraceptives in Ancient and Medieval Times." *American Scientist* 80:226.

Teitelbaum, M. S., and N. Mantel 1971. "Socioeconomic Factors and the Sex Ratio at Birth." *Journal of Biosocial Science* 3:23–41.

The Maghreb: How to ride Islam's tiger. *Economist,* July 8, 1989:52.

Tien, H. Y., Z. Tianlu, P. Yu, L. Jingneng, and L. Zhongtang 1992. "China's Demographic Dilemmas." *Population Bulletin* 47:1.

Udry, J. R., and N. H. Morris 1968. "Distribution of Coitus in the Menstrual Cycle." *Nature* 220:593–5.

Westoff, G. 1988. "Is the KAP-gap Real?" *Population and Development Review* 14:225.

Whitmire, R. 1992. "When Living and Wages don't Meet." *Tennessean,* January 5, 1992:1.

Women's value, men's worth. *Economist,* November 10, 1990:54.

Wyon, J., and J. E. Gordon. 1971. *The Khanna Study: Population Problems in the Rural Punjab.* Cambridge, MA: Harvard University Press.

Young, C. 1992. "Equal Cultures or Equality?" *Washington Post,* March 29, 1992.

7

Winners and Losers from Population Pressure

Introduction

Outcomes from population pressure vary by social and economic sector. Genetically mediated predispositions exert additional pressure. Few behavioral predispositions appear absolutely immutable, so humans select or default into any from among an array of lifestyles, family formation options, and associations. Decision making is not necessarily conscious; choices may be intuitive, quickly made, and appear inevitable.

However casually made, choices may be fatal to the individual and/or his genetic endowment. Genes that promote un-adaptive responses to the environment are likely to be eliminated from the gene pool. The real message and mechanism in Darwinian selection is that, evolution is less about what stays than what goes.

Both modern Christianity and "Cultural Marxism" have been accused of indoctrinating the European-American population with values and beliefs that lead to making un-adaptive choices. A Christian seeking to live a good life may sacrifice his own access to resources in order to help others. Cultural Marxism manipulates the Christian value system by emphasizing white European-Americans' guilt and their consequent obligation to make reparations. Americans were taught, and have learned, that reparations are owed and that altruism is good and "feels" good.

Altruism, giving to others without expectation of return, flourishes where almost everyone has enough and foresees no change in that happy circumstance. Altruism did little harm to those practicing it during the halcyon decades after World War II, a benign period of ecological release where almost every trait was good enough to get its bearer past evolution's cull.

If those assisted are genetically close, typical in small, traditional communities, the gene pool is little changed by indiscriminate giving. If those helped are not close kin, the gene pool shifts away from those giving up resources in favor of those receiving them. Repeated altruistic choices amount to genetic suicide. Larry Auster (1991) called public policy facilitating open-arms mass immigration "The Path to National Suicide."

History suggests that Christian and national values change. Were the Crusades—spanning AD 1100–1300—driven by the goal of materially helping people in lands targeted for conquest? Unlikely, when medieval Europe was in the throes of explosive population growth and periodic famines. The infamous Children's Crusade was promoted with evangelical ecstasy, but was it encouraged by pragmatists who saw benefits in removing thousands of impoverished waifs from Europe?

Several hundred years later, with the shift to commerce, Calvinism taught that one was known by one's works. That criterion came to mean material success. Values and behavioral ideals change. Where to, next?

Population Politics*

Population growth redistributes income, creating winners and losers. Nathan Keyfitz hits the mark in paraphrasing demographer Alfred Sauvy's sage analysis of ideal population size: "[T]he farmer calculating the number of cows to raise in his pasture will always arrive at a larger number than the cows themselves would prefer" (Keyfitz 1990, 730).

Indeed, economist Ronald Lee estimates that a 10 percent growth in population in preindustrial England had the effect of raising rents (investment income) by 19 percent—at the same time that it depressed real wages by 22 percent (Lee 1980).

Similarly, rapid growth in the US labor force, which occurred in the early 1970s when women of all ages and the baby boom generation simultaneously sought jobs, has been cited as a major cause of slower growth in US productivity and, therefore, wages. Since the 1970s, the increasing flow of immigration has sustained very rapid growth in the labor force. Numerous economists now think that the unskilled sector's relative lack of benefit from the 1980s' economic expansion, and the extreme vulnerability to recession of the middle class, can be explained by wage pressure from the immigrant sector. Ten percent of America's

---

*In *Population and Environment* 14(1), pp. 5–8 [September, 1992].

labor force is now foreign-born, and twenty-five percent of workers without high school diplomas are foreign-born.

Economist Donald L. Huddle is skeptical of "econometric models purporting to show that legal and illegal immigration has only a slight, if any, negative effect on U.S. labor." Huddle asks if models and field studies which do show "significant wage depression and job displacement [are] ignored and distorted . . . treated as taboos because immigration as a win-win situation is such a powerful myth?" (Huddle 1992, Abstract). So also worries Frank Morris, Dean of Graduate Studies and Urban Research at Morgan State University, Baltimore, MD. In March, 1990, testimony before the House of Representatives Subcommittee on Immigration, Refugees, and International Law, Morris stated: "My first concern is that the black community, in looking at the slow rate of growth of our numbers in the labor force and our increasing need for higher skills, may find that any encouraging assumptions we had about opportunities for young black workers and prospective workers have been sidetracked by hasty immigration policies . . . It is clear that America's black population is bearing a disproportionate share of immigrants' competition for jobs, housing and social services" (Morris 1991, 188).

Richard Estrada, editorial writer for the Dallas Morning News, concurs: "[A]pologists for massive immigration appear to blame the large-scale replacement of black workers by Hispanic immigrants in the hotel-cleaning industry of Low Angeles on the blacks themselves, instead of acknowledging the obvious explanation that the immigrants depressed prevailing wages and systematically squeezed thousands of citizens out of the industry" (Estrada 1991, 25). Established immigrants are also losers from a great influx of their own ethnic group. Estrada attributes unemployment among established and native-born American Hispanics to new arrivals who undercut wages, i.e., will work for less with fewer benefits. Jobs are systematically down-graded by labor competition so that the nostrum, "There are some jobs that Americans won't do" becomes a self-fulfilling prophesy. Bring in enough third world labor and, indeed, the wage, benefit, and safety conditions to which jobs devolve attract neither Americans nor established immigrants. Columnist David Whitmire sums it up: "A surge in immigration guarantees that the less skilled service-sector jobs remain low paid" (Whitmire 1992, 4E).

Significantly, Australia has recently reexamined its liberal, family-reunification-based immigration policy, concluding that it has been a mistake. Admissions are being curtailed in response to public pressure and a 1985 study which concluded that average long-term real wages would be higher in the absence of immigration (Smith 1991).

Economist Gary Burtless of The Brookings Institution, advocate for the American worker and author of *A Future of Lousy Jobs*, makes a similar point, noting that three countries which allow virtually no immigration and have very little population growth—Iceland, Japan, and New Zealand—can boast of relatively small wage disparity between their highest and lowest paid workers. On the contrary, the United States has the highest rates of both population growth (1.1 percent per year) and immigration of any industrialized country, and the U.S. has also the greatest disparity between highest paid executives and lowest paid labor.

Thus, a most serious effect of rapid population growth may be diminution of social equity. Rough and ready scans of world societies suggest that this possibility deserves systematic study. Consider that the one–two billion people who live in most abject poverty are in countries with the most rapidly growing populations and that each of these countries also has a handful of enormously rich families! The Philippines and El Salvador are ready examples. One must ask, does population growth cause polarization between rich and poor? A correlation cannot answer that question, but a correlation implies that searching for the direction of a causal relationship, if any, might be rewarding.

If the American working class is harmed by population growth, then legal immigration (which contributes 44 percent of annual population growth) as well as illegal immigration should be a highly politicized issue. Indeed, extreme right-wing think tanks apparently identify with Sauvy's farmer, advocating population growth and more immigration. Economist Julian Simon and his sidekick Ben Wattenberg are that policy's champions. Simon asserts that there cannot be such a thing as too many people.

Across the aisle, protests that immigration harms the American worker and keeps the poor from getting a first toe on the employment ladder are heard from public figures and labor economists alike. Vernon Briggs Jr. of Cornell University as well as former governor of Colorado Richard Lamm, a Democrat, both advocated low limits on immigration in testimony before Congress.

Nevertheless, immigration policy is more complicated and less partisan than any neoconservative versus liberal line-up implies. Democrats in Congress, the avowed champions of labor, spearheaded passage of the 1990 Immigration Reform Act which raises annual legal immigration into the United States by 40 percent. Further, Congress constantly pressures the administration to liberalize refugee admissions. By its inaction, Congress also allows unabated illegal immigration; the Congress authorizes but rarely appropriates new funds for the Immigration and Naturalization Service (INS). Only through Attorney General William P. Barr's initiative, i.e., departmentally generated funds, has the number of border patrol and drug enforcement/immigration liaison officers been increased: by 1993, personnel will have risen by about 11 percent to nearly 10,000, all told. Clearly, not all are on duty at any one time, and part of their job is guarding a border where four million illegal crossings are attempted annually.

Republican Governor of California Pete Wilson opposes the present high level of immigration on grounds that it is a principal factor busting his state's health care, education, criminal justice, and welfare budgets; and, moreover, that this multibillion dollar added burden (about $9 billion nationally in 1990) deprives native-born Americans of benefits and services even as it raises their taxes.

Republican presidential primary candidate in 1992 Pat Buchanan appears to be informed on the labor, tax, educational, and welfare safety-net effects and has made lower limits on immigration a principal campaign promise. The widely reviled David Duke, who advocates for the common man, also wants to limit immigration; his involvement with the issue plays into the hands of those who cry racism, distracting Americans from what may well be their common economic interests.

Addressing all Americans in the Keynote Address of the 1984 Democratic Party Convention, Jesse Jackson said that Americans may have come here in different ships, but "we are all in the same boat now." Although boats sink when they become overfull, Jackson was proimmigration at least until recently. No common ideological thread distinguishes among partisans or links allies in the immigration debate. But once become a subject of public discourse, the immigration issue is unlikely to drop from sight anytime soon.

Family Formation in America*

Parents, some say, are people who use the rhythm method of family planning. One might better say that parents are optimists, people who think that the present is good and the future probably better. People

---

*In *Chronicles*, The Rockford Institute, Rockford, Illinois, pp. 13–16 [May, 1999].

231

who look forward with confidence often have an extra child; those who think that their situation may worsen are cautious about increasing family size.

In fact, most people want children, but not more than can be raised well given family standards. When people believe that economic prospects are brightening, they marry early and plan to have children quickly, a phenomenon that I call the fertility opportunity effect. The perception of expanding opportunity explains the various episodes of high fertility in America.

In the colonial and frontier periods, for example, the natural wealth of the American continent invited population increase, and, indeed, very large families were common. Settlers in the New World averaged much higher fertility rates—that is, more children per woman—than were usual in the societies from which they came. Numerous authors, beginning with Adam Smith, attributed the very large family size typical in the colonies to the seemingly boundless natural resources that required human labor for transformation into wealth.

The transition from high to low fertility followed the frontier as it swept westward. Free land vanished, and good land became expensive as isolated homesteads became settlements and then established agricultural communities. Land prices became a consideration for families wishing to set up on good farms. Saving for investment in land became a barrier to early marriage and, with the foresight that it would be difficult to buy additional farms for children, was a disincentive to the early colonial pattern of very large family size. Economist Richard Easterlin has shown that denser settlement was linked to higher land prices and decreasing numbers of children per family.

In addition, cycles of prosperity saw a parallel decline or increase in the fertility rate—with the expected lag time for gestation. This relationship was clear in Concord, Massachusetts, an offshoot of the Massachusetts Bay Colony which was settled by Puritans in 1630. Lumber and agricultural exports earned Concord's early colonists the British pounds with which to import goods that they could not grow or make for themselves. They needed trade.

Initially, the bottleneck to colonial trade was the availability of shipping; hulls making the return trip to England depended upon the demand for passage by Puritans wanting to emigrate. Ironically, improvement in the Puritans' political fortunes in England brought recession and a birth dearth to Concord. Such improvement occurred in the years after 1642 when the Roman Catholic Stuart king, Charles I, was imprisoned and beheaded. Later interruptions in trade were caused by a collapse of demand and prices for raw goods in England.

Political scientist Brian Berry (1996) summarizes the relationship between colonial economic cycles and fertility rates: "These bad times of plummeting commodity prices and falling real incomes came in the 1640's, the 1690's, the 1740's and the 1790's, and are clearly identifiable in the Concord birth record."

Eventually, the American market assumed greater importance, and domestic economic cycles began to drive demographic adjustments. The long-term trends were punctuated by cycles of higher or lower fertility in response to fluctuations in the economy. Immigration entered into the relationship by late in the nineteenth century, when large flows of immigrants damped the direct impact of the labor market on Concord's established residents and their fertility rate. By the nineteenth century, most of the adjustment to poor labor opportunities in Concord took the form of reduced immigration.

Until 1930, half of the US population lived in rural areas, so agricultural sector depressions had the greatest effect on the established population. The break in farm prices in 1920, for example, was followed by a fertility decline in rural America. More than ten years later, urban fertility fell in response to the Great Depression.

The US fertility rate was reviving by the end of World War II and, in the years 1946–1962, recovered to levels not seen for decades—the fabled baby boom. Conditions favored the growth of a strong middle class. Specifically, by 1946, Americans enjoyed a surging demand in the labor market because of economic growth and the limited number of men entering the labor force. (The small generation of the 1930s, as well as the G. I. Bill, which encouraged college attendance as a near-term alternative to employment, saw to that.) The small labor force relative to job openings created excellent entry-level opportunities and accelerated promotions, while technologically driven growth in productivity checked inflation. Immigration had virtually no impact on the labor market (except for the Southwest bracero program) and was minimal until 1965.

The opportunity structure gradually changed, and, by 1962, the baby boom ended. Upward mobility stalled as the employment pipeline filled and the labor force grew rapidly, mostly from baby boomers coming of age. Vernon Briggs (1992s) observes that, "In 1964, one million more people reached the age of 18 than the year before and the entry number remained at this high level until 1980." Competition for entry-level positions stiffened, and, while many people saw their standard of living rise, progress for white Americans was significantly slower than the steamy pace that had been taken almost for granted since World War II. At the same time that inflation-adjusted income failed to rise at the accustomed pace, schools became overcrowded and taxes rose to pay for new schools and other infrastructure. At the national level, war launched the country into a renewed bout of deficit spending.

Further developments included the 1973–1974 oil embargo. Higher oil prices and spot shortages set off the "quiet depression," with productivity and wage increases much below those of the previous three decades. Pushed by inflation and recession, the economy fell from its historic growth trajectory of 3 percent per year to a modest 1 percent.

In fact, most working Americans have seen a decline in their personal economic circumstances since about 1973; the majority of working people have experienced either stagnant or declining earnings measured in inflation-adjusted, after-tax dollars. Worsening labor market conditions for blacks were initially somewhat offset by new civil rights and welfare assistance. By the 1990s, however, the impact of these programs had worn thin because an accustomed level of opportunity is not perceived as particularly good and, in fact, most blacks are among the 80 percent of Americans whose real income has not appreciably increased for twenty-five years.

Not all sectors of American society participated equally in the periods of economic growth after 1980. Only the top 20 percent of families, and especially the upper 5 percent, made significant income gains; the middle class fell into decline.

In many families, both spouses work in order to maintain accustomed amenities and educational opportunities for children. Few young couples believe that their children, if they are to receive necessary parental attention and educational advantages, can have as many brothers, sisters, and cousins as they themselves had. Small wonder that the average age of marriage has risen and that family size has declined.

Women and couples delay marriage and are cautious about expanding their family if they think that their personal economic prospects are narrowing compared to a reference standard (their own parents' lifestyle, for example). Just as the Great Depression made many people wary of childbearing, economic conditions beginning in the mid-1970s depressed family size in most sectors of American society.

Persuaded by the history of fluctuations in the fertility rate, the Advisory Council on Social Security has adopted a similar theory. Their 1994–1995 Report argues that a small birth cohort, whose members encounter ample job opportunities relative to their number, will command high wages, see rapid career advancement, and, therefore, have big families. On the other hand, a large birth cohort tends to flood the labor market, resulting in stagnant or falling wages and benefits and a decline in desired family size. Notably, the Advisory Council not only accepts the principle that perceived opportunity is a determinant of the fertility rate, but also assumes that rapid population growth depresses the earnings of the average working person.

In fact, it is well documented that a change in the size of the labor force, all else being equal, affects wages. Ronald Lee, examining preindustrial England, and Claudia Goldin, reporting on early-twentieth-century labor markets in cities heavily impacted by immigration, find that an increasing labor supply depresses both wages and conditions of work. The converse is also true: economic growth combined with the relatively small labor force after World War II raised compensation, prospects for promotion, and family size.

The predictive value of the 1994–1995 Report of the Advisory Council on Social Security is weakened, unfortunately, by failure to take into account the labor market effects of immigration. Indeed, as the example of Concord, Massachusetts, shows, these exogenous flows of labor may smooth out the native-born fertility rate, including what would have been its peaks.

The US fertility rate drifted lower through the 1960s, declined faster after the first oil price increase, and reached a new low, 1.7 children per woman, in 1976. Among whites, the fertility rate declined to approximately 1.4 children per woman. These rates are well below the number needed to replace the population. (A fertility rate of about 2.1 children per woman just replaces parents, assuming low child mortality.)

The fertility rate is now rising. In 1997, it was 2.05, essentially the replacement level. However, this statistic combines births to native-born Americans with those of the foreign-born. Among the native-born, it appears that the black fertility rate has declined to approximately replacement level, and white fertility remains at approximately 1.8 children per woman. Only immigrant fertility is high. In 1994, for example, the foreign-born were fewer than 10 percent of the population but accounted for approximately 18 percent of births.

Newcomers to the United States often do not share the trepidation of natives who sense that opportunity for themselves and their children is deteriorating and who, therefore, feel compelled to husband resources by limiting family size. Newcomers feel well off because economic opportunity is usually greater than in the country left behind, the social safety net is stronger and broader, and educational opportunities for children are often far superior. Not surprisingly, those coming from a culture where large family size is highly valued feel free to raise their childbearing target to a number closer to their ideal. Comparisons suggest that some immigrants—Mexicans, for example—have larger families in the United States than if they had remained at home where opportunities are more limited. Different perceptions of opportunity result in different fertility rates.

If native-born Americans are to replace themselves in future generations, their fertility rate should rise and immigrant fertility should fall (converging on replacement level), and immigration itself should be reduced to an annual flow no greater than the number of persons who leave the United States.

This discussion of fertility rates exposes issues that invariably raise the emotional pitch during discussions of immigration policy. Should immigration serve the national interest? If such interest is judged to be moral, how should it rank among competing interests? Is it moral to give priority to the national interest? Should American citizens define the national interest? Do American citizens have the right to define immigration policy in the light of national interest? Is the United States a nation-state in the sense that other politically defined, geographically bounded entities are nation-states? Are Americans entitled to a country, or is the United States, as Ben Wattenberg says, "the first universal nation"?

Some advocates for a high level of immigration question whether American citizens have a legitimate interest in preserving their representation in the population, arguing instead that global humanitarian goals should control immigration policy. This debate would have been familiar in the early twentieth century, as Kevin MacDonald showed in a March 1998 article in *Population and Environment*. Over the vehement opposition of mostly Jewish, self-styled humanitarians who assaulted immigration restrictionists with charges of racism, Congress passed the Immigration Act of 1924. This legislation significantly reduced the annual flow of immigrants, established quotas that reflected the European origins of the 1890 population, and remained the law of the land until 1965. The act encouraged assimilation of the large foreign population then in the United States. Over time, it also reduced prejudice against nonnorthern Europeans and created opportunity for black and white Americans from the rural South, who were recruited into well-paying industrial jobs in the North—jobs formerly filled by immigrants. The small labor force in the decades immediately after World War II—limited mostly to native-born Americans—laid the foundation for prosperity, higher productivity, growth of the middle class, and civil rights achievements which were a triumph of the American way of life.

The discouragement of middle-class Americans today stems from a combination of factors. Most worrisome to many is the growing disparity between high and low earners and the temporary nature of jobs even for those who try to remain employed. Between 1980 and 1996, median income (in 1996 dollars) rose less than $2,000, while income to the wealthiest one-fifth rose by more than $26,000. In 1980, the richest quintile had an income 10.3 times that of the poorest fifth of the population; by 1996, the multiple had grown to 13.4. This disparity is greater than in any other industrialized country, and greater than at any time since the Great Depression.

The relative decline of middle-class income and the perceived scarcity of nonfinancial resources—family time, recreational time, and community amenities, including the quality of public schools—contribute to the perception of diminishing opportunity. This trend not only discourages childbearing, it undermines the vitality of democracy, which depends upon a participating middle class with a self-conscious stake in community and country.

Population size stabilizes over time if families are small—given zero net immigration—and this adjustment might be all that is needed to restore opportunity to average Americans. One generation's low fertility gives their (few) children the advantage of reaching maturity in an economy that is probably experiencing a labor shortage. The limited supply of labor leads to a bidding up of entry-level wages. Promotion opportunities improve through better-capitalized jobs, as well as through the shortage of labor.

Step by step, tracking the improving economic prospects available to young people, the fertility rate rises. That is, the fertility rate adjusts to conditions created by the high (or low) childbearing of the previous generation; thus, both high and low fertility are self-correcting over time.

Rapid population growth in a postfrontier, postindustrial society is one cause of the many reverses in opportunity, financial security, and lifestyle that native-born Americans have experienced in the latter half of this century. The United States ended World War II with a population of 135 million. In 1950, the population was 150 million; in 1970, about 200 million. By 1995, it had reached 263 million, and the National Academy of Sciences estimates that, with a "medium" level of immigration, it will be 277 million by the millennium, with no end to growth in sight.

Such population growth has major environmental, fiscal, and economic effects. For example, the population added from 1970 to 1995, i.e., sixty-three million persons, accounted for over 90 percent of the increase in US energy use over the period. The rising demand for energy hastens the depletion of domestic oil and natural gas supplies (already the United States imports over 60 percent of its oil). The enormous dependence on fossil fuels may also exacerbate economic dislocations if, or when, the US economy is shackled by a requirement to cut carbon dioxide emissions.

Population growth also accelerates the destruction of habitat for wild species by transforming agricultural and wilderness lands to urban and suburban building. In drought-stricken areas such as Southern California, the growing demand for water by urban users threatens agricultural uses of water. Nationally, aquifers (underground water accumulated over millennia) vital to agriculture are being depleted 25–50 percent faster than the replenishment rate.

Population growth also results in crowding roads, schools, and recreational areas, and it is exceeding the capacities of water-treatment and waste-disposal facilities. The ensuing demands for new infrastructure—including roads, schools, fire, police, water and sewage treatment, electricity-generating and hospital capacity, and library and recreational facilities—result in higher local taxes. Although community development boosters often claim that new growth pays for itself, population growth actually imposes net per capita tax burdens on established residents. Newcomers' taxes cover only a fraction of the costs of infrastructure constructed on their behalf. Whether through bond issues or current taxes, established residents bear most of the costs of development that would not have been needed or even contemplated if community size remained constant.

Certain facts are indisputable. First, population growth forces established residents to pay for growth, although it is not obvious that they receive any benefits or increments to their quality of life.

238

On the contrary, some indicators show diminished quality: the ethos of a small, close-knit community, good public education, and open space is almost inevitably sacrificed to growth. And, although it is "common knowledge" that more people mean a larger market, the tax nibble on disposable income may reduce discretionary spending. The larger share of per capita earnings that goes to pay taxes, as well as the earnings-depressing effect of a rapidly growing labor market, may offset the potentially larger consumer market: poor people do not buy.

In a nutshell, population growth is the result of more births than deaths, and more immigrants than emigrants. The immigration impact is annual immigration plus births to the foreign-born, minus deaths and emigration of immigrants.

The annual share of US population growth attributable to immigration rises continuously as births to recent (post-1969) immigrants are added to the flow of new arrivals. In 1994, immigration and the children of recent immigrants accounted for over 60 percent of US population growth.

The annual flow and first-generation births do not fully represent immigration's long-run impact on national population size. The cumulative difference can be seen from the 1997 projection of the National Academy of Sciences for the year 2050. With zero immigration (beginning, hypothetically, in 1995) the population would peak a few years before mid-century and then decline to 307 million (which is just about 27 million more than today); with "very high" immigration, the mid-century population would be 463 million, with no end to growth in sight.

Note that these are only projections, not predictions. Other demographers estimate that, if current trends continue, the population of the United States in 2050 may be well in excess of half a billion. There is widespread agreement, however, that population growth in the twenty-first century would be almost entirely (over 90 percent) due to immigration, if present trends continue.

Since the cause of low fertility (below replacement level) among American women is understood, the changes needed to raise fertility are also clear. Optimism must return to the middle class. The fundamental conditions are satisfactory compensation from work (inflation-adjusted, personal, after-tax income) and pride in country and culture.

The discouragement which oppresses many young Americans is mediated through jobs, environment, community, and family; but underlying many negative signs is a single cause: rapid population growth and lack of confidence in America's right to reduce immigration. Where is the proper moral indignation when young Americans avoid occupations in which immigrants who will work for less depress wages, or when job seekers find their options narrowing?

Many of the Americans affected are the young, who have traditionally used technical specialties to get ahead. They delay marriage and childbearing until they feel established professionally. In today's employment climate, that confidence is likely to be some time coming.

Unlike trade or out-sourcing jobs, which can be stopped at any time, immigration leaves footprints. Newcomers stay, reproduce, and change both culture and community. Rapid population growth destabilizes American communities and deprives young Americans of educational and employment opportunities even as they seek to become productive members of society. The economic growth of the past decade should have brought prosperity and hope to all Americans. Instead, it has principally benefited the few.

Middle-class America would gratefully return to its traditional family way. But this is not likely to happen until conditions of work, opportunity, and national pride encourage the young to believe that America cares and that the future will be good, again.

Changing the USA's Population Signals for a Sustainable Future*

Population growth in the United States has major ramifications for the world economy, the environment, and society. If present trends continue, the population could double in less than seventy years. Immigration and children born to immigrants after arrival in the United States account for 50 percent of population growth, and this share is projected to increase steadily. Progress in deficit reduction, equity, and opportunity for all Americans, and a healthier environment would be well served by temporarily closing the door on immigration while the nation takes stock of its resources and goals.

Perhaps the most astonishing feature of the United States and the world, as the 21st century approaches, is their rapid increase in population size. It took all of human history until 1825 for world population to build up to one billion, but now population is increasing at the rate

---

* In *Futures* 26(2) pp. 138–45 [March, 1994].

of one billion in less than eleven years. Projections for future growth range from horrifying[1] to unthinkable.[2]

The United States is the fastest growing industrialized country in the world. The fertility rate of the native-born American sector is not dissimilar from European rates; but the immigration factor casts a wholly different complexion on numbers here. The United States fought World War II with a population of 135 million; in early 1994 the country is near to a population of 260 million. If present trends continue, it could be half a billion in sixty or seventy years.[3] Yet most people appear not to reflect on how this growth drives other changes in a society—changes which citizens, for the most part, deplore.

In the United States, the population expands by 58,000 people per week, equivalent to adding three million per year. This growth approaches an annual rate of 1.1 percent,[4] putting the country on track to double, if this rate continues, in sixty-four years.[5] The US Census Bureau's most recent middle projection released in December 1992,[6] shows the US population passing 400 million in the 2050s and still growing fast.[7] This middle projection represents a dramatic revision by the Census Bureau from as recently as 1990. Their former middle projection showed a high point of 300 million people and stabilization just below that level. The 1990 middle projection assumed (1) that immigrant fertility would decline to the rate of the native-born sector, and (2) that illegal immigration would be 100,000 annually. The 1992 middle projection assumes continuing high fertility in the immigrant sector and illegal immigration of 200,000 annually.[8]

Worldwide, population growth is driven by fertility in excess of deaths. An additional factor within certain countries is immigration in excess of emigration.[9] In the United States, for example, immigration and children born to post-1970 immigrants account for 50 percent of population growth. Immigration would account for a still larger share of the growth were it not for increased longevity among the native-born population.[10] The longevity of older Americans masks part of the effect of very low fertility among the native born; their low fertility since the early 1970s would be allowing the US population to stabilize were it not for recent and continuing immigration.[11]

The population futures now being contemplated take one far from former thinking about national goals. The 1972 Rockefeller Commission stated that the United States should "welcome and plan for a stabilized population."[12] Population stabilization was not expected to solve the nation's problems, but the Commission foresaw that most social and

241

environmental problems would become more intractable as the population grew.

The consequences of rapid population growth include:

- More pressure on the environment. Pollution will be worse and abatement more costly; resource scarcity (of water, energy, or fertile arable land) will become chronic; and biodiversity will be threatened.
- More urbanization and megacities.[13]
- More distant representation by government. One congressional member represented 35,000 people when the Constitution first declared the uniting of the States of America. Today, one House of Representatives member answers to nearly 600,000 constituents.
- Increasing economic disparity between rich and poor.[14] A trend where less favorable resource/population ratios lead to polarization of society is predicted from (1) the characteristic of overpopulated third world countries wherein a few very rich families dominate the mass who are very poor, and (2) Ronald Lee's analysis of the preindustrial period in Europe. Lee finds that a 10 percent growth in the labor force was accompanied by a 19 percent decline in wages and a 22 percent increase in return on land.[15] Generalizing from land to other kinds of capital, one finds that the relationship endures. Capital, being the scarcer factor of production, is better rewarded, i.e., expensive. Industry selects the cheapest combination of labor and capital and will thus prefer relatively cheap labor over expensive capital investment, a preference which gives impetus to the decapitalization of jobs, lower productivity, and lower wages. (If structural factors such as government mandates or union contracts prevent market adjustments in the wage rate and benefits, employers respond to lower labor productivity by cutting jobs from the payroll.[16])
- A downgrading of the status of women. Women's unique capacity, bearing children, is devalued wherever there is overpopulation. Women are themselves often treated as threats in overpopulated societies; their rights and freedoms shrink. This cultural response to rising population pressure is adaptive in so far as its effect is to dampen growth. Nevertheless, the process is often inhumane. Women are victimized in myriad ways which legislated efforts to protect women's rights and health status seem powerless to quell.

Women can retain status by remaining in the labor force. But, recognizing that employment opportunity is undercut when growth in the labor force outruns new investment, this strategy is itself problematic.[17]

Consequences of Immigration

Immigration as the driving force in population growth has additional consequences. Because most immigrants arrive as adults, their skill level is less likely than that of native-born workers to match the needs of the economy. The majority of the 1.3 million immigrants to whom the INS gave work authorization papers in 1992 had few skills relevant to an information economy. Immigrants now comprise 25 percent of the unskilled workforce. Thus, the influx from abroad compounds the effects of disappearing unskilled and inner-city jobs, inevitably contributing to unemployment among the United States' own poor.[18]

Early outposts attract other immigrants of their same ethnic group. In the past decades, concentrations have grown in ecologically sensitive areas, especially Florida, California, and in already explosive inner cities.

Pressure on schools and other social services is a further nontrivial effect of immigration. The high fertility and poverty of the average immigrant result in public outlays on their behalf which are significantly in excess of the taxes they pay. Primary and secondary education is the single largest cost category associated with post-1970 immigration and, in 1992, totaled $13.2 billion.[20] Immigration drives rapid growth in California's school-age population and has played a major role in moving it from first in the nation in spending per student to below fortieth place.

The dislocations to the labor market and the educational system are arguably the most serious but not the only costs of immigration. Public health and direct health care expenditures are the second and third, respectively, most costly programs used by legal immigrants. In 1992, services to post-1970 legal and illegal immigrants and their US-born children, and expenditures on behalf of Americans who are unemployed because of being displaced by immigrants, cost the US taxpayer $42.5 billion over and above what immigrants paid in taxes. These outlays were distributed among federal, state, and local levels of government.[21]

Over the next ten years, outlays for twenty-two programs analyzed are expected to total $668.5 billion over and above what immigrants pay in taxes. This estimate assumes the 1992–1993 rate of immigration and discounts costs to 1993 dollars. "Legal immigrants," states economist Donald Huddle, "will account for three-quarters of those costs."[22] Approximately two-thirds of these projected expenditures are unavoidable because of being associated with nondeportable immigrants, that is, those who have come legally or have received amnesty, asylum, or refugee status, or whose children have been born in the United States (citizen children of illegal aliens). But if immigration stopped after 1992, $220 billion would be avoided. This, an average of $22 billion per year in each of the next ten years, is the expected net public cost of immigrants coming from 1993 to 2002.[23]

Americans should be aware that the cohort which will drive these public expenditures is just beginning to arrive in the United States. Legal immigrants will account for three-quarters of future costs. The magnitude of the numbers further suggests that they should be factored into discussion of federal and state budget deficits. Under the circumstances, a national debate should encompass all facets of immigration.

Polls show that large majorities of Americans of every racial and ethnic category want to greatly reduce all immigration. The majority has been growing steadily and ranges from over 60 percent up to 85 percent in favor of curtailing immigration. The Latino Political Survey, begun in 1990, shows that 79.4 percent of Mexicans in the United States want to curtail immigration.[24]

Although legal immigrants (including refugees and those granted asylum) account for two-thirds of the number and three-quarters of the cost, it seems likely that Congress will first address only the illegal component of the annual flow. As recently as 1990, Congress increased legal immigration by 40 percent. Moreover, the erroneous perception that the illegal immigration flow is both larger and more expensive is widespread. Yet illegal immigration accounts for only one-quarter to one-third of the total number entering and settling in the United States.

The United States needs a "time-out" on immigration in order to restore some order in its cities, work on bringing minorities into the mainstream (as was pledged years ago), evaluate its environment and resources, and reduce public debt. With political will, the United States could virtually halt immigration, making exception for hardship cases, with results redounding to the benefit of all Americans. Not only would the United States' own poor be more likely to aspire again to enter the mainstream economy, a halt to immigration would contribute to reducing the national debt and would be a positive step toward economic/environmental sustainability.

Some readers would perceive that an argument relating to sustainability is self-serving. Therefore, one may ask about the effect of a changed policy on the third world, on countries that the United States tries to help. Some would argue on moral grounds that industrialized countries cannot refuse to share their relatively much better standard of living with those who are less well off.

This view is simplistic. The reality is that the major burden of "sharing" falls on the United States' own poor, many of whom are minorities. Inequities in the United States increase so long as large-scale immigration and population growth continue to add to pressure on resources.[25]

Moreover, my data presented in *Population Politics*[26] suggest that the third world is also harmed by the open-door policies pursued for the past fifty years. This harm results from a widespread but *false* belief embedded in misguided demographic transition talk—that prosperity and socioeconomic development lead to small family size.

Family Size

Many examples suggest that when people perceive expanding economic opportunity, they want more children, not fewer. A few examples are: (1) optimism and fertility both rose sharply in India and Algeria after these countries gained independence from colonial powers; (2) in Cuba, Fidel Castro's populist revolution against Fulgencio Batista—promising redistribution of wealth—was also followed by a significant increase in the fertility rate; (3) land redistribution in Turkey promoted a doubling in family size (to six) among formerly landless peasants; (4) in the United States and much of Western Europe, a baby boom coincided with the broad-based prosperity of the 1950s; (5) more water wells for the pastoralists of the African Sahel promoted larger herd size, earlier marriage and much higher fertility; (6) the introduction of the potato into Ireland before 1745 increased agricultural productivity and caused a baby boom; (7) and in the seventh century, Arabs introduced the stirrup into Europe and so popularized horses, which were then available for ploughing when the further introduction of beans put a premium on deep cultivation and triple cropping. This expansion of agricultural productivity led out of the Dark Ages to the flowering of mediaeval culture and thence on to a tripling of population size between 1000 and 1300 AD.

On the other hand, a sense of limits, or scarcity, does lead to small family size. For example: (1) the Population Reference Bureau, which in many contexts is uncritical of demographic transition talk, will sometimes link deteriorating conditions to small family size: "As a result of grim economic outlooks, birth rates are falling quickly in Eastern Europe and the former USSR. Three former Soviet republics, Estonia, Latvia, and Ukraine, already have natural decrease (more deaths than births). Recent reports suggest that Russia's birth rate has dropped to the point where the population declined in

1992." . . . ';[27] (2) the 1930s was one extreme (but not the first) period in US history when economic depression caused a decline in fertility rates. As a multitude of American families hit the soup kitchens and the road in those desperate times, women delayed marriage, on average, until twenty-four years of age; (3) the US baby boom of the 1950s petered out in the early 1960s, when people began to feel stressed and jobs were just becoming harder to find. After the 1973 oil shock, fertility fell to 1.7, well below the replacement level rate of 2.1 children per woman. Real disposable personal income (after-tax, inflation-adjusted income) has been stagnant since 1973, and native-born US fertility remains near 1.7 children per woman. The national rate has risen to 2.1, however, because it is a blend of native-born and immigrant rates and the latter are high; (4) in Ireland, land became scarce as the 1745 population of three million grew rapidly to eight million. By about 1800, traditional controls on premarital pregnancy and marriage were being reinstated, whereupon fertility retreated to its low, prepotato level. By 1830, only about half of women married while they were still of prime childbearing age; so for every mother of a large family, many remained childless (nevertheless, the momentum of growth carried the population beyond Ireland's sustainable carrying capacity, and blight of the potato crop precipitated a famine which lasted from 1845 to 1854); (5) in the Sudan and Myanmar (Burma) today—where the economy is chaotic and essentially no modern contraception is available—fertility has fallen by 20 percent because here, too, couples have begun to delay marriage. Women marry five or six years later than was common just a decade ago; (6) much of Northern Africa—where unemployment now runs at 50 percent—saw this same trend of later marriage and falling fertility develop during the 1980s;[28] (7) the economic outlook in Mexico is increasingly bleak. After years of expecting petroleum-driven prosperity, justifiable pessimism pervades most sectors of society. Indeed, unemployment rose to 40–50 percent of the labor force during the 1980s. This new outlook, probably reinforced by a TV soap opera series that dramatizes the benefits of small family size,[29] has restructured incentives, and the fertility rate recently fell from 3.8 to 3.2 children per woman. On the contrary, Mexican women who emigrate to the United States have four or five children each. The differential appears to be due to perceived opportunity in the United States compared to the situation left behind.

Environmental constraints are a useful warning, when heeded in time, to exercise marital and reproductive caution. In historical, undisturbed societies, environmental constraints are usually both heeded and anticipated.

Western efforts to help are counterproductive when they prevent people from correctly interpreting negative signals from their own environment. The signal broadcast by large-scale foreign aid through both bilateral arrangement and World Bank lending—as well as by US immigration policy—is that the Western world has enormous reserves. Why would we otherwise, by most people's reasoning, be so willing to share?

If an abundance of resources is reality, then poverty is naught but a distributional problem. This was and is, to some extent, our message. It signals to people everywhere that their poverty can be alleviated and that reproductive caution is misplaced.

On the contrary, a door temporarily closed to immigration, with exceptions for hardship cases, would be a step (among many which are required) toward showing that the United States is responding to its deficit problem as well as intending to live sustainably within the limits of its carrying capacity. Most important, the message of a closing door into the United States would be congruent with, and reinforce the signals already coming from local environments worldwide (including those within the United States). That is, the carrying capacity has been exceeded.[30] Marital and reproductive caution is the only choice.

This worldview would enhance incentives to use modern contraception. It is the responsibility and in the self-interest of the industrialized countries to make contraception available.

With or without modern contraception, fertility declines when people rediscover a sense of limits. Culture responds to the threat of overpopulation and system collapse.[31] Worldwide, traditional assumptions about scarcity are reasserting themselves after what can be most charitably described as a terrible mistake—a period of rising expectations brought on by the industrial era and the abundance promised by science, technology, and trade. Add to this mix the unimpeded opportunity to cross national borders, and the vastness of wealth seemed confirmed. But reality, returning, calls a different tune.[32]

The United States can help, both its own population and others, by becoming a model of the sustainable society. It could decide to give the lie to the words of Robert Frost, "It doesn't take man long to use up a continent." Sustainability demands that we regenerate the American continent or at least prolong using it up. For this, we must halt population growth and rein in overconsumption. In the process, responsible leaders will desist from adding to the misleading signals[33] which make it more difficult for others also to come to terms with their environment and the unalterable finitude of the planet, Earth.

Environmental and Ethical Aspects of International Migration*

Immigration policy has a beneficent intent. However, recent work suggests that the signal it sends internationally—that emigration can be relied upon to relieve local (third world) population pressure—tends to maintain high fertility rates in the sending country. This effect is counterproductive because high fertility is the primary driver of rapid population growth. In addition, it appears that the relatively open US immigration policy has resulted in a rate of domestic population growth that threatens both the well-being of American labor and cherished environmental values.

In recent years, Western industrialized countries have extended their traditions of community responsibility to encompass much that is beyond their national and even continental borders. Embracing an ideal of international beneficence does not preclude giving weight to the national interest; nevertheless, beneficence has sometimes guided US policy in directions which appear inimical to the nation.

Given so determinative an ideal of beneficence, one must be doubly confident that what is intended to do good indeed has that effect. Harm to intended beneficiaries is unconscionable, the more so when policies serendipitously entail sacrifice of the national interest, and in particular (as will be shown), threats to the environment and the well-being of this country's more vulnerable sectors.

One US policy that is believed to be beneficent in both intent and effect is the relative openness to international migration. Those who immigrate to the United States expect to improve their own lives and, often, help relatives by sending home remittances. This article contends, nevertheless, that the net consequences of international migration are negative for:

- the countries which emigrants leave;
- vulnerable sectors of the host country's labor force with which immigrants compete;

---

*In *International Migration Review* xxx(1), pp. 132–150 [1996].

- the host country's economy generally (addressed in Abernethy 1993);
- the environmental goal of conservation and minimization of pollution.

These effects would suggest that a pause in international migration deserves deliberate consideration.

The Countries Which Emigrants Leave

Emigration can be counterproductive for immigrant-sending countries in two ways at least. Emigration provides an escape for dissident and energetic elements who might otherwise provide leadership and a critical mass for change. Where would Poland be, for example, if Lech Walesa was an electrician in Chicago? How long would Fidel Castro retain control in Cuba if the opposition there stayed put?

In addition, emigration appears to alter the incentive structure so that high fertility and large family size become more desirable. Only a very rapid fertility decline, however, offers even the semblance of hope that the ordinary citizens of most third world countries will be able to enjoy a healthy and dignified existence.

Demographers usually attribute the rapid population growth which occurred after World War II to a decline in mortality. Some experts also grant a small role to rising fertility due to cultural change, acknowledging that traditional behavior patterns which depress fertility are discarded as a side effect of modernization. These real and true effects are not, however, the whole story.

Unfortunately, well-meant policies intended to implement the dominant "demographic transition" model seem also to have encouraged high fertility. The idea of a demographic transition has been popularized to incorporate certain causal assertions which are essentially unfounded but have mislead two generations of policymakers. Scholars, including historian Paul Kennedy (see Connelly and Kennedy 1994), former editor-in-chief of the *Scientific American* Gerald Piel, and politicians including Nafis Sadik of the United Nations and Vice President of the United States Albert Gore, remain in thrall to the demographic transition model. Its tenets—that prosperity, modernization, declining infant mortality and socioeconomic development produce a preference for small family size, and thus will eventually correct population growth—are based mainly on correlations. The postulated causality breaks down when tested systematically with chronological data (historical and modern) or controlled comparisons (Abernethy 1979, 1993, 1994, 1995).

Some professional demographers have long doubted the causal postulates of demographic transition theory (Teitelbaum 1975), and others have tried to illuminate the motivational aspects of reproduction. Lant Pritchett (1994) suggests that desired family size explains up to 90 percent of the variance in actual family size. Kingsley Davis (1963), Paul Demeny (1988), Charles Westoff (1988), and Sergio Díaz-Briquets and L. Perez (1981) have addressed particular motives and incentives which determine completed family size. For example, economist Richard Easterlin (1962) analyzed the US baby boom, showing that the low fertility of the 1930s depression years gave way to early and frequent childbearing, probably because of the bright economic prospects of the late 1940s and 1950s. Raymond Firth's (1956, 1957, 1967) studies of the Tikopia also support an economic opportunity explanation of fertility.

The analysis of Sergio Díaz-Briquets and L. Pérez (1981) of the baby boom in Cuba after the 1959 Fidel Castro revolution is one of the more compelling cases showing that perception of expanding economic opportunity encourages couples to raise their family-size target. The authors conclude that the spike in Cuban fertility has a "straightforward" explanation: "The main factor was the real income rise among the most disadvantaged groups brought about by the redistribution measures of the revolutionary government. The fertility rises in almost every age group suggest that couples viewed the future as more promising and felt they could now afford more children" (p. 17).

Linkages between economic/resource variables and behaviors which determine family size are usually not so conveniently ready-drawn. Investigators are just beginning to ask the questions which would establish causal sequences.

My work is synthesis, from which I propose a hypothesis to account for couples wanting either more or fewer children. A first book (Abernethy 1979) summarizes the findings from controlled comparisons of New Guinea and Eskimo societies, and various other historical and anthropological materials. For the most part, I have had to use separate sources to match the economic variables with predicted demographic effects.

I continue to find that historical and cross-cultural data point, with startling consistency, to a causal relationship between perceived economic conditions and desired family size. It appears that people who see expansive economic opportunity want and have more children; conversely, a sense of limits or contracting horizons promotes reproductive and marital caution (Abernethy 1979, 1993, 1994, 1995). I have little hesitation in stating that family size increased worldwide after World War II as a result, in part, of people anticipating prosperity and therefore wanting more children.

Perceived opportunities (postulated to raise fertility) come in the guise of new technology, widely distributed gains in income or subsistence subsidies, populist political changes, and migration. For the main rationale and data, I refer you to earlier publications. As a sample of one type of evidence, the flavor of the day, I offer a new case.

Peru embarked on over a decade of unforeseen prosperity after explosive development of the anchoveta industry, an opportunity that was unrecognized before World War II but which was taking off by 1950. A corresponding increase in fertility was to be expected and, indeed, occurred. The time sequence supports a causal explanation: plausibly, widespread prosperity from the anchoveta industry triggered the one child per woman fertility *increase*. For the record, I learned of the anchoveta industry boom and predicted the rise in fertility rate before seeking out the demographic study (Montenegro and de Muente 1990, 70–71) which, as it happens, confirms my prediction.

Fertility remained at a historically high level for some fifteen years. A fertility decline was heralded by the plateau and then, in 1972, collapse of the anchoveta fishery and associated industries. The TFR was 6.85 in 1965, 6.56 by 1970, 6.00 by 1975, 5.38 by 1980, and 4.59 by 1985 (Ferrando y Ponce 1983, cited in Montenegro and de Muente 1990). The 1995 Population Reference Bureau (PRB) Data Sheet shows Peru with a 3.5 TFR. The predictably steep fall was no doubt accelerated by guerrilla activity (El Sendero Luminoso, for example) that, before 1992, threatened to engulf Peru in anarchy.

Migration opportunity appears to be another powerful contributor to perception of expanding economic horizons. The ethos of expansionism appears to affect not only those who move toward relative prosperity, but also those who stay home and occupy niches which neighbors and relatives have vacated. Hebe Lutz (1985), past president of the Foreign Nurses Association in Japan, recounts a conversation with a Nepalese elder who spontaneously observed that the new practice of the young moving away from their birth village was creating the impression of limitless space and opportunity and was a factor in rising fertility rates.

The insights of sophisticated native informants are meaningful, but there is more. Giving examples from late-nineteenth-century Ireland

and early-twentieth-century Japan, Kingsley Davis (1963) suggests that emigration expands a country's ecological niche and, thus, allows high fertility rates to persist. Similarly, John F. May (1995) suggests that mid-twentieth-century policies of dispersing the Rwandan population to undeveloped agricultural land and neighboring countries attenuated land hunger and, thus, encouraged higher fertility rates than would otherwise have occurred. The fertility decline began in Rwanda in the late 1980s as the lands colonized twenty years earlier began to lose productivity, the economy faltered, and further population dispersal became impossible.

Some countries make export of labor a way of life and appear to depend significantly on the foreign exchange earnings and remittances sent home by émigrés. In 1990, global remittance credits reached $71 billion, nearly double from 1980 (Teitelbaum and Russell 1994). High fertility rates persist in many high emigration countries, e.g., the Philippines, India, Pakistan, El Salvador, and Nicaragua. On the contrary, fertility rates have declined rapidly when the emigration option closed, as it largely did in the CARICOM countries (formerly the British West Indies) by the early 1980s (Guengant 1985).

Systematic controlled comparisons within matched West Indian communities show fertility remaining high during the 1970s and 1980s where there was a tradition of emigration, whereas a precipitous fertility decline occurred specifically in those communities where emigration was not seen as an escape valve (Brittain 1990). Similarly, nineteenth-century English and Welsh villages from which many emigrated had continuing high fertility. In contrast, fertility declined rapidly in similar communities which absorbed their own young (Friedlander 1983). The common themes appear to be perception of opportunity (niches opening up where some leave as well as, possibly, the psychological effect of having the option to move toward beckoning prosperity).

Thus, the prospect of immigration to richer territory, even if only a few of the large number who consider it will actually make the move, appears to be one factor supporting large family size. Psychologically, the contrasting state is a sense of limits (being bottled up; crowding; and no expectation of relief).

First Do No Harm

Advocates for beneficence as a guide to foreign policy should be concerned that both inappropriate international aid and generous immigration policies signal that some regions have wealth which they are willing to share. Such misinformation fosters the belief that it is unnecessary for recipients to adjust to the limited resources of their own environment, and thus it undercuts incentives to restrict family size. The consequent slow or no decline in fertility rates leaves countries vulnerable to a very uncertain, probably dismal future. The almost inevitable rapid population growth tends to divert income into consumption, impedes capital accumulation, dooms societies to deepening poverty, and becomes an insurmountable barrier to environmental protection. Misleading signals about the long-term prospects of immigration into the United States can only add to the eventual chaos.

The Host Country

Immigration also harms Americans. Working Americans and established immigrants compete with new waves of immigrants for jobs, education, housing, and other essentials. As the American dream recedes beyond grasp, many become alienated from society and others search for redress or remedies. Every poll now shows a base of 65 percent or more of all Americans (and 79.4 percent of Mexicans in the United States [LNPS 1992]) believing that there are too many immigrants (CCN 1995; Espenshade and Hempstead 1995). Such disaffection as well as violent expressions of genuine anger echo the US' economic, fiscal, and carrying capacity woes.

Labor Market Effects. Most studies which show net negative or mixed effects on American workers are relatively recent. Economist Steve H. Murdock (1995) suggests that immigration adds to aggregate income (because of the larger labor force) but harms American families individually. Murdock concludes that, by the year 2050, average per-household annual income (in 1990 dollars) would be approximately $600 lower because of immigration. Murdock assumes continuation of present numbers and labor force characteristics of immigrants.

Economist George Borjas (1995), who originally saw no negative impact on workers, now concludes that the increased labor supply resulting from inflows into the United States costs working Americans over $133 billion annually in job opportunities, depressed wages, and deteriorating conditions of work. Symmetrically, these effects put $140 billion into the pockets of employers. The net $7 billion added to the economy comes at the cost of increasing polarization between rich and poor. This easily translates into a highly divisive and perhaps dangerous trend.

Labor economist Vernon Briggs, Jr. (1990, 1992) and political scientist Frank Morris (1990 1995) contend that immigration harms first and worst America's own poor and unskilled workers, many of whom are minorities. Briggs (1990) testified before the Congressional Judiciary Subcommittee on Immigration, Refugees, and International Law that the lower end of the US labor pool is victimized by immigration. It is disruptive for both citizens and established, earlier immigrants whose labor force characteristics resemble those of newcomers. Frank Morris (1990), Dean of Graduate Studies and Urban Research at Morgan State University, Baltimore, testified in the same hearings, "My first concern is that the black community, in looking at the slow rate of growth of our numbers in the labor force and our increasing need for higher skills, may find that any encouraging assumptions we had about opportunities for young black workers and prospective workers have been sidetracked by hasty immigration policies. . . . It is clear that America's black population is bearing a disproportionate share of immigrants' competition for jobs, housing and social services."

Indeed, Booker T. Washington pleaded for an end to immigration in his well-remembered "Put Down Your Buckets Where You Are" speech at the 1895 Atlanta Exposition. Only after immigration was effectively ended in the early 1920s did African Americans begin to take advantage of industrial job opportunities in the North.

Lind (1995:111) notes that Frederick Douglass, a prominent black leader in the nineteenth century, also saw "that European immigrants were taking entry-level jobs away from black American workers. No one who lives in a city where taxi service and many other trades are almost monopolized by new immigrants can doubt that the same phenomenon is occurring again." Richard Estrada (1991), editorial writer for the *Dallas Morning News*, concurs: "Apologists for massive immigration appear to blame the large-scale replacement of black workers by Hispanic immigrants in the hotel-cleaning industry of Los Angeles on the blacks themselves, instead of acknowledging the obvious explanation that the immigrants depressed prevailing wages and systematically squeezed thousands of citizens out of the industry" (p. 25).

Earlier immigrants also lose, even when an influx is their own ethnic group. Estrada (1990) attributes unemployment among established Hispanics to new arrivals who compete down wages and benefits, adding (1991:28), "In sum, the evidence shows that Hispanic Americans have emerged as the greatest victims of U.S. immigration policy since 1965, instead of its greatest beneficiaries. The notion that Hispanics in this country favor more immigration, while the rest of America favors less, is a false one that has poisoned the debate for too long. This distortion must be corrected, especially by those who explicitly claim to represent Hispanic Americans."

Economists George Borjas and Richard Freeman (1992) see a double-edged sword falling on labor: competition from immigrants and net imports of goods manufactured by unskilled labor outside of the United States are causes—both direct and indirect—of the deterioration in the economic position of high-school-educated US workers. High school dropouts face the most competition; in this sector, immigration and the trade imbalance together raised the 1988 effective supply of labor by 28 percent for men and 31 percent for women. The large labor supply, these economists say, accounts for up to half of the 10 percentage point decline in the wages of unskilled labor between 1970 and the late 1980s.

Demographer William Frey (1995) reinforces economic findings by showing that low-skilled black and white Americans flee states that are heavily impacted by immigration. Thus, local unemployment figures often do not reveal the extent to which Americans are displaced by foreign workers. The rapidly increasing supply of labor competes down wages and conditions of work so that whole industries—construction, meatpacking, and hotelery, for example—devolve toward jobs which it is said, "Americans won't do." But various sources suggest that Americans often do want those jobs and are excluded by immigrant networks which capture access (Huddle 1992, 1993).

American skilled labor is also under pressure, particularly in fields where fluent English is not required. Immigration is viewed by the 250,000-member Institute for Electronic and Electrical Engineers as the cause of significant increases in unemployment and underemployment among engineers. Similar labor surpluses exist in mathematics (Science 1991) and other specialties (CCN 1994). Thus, parts of the skilled sector of the labor market appear to be approaching saturation.

The national security implications of these economic trends are a concern (Wiarda and Wiarda 1986). Displacement of specialized professionals by immigrants who often will work for much lower wages threatens the viability of science education and engineering schools. Undergraduates often reject mathematics, for example, when teaching assistants are difficult to understand because of poor English language skills. And at advanced levels, students begin to doubt the economic value of a technical degree. The United States cannot afford to cede pre-eminence in mathematics, physical sciences, and engineering education.

Among these labor force trends, perhaps the polarization of society into rich and poor (Rattner 1995) should alarm one most. Historical demography shows that such polarization is an inexorable result of a rapidly growing labor force (Lee 1980, 1987). Underemployment and competing down the wages and conditions of work—as occurs when the demand for new jobs exceeds the capacity of the economy to create good (i.e., well-capitalized) net new jobs—endanger the very fabric of a society. Not only despair of ever joining the mainstream, but also crime, riots, vigilantism, scapegoating, and other signs of disappointment and anger erode civil society, tolerance, and respect for democracy. To knowingly impoverish a large proportion of one's countrymen is a betrayal of the highest magnitude.

Economic Effects. Lester Thurow, dean of the MIT Sloane School of Business Administration, postulates that "No country can become rich without a century of good economic performance and a century of very slow population growth" (cited in Lind 1995). Indeed, current US data confirm that rapid growth in the labor force negatively affects both wages, the conditions of work (see Bernstein 1994), and the wealth of the nation. Real wages stagnated for up to 80 percent of the population beginning in the early 1970s, a period coincident with women and the baby boom generation bursting simultaneously onto the labor market. That one-time surge from women and baby boomers is passed, but continuing growth in the supply of workers is driven by immigration. About three-quarters of immigrants enter the labor force, and their number nearly doubles the annual need for net new jobs. This aggravates underemployment (the unemployed plus involuntarily part-time workers), which rose from 9.8 percent of the labor force in 1989 to 12.6 percent in 1993 (Morris 1995) and is an obstacle to the absorption of a probable ten million discouraged workers, the many welfare recipients whose government benefits may end, and the 900,000 more young Americans entering than older workers leaving the labor force each year.

By 1990, immigrants were 10 percent of the total US labor force and one-quarter of all workers without a high school diploma. The US economy does not need low-skilled workers.

Immigration accounts for nearly half of the annual growth in the US labor force. In addition, immigration imposes public costs in excess of taxes paid by the immigrant sector. Costs are variously estimated to range from several billions up to $51 billion annually (CIS 1994; Huddle 1995; Vernez and McCarthy 1995). Such costs are ultimately borne by all sectors of the economy, making it more difficult to accumulate savings for investment in any productive enterprise.

Population Growth: The Ultimate Environmental Threat

The United States has the fastest population growth rate in the industrialized world. At 1.1 percent per year (and rising), the US growth rate is approaching that of some third world countries and puts the population on track to double in fifty or sixty years. A population size of half a billion by 2050 was "the most likely" variant projected by demographers Ahlburg and Vaupel (1990). The number might now be higher in contemplation of the annual flow of one million legal immigrants, including refugees and asylees, the conservatively estimated net 400,000 illegal immigrants, and the many who enter legally but overstay visas.

Demography explains much of the environmental stress in America (Arrow et al. 1995). The insatiable thirst for oil and energy (Holdren 1991), the annual erosion or paving-over of three million acres of US farmland (Pimentel and Giampietro 1994; Pimentel et al. 1995), the appropriation for residential purposes of rural habitats with an attendant loss of species (Stevens 1995), the buildup of carbon dioxide loads (Rosa and Dietz 1995), and such all indict the human load factor: too many people living in an energy-guzzling society.

Population growth, particularly as reflected in the transformation from agricultural to residential and other more intensive uses of land, is visibly connected to loss of habitat for wild species and extirpation of species. Between the 1780s and 1980s the United States lost 53 percent, or nearly 120 million acres, of its wetlands. The loss has been proportionally greatest (91 percent of wetlands lost) in California (Balance Data 1993) where, not coincidentally, the population growth rate is higher than in many developing countries. Population growth and environmental quality also clash in southern Florida (Balance Data 1994) and in the Chesapeake Bay watershed adjacent to rapidly urbanizing areas of Maryland and Virginia (McConnell 1995).

Depletion of nonrenewable and very slowly renewable resources including underground water (aquifers), the topsoil, and oil are further evidence that the US population may already have exceeded the carrying capacity of the environment. Worldwide, per capita use of oil began a precipitous decline in about 1980 (Duncan 1993) and a parallel peak followed by decline has been predicted for the United States by 2005 (Gever et al. 1986). In fact, Americans' *per capita* use of energy has already nearly ceased to increase. Most (93 percent) of a 25 percent increase in total energy use between 1970 and 1990 was driven by population growth. That is, consumption per capita leveled off, but increased efficiency and conservation efforts were, and continue to be, overwhelmed by growing population numbers (Holdren 1991). Ongoing research suggests that carbon dioxide loads, a correlate of energy use, are disproportionately large for the largest nations "across the entire spectrum of national incomes" (Rosa and Dietz 1995).

Rapid population growth magnifies the difficulty and cost of making headway or even holding past environmental gains. The resulting frustration has led to foundation support for a coalition dedicated to population stabilization in the United States. The rationale is:

> as a funder entertaining proposals from conservation groups around the country, the Foundation had seen population growth, as manifested in extensive land development and widespread environmental degradation, emerge as the primary, never-ending scourge counteracting the good work these groups were doing on the homefront every day. This was true whether a group's purpose was to clean up our bays and estuaries, protect fisheries, save our rivers, improve habitats for bird, animal and plant species, preserve important ecosystems, or defend our forests from further unwise exploitation (Laurel Foundation).

At times the Foundation asked these organizations why they had not attempted to communicate their concerns over growth, specifically population growth, to Congress and the administration. The replies, of course, varied considerably, ranging from not wanting to urge fertility reduction lest they be drawn into the abortion conflict, to fear of being called racist by proimmigration interests. However, by far the majority of answers spoke to the fact that they were small or specialized organizations working toward a specific goal and not staffed to engage in advocacy of that nature. They believe that, even if raised, their voices would be lost in the labyrinths of Washington.[34]

Well-meaning citizens have decreasing options for addressing environmental quality. Deteriorating systems are everywhere apparent. Many factors (deforestation, pollutants, infrastructure, traffic congestion) could be substituted for habitat, oil, water, and topsoil loss to illustrate stresses which population growth places upon the environment. Resources are being depleted even at the present rate of use. More people demand more resources; in using them, people create more pollution. Some systems have no substitute and, once used up or degraded, the loss is irretrievable. Other systems are remediable but at a cost—for example, $25 billion is the estimated annual cost of implementing the Clean Air Act.

In the third world and Russia, the linkage between wealth, population growth, and environmental devastation has long been evident. Protection and conservation take real money, lots of it, and such efforts are low on the list of priorities in poor countries. In the United States, the linkages between population growth and the environment have been masked by affluence. (As well as the much-reviled overconsumption, affluence lets one afford environmental protection and restoration.)

Until recently, environmentalists relied on government regulation and a mix of private and public (taxpayer) funds for environmental protection. But the cost of such programs has provoked a political backlash, revision of some environmental legislation, and possible retrenchment of Environmental Protection Agency (EPA) activities. The cost of mitigating the environmental damage done by large populations grows along with population size, but it seems likely that less money, rather than more, will be available in the future. Thus, environmentalists may have little choice but to confront the linkages between population growth and environmental quality. This appeared to be the gist of questioning by Senator Harry Reid (D-Nev) at July 13, 1995, hearings on the Endangered Species Act. Senator Reid, who also has sponsored an immigration moratorium (bills in 1994 and 1995), pressed the connection between human appropriation of wildlife habitat and species loss.

As natural wealth diminishes and population grows, human demands crowd out other values. Do people need jobs? Is housing scarce and too expensive? Forget the spotted owl! Rescind the Clean Water and Wetlands Acts!

People vote. Other species are no one's constituency.

Environmental battles are perennially refought because the needs of people and intrusion into wildlands habitat grow in proportion to the number of people. Environmental values are overwhelmed by population growth. Peoples' wants trump the environment.

259

Conservation Ethic

These few examples suggest that a conservation ethic in America should start with the goal of maintaining this country at as small a population size as possible. This goal is incompatible with a relatively open-door immigration policy. Therefore, the United States should not undertake to relieve other countries of their excess population even if such a policy were neutral to the immigrant-sending country. However, the US open-door policy probably is not neutral but actually, because of the misleading signals it sends, does harm.

Whereas equalizing opportunity within every nation remains a politically and ethically valid goal, cross-national transfers of wealth and carrying capacity jeopardize the incentive to make adjustments which only local societies and families can undertake. Americans have voluntarily limited fertility to below replacement levels. Others cannot expect to raise their standard of living without doing the same.

Even at present population size, the US environment is continually compromised despite the considerable sums spent to improve quality and mitigate harm—and present levels of expenditure may not be sustainable. Environmental and conservation programs compete with other economic and fiscal uses for resources and money.

In fact, environmental protection is probably a luxury available only to relatively rich nations with stable populations. Nations, institutions, families, and individuals can afford and are likely to conserve only if income is sufficient to support the expected quality of life. At the extreme of poverty where consumption hovers near subsistence level, individuals are compelled to consume their wealth, including natural capital, as a last-ditch survival strategy. A tragic testament to today's destitution and overpopulation is that those who believe they can afford to conserve may be in the minority.

Wealth facilitates but does not guarantee conservation. Control over some critical minimum of resources as well as secure rights to benefit from them in the future—in order to avoid the mentality of the commons (Hardin 1968)—are necessary conditions for conservation, but alone they may not be sufficient (Abernethy 1993). For most people, privatizing wealth to generate future income takes priority over conservation of the commons and will lead to overexploitation of resources whenever rights to future benefits are insecure.

V. S. Naipaul (1989), a widely read commentator on the third world, states that the element of society most upsetting to him is "cynicism."

He explains cynicism as, "fouling one's own nest at home and feathering another abroad. The cynicism, bred perhaps by this availability of emigration abroad . . . is very demoralizing. People are able to create a mess at home, build dreadful skyscrapers in cities like Bombay, yet buy nice apartments for themselves in foreign countries that are better organized" (p. 48).

The very rich have global mobility, and increasingly neither people nor corporations appear to have the loyalty to country that economists such as David Ricardo and John Maynard Keynes took for granted. Citizens of the world may be patriots of nowhere.

For example, virgin timber is a core element of national wealth and exports represent depletion of barely renewable natural capital, but until recently Brazil regarded as intrusive offers of international assistance in protecting the rain forest. Tax policy rewarded those who exploited the trees because exports earn foreign exchange; wealthy Brazilian nationals and foreigners jointly lumbered off the rain forest, shipped whole logs to countries which import carrying capacity (e.g., Singapore and Japan), sold the denuded land, and deposited untaxed profits in offshore banks. This treatment of forest lands as "resources to be exploited and as space for its fast-growing population" was ostensibly a public response to populist demand, writes an appropriately skeptical *Wall Street Journal* staffer (Cohen 1989).

In part, as well, the deforestation and earnings repay international debt. Excusing the debt as lenders often are urged to do would, nevertheless, be wrong. The great, original harm of the loans (besides their misappropriation) was that government leaders used funds for consumption subsidies which probably misled ordinary people into believing that larger family size was affordable (Abernethy 1993, 1994, 1995). Excusing the loans would have the perverse effect of, again, suggesting an abundance of international resources to be tapped, ad lib, for consumption.

Certain industrialized countries' business interests and multinational corporations also espouse globalism at the expense, it sometimes appears, of their own country. The export of high-value-added jobs and especially the import of cheap labor to compete with one's own show a disregard of country. Such business practices amount to letting the few ruin one niche before moving on to the next. Not only does this happen, but globalism is held before us as an ideal.

In my view, the incentive system and ethics have gone awry. And for this, opinion makers, the intellectual elite, and the government bear major responsibility. Critical liberal or conservative voices are a welcome but rare and recent counter note (see Lind 1995).

Economists John Culbertson (1989) as well as Herman E. Daly writing with ethicist John B. Cobb (Cobb and Daly 1990) tackle the problem. A consensus is growing that the neoclassical myth of perpetual economic growth underlies the business community's addiction to globalism. Culbertson, Daly, Cobb, and many others challenge the possibility of perpetual growth, calling not only upon ecology's concept of "carrying capacity"[35] but also on David Ricardo, the father of classical economics. Ricardo understood limiting factors (land). He also assumed that virtually all investment would be national. John Maynard Keynes concurs with the desirability (and still in his time the apparent inevitability) of primarily national investment.

Cobb and Daly (1990) follow classical—not neoclassical—economics. With this paradigm, free trade and an open-arms immigration policy are exposed as a betrayal of both the environment and the interests of wage earners in countries with a relatively higher standard of living. Free trade may result in exporting jobs, and immigration brings surplus labor and additional population. Cobb and Daly write that either strategy runs the risk of undermining "the national community that embraces both labor and capital." Immigration has the more lasting negative impact because people are not easily sent away. Both strategies, however, irresponsibly undercut a cornerstone of the conservation ethic, the confidence that one can benefit tomorrow from what one saves today.

Behaviors are subtly shaped, I think, by the (mostly) subliminal sense that the United States has become a commons. Waste and degradation of natural resources become normal practice when the private, local incentive to conserve the carrying capacity disappears. If everyone owns or uses a resource, if many can enter and claim a share, who will conserve? Overconsumption and loss of natural capital are inevitable when ownership is ambiguous. The key to conservation appears to be accountability and appropriate incentives. Without control, without secure rights to long-term benefits, with the possibility of moving on, or with gain unrelated to risk,[36] conservation is a sometime thing.

The mobility of monetized capital makes it difficult to envision a sufficient incentive, or workable enforcement mechanism, to tie wealthy individuals to land or any particular natural resource so that they have a stake in conserving its long-term productivity. Yet this must eventually be part of a solution. Whereas conspicuous consumption has been a sign of wealth, conservation would ideally be tomorrow's status symbol.

When the condition of irrevocable linkage to country and rights to land are not in place—and in the global economy and with ambiguity of national borders they increasingly are not—ways to promote connectedness and conservation are not obvious. The essential element of conservation, nonetheless, is a climate in which citizens can trust that their own and their children's rights to future use of assets will remain secure. Without this confidence, efforts falter through a failure of will, and then collapse under the pressure of continuing population growth.

If and when adjustments in national migration policy are made, environmental progress still depends upon the willingness of business to be a partner. The wealth generated by business, large and small, is the source of income which affords the United States the environmental protection undertaken thus far and the possibility of continuing care. Possibly, a shift of regulatory authority from federal to State and local government is the trade-off which business should exact from a country that values its capitalist, entrepreneurial, wealth-generating sector.

Regardless of the means used to encourage conservation and discourage pollution, business justifiably fears that the costs of federally mandated environmental protection and labor standards jeopardize their competitiveness in the global economy—where globalism is a reality even if not an ideal. With "free" trade, capital investment and jobs do flow to countries that accept environmental degradation, just as they flow to countries with low labor costs. Witness China, Korea, Thailand, and Mexico.

The answer cannot be to lower one's own standards for environmental quality, no more than to undercut American workers' wages with cheap immigrant labor or to accept unlimited goods from countries that produce at any human cost. As an industrialized country, the United States can compete through innovation, automation, and employment of a skilled labor force, plus protection of its markets against industrialized countries that resort to exclusionary trade practices. Bilateral trade agreements should aim for equal trade in the sum of high value-added goods—in short, "fair" trade. From a parallel perspective, permitting immigration from countries which have higher than replacement level fertility *imposes on the self-restraint of American citizens who limit reproduction;* it is unfair. And it should stop.

The American way is to let incentives work. Citizens, labor, and business alike will protect and conserve land, resources, and environmental quality where they have a stake and secure rights in the future benefits that flow from their effort, caution, low fertility rates, and frugality.

Notes

1. M. Atiyah and F. Press, *Population Growth, Resource Consumption, and a Sustainable World* (Washington, DC: Royal Society of London and National Academy of Sciences, February 1992).

2. Heinz Von Foerster, P. M. Mora, and L. W. Amiot, 'Doomsday: Friday, 13 November, AD2026', *Science*, 132(3436), 1960, pages 1291–95. Von Foerster et al fit a curve to historical population data; the resulting equation shows a mathematically impossible result being reached by the year 2027 which, in turn, suggests that the population curve will enter a 'region of instability' by around 2015. See also Stuart Umpleby, 'Will the optimists please stand up?', *Population and Environment* 10, no. 2 (1988): 122–32.

3. Dennis Ahlburg and J. W. Vaupel, "Alternative projections of the US population," *Demography* 27, no. 4 (1990): 639–47.

4. The Population Reference Bureau puts the growth rate at 0.8, a difference which can arise from relying on the unadjusted 1990 US Census and on the Census Bureau's 1990 projections including outdated assumption about the immigrant sector. See Dennis A. Ahlburg, "The Census Bureau's new projections of the US population," *Population and Development Review* 19, no. 1 (1993): 159–74.

5. Doubling time is computed by dividing the rate of growth into 70. Thus, 70 ÷ 1.1 = 63.63. . . .

6. US Bureau of the Census, *Population Projections of the United States by Age, Sex, Race, and Hispanic Origin: 1992–2050*, Current Population Reports (Washington DC: Government Printing Office, 1992), 25–1092.

7. Projections are a construct based on demographic assumptions. They differ from predictions in taking no account of exogenous factors, e.g. climate change, war, epidemics, etc.

8. The estimate of 200 000 illegal immigrants annually is unduly conservative. Apprehensions were 1.1 million in 1992, and it is estimated that three to four cross US borders for each one apprehended. Sources estimate that 300 000–800 000 each year come to stay. Possible extension of the lifespan through applications of a new biology that inhibits the ageing process is a further factor which suggests that the 1992 Census Bureau Projections for population size are still unrealistically low. Theodore J. Gordon et al., ed., *Life Extending Technologies: A Technology Assessment* (Elmsford, NY, Pergamon, 1980).

9. Australia and Germany both had relatively open-door immigration until recently; Germany virtually eliminated provisions by which non-Germans had been gaining entry, and Australia has reduced its total number of immigration visas in each of the past few years. (Rosemary Jenks, 'Country immigration policies', Washington, DC, Center for Immigration Studies, 1992). Canada admits 250 000 annually (Daniel Stoffman, 'Pounding at the gates: why Canada must reassess its wide-open immigration policy', *Toronto Star*, 20 September 1992, pages B1, 4, 5).

10. Robert M. Veatch, ed., *Life Span: Values and Life-Extending Technologies: A Hastings Center Report* (San Francisco, CA: Harper and Row, 1979); Roland H. Ebel, "Get Ready for the L-bomb: a Preliminary Social Assessment of Longevity Technology," *Technological Forecasting and*

Social Change 13, no. 2 (February 1979): 131–48; Gordon et al., *Life Extending Technologies.*

11. Leon Bouvier, *Peaceful Invasions* (Lanham, MD: University Press of America, 1992).

12. President's Commission on Population Growth and the American Future, Population Growth and the American Future (New York, Signet Books/New American Library, 1972), p. 192. The report estimated that the population was likely to stabilize at 278 million in about 50 years (page 195).

13. J. D. Kasarda and A. M. Parnell, *Third World Cities: Problems, Policies and Prospects* (Newbury Park, CA: Sage, 1993).

14. Kevin Phillips, *Boiling Point: Republicans, Democrats, and the Decline of Middle Class Prosperity* (New York: Random House, 1993).

15. R. D. Lee, "A Historical Perspective on Economic Aspects of the Population Explosion: The Case of Preindustrial England", in *Population and Economic Change in Developing Countries*, ed. R. E. Easterlin (Chicago, IL: University of Chicago Press, 1980), 517–56. See also R. D. Lee, "Population Dynamics of Humans and other Animals," *Demography* 24, no. 4 (1987): 443–65.

16. Virginia Abernethy, "Jobs, Politics and the Labor Force," *Chronicles*, (in press), October 1993.

17. Virginia Abernethy, "The World's Women: Fighting a Battle, Losing the War," *Journal of Women's Health* 2, no. 1 (1993): 7–16.

18. Abernethy, "Jobs, Politics and the Labor Force"; Virginia Abernethy, *Population Politics: The Choices that Shape Our Future* (New York: Plenum Press/Insight Books, 1993. Reprinted by Transaction Publishers 1990); Barbara Vobejda, "Poor Americans Are Seen Fleeing some States as Immigrants Move In," *The Washington Post*, September 12, 1993, A3.

19. Robert Fox and Ira Melman, *Crowding Out the Future* (Washington, DC: Federation for American Immigration Reform, 1992).

20. Donald L. Huddle, *The Costs of Immigration*, 20 July Update (Washington, DC: Carrying Capacity Network, 1993).

21. Ibid.

22. Ibid., 2.

23. Ibid.

24. 'Immigration Unpopular in Poll', *San Francisco Chronicle*, June 5, 1990, A10; Gallup Poll, "Americans Respond to Immigration Queries," March 1, 1992; Robert Suro, "Hispanic Pragmatism Seen in Survey," *New York Times*, December 15, 1992, 4; Had they been released in time, The Latino National Political Survey findings might have had a bearing on the 1990 Immigration Reform Act, which raised legal immigration by 40%. The study was conducted by Rodolfo de la Garza of the University of Texas with funding from the Rockefeller and Ford Foundations; *USA Today*/CNN/Gallup Poll, "65% Want Immigration Cut Back," *USA Today*, July 15, 1993, 8A.

25. "Native-born Poor Being Displaced," *San Francisco Chronicle*, September 13, 1993, 3.

26. Virginia Abernethy, "Jobs, Politics and the Labor Force."

27. Population Reference Bureau, *Population Today*, 21(6), June 1993, page 2.

28. Algeria illustrates the cycle. Fertility rose after achievement of independence from France in 1962. In 1991, some 30 years later, 70% of the population was under 30 years of age. Unemployment and underemployment increasingly

underlie social and political unrest, while both acceptance of modern con-traception and religiously inspired revival of emphasis on female virginity and arranged marriage contribute to a declining fertility rate.

29. William Ryerson, "Population Communications International and Its Role in Family Planning Soap Operas," *Population and Environment* 15, no. 4 (1994): 255–64.

30. Lindsey Grant, ed., *Elephants in the Volkswagen: Facing the Tough Questions About Our Overcrowded Country* (New York: W. H. Freeman, 1992).

31. Abernethy, "Jobs, Politics and the Labor Force"; Virginia Abernethy, *Population Pressure and Cultural Adjustment* (New York: Human Sciences Press [now Plenum Press], 1979).

32. Donella Meadows, Dennis Meadows, and Jorgen Randers, *Beyond the Limits: Confronting Global Collapse, Envisioning a Sustainable Future* (Post Mills, VT: Chelsea Green, 1992).

33. US-produced TV bears much responsibility for sending the message of affluence and renewable abundance to the corners of the Earth.

34. For information regarding the coalition, contact Population-Environment Balance, www.Balance.org .

35. Carrying capacity refers to the number of individuals who can be supported without degrading the physical, ecological, cultural, and social environment, i.e., without reducing the ability of the environment to sustain the desired quality of life over the long term.

36. US domestic policies often support unwise exploitation of natural capital. For example, sale of cheap (below market price) crop insurance encourages planting grain in the fragile, drought-prone prairie grasslands of Oklahoma and other dry states. When the crop fails, the US taxpayer pays for it. Meanwhile, the soil erodes and irrigation drains underground aquifers at unsustainable rates. Similarly, water subsidies throughout the US West encourage agriculture in areas that are naturally desert. Given the price incentives, flood irrigation—which wastes water—will continue.

References

Abernethy, Virginia Deane. 1979. *Population Pressure and Cultural Adjustment.* New York: Human Sciences Press (Plenum Press).

Abernethy, Virginia Deane. 1993. *Population Politics: The Choices That Shape Our Future.* New York: Plenum Press.

Abernethy, Virginia Deane. 1994. "Optimism and Overpopulation." *The Atlantic Monthly*, December, 84–91.

Abernethy, Virginia Deane. 1995. "Crowd Control: Review of Critical Masses." *Scientific American*, July, 92–93.

Ahlburg, D. A., and J. W. Vaupel. 1990. "Alternative Projections of the U.S. Population." *Demography* 27 (4): 639–47.

Arrow, K., B. Bolin, R. Costanza, P. Dasqupta, C. Folke, C. S. Holling, B.-O. Jansson, S. Levin, K-G. Maler, C. Perrings, and D. Pimentel. 1995. "Economic Growth, Carrying Capacity, and the Environment." *Science* 268:520–1.

Auster, Lawrence. 1991. *The Path to National Suicide: An Essay on Immigration and Multiculturalism.* Monterey, VA: American Immigration Control Foundation.

Bernstein, A. 1994. "Inequality: How the Gap Between Rich and Poor Hurts the Economy." *Business Week*, August 15, 1994, 78–83.

Berry, B. J. L. June 1996. "From Malthusian Frontier to Demographic Steady State in Concord, 1635–1993." *Population and Development Review* 22 (2): 207–30.

Borjas, G. 1995. "Know the Flow." *National Review*, April 17, 44–49.

Borjas, G., and R. B. Freeman. 1992. *The Economic Effects of Immigration in Source and Receiving Countries*. Chicago, IL: University of Chicago Press.

Briggs, V. M., Jr. 1990. Testimony before U.S. House of Representatives Judiciary Committee Subcommittee on Immigration, Refugees and International Law. Congressional Record. March 13.

Briggs, V. M., Jr. 1992. *Mass Migration and the National Interest*. Armonk, NY: M.E. Sharpe, Inc.

Briggs, V. M., Jr. 1992. *Mass Migration and the National Interest*. Armonk, NY: M.E. Sharpe, Inc.

Brittain, A. W. 1990. "Migration and the Demographic Transition: A West Indian Example." *Social and Economic Studies* 39 (3): 39–64.

Burtless, G., ed. 1990. *A Future of Lousy Jobs*. Washington, DC: The Brookings Institution.

Carrying Capacity Network (CCN). 1994. "Sharp Increase in Science and Engineering Immigrants Results in Unemployed American Ph.D.s," *Clearing House Bulletin*, p. 3. November.

Carrying Capacity Network (CCN). 1995. *Polls Show Most Americans Want Immigration Levels Reduced*. Washington, DC: Carrying Capacity Network.

Center for Immigration Studies (CIS). 1994. *The Costs of Immigration: Assessing a Conflicted Issue*. Washington, DC: Center for Immigration Studies.

Cobb, J. Jr., and H. Daly. 1990. "Free Trade versus Community: Social and Environmental Consequences of Free Trade in a World with Capital Mobility and Overpopulated Regions." *Population and Environment* 11 (3): 175–92.

Cohen, R. 1989. "Brazil." *Wall Street Journal*, A6, April 10.

Connelly, M., and P. Kennedy. 1994. "Must It Be the West against the Rest?" *The Atlantic Monthly*, pp. 61–84. Dec.

Culbertson, J. 1989. "'Economic Growth,' Population and Environment." *Population and Environment* 11 (2): 83–100.

Davidson, J. 1995. "Panel's Proposals to Slash Immigration Spur Intense Opposition by U.S. Business," *Wall Street Journal*, B4. June 9.

Davis, K. 1963. "The Theory of Change and Response in the Modern Demographic History." *Population Index* 29 (4): 345–65.

Demeny, P. 1968. "Early Fertility Decline in Austria-Hungary: A Lesson in Demographic Transition." *Daedalus* 97 (2): 502–22.

Demeny, P. 1988. "Social Science and Population Policy." *Population and Development Review* 14 (3): 451–80.

Diaz-Briquets, S., and L. Perez. 1981. *Cuba: The Demography of Revolution*. Washington, DC: The Population Reference Bureau.

Duncan, R. C. 1993. "The Life Expectancy of Industrial Civilization: The Decline to Global Equilibrium." *Population and Environment* 14 (4): 325–58.

Easterlin, R. 1962. *The American Baby Boom in Historical Perspective*. Occasional Paper No. 79. New York: National Bureau of Economic Research.

Espenshade, T. J., and K. Hempstead. 1995. "Contemporary American Attitudes toward Immigration." Presented at Population Association of America Annual Meetings, San Francisco, CA, April 6–8.

Estrada, R. 1990. "Less Immigration Helps Hispanics." *The Miami Herald*: 13A. July 24.

Estrada, R. 1991. "The Impact of Immigration on Hispanic Americans." *Chronicles*, 24–28 July.

Estrada, R. July, 1991. "The Impact Of immigration on Hispanic Americans." *Chronicles*, 24–28.

Firth, R. 1956. *Elements in Social Organization*. London: Watts.

Firth, R. 1957. *We the Tikopia: A Sociological Study of Kinship in Primitive Polynesia*. Boston, MA: Beacon Press.

Firth, R. 1967. *Tikopia Ritual and Belief*. Boston, MA: Beacon Press.

Frey, W. 1995. "Immigration and Internal Migration 'Flight': A California Case Study." *Population and Environment* 16 (4): 353–75.

Friedlander, D. 1983. "Demographic Responses and Socioeconomic Structure: Population Processes in England and Wales in the Nineteenth Century." *Demography* 20:249–72.

Gever, J., R. Kaufmann, D. Skole, and C. Vorosmarty. 1986. *Beyond Oil: The Threat to Food and Fuel in Coming Decades*. Cambridge: Ballinger.

Guengant, J. P. 1985. *Population and Development in the Caribbean: A Demographic Survey*. New York: Inter-American Parliamentary Group on Population and Development.

Hardin, G. 1968. "The Tragedy of the Commons." *Science* 162:1243–8.

Haub, C. 1994. "Population Change in the Former Soviet Union." *Population Bulletin* 49 (4). Washington, DC: Population Reference Bureau.

Holdren, J. P. 1991. "Population and the Energy Problem." *Population and Environment* 12 (3): 231–56.

Huddle, D. 1992. "Immigration and Jobs: The Process of Wage Depression and Job Displacement." Abstract. Paper presented at the Society for the Advancement of Socio-Economics annual meeting, March 27–29, 1992. Irvine, CA.

Huddle, D. L. 1992. *Immigration, Jobs and Wages: The Misuses of Econometrics*. Teaneck, NJ: Negative Population Growth.

Huddle, D. L. 1993. "Dirty Work: Are Immigrants Taking Jobs That the Native Underclass Do Not Want?" *Population and Environment* 14 (6): 515–38.

Huddle, D. L. 1995. *The Net National Costs of Immigration in 1994*. Washington, DC: Carrying Capacity Network.

Huddle, D. L., and D. Simcox. 1994. "The Impact of Immigration on the Social Security System." *Population and Environment* 16 (1): 91–98.

Kaplan, R. D. 1994. "The Coming Anarchy." *The Atlantic Monthly*, February, 44–75.

Keyfitz, N. 1990. "Alfred Sauvy: In Memoria." *Population and Development Review* 16 (4): 727–33.

Krugman, P. 1994. "The Myth of Asia's Miracle." *Foreign Affairs* 73 (6): 62–78.

Latino National Political Survey (LNPS). 1992. New York: Ford Foundation Program for Governance and Public Policy.

Lee, R. D. 1980. "A Historical Perspective on Economic Aspects of the Population Explosion: The Case of Preindustrial England." In *Population and Economic Change in Developing Countries*, edited by R. E. Easterlin, 517–56. Chicago, IL: University of Chicago Press.

Lee, R. D. 1987. "Population Dynamics of Humans and Other Animals." *Demography* 24 (4): 443–65.

Lee, Roland D. 1980. *Population and Economics Change in Developing Countries*. Edited by R. E. Easterlin, 517–56. Chicago, IL: University of Chicago Press, Chicago.

Lind, M. 1995. "America by Invitation." *The New Yorker*, April 24, 107–12.

Lutz, H. 1995. Personal communication, AWHONN Conference, Nashville. June 8.

May, J. F. 1995. "Policies on Population, Land Use, and Environment in Rwanda." *Population and Environment* 16 (4): 321–34.

McConnell, R. L. 1995. "The Human Population Carrying Capacity of the Chesapeake Bay Watershed: A Preliminary Analysis." *Population and Environment* 16 (4): 335–52.

McCracken, P. W. 1991. "The Big Domestic Issue: Slow Growth." *Wall Street Journal* A14, October 4.

McCracken, P. W. 1992. "The Best Recession Policy: Investment." *Wall Street Journal*, Editorial Page.

Montenegro, A. V and P. M. de Muente. 1990. *La Situacion Poplacional Peruvana: Balance y Perspectivas*. Lima, Peru: Instituto Andino de Estudios en Población y Desarrollo (INANDEP).

Morris, F. L. 1990. Testimony before the U.S. House of Representatives Judiciary Committee Subcommittee on Immigration, Refugees, and International Law. Congressional Record. March 13.

Morris, F. L. 1995. "Illegal Immigration and African American Opportunities." Testimony before the U.S. House of Representatives Judiciary Committee Subcommittee on Immigration and Claims. April 5.

Morris, Frank. 1991. "Re Legal immigration reform: Testimony before the House Subcommittee on Immigration, Refugees, and International Law." *Social Contract* 1 (4): 188.

Murdock, S. H. 1995. *America Challenged: Population Change and the Future of the United States*. Austin: University of Texas Press.

Naipul, V. S. 1989. "A Miraculous Achievement." *Newsweek* (European Edition), 48, July 3.

Pimentel, D. and M. Giampietro. 1994. *Food, Land, Population and the U.S. Economy*. Washington, DC: Carrying Capacity Network.

Pimentel, D., C. Harvey, P. Resosudarmo, K. Sinclair, D. Kurz, M. McNair, S. Crist, L. Shopritz, L. Fitton, R. Saffouri, and R. Blair. 1995. "Environmental and Economic Costs of Soil Erosion and Conservation Benefits." *Science* 267:1117–23.

Population-Environment Balance. 1993. *Wetland Losses and Population Growth April 1993*. Balance Data. Washington, DC: Population-Environment Balance.

Population-Environment Balance. 1994. *Not a Drop to Drink*. Balance Data. Washington, DC: Population-Environment Balance.

Porter, M. E. 1990. "The Competitive Advantage of Nations." *Harvard Business Review* 90 (2): 73–93.

Pritchett, L. A. 1994. "Desired Fertility and the Impact of Population Policies." *Population and Development Review* 20 (1): 1–55.

Rattner, S. 1995. "GOP Ignores Income Inequality." *Wall Street Journal*, A22, May 23.

Rivera, M. N., and T. J. Espenshade. 1995. "Peru's Coming Baby Boomlet." *Population and Environment* 16 (5): 399–414.

Rosa, E. A. and T. Dietz. 1995. "Letter." *Science* 268:1551.

Rubenstein, E. 1995. "Missing the Point." *National Review*, 16, February 20.

Rukstad, M. G. 1989. *Macroeconomic Decision Making in the World Economy*. Chicago: Dryden Press.

Science. 1991. "Math Ph.D.'s: A Bleak Picture, 1991." *Science* 252:502.

Smith, Joseph Wayne. 1991. "Population, Immigration and the Limits to Australia's Growth." In *Immigration, Population, and Sustainable Environments*, J. W. Smith, 1–43: South Australia: Flinders Press.

Stevens, W. K. 1995. "Entire Ecosystems on Endangered List." *San Francisco Chronicle* (Nation). February 14.

Teitelbaum, M. S. 1975. "Relevance of Demographic Transition Theory for Developing Countries." *Science* 188:420–5.

Teitelbaum, M. S., and S. S. Russell. 1994. "International Migration, Fertility, and Development." In *Population and Development: Old Debates, New Conclusions*, edited by R. Cassem, 229–52. New Brunswick: Transaction Publishers.

Teo, P. 1995. "Population Planning and Change in Singapore." *Population and Environment* 16 (3): 237–52.

Van Zandt, H. F. 1981. "Efforts of Japan and the United States to Solve Common Problems." Kokusai Denshin Denwa, Tokyo.

Vernez, G. and K. McCarthy. 1995. *The Fiscal Costs of Immigration: Analytical and Policy Issues*. DRU-958-1-IF. Santa Monica, CA: The Rand Corporation.

Westoff, C. 1988. "Is the KAP-Gap Real?" *Population and Development Review* 14 (2): 225–32.

Whitmire, R. January 5, 1992. "When Living and Wages Don't Meet." *The Tennessean*, 1,4E.

Wiarda, I. S., and H. D. Wiarda. 1986. *Population, Internal Unrest, and U.S. Security.* Amherst: University of Massachusetts Internal Area Studies.

8

Marriage, Motherhood, and Power

Introduction

The prism of reciprocal rights, duties, privileges, and responsibilities illuminates virtually all interpersonal relationships. The interplay of give and take is seen not only within marriage and parenthood but also in nonfamilial settings. The doctor-patient relationship—particularly when hospitalization highlights a patient's relative helplessness—is hedged in with expectations about rights and obligations appropriate not only to roles but also to age. The case described below may have had some small influence on subsequent medical practice.

Interpersonal exchanges revolve around multiple axes. Power, trust and caring [among other relationship elements] can be viewed as mediums of exchange. For example, power is not only exerted but allowed: even if disadvantaged, one can resist the power that another tries to wield. Equally, caring and affection can be given or withheld, and the giving may entail a trade-off for power.

Trust is commonly thought to be an affirmation that one earns. But again, it can be viewed as an exchange good, particularly if the pretense of trusting or being trustworthy can be passed off as real.

Most people learn to navigate the intricacies and shoals of interpersonal relationships. Because of a lesser need for closeness, or a preference for independence and even solitude, some may be slow learners. But virtually everyone who lives within society develops a strategy for rubbing along.

Preferences, behavior and strategies may be modified as economic, social, cultural or even health circumstance change. Adaptability is continuously tested.

Marriage is unique because of being an organizing principle of society. Nonetheless, its importance varies because it may have many or few functions. In the post-modern United States, as much as half of a traditional marriage's value—including its political and most of its economic meanings—have been lost. What remains are emotional and procreative functions.

The current culture has introduced the view that marriage's emotional value should not be limited by heterosexuality. What remains exclusively to heterosexual couples is the procreative function of marriage.

I *predict* that special terms will be invented, and soon, to denote a form of marriage where the explicitly stated intent is to have and raise children. The terms will connote aspiration and moral purpose. Inching farther out on the proverbial limb, I foresee that the *normal pattern* will be to delay marriage sacraments until a prospective bride's pregnancy begins to show. Recall the Old Dutch Masters whose portrayals pridefully reveal both material wealth and a woman's swelling form.

Driven by people, ideas, and environments, culture changes. Feedback loops then force further change and adaptation.

Compassion, Control, and Decisions about Competency*

A competent patient has the right to refuse any medical intervention. However, hospitalized patients who refuse treatment sometimes find their competency challenged. The author describes the grounds for deciding that an elderly woman who resisted amputation "lacked capacity" to refuse the intervention, so that custody was conditionally awarded to a state social service department. Questions are raised about the evaluation process. The author suggests that the standard for finding a patient not competent to refuse treatment should be no less than generalized incompetence, including clear evidence that a patient is uninformable on emotionally neutral issues and cognitively incapable of making ordinary decisions on matters unrelated to the crisis at hand (*Am J Psychiatry* 141:53–58, 1984).

The definition of mental competency is elusive. Defining it is a compelling quest, nonetheless, because a patient's right to exercise autonomy with respect to decisions about his or her medical care is conditional on the patient's competency (Abernethy and Lundin 1980; Reiser 1980).

The root premise that elevates the importance of evaluating competency, fundamental in the American jurisprudence system, is that "every

---

*In *American Journal of Psychiatry* 141(1), pp. 53–58 [January, 1984].

human being of adult years and sound mind has a right to determine what shall be done with his own body" (*Canterbury v Spence* 1972).

The patient has the right to "forego treatment or even cure if it entails what for him are intolerable consequences or risks, however warped or perverse his sense of values may be . . . so long as any distortion falls short of what the law regards as incompetency" (*2 F Harper and F James* 1968).

There is a legal presumption, but of uncertain magnitude, in favor of finding that an individual is competent; that is, the burden of proof is on those who allege that the patient is not competent. The standard required to overcome the presumption of competency in civil cases was stated, in one decision, to be "clear, cogent and convincing evidence" (*Grannum v Berard* 1967). Similarly, disorientation, mental illness, irrationality, or commitment to a mental institution are not conclusive proof of incompetency (*Winters v Miller* 1971).

Although the courts and the medical profession are frequently required to make judgments about competency, there is often great difficulty in implementing the concept. Real complexity in evaluating patients' mental function may be further clouded by conflicts over value systems. To the extent that the outcome of saving life is raised above alternative values such as autonomy, the patient who makes decisions that appear contrary to his best medical interests is likely to be seen as not deciding in a cognitively rational manner and, therefore, as incompetent. In this paper I explore competency in the context of an actual case and recommend conditions that must be met before finding that a patient cannot decide for himself.

Case Report

Ms. A was seventy-two years of age at the time her story became front-page news. She was described as athletic looking, as appearing much younger than she actually was, and also as dirty and soot-covered. She lived with her six cats in one garbage-strewn room heated by a wood fire in the formerly luxurious house in which she was raised (Abernethy and Lundin 1981).

In January 1978, a fire in Ms. A's house led to her being escorted to a hospital by the police. The emergency room doctor noted that she was "mentally competent for her age [and] a very self- and strong-willed individual, very determined-minded person and definitely was not insane" (Abernethy and Lundin 1981, 11–12, police report). Ms. A insisted on returning home after spending only the night of the fire with neighbors. Both they and a mayoral aide, who earlier had become aware of Ms. A's lifestyle, became concerned as January temperatures dipped toward zero. On one occasion when the neighbors brought food, they noted that Ms. A's feet were black, blistered, and bleeding. She rejected offers of aid or shelter (she had once met a social worker with a shotgun and refused him entry). Ms. A refused even food unless she was allowed to pay for it (Abernethy and Lundin 1981). Finally, the mayoral aide used her influence to mobilize the police. With the aide's repeated urgings and under a broad interpretation of the principle that police can intercede when a person is harming herself, the police made four visits, eventually broke down doors, physically overwhelmed Ms. A, and transported her against her will to the hospital.

Once hospitalized, Ms. A was treated for pneumonia. One week later, gangrene was recognized, and the surgeons advised bilateral, below-the-knee amputation, citing a 50 percent chance for life with amputation and a 5–10 percent chance without the operation. Ms. A adamantly refused amputation. At the surgeons' request, hospital social workers called in the state human services department to assist in persuading her to have the operation. Ms. A still refused, allegedly saying that her feet were just black from soot, so the department sought guardianship under a state law covering protective services for the elderly. (In October 1981 a similar statute became law in New York state.) Grounds for the custody petition were that she was "in imminent danger of death" and "lacked capacity to consent" to treatment (Abernethy and Lundin 1981, 5, 6, statute).

The case evolved into an effort to determine whether Ms. A was competent to refuse amputation and was heard subsequently at four judicial levels. The state appeals court held an unprecedented hearing at Ms. A's bedside. This yielded the only transcript of evidence or of Ms. A's own words. On this occasion, she was willing to discuss her feet and at no time claimed that their color was attributable to soot. Instead, she pointed out that the feet and legs had been a cause of concern, and she marshalled evidence of improvement. The following material is from the transcript (Abernethy and Lundin 1981, 10).

> Judge: I understand that you had a little problem of getting too cold out there at your house.
>
> Ms. A: Yes. It's a point of this, the swelling in my foot was . . . very dangerous looking. . . . So that's what caused most of the trouble. It's starting to go down. Give it a chance; it is starting to go down and it's almost. . . . .

> Judge: You remind me of my mother. She's a good deal older than you are, and she lives by herself, but I go by and see her every morning and sometimes every afternoon.
>
> Ms. A: Yes.
>
> Judge: Keep mighty close watch on her.
>
> Ms. A: Well, these ankles and along these legs have gone down wonderfully.

In addition, Ms. A noted that she could move her toes. Several years before, she had experienced natural recovery from blackening and ulceration of her feet secondary to winter freezing; the experience also contributed to her conviction that the feet would recover. An account of a similar discussion was reported in the narrative, a reconstruction of lower court proceedings. The guardian ad litem appointed by the court to represent Ms. A described the first interview with her client: "[She told me that] the swelling in her feet was going down, she was getting better, and the doctors were wrong about her situation. [Ms. A] said that she felt it was a terrible thing when they can take a person's two feet with the person being denied the right to make that decision" (Abernethy and Lundin 1981, 26, narrative).

The surgeons did not dispute the reality of the physical signs to which Ms. A called attention, and the appeals court was, in addition, aware of her repeated experiences with frostbite. Nevertheless, the court accepted both (1) the surgeons' formulation that the only significant chance for life lay with amputation and (2) the idea that a competent person should be willing to make a choice between dying and amputation (Abernethy and Lundin 1981). The judges' attempt to force a decision within this surgically defined, two-choice world emerges in the following dialogue (Abernethy and Lundin 1981, 73–75, transcript).

> Judge: . . . should we let you die, or would you rather live your life without your feet?
>
> Ms. A: I am giving my feet a chance to get well.

> Judge: If the time comes that you have to choose between losing your feet and dying, would you rather just go ahead and die than to lose your feet? If that time comes?
>
> Ms. A: It's possible. It's possible only if I . . . just forget it. You are making me sick talking.

Judge: I know. I am sorry. You'd be willing to say to me that you just don't want to live if you can't have your feet. Is that the way you feel?

Ms. A: I don't understand why it's so important to you people, why it's so important.

Judge: I believe, [Ms. A], that you have made your point that you don't want to live if you can't have your feet. Isn't that it?

Ms. A: That's possible. It's possible to see it that way, to have that opinion.

Judge (frustrated): She wants to live and have her feet.

Ms. A's friend: That's exactly what she wants.

Ms. A: This is ridiculous. I am tired. Ridiculous, you know it is.

In other circumstances, Ms. A's avoidance of the key question might have been seen as canny. The guardian ad litem later noted, "She was not going to let them put her in the position of saying, 'Yes, when I become unconscious, you can do it.' This was a smart lady. I've seen people on a witness stand say things that hurt them worse. This woman was being cross-examined by an appellate judge, and she wasn't going to give him what he wanted" (Abernethy and Lundin 1981, 100, interview).

Nonetheless, Ms. A's failure to appreciate or accommodate to what was wanted inspired the judge to write: "The patient has not expressed a desire to die. She evidences a strong desire to live and an equally strong desire to keep her dead feet. She refuses to make a choice" (Abernethy and Lundin 1981, 82, appellate court opinion).

The mutual frustration and misunderstanding are palpable. In the parting moments, one judge gave Ms. A a final opportunity to consent to amputation, asking to leave her with a "little thought." He started the parable "If thine eye offend thee. . ."; she correctly completed it, and the judge suggested that she apply the moral to her feet. Ms. A thanked him appropriately and added her metaphor: "Let me leave you with one. Of spirits and ancient inspiration. Well, they're all my facts yet, and I am not going to throw my inspirations and everything away" (Abernethy and Lundin 1981, 75, transcript).

Her rejection of the two-choice model became the grounds, finally, for concluding that Ms. A was not competent to refuse amputation. Her hope for a third outcome, that the feet might recover, became the primary evidence of denial and, ipse dixit, her incompetence: "If, as repeatedly stated, this patient could and would give evidence of a comprehension of the facts of her condition and could and would express her unequivocal desire in the face of such comprehended facts, then her decision, however unreasonable to others, would be accepted and honored by the courts and her doctors. The difficulty is that she cannot or will not comprehend the facts" (Abernethy and Lundin 1981, 83, appellate court opinion).

The court wrote that Ms. A did not "comprehend the facts," although it had heard contrary testimony from a surgeon (Abernethy and Lundin 1981, 61, transcript):

> Questioner: Has she ever by statement to you indicated that she comprehends that, in your opinion, her feet are dead and that her life is threatened?
>
> Surgeon: She understands it very well, but I don't think she believes it.

The judges' appreciation of this distinction was apparently dulled by their fixation on a forced choice between amputation and death. Moreover, they chose to ignore both their own observation that the "respondent is an intelligent, lucid, communicative individual . . . and apparently of sound mind generally" (Abernethy and Lundin 1981, appellate court opinion) and their awareness of a logical problem: Ms. A's alleged incompetence was linked to her refusal of amputation; that is, had Ms. A consented, it was generally agreed that she would have been competent to consent. A judge held the following sworn interchange with the psychiatric consultant (Abernethy and Lundin 1981, 68, transcript):

> Judge: Please don't think I am trying to make you appear ridiculous because I am not. I want to point out a problem that you have and we have, too.
>
> In some aspects, she has the capacity to consent and she is competent if she consents?
>
> Psychiatrist: That is correct.
>
> Judge: But in her very refusal to consent, she is not competent; isn't that really the unusual conclusion we reach from the unusual circumstances?
>
> Psychiatrist: I think that's correct.

The appeals court upheld the lower court custody award to the human services department but conditioned amputation on the written statement of two physicians that Ms. A was "in imminent danger of death." Those letters never were forthcoming because she survived the gangrene. The case rose finally to the US Supreme Court as a challenge to the constitutionality of the state law, but before it was heard, Ms. A died of a pulmonary embolus. A contributing factor may have been her refusal of medication (heparin sodium) to control blood clot formation in her still unhealed (but nongangrenous) feet.

The Decision Process

The court concluded that Ms. A was incompetent because she refused to choose between death and amputation. This decision relied heavily on testimony of mental health professionals that Ms. A was using denial as a psychological defense against reality. One psychiatrist wrote, and a second psychiatrist and a social worker apparently concurred, that Ms. A was employing "psychotic denial."

The greater part of the first psychiatric consultant's written report to the lower court described an alert, intelligent, logical, and (initially) pleasant woman but concluded that Ms. A was, after all, using a psychotic defense mechanism (Abernethy and Lundin 1981, 2, letter to lower court): "Nonetheless, I believe that she is functioning on a psychotic level with respect to ideas concerning her gangrenous feet. She tends to believe that her feet are black because of soot or dirt. She does not believe her physicians about the serious infection. There is an adamant belief that her feet will heal without surgery, and she refused to even consider the possibility that amputation is necessary to save her life . . . My impression is that she does not appreciate the dangers to her life. I conclude that she is incompetent to decide this issue. A corollary to this denial is seen in her unwillingness to consider any future plans. Here again I believe she was utilizing a psychotic mechanism of denial."

In the appeals court hearing, the psychiatrist testified further: "She can [consent] but she won't. She won't because there is a tremendous amount of emotional investment going on here" (Abernethy and Lundin 1981, 66, transcript).

Other evidence for incompetence brought out at the lower court level was a social worker's opinion that Ms. A was "[not] capable of making the decision regarding surgery on her feet [because] . . . she refused to discuss the question and did not believe the doctors' reports [but] felt that they were making it more serious than it really was." On questioning, he said that she was not senile and was "generally capable of making decisions regarding herself except with regard to the decision involving her feet" (Abernethy and Lundin 1981, 24–25, narrative).

A second psychiatrist was retained by an amicus curiae but made no official report because he concurred with the negative evaluation of Ms. A's competence.

In brief, to the extent that examiners focused on the feet and on saving life, the patient was placed in a "no win" situation. She was competent so long as she consented to amputation and incompetent if she refused. Under either circumstance, the patient would lose her feet. Even the more sophisticated formulation picked up by the judges allowed Ms. A a choice only so long as she agreed to deal with predetermined categories: amputation or death.

The controversial nature of the ultimate decision suggests that forces other than dispassionate objectivity may have been at work. Three aspects of the case heighten skepticism. There was, first, an aura of medical emergency that pervaded the psychiatric consultations and the judicial process. In addition, Ms. A herself was quick to anger and clearly regarded most interactions with medical personnel as adversarial. Last, one might ask if her hostility engendered reactive anger in those charged with evaluating her competence.

The aura of medical emergency is easily documented. The lower court judge later noted: "I believe I was misled, and I'm sure not intentionally, but misled in the way the human services department presented the case to us. This was as something that has to be done right now. I constantly was led to believe that the doctor was waiting with his scalpel in his hand by the telephone. That is what was presented to me. I was asking about calling the surgeons to see if we could get a little more time. I set the first hearing early in the morning before court opened" (Abernethy and Lundin 1981, 40, interview).

The psychiatric consultant also believed that a medical emergency existed. He pressed through a snowstorm to see Ms. A (as did the judge on the following morning to personally collect the psychiatric evaluation) and later stated that so long as Ms. A refused amputation, the doctors should decide because, "we were faced with a life-threatening situation. We have to make a decision on the basis of the facts at hand now" (Abernethy and Lundin 1981, 50, interview).

In court, the psychiatrist, when asked if he had "adequately evaluated her," replied: "No. I felt I was under the crunch of time. . . . I still feel that her denial of the problem with her feet is a denial of psychotic proportions" (Abernethy and Lundin 1981, 66, transcript).

The second disruptive factor was Ms. A's anger. Her sense of being under attack dated realistically to a year earlier when efforts had been made to condemn her home. Her fears and outrage could not have been lessened by the police breaking in and taking her to the hospital. The news that she must have her feet amputated was met with refusal and then, as attempts to persuade her mounted, with increasing anger. Both psychiatrists, one nurse, and a surgeon were among those summarily turned out of her room on at least one occasion (Abernethy and Lundin 1981). Her angry feelings were manifested on various levels, including the slight alteration of one surgeon's name to "Dr. Tacky."

Such wit and sarcasm are documented features of Ms. A's communication style (Abernethy and Lundin 1981), but in the context of an emergency psychiatric evaluation and her (by then) adversarial response to anyone appearing to coerce her into consent, the sometimes fanciful dismissal of problems with her feet facilitated misunderstanding. The psychiatrist later recalled an interchange that occurred near the stormy end of the evaluation: "She ignored, or denied, that there was anything wrong with her feet at first. Then when I said, 'Well, you know, that doesn't seem to be the case', she said, 'Well, there's just some soot on them'" (Abernethy and Lundin 1981, 46, interview).

Finally, one may ask whether the evaluation process was disrupted because Ms. A's anger sparked a like emotion in those she berated. Professionals who think of themselves as altruistic, or at least benevolently motivated, may be particularly sensitive to hostility because they feel deserving of gratitude. Did it, therefore, make a difference that the social worker was the same person whom she once had run off with a shotgun? Similarly, the psychiatrist considered himself "pretty good at interviewing folks that other people have trouble with, [but] forty-five minutes was all the time that she gave me before she verbally threw me out" (Abernethy and Lundin 1981, 45–46, interview). The second psychiatrist to see Ms. A had a quicker exit. He was dismissed almost immediately but continued the interview from behind the door, using as intermediary Ms. A's trusted friend (Abernethy and Lundin 1981). Could any negative affect have influenced their evaluations?

This background at least supports a question about the objectivity of professional decision making. Part of the disruptiveness here is attributable to Ms. A's personality and part to social and health care systems that demand acquiescence from even the shanghaied client or patient. It also is no small matter that the courts became the agent of the health care system in its coercive rush to do good.

Discussion

An alternative conclusion to that reached by the courts is that Ms. A's conversation (as recorded in the extensive transcript), other testimony, and the judges' own description of her as an "intelligent, lucid, communicative individual . . . of sound mind generally" reveal Ms. A to have been competent, entitling her to make the one decision that mattered most to her, for whatever reason or guiding inspiration she might have had. Hoping for recovery even against great odds is not a criterion of incompetence in this schema.

That judgment requires one to accept that hope (disbelieving the physicians' pessimistic prognosis) is not a criterion of psychotic denial. Hackett and Cassem (Hackett and Cassem 1974) suggest that denial of the seriousness of medical illness is common among dangerously ill patients, and they do not call this defense mechanism psychotic. Indeed, they note a convergence of psychoanalytic formulations in which denial is seen as the goal of assorted defense mechanisms and tactics. Moreover, they report that, at least for coronary patients, denial is associated with better outcomes during the course of hospitalization.

The possibility still may be raised that the patient is delusional on the issue of the medical decision only, while demonstrating apparent organization in other domains. It is this very problem that the paper has attempted to address: the criterion of a focal delusion is dangerously liable to error because a patient can easily be seen as delusional in an emotionally charged interchange, when in other circumstances he addresses the same issue appropriately. This contrast is clear in the verbatim transcript in which Ms. A gives a cogent account of her feet, their "dangerous" look, and their visible improvement.

If it is granted that Ms. A was competent, discussion of those logical contortions seen in the decision process has been appropriate. It is legitimate to ask why mental health professionals repeatedly stated that Ms. A was incompetent to decide about her feet but only for so long as she refused amputation. Similarly, why did the appeals court formulation make competence depend on choosing between predetermined categories?

It is not self-evident that a patient should be required to address any particular question as a test of competence. On the contrary, the opposite can be inferred from the dubious constitutionality of using the substance of a decision, or outcome, as the criterion that determines the competence of the decision maker. A 1964 opinion by Judge

Warren Burger, later to be Chief Justice of the US Supreme Court, speaks to this point: "Mr. Justice Brandeis, whose views have inspired much of the 'right to be let alone' philosophy, said. . . : 'The makers of our Constitution . . . sought to protect Americans in their beliefs, their thoughts, their emotions and their sensations. They conferred, as against the government, the right to be let alone . . . the most comprehensive right and the right most valued by civilized man.' Nothing in this utterance suggests that Justice Brandeis thought an individual possessed these rights only as to sensible beliefs, valid thoughts, reasonable emotions, or well-founded sensations. I suggest he intended to include a great many foolish, unreasonable and even absurd ideas which do not conform, such as refusing medical treatment even at great risk" (Abernethy and Lundin 1981, amicus curiae brief).

The implications of the Brandeis-Burger formulation may be difficult to accept precisely because many health care professionals are outcome oriented. Doing the best for the patient is a mandate that makes it repugnant to allow a patient to self-destruct in the name of the ofttimes conflicting value, autonomy. Yet, declaring Ms. A incompetent because of what she decided might have been seen as a violation of her constitutionally protected rights had the case reached the United States Supreme Court. The thrust of evolving law suggests that autonomy will be protected (Abernethy and Lundin 1980, 1981; *Canterbury v Spence* 1972; *2 F Harper and F James* 1968; *Grannum v Berard* 1967; *Winters v Miller* 1971; Miller 1981).

This issue is further brought into perspective by considering that, in practice, the competence of marginally delirious or demented patients who consent to a treatment is rarely challenged. The invisibility of these consenting patients raises an awkward ethical question, and, practically, makes it difficult to think about what level of mental function, or understanding, is consistent with a challenge to competency.

Thus, the complexities of evaluating competence are imposing even in the absence of value conflicts. When there is, in addition, the latent tension between an outcome orientation and commitment to honor the autonomy of persons, the judiciousness of the system appears overly strained. This case demonstrates the fragility of both clinical and legal processes.

If decisions about competence are in reality so vulnerable to extraneous circumstance, it becomes important to specify strict criteria for determining that a patient is incompetent so that the constitutionally protected right not to be touched is safeguarded. Thus, I recommend that the presumption of competence should be overcome only when significant dysfunction in an array of cognitive and interpersonal domains can be demonstrated. Good overall cognitive skill would be incompatible with a judgment of incompetence, no matter how (by what intrapsychic process) or what the patient decided about medical interventions. A patient who was informable and cognitively capable of making ordinary decisions on matters unrelated to the crisis at hand would be held competent to refuse or accept medical interventions.

Competence is presumed and does not have to be proved. Incompetence must be proved. A high standard of proof is needed as a safeguard of the right to be let alone, because patient autonomy is too easily thrust aside by the double-barreled salvo of medical crisis and interpersonal conflict. A patient may have hope, or may have quality of life priorities that outweigh life itself, and a competent patient should have the scope to express these idiosyncrasies.

American Marriage in Cross-Cultural Perspective*

Marriage is one of the few institutions that exist in all human societies. The recognition of marriage as an institution implies that it is a culturally patterned adaptation of individual and group needs within the context of particular environments and technologies. The orderliness of society and the security of the individual are enhanced to the degree that a culture recognizes the legitimacy of some form of social organization that clarifies the sexual and economic rights and obligations of men and women, and, through reproduction, provides for the continuity of the social group. The universality of marriage is thus perceived in the cluster of functions that it performs for persons and societies.

Specifically, marriage regulates and stabilizes sexual relationships within a society: unlike other primates, no human group allows sexual access to depend principally on male dominance hierarchies. Secondly, marriage is a solution to the problem of replacement or recruitment in society: it legitimizes children born to a woman and, in so doing, tries to ensure that responsible adults will provide for the care and socialization of the young. Lastly, the rules governing marriage organize division of labor between sexes, which is the most rudimentary and the only universal form of occupational specialization: although cross-culturally, few tasks are consistently assigned either to male or

---

*In *Contemporary Marriage: Structure, Dynamics, and Therapy,* edited by Henry Grunebaum and Jacob Christ, Little Brown and Co., pp. 33–51 [1976].

female, marriage as an economic arrangement capitalizes on the ability to learn complementary skills that are then stereotyped as sex roles.[1]

Shifting to the permutations of these functions as seen from the perspective of an individual in a particular society, one may again ask, what is marriage for? What are the objectives of this legal contract that binds principals alone or the principals and their relatives to a bundle of reciprocal rights, duties, obligations, and privileges? Is marriage for the purpose of having children? For the mutual happiness of the man and woman who marry? Is marriage a way of cementing alliances between groups? Does marriage provide an economic and social framework that is a springboard to other activities?

Cultures vary in the emphasis accorded each objective, and in some societies one or more objectives may be absent altogether. The manifestations and range of cultural attitudes to the "goods" of marriage can illuminate some strains intrinsic to marriage in particular societies, and therefore it is to a study of societies that we now turn. A review will locate modern Western marriage along the continua of emphasis on (1) individual happiness; (2) alliances between politicofamilial units; (3) means of access to socioeconomic benefits; and (4) children as a goal of marriage.

American Marriage in Perspective

Cross-cultural comparison suggests that the normative pattern for marriage in the United States is unusual in the degree to which it emphasizes happiness as an individual "right" and equates this state with emotional attachment between spouses. The conjugal relationship is seen as a contract exclusively between consenting individuals, rather than as a politicoeconomic alliance that links families.

Marriage for Happiness

Reviewing research on marriage in the United States during the 1960s, Hicks and Platt conclude that, "In our society marriages are assessed by two norms: happiness and stability" (Hicks and Platt 1970).

The criterion of happiness identified by professional students of the family appears consistent with the pervasive lay ideals of romantic love as prerequisite to marriage, and continuing conjugal affection as a major goal. This enshrinement of emotions is a comparatively recent development and distinguishes present marriage norms from nineteenth-century dictates of rationality, which stressed good health, strong character, and similarity of religion as reliable guides to mate selection (Gordon and Bernstein 1970).

Barring a national crisis, there is little ground for anticipating a return to traditional criteria and expectations. The earlier standards were based on spouses' pressing need for each other as working partners in agricultural or home-centered enterprises. Whereas at agrarian levels of technology, husbands and wives are often nonreplaceable by other personnel and make complementary contributions to subsistence, the economy of more developed societies allows most goods and services to be obtained commercially—in markets, restaurants, and laundries, from electricians, gardeners, housekeepers, and so on. Given that finances are adequate, both specialization of labor and the impersonality and transferability of money and services are factors that make dissolution of marriage comparatively easier.

Thus, by default of subsistence pressure as a stabilizing force, the burden of binding marriage partners comes to rest on personal and emotional attachment. In wealthy industrial nations this fragile bond of conjugal emotion is invoked and supported through the romanticism of the mass media, the cosmetic industry, marriage counseling, and psychotherapy directed toward improved communications and interpersonal relationships.

Ironically, the crisis of modern marriage is intrinsic to its main support: great expectations for emotional fulfillment in marriage lay the groundwork for later disappointment. The nation's high divorce rate may understate the disillusionment; a reservoir of discontent and feelings of having been cheated by marriage probably does not find legal expression (Cuber and Harroff 1965; LeMasters 1959).

Marriage as a Political or Economic Alliance

When the extended family has corporate functions in ownership of land or business, marriage partners are frequently co-opted as representatives (or even de facto hostages) for their respective kinship units. For instance, the bride and groom may be scions of banking houses, trading partners, or adjoining farms or kingdoms, with the marriage becoming a vehicle for consolidating wealth or confirming politicoeconomic arrangements. Such interlocking of kinship with economic and political relationships is most common in preindustrial societies where the economy is dominated by agrarian or relatively small-scale financial and manufacturing enterprises. In the circumstances described, where marriage may be an instrument of family strategy in its external power relationships, the stability of the conjugal tie becomes a vital family concern.

By contrast, there are few instances in modern Western society of the marriage alliance's being economically or politically significant to the couple's families. In the United States, for example, ownership in major productive enterprises is distributed through large sectors of the population, and rarely would a marriage forge a controlling interest in a big company or divorce dissolve such. In the political domain, the rare marriages between offspring of prominent families occur amidst great publicity and could, through informal channels, be advantageous; however, in a democratic system of elected officials, only machine politics can provide the continuity to give extended family alliances long-term impact. Within the military establishment, marriage may consolidate the influence of families that for generations have been "Army" or "Navy"; but again the network is informal and in no sense rigid. Consequently, even in these cases, the threat to vested interests posed by marital dissolution is limited and, although relatives may counsel against divorce as disruptive to individual careers, seldom are sufficient forces mobilized to overwhelm the couple's inclinations.

An outstanding exception in the modern Western world is the British royal family, whose aversion to divorce is well known. Insofar as the monarchy has survived and justifies continuing privilege in terms of a symbolic contribution to British identity, instability within royal marriage could undermine its remaining function. Thus, reports that pressure from royalist interests has been sufficient to prevent marriage between royalty and divorced persons and to remove an offender from line of access to the throne is not suprising (Edward VIII 1951).

The atypical examples cited serve principally to illustrate that in the postindustrial period, politicoeconomic interests are comparatively isolated from marriage; natal families rarely expect material benefits to accrue from their children's marriages.

Western marriage tends to be a contract between individuals only; the families of bride and groom may not meet until the engagement party or wedding. They hope to like each other, but are themselves as far from feeling party to a contract as they are unlikely to have vested interests in the alliance. It is enough that a daughter marries a fine-looking boy who has a promising future.

If and when marital dissolution appears imminent, the couple's parents may weep (for their grandchildren?), but they are unlikely to rave or threaten. Only rarely in modern Western society are the extended families of a couple bound by the latter's marriage or do they feel themselves so threatened by its demise that significant forces will be mobilized to forestall the event.[2]

Concluding, some currents of writing on the contemporary family stress that, although particular marriages lack continuity or stability, remarriage of divorced persons is common; and therefore marriage is shown to retain its importance as the preferred basis for household formation. The new pattern is congruent with the reality that kinship is no longer a major instrument of familial politicoeconomic strategy. This function of marriage is not important in postindustrial societies, and thus is not available to sustain marriage as a dominant institution of the society.

Marriage as Springboard

To some extent, all societies regard marriage as a preferred framework within which, or from which, individuals conduct other activities. The American norm in this respect is unremarkable in being approximately intermediate between (1) the rigid prescription of the Muslim culture, in which, essentially, a woman must marry to be respectable (Lee 1971), or of most hunter-gatherer groups, whose subsistence technology makes it virtually impossible for either a man or woman to live alone and (2) the opposite extreme, as illustrated in Ireland, of institutionalized alternate lifestyles featuring very late marriage or celibacy (Connel 1955–1956).

Until recently,[3] wedlock was the undisputedly preferred, as well as the statistically normative, state for American women. All periods between 1880 and 1969 have seen over 75 percent of the female population fourteen years of age and over married, widowed, or divorced. In 1969, almost 90 percent of women eighteen years old and over were or had been married (US Bureau of the Census 1960, 1970). The value placed on marriage for women is integrally related to other societal patterns, such as the banning of females from many occupations (Rossi 1964, 1965) and lone (unmarried or otherwise) women from public places and from social participation (Friedan 1963; Rossi 1964).

Not only American women, but also American men, have traditionally considered marriage to be a helpful framework for the conduct of a full life. Apart from providing domestic comfort and a ready partner for social and sexual activity, marriage enhances a man's attractiveness to employers who value settled reliability. Marriage may also increase upward mobility if business is conducted through the skillful entertaining of clients or associates; and it is commonly believed to enhance the political profile of candidates for public office.

Thus, there is small doubt that, for society at large, marriage presently retains its preeminence as a springboard to other activities. However, close scrutiny suggests that these secondary benefits of marriage derive to some extent from the value placed on marriage: a married status facilitates movement through countless social, economic, and political domains only because it is commonly acknowledged that it is good to be married. The circularity is apparent and suggests the query, "If the value placed on an institution lacks foundation in real adaptive advantage, will it persist?"

Presently, heterosexual marriage is under attack by diverse interest groups that include hippies, communes, the Gay Liberation Movement, and the Women's Liberation Movement. Their advocacy of alternate lifestyles appears to be having an impact that varies with region and socioeconomic level (*Time* 1970; Winch 1970). At the least, the rhetoric of Women's Lib is likely to support the decision of a number of young women to delay, redefine the terms of, or forgo marriage in favor of other commitments. Slowly emerging patterns that are conducive to a reduction of pressure on women to marry include a newfound social freedom for "singles," the companionship offered by communal living styles, and community tolerance of heterosexual cohabitation without adherence to legal formalities (Winch 1970).

The foregoing discussion has touched on the intrinsic weakness of modern Western marriage because it depends almost entirely on the emotional attachment between spouses. Marriage is relative unimportant politically and economically; neither families protecting vested interests nor subsistence pressures are a significant stabilizing force. Moreover, the benefits conferred by marriage as a framework for other life pursuits seem to depend on the positive valuation of marriage; but a value unsupported by real adaptive advantage is on a fragile foundation.

In only one of its functions does traditional marriage retain a monopoly. That one is legitimate reproduction.

Marriage and Children

On no other objective of marriage is there greater consensus the world over: children are a desired outcome of marriage, and everywhere marriage legitimizes the children born to a woman (Gough 1968). The positive valuation of children can be inferred both from most informants' statements and from the rules governing disposition of children in the event that the usual family structure is disrupted, as by divorce or death. The issue typically turns on who has "rights" to children.

Cross-cultural study of marital dissolution reveals that rights over children are assigned across a wide range of possibilities. For instance, bride-price is often, but not necessarily, conceptualized as the purchase of the woman's procreative powers and thus predictive that rights to children are retained by the male parent or his relatives or both. Place of residence after marriage is also a good, but by no means invariable, clue to the disposition of children after death or divorce. The following examples suggest that a society's attitudes toward children may be viewed on a continuum, having as its logical endpoints the preeminence of either maternal or paternal rights in regard to progeny.

Among the Hopi Indians of the southwestern United States, a child's economic, legal, and residential affiliation stays unalterably with the mother's family, although the child remains bound to the father's family by strong emotional ties. This society traces *descent* (relationship by birth as opposed to relationship by marriage) through the female line. Marriage is usually between a man and a woman of the same village (or mesa); there is neither bride-price nor dowry; and after marriage both husband and wife live with the wife's family. The husband works his wife's family's fields, but he is in no sense an authority figure in the household. Rather, this position is held by the wife's brother or wife's mother's brother, although both of these men actually live elsewhere, namely, with their wives' families! Approximately 40 percent of Hopi marriages end in divorce. After divorce, a man ceases to till his divorced wife's fields and returns to live with his mother's or sister's family. The parents' marital status notwithstanding, affectionate, nonauthoritarian relationships between father and children are expected to persist, and a network of continuing ritual privileges and obligations bind children to other members of the father's family (Titeiv and Old Oraibi 1944).

The Tlingit of the northwest Canadian coast illustrate a second variant of the children's belonging to the mother's family. In this society, descent and inheritance are traced through the female line, but residence after marriage is with or near the husband's family. In case of divorce, the wife and children return to her family's village, which, because of the conjunction of matrilineal descent and virilocal residence, will be her brother's home (Lowie 1920).

Legal rights to children are also unequivocally retained by the mother and her kin among the Kai of New Guinea. This arrangement is somewhat unusual in its association with both patrilocal residence after marriage and institutionalized bride-price, payable by the groom's family to the woman's father, brothers, and maternal uncles.

Observation of marital dissolutions, however, reveals that bride-price confers only exclusive sexual rights over the wife and that this is distinct from rights over her procreative powers. Thus, in an ordinary divorce (one in which fault cannot be clearly assigned), a man does not retain rights to his children's labor, nor can he claim jurisdiction over them, nor is he entitled to return of the bride-price. The bride-price would be forfeited by the woman's family only if the divorce was precipitated by her elopement or adultery (Lowie 1920).

Proceeding along the world continuum, one finds that the rules governing rights to children are often flexible, allowing such factors as age of the child, ability of a parent to care for the child, and sex of the child to influence outcomes. The common denominators of societies making do with ad hoc arrangements of this order are the related circumstances that (1) there is little reliance on children's contribution to subsistence, and (2) the economy is not "labor -intensive."

Most hunter-gatherer groups as well as technologically advanced nations meet these criteria: in all but the harshest environments, hunter-gatherers appear to amply satisfy their limited wants with a leisurely work style involving only adults in their prime; similarly, the automated industries of modern nations have minimal use for (unskilled) child labor. Moreover, in technology-oriented societies, individual contributions to the economy may be delayed until after the long period required to learn specialized skills.

The latter constellation is familiar in the United States, where most children remain an economic liability, rather than an asset, well past adolescence. Inevitably, the issue of rights over children assumes a different flavor when children are unable to contribute to the family economically or when such a contribution could undermine the parents' self-esteem. Under conditions of divorce or separation, the father's rights over children frequently are transformed into the father's obligation to continue financial support. The physical care of younger children is most often entrusted to the mother, and in this sense she has rights, which are rarely waived. So long as the children must be supported by their father, she gains a measure of financial security by caring for them. The usual disposition of children to the mother reflects both (1) the imperative that the father earn enough to support them, which typically entails work away from home and (2) the cultural emphasis on preserving emotional bonds: the mother's presumably greater affective involvement with children is felt to justify her claim to priority in regard to their physical custody.

Continuing with a cross-cultural overview, one discovers the parochial nature of the Western assumption that a mother's emotional commitment to the child confers a legitimate legal claim. On the contrary, a great number of societies recognize the strong affectional mother-child ties but do not find in them a basis for granting a woman prior rights to her children. Legitimate claims to children are often reserved to the father and his family, and such was accepted practice in the United States until the early twentieth century.

Among the Kwaio a widow must usually relinquish her children if she chooses to leave a deceased husband's village to return to her natal home. Exceptions do occur, however, when the husband's relatives who contributed to her bride-price are also deceased or otherwise unavailable to assert their claims, or if the mother's family offers to repay a portion of the bride-price, thus buying back rights over the offspring. This is an example of bride-price explicitly securing rights to procreative powers (Keesing 1970).

Transference of the women's procreative powers through bride-price is also seen among the Thonga of South Africa. In this society, a woman's offspring belong to her family only in the rare case that the bride-price remains unpaid. Normally, her issue belongs unequivocally to the father's family, and should she die childless, her family would be obliged to return the bride-price (Lowie 1920).

In extreme cases of the preeminence of father rights, there are no exceptions or institutionalized arrangements whereby the mother's family can reassert rights to children. Exemplifying this extreme are the Guari Katchin of Burma, where, in the unusual event of divorce, the woman returns to her natal village while the children remain with the father. A nursing infant goes with its mother, but this necessity is time limited, and after weaning, the child returns to the paternal domicile (Leach 1957).

Cross-culturally, then, children are a primary objective and desired outcome of marriage. Children of one or both sexes may be valued for their contributions to the work force. In addition, males add to the fighting strength of the society, and females may be prized as sources of income (bride-price) or, by fathers, as tradable assets in securing a wife for oneself or a son. However, rights and responsibilities in regard to children are differentially assigned to spouses and their relatives, and, as a corollary, the importance of children to the several parties in a marriage contract may vary considerably.

Weighing the importance of factors that account for the positive valuation of children, one finds that in agricultural societies even very young children contribute substantially to subsistence, whereas the general pattern in a technology-oriented society is that immature offspring are not an economic asset but are valued primarily because they are objects of affection (Lerner 1957). The phenomenon can be logically related to the impersonality of the communities in which a large proportion of the population lives. A technological orientation is frequently associated with social and geographic mobility that shatter the continuity of friendships. Except in crisis situations, supportive relatives tend to be unavailable.[4] Therefore the small family unit turns inward to satisfy emotional needs, and the adding of children to this elementary family grouping assumes urgency.

However, an additional and more subtle motive may be the popular view that parenthood is a rewarding emotional experience. Perhaps this theme represents rationalization of the reality that, rather than being an asset, children are a financial and, occasionally, even an emotional, liability. Since children cost so much, they must be good.

Mature industrialized societies go to the extreme of asserting that children should not be an economic asset: child labor is forbidden, and the old person who becomes financially dependent on an adult son or daughter may be stigmatized. The reality that many old people are at least partially dependent on children in no way contravenes the value placed on independence or the shame associated with becoming a burden (Brown 1969). The covert wish that children function as old-age security no doubt exists at some level but is a culturally illegitimate expectation in Western society; it can be articulated only by "undesirables" such as the cockney renegade in *My Fair Lady*: I'll be supported by my children . . . and never have to work again" (Lerner and Loew 1956).

The refusal of economic contributions from children should not be mistaken for an absence of demands on children. The demands unmistakably exist, but are attuned to psychological, rather than material, goods. Emphasis on children as a major satisfaction in marriage appears to increase as opportunities for reciprocal giving and receiving in an industrial and migratory society decrease (Luckey and Bain 1970). To a degree which is often unrealistic, children are expected to satisfy a woman's emotional cravings, affirm, if not create, her identity, give meaning to her life, and cement a marriage (Friedan 1963).

A man's social identity depends on children to a lesser degree, and meaning for him may hinge on giving children more than he had when he grew up or on having heirs to benefit from his achievements.

Self-recognition and evidence of prepotency are added factors in the chip-off-the-old-block boast.

Insofar as children are valued as objects of affection, it follows that they will be expected to reciprocate love. Mother's Day and Father's Day are institutionalized opportunities for children to express appreciation for all that has been done for them.[5] It is thus a consistent and culturally legitimate expectation that children should forebear from distancing themselves and should provide emotional security for their aged parents (Streib 1965).

Nevertheless, a source of conflict for many an insightful parent is that parents' demands for closeness from their children may be self-defeating. Indeed, the isolation of old people, as well as the present demand for (and conditions in) nursing homes,[6] suggests that, paradoxically, a generation dedicated to making life easier or better for their young is not receiving the hoped-for spontaneous warmth from the beneficiaries of the hard work and self-denial. Even when parents are old and growing feeble, the attitude that parents ought not complain is pervasive. Lifetime values and obligations persist, and the ethos that children should not be burdened supports the old person in behavior that shields the son or daughter from responsibility and guilt (Brown 1969; Streib 1965).

Given these conditions, some of today's adolescents and young married couples can hardly fail to conclude that one benefit supposedly accruing to parenthood is evanescent: the much publicized failure of communication between generations and the unwillingness and inability of mobile families to care for an old person must, inevitably, shake the belief that children are rewarding in the long run.

Moreover, the circumstances under which many present-day mothers raise their children often lead to disillusionment with the maternal role itself. Some of the frustration produced by childrearing responsibilities derives from geographic mobility and the consequent disruption of intimate and close-knit relationships within the community. Maintaining relationships with old friends despite a move is hampered by physical distance; and the lesser level of intimacy and trust inherent in new friendships in a new community is less emotionally rewarding. Also, friends will not infrequently favor different childrearing objectives, techniques, and values. The mobile mother is thus exposed to numerous variants in childrearing theory and practice, which may be confusing to a parent and, if conflicting strategies are utilized, also to the child. The mother's initial uncertainty and the predictable

293

fractiousness from a confused child interact to reduce confidence and competence in implementing any approach, and thus lead directly to maternal frustration (Abernethy 1969).

In regard to childrearing, the contrast of our society with traditional, more stable societies is marked. In other cultures, the sharing of an experience within an intimate circle leads to a common interpretation and thus to a consensus on meaning and appropriate action. Although such closure of the communications network, or parochialism, entails a reduction in information and alternatives, it also fosters certainty. In childrearing this means that a woman is sure of objectives for herself and for the child and has confidence in the techniques for achieving her goals (Abernethy 1969).

Cooperation in exchanging childcare responsibilities becomes practical only when mothers share values and utilize them similarly. Children of women in tightly knit, traditional networks are accustomed to similar demands and constraints and thus do not challenge or disrupt the modus operandi of the household they visit. Under these circumstances, it is not difficult to care for a friend's or a relative's child. On the other hand, children's expectations about permissible deportment or entertainment are unlikely to be similar if their mothers have different models for childrearing. Faced with caring for a child who has been taught by other standards, a mother has the alternatives of constant policing or of ignoring a breach of discipline while her own child's behavior is "corrupted" (Abernethy 1969).

As numbers of women follow ambitious, job-oriented husbands into new communities and attempt to raise children in unfamiliar, if not alien, surroundings, the crisis of motherhood will mount. Mothering may be increasingly characterized by uncertainty, rigidity, bookishness, and frustration.

The effect of the first child on the conjugal relationship is a further factor that will be assayed in the ongoing cultural valuation of children. Intimacy and affection between spouses is a highly valued objective in modern marriage, but recent studies tend, with increasing consistency, to the conclusion that parenthood is negatively related to this desired state of man-woman bliss (Laws 1957, 1971). Family life cycle literature consistently shows that high initial satisfaction in marriage is followed by decreased satisfaction that coincides with the advent of children and which is most pronounced during the preschool years. The literature shows, finally, a gradual resurgency of satisfaction in the "empty-nest" phase of the marriage (Blood and Wolfe 1960; LeMasters 1967; Rollins and Feldman 1970; Rossi 1968). These fluctuations appear to be more pronounced for wives than husbands (Laws 1971). Case studies also suggest that parenthood threatens communication, intimacy, and mutuality in marriage (Gavron 1966), that husbands may anticipate parenthood with ambivalence (Meyerowitz 1970), and that immature wives regress into pathological states under the stress of motherhood (Cohen 1966). These findings are consistent with survey data from a large, representative sample in which childless couples report higher marital satisfaction than do parents (Renne 1970).

However, an earlier study suggests that satisfaction in marriage is not related to the presence or absence of children (Burgess and Wallin 1953), a finding that may be explained by independent data showing childless couples at either extreme of marital satisfaction, whereas parents tend to be average on this dimension (Landis and Landis 1963). Satisfaction aside, stability of a marriage appears to be increased by the presence of children (Luckey and Bain 1970; Renne 1970). With so fraught a subject and the extensiveness of variables, if may be that definitive research will never be available.

Trends in Parenting

The feelings engendered by the nonexistent economic benefits of children and the waning emotional rewards of parenting appear to be making a natural alliance, in our society, with the demographic warning that we face a population crisis. The author suspects that the recent spate of liberalization in abortion and contraceptive legislation and judicial decision could not have occurred without impetus from both sources: the disillusionment with parenthood and the Malthusian threat of overpopulation.

The impact of these developments on marriage has yet to be widely felt. However, a vision of the future may exist in the ethos of couples who live together, put off childbearing, and deny the need of entanglement through marriage. When a child is desired, such couples will usually enter into the formality of a marriage contract. It now appears that the viability of a male-female coalition independent of marriage should be considered (Mead and Heyman 1965); the highly valued emotional core of modern marriage can apparently exist without institutional formalities (Laws 1971). Marriage proper, with its defining function of legitimizing and guaranteeing to the society the responsible rearing of children, will be relevant only to those couples desiring children.

An underlying assumption is that the decision to have children can be brought under rational control through contraception. The soundness of this premise may be questioned, however, in view of the Bumpass and Westoff estimate that one-fifth of all births between 1960 and 1965 were unwanted (Bumpass and Westoff 1970). This pattern appears to be changing (Commission on Population Growth and the American Future 1971), perhaps as a result of improved contraceptives and post-conception technology (the morning-after pill), but nonetheless one may take note of unconscious motivations that appear to impel a woman or couple toward parenthood. Ineffective birth control despite an avowed intention to avoid pregnancy may be related to such traits as an exaggerated dependency need, a passive-aggressive mode of relating to others, and denial as a defense mechanism (Abernethy and Grunebaum 1970).

The generality of such unconscious motivations in the population at large is unknown. There exists the probability that a need to give nurturance is innate rather than a pathological expression of dependency needs. In this event, a block on reproduction, a major outlet for nurturance, could persist in a healthy individual only in conjunction with learned sublimations that might range from work in the helping professions (e.g., medicine, nursing, teaching) to gardening, animal husbandry, or simply keeping a pet.

Summary

Cross-culturally, marriage is defined by its functions. This article discusses the extent to which marriage is losing functions—losing its adaptive advantage as a way of life—in our society. Marriage has much diminished in significance both for organizing labor to meet basic subsistence needs and as an adjunct to politicoeconomic strategy. Only the human longing for others with whom to share and enjoy is still met for the majority by the spouse and children of nuclear family marriage. Nonetheless, the danger inherent in investing a great part of oneself in these narrowly circumscribed and possibly antagonistic relationships is increasingly recognized and finds voice in fringe groups of protesters and social innovators. The decrease in the functions of marriage and the emotional demands placed on the heterosexual-pair relationship should perhaps be considered as significant and nonreversible factors in the twentieth century. Together, they lend impetus to today's search for alternative modes of living and loving.

Notes

1.   Recent anthropological writing suggests that a dichotomy based on having or not having childrearing responsibilities is more accurate than the male-female distinction in predicting what other activities will be performed by a member

of a society. That is, childless females and males tend to follow pursuits that are similar to each other's but distinct from those of individuals charged with childcare. This analysis of human societies is consistent with observations of feeding and traveling groups of chimpanzees (Williams 1971).

2. This freedom of principals to a marriage contract from accountability to their natal families is observed in many hunter-gatherer as well as in highly industrialized societies. Despite the disparity in technological level, a common denominator is minimal investment by the family, qua family unit, in the factors of production.

3. Statistics from the US Bureau of the Census show nearly one-half of women aged twenty-one in 1970 to be single, compared to approximately one-third in 1960.

4. Although mother-daughter visiting is reportedly frequent in some classes (Cohler 1970), it appears to be diminished by social mobility (Aldous 1967). Moreover, kinship ties become increasingly vulnerable to mobility as genealogical distance increases and, beyond primary relatives, visiting, may lapse altogether as one family rises or falls on the social status ladder (Aldous 1967).

5. But LeMasters and Riesman conclude that children are rarely appreciative (LeMasters 1970; Riesman 1961).

6. In a paper presented in 1971 at the Harvard Center for Population Studies, Dr. Rashi Fein noted that in 1969 the United States spent $3.3 billion on nursing home care (Fein 1971).

References

2 F Harper and F James. Law of Torts, 61 n15 (Supp 1968).

Abernethy, V. 1969. Husband, Mother, and Social Network in Relation to the Maternal Response. Ph.D. dissertation, Harvard University.

Abernethy, V., and H. Grunebaum. 1970. Psychological interference with fertility control. Unpublished.

Abernethy, V., and K. Lundin. 1980. "Competency and the Right to Refuse Medical Treatment." In Frontiers in Medical Ethics, edited by Abernethy V. Cambridge, MA: Ballinger.

Abernethy, V, and K. Lundin 1981. The Mary Northern Case: Public Compassion and Private Rights. Santa Monica, CA: R and Graduate Institute.

Aldous, J. 1967. "Inter-generational Visiting Patterns: Variations in Boundary Maintenance as Explanation." Family Process 6:235.

Benedeck, T. 1959. "Parenthood as Developmental Phase." Journal of the American Psychoanalytical Association 7:389.

Benson, L. 1968. Fatherhood. New York: Random House.

Blood, R., Jr., and C. Wolfe. 1960. Husbands and Wives: The Dynamics of Married Living. New York: Free Press.

Bronfenbrenner, U. 1970. "Interview." Time, December 28, 1970, 37.

Brown, R. 1969. "Family Structure and Social Isolation of Older Persons." Journal of Gerontology 15:170.

Bumpass, L., and C. Westoff. 1970. "The Perfect Contraceptive Population." Science 169:1177.

Burgess, E., and L. Cottrell. 1939. Predicting Success or Failure in Marriage. New York: Prentice Hall.

Burgess, E., and P. Wallin. 1953. *Engagement and Marriage*. Philadelphia, PA: Lippincott.

Burr, W. 1970. "Satisfaction with Various Aspects of Marriage over the Life Cycle: A Random Middle-class Sample." *Journal of Marriage and the Family* 32:29.

Canterbury v Spence, 464 F 2d 772, 781 (DC Cir); cert denied, 409 US 1064 (1972).

Cohen, M. 1966. "Personal Identity and Sexual Identity." *Psychiatry* 29:1.

Cohler, B. 1970. Mothers and grandmothers: Personality and child care in two generations. Unpublished.

Commission on Population Growth and the American Future, An Interim Report. Washington, DC: U. S. Government Printing Office, 1971.

Connel, H. 1955–56. "Marriage in Ireland after the Famine: The Diffusion of the Match." *Journal of Statistical and Social Inquiry Society of Ireland* 19:82.

Cuber, J., and P. Harroff. 1965. *The Significant Americans*. New York: Appleton-Century-Crofts.

Dyer, E. 1963. "Parenthood as Crisis: A Re-study." *Marriage and Family Living* 25:196.

Edward VIII. 1951. *A King's Story*. New York: Putnam's.

Fein, R. 1971. Paying for medical care in the United States. Unpublished.

Friedan, B. 1963. *The Feminine Mystique*. New York: Norton.

Gavron, H. 1966. *The Captive Wife: Conflicts of Housebound Mothers*. New York: Humanities Press.

Gordon, M., and M. Bernstein. 1970. "Mate Choice and Domestic Life in the Nineteenth-century Marriage Manual." *Journal of Marriage and the Family* 32:665.

Gough, E. 1968. "The Nayars and the Definition of Marriage." In *Marriage, Family and Residence*, edited by P. Bohaman. Garden City, NY: Natural History Press.

Grannum v Berard, 422 P 2d 812, 814 (Wash 1967).

Grunebaum, H., N. Neiberg, and J. Christ. 1959. "Diagnosis and Treatment Planning for Couples." *International Journal of Group Psychotherapy* 19:185.

Hackett, T. P., and N. H. Cassem. 1974. "Development of Quantitative Rating Scale to Assess Denial." *Journal of Psychosomatic Research* 18:93–100.

Hicks, M., and M. Platt. 1970. "Marital Happiness and Stability: A Review of the Research in the Sixties." *Journal of Marriage and the Family* 32:553.

Hobbs, D., Sr. 1965. "Parenthood as Crisis: A Third Study." *Journal of Marriage and the Family* 27:367.

Keesing, R. 1970. "Kwaio Fosterage." *American Anthropology* 72:991.

Landis, J., and M. Landis. 1963. *Building a Successful Marriage*. Englewood Cliffs, NJ: Prentice-Hall.

Laws, J. 1957. "Parenthood as Crisis." *Marriage and Family Living* 19:352.

Laws, J. 1971. "A Feminist Review of Marital Adjustment Literature: The Rape of the Locke." *Journal of Marriage and the Family* 33:483.

Leach, E. 1957. "Aspects of Bridewealth and Marriage Stability among the Katchin and Lakner." *Man* 57:50.

Lee, L. 1971. "Law and Family Planning: A Publication of the Population Council." *Studies in Family Planning* 2 (4): 81.

LeMasters, E. 1959. "Holy Deadlock: A Study of Unsuccessful Marriages." *Sociological Quarterly* 21:86.

LeMasters, E. 1967. "Parenthood as Crisis." *Journal of Marriage and the Family* 19:352.

LeMasters, E. 1970. *Parents in Modern America*. Homeward, IL: Dorsey Press.

Lerner, A., and F. Loew. 1956. "Get Me to the Church on Time" (song). *My Fair Lady*. New York: Schappel.

Lerner, M. 1957. *America As a Civilization*. New York: Simon & Schuster.

Lopata, H. 1971. *Occupation Housewife*. New York: Oxford University Press.

Lowie, R. 1920. *Primitive Society*. New York: Horace Liveright.

Luckey, E., and J. Bain. 1970. "Children: A Factor in Marital Satisfaction." *Journal of Marriage and the Family* 32:43.

Mead, M., and K. Heyman. 1965. *Family*. New York: Macmillan.

Meyerowitz, J. 1970. "Satisfaction during Pregnancy." *Journal of Marriage and the Family* 32:38.

Miller, B. L. 1981. "Autonomy and the Refusal of Lifesaving Treatment." *Hastings Cent Report* 11 (4): 22–28.

New York Times. 1971. "Population Growth in the U.S. Found Sharply Off." November 5, 1971, 1.

O'Neill, W. 1967. *Divorce in the Progressive Era*. New Haven, CT: Yale University Press.

Orden, S., and N. Bradburn. 1968. "Dimensions of Marriage Happiness." *American Journal of Sociology* 73:715.

Poloma, M., and T. Garland. 1971. "The Married Professional Woman: A Study in the Tolerance of Domestication." *Journal of Marriage and the Family* 33:531.

Rapoport, R., and R. N. Rapoport. 1969. "The Dual-career Family: A Variant Pattern and Social Change." *Human Relations* 22:3.

Reiser, S. J. 1980. "Refusing Treatment for Mental Illness: Historical and Ethical Dimensions." *American Journal of Psychiatry* 137:329–331.

Renne, K. 1970. "Correlates of Dissatisfaction in Marriage." *Journal of Marriage and the Family* 32:54.

Riesman, D. 1961. *The Lonely Crowd*. New Haven, CT: Yale University Press, 1961.

Rollins, B., and H. Feldman. 1970. "Marital Satisfaction over the Family Life Cycle." *Journal of Marriage and the Family* 32:20.

Rossi, A. 1964. "Equality between the Sexes." *Daedalus*, Spring.

Rossi, A. 1965. "Barriers to the Career Choice of Engineering, Medicine or Science among American Women." In *Women and the Scientific Professions: The MIT Symposium on American Women in Science and Engineering*, edited by J. Mattfield and C. VanAken. Cambridge, MA: MIT Press.

Rossi, A. 1968. "Transition to Parenthood." *Journal of Marriage and the Family* 30:26.

Streib, G. 1965. "Intergenerational Relations: Perspectives of the Two Generations on the Older Parent." *Journal of Marriage and the Family* 27:469.

Time Essay. 1970. "The American Family: Future Uncertain." *Time*, December 28, 1970, 34–39.

Titeiv, M. 1944. "Old Oraibi: A Study of the Hopi Indians of Third Mesa." *Cambridge Papers of the Peabody Museum of American Archaeology and Ethnology* 22(1), 1944.

U.S. Bureau of the Census. 1960. *Historical Statistics of the United States, Colonial Times to 1957*. Washington, DC: U.S. Government Printing Office.

U.S. Bureau of the Census. 1970. Statistical Abstract of the United States: 1970 (91st ed.). Washington, D.C.: U.S. Government Printing Office.

Walters, J., and N. Stinnett. 1971. "Parent-child Relationships: A Decade Review of Research." *Journal of Marriage and the Family* 33:70.

Williams, S. 1971. "The Limitation of the Male-female Activity Distinction among Primates." *American Anthropology* 73:805.

Winch, R. 1970. "Permanence and Change in the History of the American Family and some Speculations as to Its Future." *Journal of Marriage and the Family* 32:6.

Winters v Miller, 446 F 2d 65 (2nd Cir 1971).

9

Seeds of Conflict

Use it up, Wear it out.
Make it do, Or do without.
—Nineteenth century, New England

Introduction

The United States and most of the world are confronted with crowding and perceived or real scarcity of both essential and culturally valued goods. Some people secure space and privacy, but the majority are urban by choice or necessity.

Access to wilderness is an almost unknown privilege for many Americans, but the American experience began with wilderness. Isolation and wilderness foster independence and self-reliance. Necessity becomes love. My father introduced me to mountain springs, fishing, and tracking—a pale shadow of his boyhood days, roaming alone in the Blue Ridge Mountains of Virginia.

The American Dream, post–World War II's equivalent of Manifest Destiny, saw cautious frugality replaced by abundance and a consumer society's discovered needs. The middle class came to believe that each generation would be more prosperous than those preceding. A sense of economic security changed values: self-reliance and community-centeredness morphed into demand for immediate gratification, idealization of global sharing and redistribution, and belief that benevolence is both duty and feels good.

Prosperity was fleeting. The United States is the most indebted nation in the world. Not-always-friendly governments hold trillions of dollars in US government debt, and total federal debt exceeds annual GNP. Unfunded future federal government liabilities are said to exceed $100 trillion. Several large cities have ruinous pension liabilities. Detroit, Michigan, emerged from bankruptcy after repudiating obligations to public employees. In May, 2015, Moody's rating agency down-graded Chicago bonds to "junk." Many Americans use debt to maintain their standard of living. Student debt overwhelms many, although earned academic credentials are sometimes financially worthless. Twenty percent of American children live in poverty. Hunger and homelessness have returned. The middle class is squeezed by the threat of joblessness, higher prices on food and housing, and higher taxes on those who work and save.

Despite growth in energy production through fracking, the United States imports 50 percent of the crude oil it uses. Further, the depletion rates for oil produced via fracking are much higher (e.g., 60–80 percent per year) than from conventional wells, and fracking is also more capital and energy-intensive.

Periodic droughts and visibly declining water tables (even as combined ground and surface water estimates may be overstated because sources are conflated) and volatile energy prices confront Americans with absolute limits of slowly or nonrenewable natural resources. Oblivious, US policymakers push mass immigration that spreads poverty and increases population pressure on natural resources.

The social and economic harms of mass immigration are widespread and were manifested long ago. In the 1990s, Morgan State dean Frank Morris testified several times before Congress on the harm that mass immigration does to African Americans. The late journalist Richard Estrada wrote on the harm done to both black and newly established Hispanic citizens.

Doubters that mass immigration drives population growth, poverty, inequality, resource depletion, and polluting emissions that overwhelm nature's restorative capacity do still exist. Attitudes are unlearned slowly, and new expectations acquired gradually. Denial lives. Nevertheless, when scarcity is many people's dominant experience, the cultural kaleidoscope eventually falls into a new design.

Government for the People?*

Not since 1953 have as many as 10 percent of Americans wished to increase immigration. But in 1965, 1980, 1986, 1989, and 1990 Congress progressively opened America to increasing numbers of legal and illegal immigrants and refugees. That 10 percent who want more must be concentrated on Capitol Hill. Regarding Congressional refusal to heed most Americans' wish to limit immigration, former California Congressman

---

* In *Conservative Review* 5(6), pp. 7–8 [November–December, 1994].

Bill Dannemeyer states, "Frankly, the institution of Congress shows a face of contempt for the American people" (Dannemeyer 1994).

A selection of new books points out that immigration represents one of several policies through which the country's elite sells out the American middle class. An immigration-driven surge in the labor force worsens underemployment; population growth heightens environmental stress and social fragmentation; and all rouse latent ethnic conflict (Dalton 1993; Francis 1993; Gottfried 1993; Luttwak 1993).

First to be impacted are jobs, although the fact has been disputed because Americans displaced by foreign workers often move to another State and are overlooked in reports of local unemployment (Frey 1993). Further, deterioration in the ratio of invested capital to labor—undercut overnight by the North American Free Trade Agreement (NAFTA) and steadily eroded through immigration—means that the average new job is backed by less investment today than formerly.

Rapid growth of the labor force and the need for net new jobs are outpacing the economy's ability to save, i.e., create capital. Moreover, the education of American and immigrants' children—approaching crisis budgetary constraints in states like Texas, Florida, and California—competes for savings against the private, job-generating sector. The result is that new jobs have less capital behind them than the average of existing jobs, a process also known as deindustrialization. On the contrary, a competitor country, Japan, has adapted (for thirty years) to relative labor shortage; their industrial strategy is to put more capital behind each job, substituting technology for labor.

Undercapitalized jobs are a drag on labor productivity and thus on wage levels. So no surprise: over two decades, 80 percent of American workers—those below supervisory levels—have experienced incremental erosion of real disposable personal income.

The working man or woman is most valued when genuinely hard to replace, reflecting that labor is scarce. Immigration creates labor surplus and thus a power imbalance. The weakening of labor's negotiating position promotes a search for political remedies which ultimately benefit neither business nor labor. Minimum wage laws, laws outlawing permanent replacement of strikers, and government-mandated benefits and protections are no substitute for a "seller's market" in labor.

Big business is myopic in its support for immigrant advocacy groups. In 1989, according to Washington, DC, citizens' watchdog Capital Research Center, corporations including American Express, Chevron, Exxon, Ford, General Electric, General Mills, General Motors, GTE,

Johnson and Johnson, Mobil, Southwestern Bell, US West, Amoco, Dayton Hudson, Campbell Soup, Circle X, Coca-Cola, and Motorola each gave $10, or more to the League of United Latino-American Citizense (LULAC) or the Mexican American Legal Defense Fund (MALDEF), or the National Council of La Raza (NCLR). Further, according to the Annual Report of the Ford Foundation, this institution's charitable giving in 1993 included nearly $6 million distributed among six major open-border organizations: La Raza, ($2,850,000), MALDEF ($850,000), LULAC ($300,000), National Lawyers Guild ($100,000), the National Immigration Forum ($567,900), and the Urban Institute ($1,115,282).

Such liberality is shortsighted at best and could be seen as demonstrating a malicious intent to undermine the integrity of the nation. No American interest long escapes the penalties of population growth. These include environmental degradation and clean-up costs, higher taxes for infrastructure, education, healthcare and welfare, social alienation and crime, and a populace too impoverished to sustain accustomed consumption patterns and quality of life.

Both misbegotten open-arms immigration and free trade policies can level American workers to third world standards. Wage rates in some industries, particularly cottage (garment-type) industry and the unskilled service sector, have fallen so low as to bring into common usage a new category: the working poor. Yet most Americans believe that their birthright is the opportunity for honest work that will produce a good living. What politician would say this is not so? Not those, certainly, who enact the very legislation which puts the American Dream beyond reach for multitudes.

I question if democracy and mutual tolerance for our diversity can survive the dawning realization of a big cheat. Many will be enraged that government, the media elite, and multinational corporations have governed in their own interests, in crass disregard for the well-being of the average, loyal American. Others, less sophisticated, will sense only their own alienation from society and a near-total absence of a stake in its peaceful continuance. Demagogic leaders could mobilize this mass in the usual way—scapegoating, myths, promises—and the America we know and honor would become history.

America's means are finite and the people's expectations are very high. Here may lie the vulnerability of representative forms of government. De Tocqueville saw 150 years ago that the roots of America's democracy were planted in the natural wealth of the continent. With fewer than fifty million people, citizens could prosper through work, and their prosperity bound them to the commonweal. Democracy has a chance when each man and woman can create wealth from a bounteous Nature.

Perhaps our population size and extractive attack on Nature have, already, put us beyond redemption. The Rockefeller Report on the President's Commission on Population Growth and the American Future foresaw that continued population growth would make our myriad national problems more intractable (President's Commission 1972). At that time, memories still were fresh that America fought and won World War II with 135 million people. Now with 263 million people (in late 1994), the US population has nearly doubled.

This explosive growth and the burgeoning environmental and social problems it brings cannot be derailed without a moratorium on immigration. But has Congress the stomach to act in the interest of the United States?

Census Bureau Distortions Hide Immigration Crisis, Part II*

Implications of Rapid US Population Growth

Ecologists and certain conservationists and labor economists say that rapid population growth, regardless of its source, is a danger. Their concern departs from United Nations, *Financial Times*, *London Economist* and *Wall Street Journal* views, which lament European and Japanese economic and social futures because these countries' populations are on the verge of stabilizing.

One might ask what, if anything, is wrong with population stabilization?

First, native-born Americans spontaneously chose small family size starting, approximately, in 1970. The majority would probably be better off economically and ecologically today if, congruent with the recommendations of the 1972 Rockefeller Report (President's Commission 1972), the US population had begun to stabilize thirty years ago.

Second, current population growth is being forced on native-born Americans by immigration. Approximately 90 percent of growth results from the annual immigration flow and the descendants of post-1970 immigrants (Camarota 2005).

---

*Online in *Population-Environment Balance* www.balance.org [2006].

Births to immigrant women represent births that, but for immigration, would not have been US births. The Associated Press reports that Mexican women in Georgia and North Carolina average 180 births per 1,000 women of reproductive age (Hispanic Birthrate Soars in Southeast 2006). This is nearly three times the rates of native-born American women. In 2004, the fertility rate of non-Hispanic white women was 58.5 per 1,000 women of reproductive age; of non-Hispanic black women, 66.7 per 1,000 women of reproductive age (National Vital Statistics Reports 2005).

Moreover, immigration accelerates world population growth. Steven Camarota of the Center for Immmigration Studies (CIS) writes, "Analysis of data collected by Census Bureau in 2002 shows that women from the top-10 immigrant-sending countries living in the United States collectively tend to have higher fertility than women in their home countries. As a group, immigrants from these countries have 23 percent more children than women in their home countries, adding to world population growth . . . Among Mexican immigrants in the United States, for example, fertility averages 3.5 children per woman compared to 2.4 children per women in Mexico. Among Chinese immigrants, fertility is 2.3 in the United States compared to 1.7 in China. Immigrants from Canada have 1.9 children compared to 1.5 children in Canada" (Camarota 2005).

Third, current immigration comes overwhelmingly from third world countries that have cultures vastly different from ours. These immigrants may not wish to assimilate and, indeed, may have difficulty adjusting.

The territorial integrity of the United States may develop into a further contentious issue that divides citizens from Mexican immigrants. A June 2002 Zogby poll reveals that a "substantial majority of Mexican citizens believe that southwestern America properly belongs to Mexico" (Barrett 2005).

Fourth, rapid increases in the labor force have resulted in a thirty-year trend toward lower real, inflation-adjusted income for the 80 percent of Americans who depend on wages and salaries. Immigration drives most of labor force growth and thus accounts for virtually all of the recent income depression.

Economist George Borjas observes that immigration depresses wages and displaces Americans from jobs, costing native-born American workers $195 billion annually (Borjas 1999, 2004). In 2000, immigration reduced the wages of native-born American workers by an average 3.2 percent (Borjas 2003).

The impact is not even. Citing a current Northeastern University study, the *New York Times* states that "illegal immigrants contributed to a sharp decline in employment of teenage and young adult Americans" (Preston 2006). The effect on young and less-educated workers is not new news. Most recently, however, Borjas reported that the wage impact is "most intense" at the two ends of the native-born education range (Brimelow 2003).

In addition to depressing wages, immigrant workers displace Americans. Steven Camarota analyzes Census Bureau data, finding that "between March 2000 and March 2004, the number of adults working actually increased, but all of the net change went to immigrant workers" (Camarota 2004). Andrew Sum and his colleagues at Northeastern University concur. Since 2000, immigrants have taken more than 100 percent of net new jobs, that is, both capturing new jobs and displacing Americans from existing jobs (Sum 2004).

A further, fiscal, problem is that many third world immigrants are very low skilled. Consequently, they do not pay taxes commensurate with the costs they impose on communities and States.

Professor Donald Huddle estimates that between 1996 and 2006, immigrants cost taxpayers an average of $93 billion annually, net of any taxes immigrants pay (Huddle 1996). In view of the unexpectedly high flow of immigrants, Huddle's numbers would, today, be adjusted higher.

The NRC's well-received report, *The New Americans*, estimates that each legal or illegal immigrant without a high school education imposes a net (after subtracting all taxes the immigrant pays) lifetime cost on taxpayers of $89,000 in direct services. With a high school education, the average fiscal impact per immigrant is still negative, $31,000 (National Research Council 1997). The figures are significant insofar as the average Mexican and Central American immigrant has less than an eighth-grade education.

Economist Lester Thurow's 1990s analysis of the cost of population growth—without reference to whether the growth is organic or from immigration—concludes that maintaining the quality of infrastructure requires a nation to commit 12.5 percent of its GDP for each 1 percent of population growth (Sundquist 2000). A community study on infrastructure costs associated with population growth is congruent. Eben Fodor calculated in the 1990s that each new three-person residential unit burdened local taxpayers with an average of more than $15,000 in new requirements for capital improvements, not counting annual operating costs (Fodor 1997).

Less immediately evident but powerfully important in the long run, population growth harms the nation through depleting its natural wealth—as documented by Carrying Capacity Network, a nonprofit grassroots organization that advocates an immigration moratorium. One acre of land is lost to highways and urbanization for each person added to the US population; each person uses 2,800 gallons of oil equivalents and 530,000 gallons of water per year (Pimentel, David, and Pimentel 1996; Pimentel, Berger et al. 2004; Pimentel 2006; Worldwatch Institute 2004).

One hesitates to mention the contentious Kyoto Treaty, which would require the United States to cut its total greenhouse gas emissions to 7 percent below the 1990 level. With population growth, this target becomes ludicrous. Instead of an average 7 percent per capita emissions reduction—as would have been the target with a 1990s-size population size—required restrictions become ever more stringent as the population grows.

Such ecological losses and challenges are separate from the loss of community public spiritedness that follows rapid growth and multiplying languages and cultures. Immigration advocates are challenged to show one fast-growing, multicultural society that is cohesive, democratic, and smoothly functioning.

Subjectively, many Americans see their communities, schools, and hospital emergency rooms flooded with people who speak a language different from their own. They see both hospitals close from skyrocketing costs for uncompensated care and also rising tax bills to fund services for aliens who lack health care insurance. The medically uninsured appear to increase by approximately one million annually. How many are illegal aliens? How many are among the least fortunate Americans or established immigrants displaced from jobs by illegal aliens? How many Americans become ill with infectious diseases that had long been eradicated from the United States but have been reintroduced through mass immigration? (Cosman 2005)

The tally of losses from mass immigration suggests that a large price is paid for so-called cheap labor and for advancing the financial and political elite's agenda of erasing borders and integrating Canada, Mexico, and the United States into the Partnership for Prosperity and Security, a.k.a. North American Union (Corsi 2006). Middle-class Americans, possibly to be joined by Canadians, would pay the greater part of the bill.

A healthy respect for probable errors in Census Bureau data advances the case for putting enforcement with the purpose of stopping illegal immigration and dramatically reducing legal immigration at the top of the legislative and executive branch agenda. A catch-our-breath moratorium on all immigration should be a further goal of domestic policy. Immigration legislation should be debated on the basis of accurate demography as well as economic and social data that recognize costs associated with population growth, the role of immigration, and the costs and benefits of additional immigration.

Book Review of *Ethnic Politics* by Milton J. Esman[*]

Ethnic Politics addresses the risks, sources of conflict or accommodation, and likely channels of protest or control which accompany the presence of several minorities together or, alternately, a minority and majority group residing within one territory. This is an ambitious subject, and Milton J. Esman is very thorough in examining the possible permutations and combinations such as, for example, whether the minority is the intruder or a people who regard the shared territory as their homeland.

Esman devotes much attention to the issue of competition for resources and access to opportunity, and he assesses the probability of such competition becoming violent in terms of (1) the scarcity of resources; (2) the strength of the state which mediates between parties and, to some extent; (3) the control of the state by minority interests. In addition, diversity becomes more problematic if a nation's institutions allow, even encourage, the mobilization of minorities by "ethnic entrepreneurs." If the state has an interest in containing violence, increasingly authoritarian measures will be required as the population/resource ratio becomes less favorable.

"Where the state loses control of ethnic relations, the result is likely to be protracted violence and civil war as in Bosnia, Sri Lanka, and Sudan" (p. 255). The general progress of events worldwide appears to bear out Esman's contention regarding the probability of violence, be it civil disorder, armed conflict or persecution. Esman reports that, "the single most important human rights concern has become the relative status and rights of ethnic collectivities, not atomized individuals" (p. 254).

Esman suggests that the presence of minorities invariably creates strain, so the implicit or explicit goal of a vigorous society is to minimize diversity. He writes, "The classic approach to depluralization

---

[*] In *International Migration Review* xxix(3), pp. 835–836 [Fall, 1995].

is the encouragement of individual assimilation" (p. 255), although deteriorating economic opportunity makes this more difficult. "The pendulum has begun to swing, with gradual recognition that the intensity of ethnic hostilities may preclude individual assimilation as a viable goal" (p. 253).

An interesting sidelight for Americans is the alternative of regionalization, both because our neighbors to the north seem likely to fission into the separate countries of Canada and Quebec, and because an eminent American statesman, George Kennan, appears to advocate regionalization into highly autonomous units for the United States itself (see *Around the Cragged Hill*). Kennan's reasoning is that the United States has become both too populous and too diverse for effective governance. Esman would probably question, however, whether loose confederalization could be accomplished peacefully: "Because it involves loss of territory, secession is seldom acceptable to state elites even when it might contribute to their goal of depluralization" (p. 255).

The major conclusions of *Ethnic Politics* are illustrated through very detailed accounts of ethnic relations in Malaysia, South Africa, the disputed Israeli and Palestinian real estate, Canada-Quebec, and the general topic of "international migration and labor diasporas."

The United States, which sometimes defines itself as a nation of immigrants, appears as the single greatest contrary example to Esman's principal themes. Yet on closer inspection, much of American history is congruent with the analysis of *Ethnic Politics*. For example, the favored strategy regarding immigrants has been assimilation. During periods of economic and territorial expansion, this was accomplished harmoniously because resources and opportunities were plentiful. Yet ethnic riots erupted, such as between Irish and freed African Americans in New York City during the 1860s, and in periods of economic recession. The competition for opportunity was to be long-lasting and, in his famed "Put Down Your Buckets Where You Are" address at the 1895 Atlanta Exposition, Booker T. Washington pleaded for an end to immigration so that poor white and black Americans would be recruited for the new jobs in burgeoning northern and western industry.

Ethnic riots in the United States also involve newly arrived immigrant groups who compete with established minorities for jobs, housing, and recognition. The use of police and military power to quell such disturbances are foreshadowed in Esman's observation that authoritarian governments are most successful (and maybe essential) in keeping control of ethnic relations. Indeed, the strains of growing pluralism could destabilize a government that was not authoritarian.

Readers will find Esman's book to be both informative and very readable. The tone is objective and subdued in spite of the highly charged nature of the subject.

References

Borjas, George. 1999. *Heaven's Door*. Princeton, NJ: Princeton University Press.

Borjas, George. 2003. "The Labor Demand Curve is Downward Sloping: Re-Examining the Impact of Immigration on the Labor Market." *Quarterly Journal of Economics*, Fall, 2003.

Borjas, George. May 2004. Increasing the Supply of Labor Through Immigration, CIS Backgrounder.

Brimelow, Peter. 2003. "New Borjas Bombshell: Immigration Now Impacting College Grads' Incomes." www.Vdare.com August 29, 2003.

Camarota, Steven A. 2004. *A Jobless Recovery? Immigrant Gains and Native Losses*. Washington D.C: Center for Immigration Studies, October, 2004.

Camarota, Steven A. 2005. *Birth Rates Among Immigrants in America: Comparing Fertility in the U.S. and Home Countries*. Washington, DC: Center for Immigration Studies.

Camarota, Steven A. 2005. *Births to Immigrants in America, 1970 to 2002*. Backgrounder, Center for Immigration Studies, Washington, D.C. July, 2005; Center for Immigration Studies, Immigration Statistics. Washington DC, various dates.

Cited by Tom Barrett. Publisher@ConservativeTruth.org April 18, 2005.

Corsi, Jerome R. 2006. *The New World Order*. Canadians Protest New World Order. www.WorldNetDaily.com September 9, 2006.

Cosman, Madeleine. 2005. Illegal Aliens and American Medicine, Journal of American Physicians and Surgeons 17(1) (Spring, 2005); www.JAPANDS.com.

Dalton, H., ed. 1993. *Will America Drown? Immigration and the Third World Population Explosion*. Washington, DC: Scott-Townsend.

Dannemeyer Backs Immigration Control. May, 1994. *Border Watch*, 5.

Fodor, Eben. 1997. "The Real Cost of Growth in Oregon." *Population and Environment* 18 (4): 373–88.

Francis, Sam. 1993. *Beautiful Losers: Essays on the Failure of American Conservatism*. Columbia, MO: University of Missouri Press.

Frey, W. H. 1993. *Interstate Migration and Immigration for Whites and Minorities, 1985–90: The Emergence of Multi-ethnic States*. Research Center. Ann Arbor: University of Michigan.

Gottfried, P. 1993. *The Conservative Movement*. New York: Twayne/Macmillan.

Hispanic Birthrate Soars in Southeast. Associated Press, August 15, 2006.

Huddle, Donald. 1996. The Net Costs of Immigration: The Facts, the Trends, and the Critics. Carrying Capacity Network, October 22, 1996.

Luttwak, E. N. 1993. *The Endangered American Dream: How to Stop the United States from Becoming a Third World Country*. New York: Simon and Schuster.

National Research Council. 1997. *The New Americans*, 334. Washington, DC: National Academy Press.

National Vital Statistics Reports: Preliminary Data for 2004. Births: Vol. 54(8), December 29, 2005. National Center for Health Statistics, Hyattsville, MD.

Pimentel, David. 2006. Personal Communication, September 14, 2006.

Pimentel, D., B. Berger, et al. 2004. "Water Resources: Agricultural and Environmental Issues." *BioScience* 54 (10): 909–18.

Pimentel, David, and M. Pimentel, eds. 1996. *Food, Ecology, and Society*. Niwot: University Press of Colorado.

President's Commission on Population Growth and the American Future. Population Growth and the American Future (the Rockefeller Report). New York: New American Library, 1972.

Preston, Julia. 2006. Illegal Workers Supplant U.S. Ones, Report Says. *New York Times*, September 22, 2006.

Sum, Andrew, et al. 2004. "Foreign Immigration and the Labor Force of the United States." Center for Labor Market Studies, Northeastern University, July, 2004.

Sundquist, Bruce. 2000. *Immigration Economics*, 2nd edition, May 13, 2000.

Worldwatch Institute, State of the World 2004, pp. 27, 50.

10

Restoring the Tradition

Introduction

Multiculturalism, framed in terms that capture the imagination of well-meaning people, has been sold as an ideal toward which all should aspire. But multiculturalism is a textbook plan for destruction of a nation. Military strategist William S. Lind addresses multiculturalism, a facet of Cultural Marxism, on the Carrying Capacity Network Action Alert website (www.carryingcapacity.org/alerts/alert0210a. html, February 2010). Lind's piece is a detailed critique of policies, media misdirection, and popular culture that substitute self-destructive values and behaviors for mainstream American tradition.

Examples of subversion are legion. One handout entitled "Recognizing Microaggressions and the Messages They Send" from University of California President Janet Napolitano exhorts the faculty to desist from offending minorities. The handout—part of Diversity in the Classroom, UCLA Diversity and Faculty Development, 2014—*warned against* phrases such as, "I believe the most qualified person should get the job" and "American is the land of opportunity." Are attacks on merit, competition, and achievement precursors to worse perversion of traditional values?

The essence of multiculturalism is the primacy of ethnic identity, ethnic separatism, and ethnic power. The new set of rules asserts privilege and power for ethnic groups rather than individuals, a doctrine that persuades whites to accept their own defeat. In the public schools and the popular culture, multiculturalism has replaced the honored motto of by-gone years: *e pluribus unum*—out of many, one. Not to mention scrubbing from memory the Horatio Alger ethic of success through one's own integrity and hard work.

Few who experience cultural transformations from the inside would deny that European-Americans, especially straight men, are discriminated against in educational and employment venues, in the media, and by the criminal justice system. Job insecurity and slanderous charges of racist, anti-Semite, neo-Nazi or worse are used to silence people who do not go along with the multicultural program. And, *when was assault of a white by a minority a front-page hate-crime story above the fold?*

My epiphany on multiculturalism developed from being falsely labeled "a white supremacist" during the 2004 campaign for passage of Protect Arizona Now's Proposition 200. I said, "No, I am a European-American separatist," and PAN's Kathy McKee lobbed the key question, "How can you be against separatism? Do you want to empty all the Chinatowns, shut down little Havana, raze the barrios, disperse the population of Skokie, Illinois, and Brighton Beach, Brooklyn, sometimes called 'little Odessa'? Do you want to squelch MALDEF, La Raza, LULAC, the Anti-Defamation League, Hillel, JINSA, ZOA, AIPAC, or the American Jewish Congress—because they are separatist? If you are against separatism, aren't you against all of those?" Is it not true that only European-Americans are denied the right to assert a preference for separateness manifested, for example, in on-campus clubs?

Americans as a people with a long and honorable history have yet to claim pride in their unique accomplishments and heritage. Under the bruising barrage of multicultural propaganda, a historic ethnic majority hesitates to assert itself. The middle class is uneasy and confused by media messages that undercut traditional values; and policymakers disappoint by promising much, delivering little, and usually acquiescing in the anti-American multicultural agenda. Government has become a handmaiden to multiculturalism and an obstacle to a prosperous American future.

Report Confuses "Diversity," "Multiculturalism"*

[The following letter was distributed to the Vanderbilt University Board of Trust.]

Anyone who believes that the Report of the University Committee on Diversity (April 1991) is about who belongs to what country club (Tennessean, April 10, 1991) should look again. The report is about what is taught and who teaches it. These decisions determine what information, analytic competence, and values are transmitted to future

---

*In *Viewpoint: The Vanderbilt Register*, Vanderbilt University, Nashville, TN [April 22, 1991].

generations of university students. The Board of Trust, administration, faculty, students, parents, and alumni all have a stake in this debate.

As a faculty member, an anthropologist teaching in the School of Medicine and a concerned citizen, I feel obligated to state my opinion of the report. I think it is misguided, mischievous, and unintentionally revolutionary beyond the contemplation of any student who thinks that revolution, on its face, is rather fun. The report achieves all this by confusing diversity, which may refer to individuals who have different cultures, with multiculturalism, which asserts that all cultures have equal relevance and validity for Americans.

US education is being undermined by multiculturalism. The question is, should Vanderbilt fall into step? Will students come to Vanderbilt to study "Writings of White Males" (a course offering at Columbia University) which covers many of the same texts as Nineteenth-Century English Literature but treats them as examples of political oppression? Quite aside from the academic credibility of this approach, would the typical parent pay for this? Would the alumni give? Would the Board of Trust run (not walk) from their volunteer service to the university?

Is it a university function to change society by advancing doctrine? Or is its function to transmit the majoritarian culture that is the cradle, after all, in which its own existence, science, and free inquiry have long been nourished? Free inquiry invites diversity . . . diversity of every kind.

Multiculturalism has little in common with free—liberal arts or scientific—inquiry. The principle underlying multiculturalism is that there is no reality except in the eyes of the beholder. Words like deconstructionism," "postmodernism," and "hermeneutics" identify the intellectual provenance of this assertion. Deconstructionism and these other terms imply that every beholder is entitled to create, even invent, his/her own reality. Whose reality prevails is then determined by political power. Is this scholarship?

Closely linked to the academic implications of multiculturalism is a threat to American individualism and equal opportunity. Specifically, individual rights are to be supplanted by group rights. Group rights easily become the tyranny of quotas.

For example, in order to ensure representation of the greatest number of versions of reality, claims to a university position or tenure would be based in part on gender or membership in a particular sexual preference, ethnic or racial group. Arguably, personal excellence in one's discipline could become secondary. The recent dispute in the San Francisco Fire Department is analogous. There it had been decided that the next chief would be Hispanic. It only remained to be determined whose Hispanicism could stand up to scrutiny by the newly formed San Francisco Ethnic Purity Review Board.

It is easily seen, in this light, how recommendations of the report, e.g. use racial/ethnic group membership and gender criteria in making hiring and promotion decisions, have, as their true goal, a shift in political power. This path leads far from the objectives of fairness and evaluations of individuals on merit.

Advocacy of group rights is racist, sexist, and ethnist. Advocacy for group rights is not a natural extension of antidiscrimination activism. Discrimination is wrong because people are judged on traits that are irrelevant to their competence. Group rights implies a similar disregard for individual competence, so how can it be proper?

I write out of unabashed patriotism as well as concern for the university. This is a time that tries men's and women's souls. We are fast becoming ethnically diverse because of the immigration policies devised by Congress. But that is a far cry from saying that we as a nation or a university ought to adopt multiculturalism. Immigrants have assimilated before. Why not now?

Multiculturalism was in action in the case of a New York City judge who commuted the sentence of a Chinese immigrant convicted of beating to death his wife. She was a self-confessed adulteress, and the defense successfully argued that the husband's action was just within the context of his own culture. Do Americans need more of this?

I, as an anthropologist, would be the last to denigrate the values and institutions of other peoples. But values, assumptions, and behavior that seem appropriate to others are not appropriate in the United States. We should be proud of what we have and feel entitled to defend it.

Our biblical, Graeco-Roman and Northern European traditions enriched by the contributions of native-American Indian and African peoples produced a fabric that has served the nation well. The American values of individualism, conscience, self-reliance, work ethic, and community service are a combination unique in today's world. Our culture is the basis of a form of government that, while not perfect, is widely envied. One of its strengths is its capacity for measured, evolutionary change. All citizens are able to contribute, benefit, and succeed within this system.

Individual rights are an integral part of the system. Group rights are an aberration that could sink it. Why give up the ship? Why let the university step into the front rank of subversion?

True, opinions like mine are usually drowned with charges of "racist." In advance, my response is that such allegations are anticipated, politically motivated, baseless, and untrue. I can buttress my views on multiculturalism with published papers by a variety of authorities among whom liberal credentials abound.

Above all, it is not racist to advocate individual rights.

Concessions to group rights strike at the very core of the American value system and culture (although I am sure that those at Vanderbilt who fashioned this fairly mild document had no such project in mind and could be guilty of no more than borrowing a fashionable idea).

Nevertheless, good intentions do not mitigate bad effects when the latter can be easily foreseen. Group rights as pressed in many esteemed quarters of academia and public life have the potential to lead this country down the path of tribalism. The divisiveness of language as in Quebec or of ethnic group as in Yugoslavia, Iraq, and the USSR could plunge even our country into a dark night of self-doubt, combat, and misery and might extinguish forever in the world the light of democracy.

Promotion in the San Francisco Fire Department*

Captain Thomas Santorno, who aspired to be chief of the San Francisco Fire Department, recently achieved fame, or notoriety, by claiming he legitimately changed his self-identification from Caucasian (his father) to Hispanic (his mother). But Captain Roybal, also of the San Francisco Fire Department, alleged that Santorno falsified the grounds on which he claimed to be Hispanic. There is no disagreement at all about two points: one, that the next chief was to be Hispanic; and two, that Roybal, who is the genuine article, scored below Santorno and others (fortieth, in fact) on the qualifying test. Roybal's shot at the job would improve if other candidates' Hispanicism could be impugned.

This case shows that the multiculturalism taking root in our universities is bearing fruit. There is genuine acceptance of making ethnicity central to job qualifications. If two qualified persons go toe-to-toe and the employer is large enough to be noticed, the minority candidate gets the job even if the other is better qualified.

This case hits close to home. I am myself on the verge of proclaiming that I am Hispanic. I have every right. I was born in Cuba. Spanish is, literally, my first language. Until age eighteen, I had dual US and Cuban

---

*In *Chronicles*, The Rockford Institute, Rockford, Illinois, p. 8 [December, 1991].

citizenship. When I went through immigration at the Havana airport (before Fidel Castro), my papers were processed in the first batch while other American citizens waited.

Hispanicism should be recommended to any American who has grounds. My new designation will be a great boon to my employer [who can now list another minority hire], and possibly I will be rewarded for my additional contribution. My children may benefit in their chosen professions, but the real boons are reserved for my grandchildren.

If current trends toward political correctness and quotas are any guide, my grandchildren may expect scholarships and significantly lowered admission requirements at top universities. Minority scholarships from federal sources were reinstated when Lamar Alexander was confirmed as Secretary of Education and, in any case, still abound from private sources like Fiesta Bowl sponsors. At the university level, my grandchildren will have multicultural curricula designed specifically for them, to enhance their self-esteem. In the workplace, they will benefit from preferential employment practices including race norming. Hispanicism will follow my grandchildren through life and, as English-speaking minorities, they should prosper.

I am not overly concerned that my grandchildren's Hispanicism would be challenged so long as my status is confirmed. One-quarter Hispanic (a grandchild's share) should be enough. In New Zealand, for example, being one sixty-fourth Maori qualifies one for benefits including concessionary, government-subsidized interest rates.

I am in the process of submitting my own ethnic claim to adjudication by higher authority. The authorities from whom I seek a ruling include Fidel Castro's Cuban Immigration and Naturalization Service in Havana, the Cuban government-in-exile in Miami (I would appreciate help with this address), the newly formed Beleaguered Americans Legally Oppressed Never Ever Yielding (BALONEY, 260 W. Main Street, Suite 104, Hendersonville, TN 37075), and the also new Ethnic Purity Review Board in San Francisco.

Perhaps I am not alone with this dilemma. Can others help?

NOTE: My experience with Cuban Immigration on entering and leaving Cuba in December, 2015, was spectacular. I learned that, because of being born in Cuba, a special visa to re-enter was required; so I was held up for an hour both arriving and leaving. Agents and supervisors with whom I spoke at the airports could hardly have been nicer [all assured me that the visa problem would be worked out, and one winked at me], but Havana officialdom had to be notified of the irregularity. Documentation that I was in Argentina by age three no doubt helped, but the over-riding issue was, "Usted es Cubana". I think that Cuba would give me a passport! And Hoorah! My grandchildren and their children can claim minority privilege with a clear conscience.

Responsibility—The Lost Virtue*

On March 23, 1998, the social engineering and pedagogy of thirty years came home to roost. A generation and a half with rights but no responsibility, relative deprivation but no answerability, and power but no accountability came into its own. An eleven-year old and a thirteen-year old in Jonesboro, Arkansas, joined forces to steal guns from parents and grandparents (taking what was put away unlocked after trying vainly to pry and torch open locked gun cabinets), steal a family van, set off their school fire alarm, and shoot four fellow students and a teacher as the building was evacuated.

The nation wants to know why, because if we understand it we can substitute pity for judgment. Certainly the young perpetrators of this crime had an excuse. We cannot believe that they are bad actors. Or such is the prevailing ideology.

I can provide the explanation. These children were raised with only half of their traditional culture. They learned pride, self-reliance, love of hunting, respect for and skill with guns, but no sense that what they did and what they became in life was ultimately their responsibility.

The culture no longer teaches responsibility. If you have an accident, you are not a damn fool but probably the entitled grievant in litigation against whomsoever has the deepest pockets. If you behave insanely, you are certainly not schizophrenic although you may *have* schizophrenia. If you beat your spouse, well, you were abused as a child. If you commit criminal acts, you are not a criminal but a victim of the circumstance in which you were raised.

Traditional American culture was not like this. Whatever you did, even if harm to others was inadvertent, you were supposed to own up to it and take responsibility. Others might exonerate you, but you did not blame your family or exonerate yourself. One of the boy's grandfathers in the Arkansas case took the responsible way—he said that yes, the stolen guns were his. This is the older generation, raised when

*Editorial in *Population and Environment* 20(3) pp. 189–99 [January, 1999].

American culture was intact. President Harry S. Truman famously said, "The buck stops here."

Taking responsibility requires a certain kind of pride. Not bravado, but the quiet certainty that one is a free man or woman, as good as any other, and that pride has to be earned, and confirmed, by courage and right-doing. Respect for self begins with respect for others. This prideful self-respect has been witlessly squandered by social engineers and reflexive do-gooders who know no standard of individual behavior or accountability, and teach that society owes miscreants instead of the other way around.

Perhaps the nation is lost and it is just a painful scrape downhill all the way from here. Democracy cannot function without a majority of citizens who accept its laws and the concepts of right and wrong, honor, respect for others matched with a demand that they, too, observe rules of good conduct and individual accountability.

This was the culture of the nation, and some Americans think that there is a way back. Until half a century ago this was a religious nation. A return to the Ten Commandments and the (yes, vengeful) God of Our Fathers may help the United States of America get back on track.

Granted that, if all children were philosophers, an education in ethics might do, a religious nation more reliably raises most children to be citizens who have an internalized locus of control and a sense of accountability. Belief that individual rights and privilege are balanced by humility and personal responsibility are further elements of what was once called "character."

Character sustains us when circumstances require that we—individually or collectively—become stiff-necked, noncompromising patriots, protectors of liberty, and judges of virtue. Character can sustain us in becoming again worthy of the power with which God and our forebears endowed us.

Marriage and Reproduction Make Sense After All*

When has a married woman been encouraged to bear children by a succession of lovers but not by her husband? This was southwest India's nineteenth-century Nayar pattern, probably popularized because it blocked a husband's usurping his wife's estate—ostensibly on behalf of their children—while her brother was off to war. The near-fictional marriage-without-consummation lasted little longer than needed to

---

* In *The Family in America*, www.familyinAmerica,org pp. 6–7 [October, 1997].

mobilize for regional defense. Marriage has purpose, although seldom is that purpose war.

A nation which expects to endure must accomplish certain tasks. Major ones are recruitment and socialization of new members. "Recruitment" usually means childbearing, that is, replacing members from within its own ranks. "Socialization" means training and educating the young, and not only in a body of knowledge, but also in the values and assumptions of their parents' culture. If a society fails in these tasks, its people and its traditions will be supplanted by others. Without exception, societies so weary or unaware of their tradition, or so lacking in self-confidence that they do not reproduce and instruct the young, have withered away or been overrun.

Marriage between man and woman is the time-tested institution in which all Western societies and most others worldwide bear and raise children. Experiments that try to disrupt identification with a natal family by substituting statist or communal loyalties have been short-lived. No, a "village" cannot raise a child; families can, and do.

The two-parent heterosexual family is the principal channel for transmitting a nation's culture from one generation to the next. In America, such families transmit the ideal of liberty and the common understanding of bedrock constitutional values, all of which nourish the nation's spirit and require unceasing vigilance.

America's own children should be taught by parents to love self-reliance, liberty, community, and country in order to become the responsible guardians of America's future and freedom. Undermining the major institution for transmitting America's values could dissipate the very commitments which presently protect our right to be let alone and the ideal of republic that we cherish.

Some, such as biologist Paul Ehrlich, argue that Americans should diminish their own birthrate in order to make way for more immigrants. This proposal—which strikes most Americans as absurd—highlights better than all else just what traditional marriage is and does. The job is not only the birthing of children, but also the teaching of children from their earliest hours in the ways and values of their nation's forebears. Immigration cannot substitute for recruiting new members from within, that is, begetting American children, because immigrants are less likely than native sons and daughters to understand and accept the traditional culture. In a nation where immigration is symbolic, a decision to grapple seriously with this challenge is overdue.

The continuation of a people and their culture cannot be taken for granted, yet many Americans seem unaware that incremental changes lead, in time, to a system which they would not want. The Republic, as conceived, protects privacy, "alternative" lifestyles, speech, and the right of assembly. Women, minorities, and those who are homosexual have as great a stake as any other in this foundational idea.

Nevertheless, some major beneficiaries of America's unique liberties use freedom counterproductively, making claims which can only weaken the very tradition which guarantees them protection. One such claim relates to the granting of recognition under the law to same-sex "marriage."

Giving standing to all proposed forms of marriage has been presented as an embodiment of the notion of tolerance, or a mere extension of individual autonomy. But it is much more than that. Diluting the legal primacy of heterosexual marriage would undermine a major bulwark of American freedom, because marriage between a man and woman, a union whose chief undertaking is to bear and raise young who carry forward their parents' culture, is central to the continuance of any nation.

The basic question is how resistant to legitimizing other forms of "marriage"—polygamy, same-sex marriage, or other arrangements—ought one be? Can different marriage patterns coexist, each with equal honor and judicial standing?

Not likely. Virtually every society, historically and cross-culturally, esteems heterosexuality and its marital privilege above others. This is not surprising, because as efficiently as any system yet devised by or for mankind, heterosexual, monogamous marriage accomplishes both reproduction and socialization.

Moreover, a society which does not back up its traditional standards of value and behavior is changing, not necessarily for the better. Not only is such indecision or passivity a sign of weakening but also, when so central an institution as marriage is attacked, hesitancy to defend can hasten and intensify the transformations. The essence of a society is to build and maintain specific traditions, without which a population would be a mere accident.

A society manifests preferences by granting or withholding its imprimatur. Selectivity works because the accumulated knowledge, values, and institutions of a people—their time-tested cultural moorings—are proven strong rocks on which the young can build. Following culturally legitimated paths and milestones helps one acquire rights to social and legal standing, rights which are generally unquestioned by members of the society and which may not accrue to other pursuits and lifestyles.

A nation cannot renounce its duty and privilege to exercise preference in defining the forms of behavior necessary to its future and well-being.

Reference

Katel, Peter. March 26, 1998. Arkansas Boys Stole Family Guns. *USA Today*, 1.

Epilogue

Reality testing is in order. World population grows by eighty million annually, fast approaching a total eight billion. Sixty years of humanitarian interventions that included best contraception and family planning technology plus information and supplies barely slowed, if at all, the momentum of growth. Many humans survive by living on resources that are virtually nonrenewable. Clean fresh water and energy grab headlines, but the fragile bit of dirt covering our planet, the topsoil, is equally essential to life. Iowa topsoil, twelve feet deep when intensive agriculture began, is now measurable in those same places in inches.

Not everyone is disturbed by the impending calamity, even in countries seen as prosperous. But our attention has seldom been more needed, because the next generation, if not the current one, faces an existential crisis. While popular culture and political, religious, and business enterprises continue along ways likely to cloud focus.

The blithe ones, unaware and unafraid, enjoy the free fall from the penthouse roof—until everything changes. I recently met one of the breed: rich, influential, immersed in banking and East Coast culture, he is secure in a worldview that to others may seem dazzlingly shortsighted.

The gentleman is aware of California's multiple-year drought. He knows that almond growing is water-intensive and he demonstrates environmental credentials by refusing slivered almonds in a bowl of oatmeal. He deplores impounding any of California's water for the benefit of fish. Oblivious to the interconnectedness of natural systems, he thinks that as much water as needed should be allocated to people.

Nature's limits and the need for lifeboat ethics elude those who put people's immediate needs first. Seeing open spaces seemingly without limit, they draw a curtain between use of scarce resources and the inevitable consequence: overuse and eventual destruction of those resources and of the resident population that depends on them.

A question intrudes. Can the United States survive denial of ecological reality? Can those who grow the food, know the quantities of water, fossil-fuel-based fertilizer, and fertile land needed for crops, and know that year-round maintenance of one cow-calf unit requires thirty acres of Wyoming rangeland—or in Navajo country, fifty acres for the maintenance of one ewe-lamb unit—be ignored? Should those who think that fish and migratory water fowl should be let die so that more people can be supported in California carry the day?

Some condemn the ecological view and its lifeboat ethics for selfishness and inhumanity. But others think that indiscriminately putting people first is self-righteously delusional and unsustainable.

Factoring in the loss of carrying capacity, degrading infrastructure, weight of national and local government debt, poverty in large parts of flagship cities, alienation of whole sectors of Americans who think they have no stake in its future, together with broad anger at the political class, can one believe that the United States remain lands of opportunity and plenty? Do these interlocking difficulties suggest that the United States—most of them—are on the brink of calamity?

While problems fester, the media and government bureaucrats manufacture disinformation. Data on US population size, growth rate, and fracture of the national culture are shoved from view. And why? Do some fear raising popular resistance to special interests, multiculturalism, mass immigration, and the big-government one-world agenda?

The refugee invasion of Europe in 2015 and the ongoing invasion of the United States by migrations of largely impoverished people—invasions that governments seem unwilling to prevent—open a vision of the future. Fully revealed is unparalleled denial that blocks acknowledging that cracking open the migrant door precipitates human tsunamis.

When Australian prime ministers Kevin Rudd and Julia Gillard permitted boatloads of refugees to land on the mainland, the initial wave of Indonesians was soon followed by triple numbers of Afghanis, Pakistanis, and would-be migrants from much of Southern Asia. The successor prime minister, Tony Abbott, stopped the flotillas by ordering the Coast Guard to tow boats back to ports of origin and, for those immigrants landing, internment on a distant island. The current Liberal Party prime minister, Malcolm Turnbull, expects to follow this Abbott policy. The boats no longer come, but Australians had seen a specter: the deluge which follows any glimmer of opportunity to migrate.

The planet collapses under the weight of eight billion, mostly in the third world. A not far-fetched guess is that half of these unfortunates would like to move to the more prosperous, less crowded, and better organized countries of the West. Polls show that nearly half of Mexicans would like to move to the United States.

Will Europeans allow the refugee invasion of their countries to continue? Will refugees along with economic migrants be deported? Will Americans allow mass immigration to continue? Who would want their own and their children's life chances sacrificed so that others may live? The question is real and existential. The Earth's population has exceeded the carrying capacity and many are doomed. Who shall it be? Those who advocate opening our national doors are choosing that the doomed shall include you, me, our children, most Americans.

The culture makes heroes of those who give their life so that another may live. Modern Christianity teaches that sacrifice is a required ethical choice. But some Christians disagree. When an ideology leads to the death of—or leaving no offspring by—those who follow its teachings, the ideology itself will die. Can anyone of faith rationally and morally choose to act in a way that causes his faith to disappear? Is consent to personal or cultural suicide immoral?

If those believing that the United States can absorb more immigrants prevail (as until now they have), how will the United States (and for that matter, Europe) survive? How long will the American grassroots tolerate destruction of their wilderness, livelihoods, culture, hopes, and dreams? How long will they tolerate their own children and grandchildren being disinherited for the benefit of foreign peoples?

When will Americans reject official lies and disinformation that cloud the reality that the middle class is being impoverished and, therefore, will not reproduce itself? When will the public catch on that small gains in Gross National Product hide the arithmetic fact that GNP divided among many more people amounts to smaller shares for each?

When will real wealth—the cleanliness of air and water, the richness of soil, the expanse of tillable land and healthy forests, and sound infrastructure—be valued separately from National Income however distributed?

Who will resist lies and invasions? Who will pursue Truth? Who will persist in coming to the aid of kin, class, and community?

Index

Grant, Lindsey, 19
Gross National Product [GNP], 14, 15, 327
Guatemala, 19, 107–109 [see also Central America]

Haiti, 19 [see also Central America]
Handwerker, Penn, 159, 211
Hardin, Garrett, 35, 49, 54, 55, 91, 158, 181
Heinen, Joel, 65
Hern, Warren, 88, 89
Hispanic, 13, 16, 22, 254, 255, 317, 318
La Raza, 45
MALDEF, 45
HIV-AIDS, 131–134, 213 [see also disease]
Homeland Security, Department of, 21
Hong Kong, 124–148 [see also Asia]
Huddle, Donald, 28, 179, 229, 307
Hudson Institute, 3
Hungary, 116
Hunt, E.E., 204
hypothesis testing, 111–147, 250

Ikle, Fred Charles, 60
Immigration Act of 1924, 236, 237
Immigration Act of 1965, 5, 7, 16 [see also immigration]
Immigration and Naturalization Service [INS], 1, 2, 5, 7, 10, 15, 43, 231
Immigration Act of 1987, [see illegal immigration]
Immigration Reform Act of 1990, 4, 13–15, 230
immigration, 2, 5, 6, 10, 57, 170, 171, 233–238
asylees, 16
costs of, 7, 23, 28, 29, 173–180, 231–247, 256, 257, 262, 263, 307, 308
disproportionate burden, 180, 228, 240, 248, 253, 254, 256, 307, 308
disease, 15, 25–30, 213, 308
education, 13, 316, 321
jobs, 302
H1-B visa, 7, 14, 303, 304
illegal, 17–22, 25, 170, 171
incentives, 173, 174, 240–244, 249, 260, 261
lobbyists, 45
media coverage, 45
moratorium, 24, 40, 185
policy, 248, 303, 304, 307, 308

population growth, 10–13, 21, 22, 59, 105, 154, 239, 256, 305, 306
poverty, 15, 23, 61, 230, 237, 302, 326
public opinion, 42, 253, 302, 326
refugees, 16, 40, 185, 231
visa overstayers, 19, 20
India, 19, 26, 95, 152, 156, 166 [see also Asia]
Khanna, 164, 200, 206, 320
Indonesia, 118, 126–148 [see also Asia]
infanticide, 84–87, 122, 165, 203, 205
Iran, 92
Ireland, 78, 119, 152
Ivanhoe, L.F. 52

Jackson, Jesse, 231
Japan, 1, 95, 118, 119, 124–148, 199, 200, 303 [see also Asia]
Journal of the American Medical Association, 26

Kalipeni, Ezekiel, 76, 112, 175, 176
Kennan, George, 310
Kennedy, Paul, 151
Kennedy, Paul, 249
Kennedy, Sen. Edward, 9
Kenya, 115, 212 [see also Africa]
Keyfitz, Nathan, 41, 119, 228
Keynes, John Maynard, 261, 262
King, Maurice, 164
Knodel, John, 165
Korea, 1, 118
Krugman, Paul, 60
kuru, 203 [see also, Indonesia]

labor [see also immigration]
blacks, 180, 229, 234, 237
Commerce Department, 8, 9
discouraged worker, 2, 5
General Accounting Office, 8, 9
Information Technology Association, 8, 9
labor supply, 2–6, 24, 104, 233, 234, 237, 253–256, 302, 303
STEM workers, 4, 24, 255, 256
unemployment, 1–5, 9, 24, 254
wages, 2, 6–9, 15, 23, 29, 61, 228, 234, 237, 253, 306
women, 211, 212, 234
Lamm, Richard, 230
Laos, 125 [see also Asia]